EARLY SUPERSONIC FIGHTERS of the West

EARLY SUPERSONIC FIGHTERS of the West

BILL GUNSTON

LONDON

IAN ALLAN LTD

First published 1976

ISBN 0 7110 0636 9–103/74

Published by Ian Allan Ltd, Shepperton, Surrey, and printed in the United Kingdom by Morrison & Gibb Ltd, London and Edinburgh

Contents

Preface

The fighter aeroplane is one of the most exciting of man's vehicles. It is also a noble military weapon. It is at least nominally defensive in nature, and certainly does not usually wage war against civil populations. More than this, it has a unique personal quality. Locked up inside its thunderous frame is a man—indeed, a superman—and, once he has joined combat, the battle he fights is every bit as individual as that of the knight at the jousting tourney. There is another romantic parallel, in that many fighters have been emblazoned with colourful heraldic devices of their units and pilots—and often with choice artwork never approved by the College of Heralds. Stirring tales can be read of famous Camels and Spads, scarlet triplanes and yellow-nosed Messerschmitts. Much less has been written about the first generation of fighters capable of flying faster than sound.

A quarter-century ago supersonic flight was very difficult to achieve, even by a research aeroplane designed to do nothing else. Almost certainly the first fighter to 'break the barrier' was the F-86A Sabre, which could make a beautiful bang merely by rolling on its back and pulling round the second half of a loop at full power to go back the way it had come but 10,000 feet lower. Trading altitude for speed has its limitations. In contrast, the fighters in this book were designed to exceed the speed of sound merely by pushing the power lever all the way forward. Some just made it beyond Mach 1, most could gradually work up near to Mach 2, and the almost wingless F-104 maintained high acceleration until the engine overheat warning showed at Mach 2.2. Twenty years ago it seemed natural to reach out to the highest practical speed, and if a designer had discovered a reasonable way to reach Mach 3 he would have taken it. More speed and more height had been primary goals of the fighter designer ever since the colourful fighting scouts of 1916. The vision of the future fighter was of a projectile arching through the stratosphere at something beyond Mach 2.

The fighter pilots and designers of 1955 would have given much to have a glimpse of aerial fighting in 1975. Would it reach Mach 3? Mach 4? Would fighters have become aerospace planes, able to soar out into the black void far from the Earth and manoeuvre on the thrust of rockets?

The astonishing fact is that development has gone just the other way. There have been thousands of air combats in the past ten years, and almost every one has taken place at subsonic speed at below 20,000 feet! Though a few fighters do carry long-range missiles which can be deadly when fired from 100 miles away, almost all recent engagements have become intimate dog-fights in which it is impossible to pull round short-radius turns and also fly fast. Speed helps in catching the enemy or getting away from him, and excess engine thrust is essential for sustaining violent manoeuvres, but supersonic combat appears to be almost a contradiction in terms. Moreover, the gun has been restored to its rightful place as vital armament for every fighter. In addition, the finest possible radar, with great power and enormous cunning, is well worth its cost and weight even in CAVU weather; and ECM (there is a glossary on p. 10) can mean the difference between life and death, especially when over hostile territory. In any case, air-to-air fighting is today held to be the least cost/effective way of destroying enemy air power; the best answer is to clobber it on the ground.

In view of these recent trends I could easily pour scorn on these early supersonic fighters designed back in the 1950s. By 1975 standards they are crude, for their methods of employment, and often their equipment, show little advance over many fighters of World War 2. Often their basic concept was ill-founded. How could anyone, even 20 years ago, give serious consideration to a fighter designed to fly at Mach 2 in the stratosphere with no radar save a gunsight with a range of about a mile? Flying such a fighter one did stand a chance of destroying enemy aircraft, because it might have proved impossible to avoid a mid-air collision.

Yet a snide and superior attitude would be mistaken. Today's fighters are possible only because of enormous advances in structures, propulsion, systems, and especially in avionics, which the superficial observer—concerned only with Mach performance—might overlook. The aircraft in this book were all designed in what seems today to be almost a prehistoric age. They were created at a time of extreme world tension, usually under extreme pressure and always whilst overcoming great difficulties. Some succumbed to the difficulties, becoming the first of many military aerospace programmes to be bogged down by political mismanagement, wildly escalating costs and a declining national will.

The decline is certainly visible in the West. It is less evident in the Soviet Union, but as in earlier volumes in this series I have for obvious reasons been unable to include such Russian aircraft as the Mig-19, Mig-21, Su-7 and Yak-28. I have also omitted several other types such as the F-101 Voodoo, F11F Tiger, Egyptian HA-300 and Indian HF-24 Marut. Selection was not easy, but I think this book includes the pick of a fine bunch. Most have a proud record of combat over the Middle East, SE Asia, the Indo-Pakistan frontier or elsewhere. Others are of outstanding interest from the technical and political points of view, serving to prove (again) that aerospace is no place for cultured amateurs.

It was my privilege to know all these programmes at first hand. Each dates from a time when a supersonic aeroplane of any sort was an intensely exotic species. It was something new to feel the chest-vibrating thunder of big afterburners, and then to watch a high contrail approach silently at unnatural speed and receive a splendid double boom some while afterwards. I apologise to the environmentalists for getting a kick out of such things.

Haslemere, 1974 Bill Gunston

Glossary

Again I think it will be helpful to spell out some of the abbreviations and technical terms, as in the two previous books in this series. On this occasion I have left out such familiar things as 'RAF' and 'NATO'.

AAEE Aeroplane & Armament Experimental Establishment (UK)

ACAS(OR) Assistant Chief of the Air Staff (Operational Requirements)

ADC Air Defense Command (US Air (Force)

AEDC Arnold Engineering Development Center (US Air Force)

AFB Air Force Base (US)

AFFTC Air Force Flight Test Center (US)

AFHQ Air Force Headquarters (US)

afterburning reheat (q.v.)

AI airborne interception

ANG Air National Guard (US)

Area Rule a rule for shaping aircraft for minimum transonic or supersonic drag

ASI air-speed indicator

BLC boundary-layer control, for example by flap-blowing.

BuAer Bureau of Aeronautics (US Navy)

CA Release release for operational service of a new type of aircraft by the Controller, Aircraft (UK)

CAS Chief of the Air Staff (UK)

CAVU ceiling absolute, visibility unlimited, ie perfect weather

CEV Centre des Essais en Vol (Flight-test centre) (France)

CFE Central Fighter Establishment (UK)

c.g. centre of gravity

c.p. centre of pressure, through which the resultant aerodynamic force on the wing acts

c.t.p. chief test pilot

DCOS Deputy Chief of Staff (US)

DDAW Deputy Director of Air Warfare (RN)

DNAW Director of Naval Air Warfare (RN)

DoD Department of Defense (US)

dry thrust Thrust without reheat or other boost system

ECM electronic counter-measures

FAC Forward Air Controller

FAI Fédération Aéronautique International

FBS, FBW Fighter Bomber Squadron, Wing (US Air Force)

FDS, FDW Fighter Day Squadron, Wing (US Air Force)

FFAR folding-fin aircraft rocket, an unguided spin-stabilised missile

FIS, FIW Fighter Interceptor Squadron, Wing (US Air Force)

FR flight-refuelling

g.a. drawing three-view general-arrangement plan of proposed aircraft

HTP high-test peroxide

HVAR high-velocity aircraft rocket, heavy weapon for surface attack

IAS indicated air speed, which varies with air density and so is very low at high altitudes

IFF identification friend or foe

ILS instrument landing system

IR infra-red (i.e., heat)

ITP Instruction To Proceed, formal notification to a manufacturer to do work in advance of a contract

LLTV low-light TV system, for 'seeing in the dark'

MAC Military Airlift Command (US Air Force)

MAP Mutual Aid Program (US), Ministry of Aircraft Production (UK)

MDAP Mutual Defense Assistance Program (US)

MIL power Military rating of a turbojet or turbofan engine; often maximum unaugmented (non-afterburning) thrust

MMH/FH maintenance man-hours per flight hour

MoA, MoD, MoS Ministries of Aviation, Defence and Supply (UK)

MTBF mean time between failures

MTI moving-target indication, a radar display which automatically eliminates static 'clutter'

MWDP Mutual Defense Weapons Program (US)

NACA National Advisory Committee for Aeronautics (US)

NAS Naval Air Station (US)

NASA National Aeronautics and Space Administration (US)

NRC National Research Council (Canada)

OCU Operational Conversion Unit (UK)

q-feel Feedback control force proportional to air density and air-speed

RAE Royal Aircraft Establishment (UK)

RCAF Royal Canadian Air Force

R&D research and development

RDF radio direction finding

reheat thrust-boost system for air-breathing engine, such as a turbojet or turbofan, by burning additional fuel in the jet pipe

RFNA red fuming nitric acid

RFP request for proposals (US)

RPV remotely piloted vehicle

RRE Royal Radar Establishment (UK)

RSAF Royal Swedish Air Force

R/T radio telephone

SEP specific excess power, thrust available for climb or manoeuvre

SHAPE Supreme Headquarters Allied Powers Europe

SLAR sideways-looking aircraft (or airborne) radar

STOL short take-off and landing

TAC Tactical Air Command

t/c ratio of wing thickness to chord (distance from leading to trailing edge)

TFS, TFW Tactical Fighter Squadron, Wing (US Air Force)

USAFE US Air Force, Europe

USS United States Ship (US Navy)

VMC visual meteorological conditions

Zell zero-length launch: aircraft rocket-boosted launch with no ground run

BAC Lightning

It is a scarcely credible fact that the total number of types of all-British supersonic aircraft ever to go into operational service is one—and there is not the slightest sign, or likelihood, of a second. One might deduce that the type concerned must have some remarkable qualities—which, in relation to its timescale, it does—but the reason it stands alone is that the other 12 types of supersonic aircraft planned for the RAF or Royal Navy between 1953 and 1965 were all cancelled before their development had been completed. Indeed, if the aircraft described in this chapter had not been started soon after World War 2 it would probably have followed the others into oblivion. This is because in 1957 the government said that instead of fighters and bombers the RAF would buy only nice cheap missiles. When it discovered this was an error of titanic proportions it placed contracts for a range of challenging British aircraft; when these were almost ready it cancelled them and bought American ones, and finally decided to buy aircraft from European partnerships. The Lightning slipped through the flailing Whitehall choppers, partly because it was already well advanced in development and partly because in 1957 the wonderful missiles weren't quite ready to replace it. So the Treasury grudgingly let it continue, but took care nobody spent any money on improving it.

Despite this pathetic political background the Lightning is a thoroughly splendid aeroplane which every 'fighter jock' from Tashkent to Timbuktu would dearly like to get his hands on. Today they don't often see one back at the Warton plant, but if one does arrive the test pilots put down their Jaguars and MRCAs and try to scrounge any Lightning checks that may be needed. This is rather remarkable because the design of the Lightning was begun before almost all of them were born. The basic conception was unique, and never repeated in any other aircraft, but it was so basically right that the Lightning triumphed over the errors of the officials and their expert advisors and ultimately even over the non-decisions and wrong decisions of the Air Staff. Had the Ministers and air marshals been able to see beyond their noses something over 1,000 Lightnings would have been built, and possibly twice that number, instead of 340. As it was, as soon as the RAF finally realised (in 1965) that the manufacturer had been correct all along, millions of pounds were spent in modifying the RAF aircraft the way they should have been built, and BAC was able to land what was at that time the biggest export deal in British history—a deal which in 1973 brought a further support contract worth a cool £250 million.

Of course the dedicated men I am criticising so harshly would claim that the duty of the RAF is to defend Britain, not to bother about exports. My complaint is that if they had not fought so hard to prevent the Lightning from being a long-range multi-role aircraft it would have been far better for the RAF too. In any case, the need to look at world markets has now been thumped home so hard with both military and civil aircraft that I need hardly belabour the point.

So let us go back to July 1949, and to the rain-sodden railway station at Preston, Lancashire. Just a year earlier, in one of the noisome toilet cubicles on that station, I had taken off my RAF uniform for the last time and put on my unfamiliar 'demob suit'. Now I was back as an undergraduate looking forward to a 14-week vacation course at the English Electric factories at Warton and Samlesbury, where lay Britain's production line of de Havilland Vampires—one of which had been the last aircraft that I flew in the Service. In the course of those 14 weeks I was privileged to be summoned to the office of Mr W. E. W. Petter, the renowned chief engineer. Teddy Petter's masterpiece was the blue-painted 'A.1' bomber prototype which chief test pilot R. P. 'Bee' Beamont flew with such verve, and which was later to go into production as the Canberra. But I had the nerve to ask Petter 'Could you tell me anything, sir, about the English Electric fighter?' His reply was 'I'm sure you have heard rumours of this project. People are saying in the works that we are now going to build the only fighter that will be able to shoot down our jet bomber. . . . I can only tell you that we hope to build an aeroplane that will fly faster than sound. Whether it will lead to a fighter that will serve with the Royal Air Force I do not know. It is a credit to our design organisation that we have been entrusted with this work, which of course must not be mentioned outside these works.'

I kept hoping to find tangible evidence of this project, but at that time it was confined to pieces of paper and models in restricted areas where snooping undergraduates were not allowed. But I met some of the designers. There was Freddie Page, who was soon to get the No 1 job when Petter went to Folland to build the Gnat. There were Ray Creasey, D. L. Ellis and F. D. Crowe—all seemed experienced, eager and very good indeed. The only comment on the 'fighter' I could draw was 'Now that the bomber is in the air it is logical for the project team to be considering something else'. I doubt if they would have credited that that same bomber would keep the project office busy for a further 25 years in creating new versions for customers all round the world. Even if they had, it was still prudent to have a completely new product-line. But in fact a new product was a very long way off.

At that time supersonic flight was officially regarded in Britain as almost contrary to some law of nature. In 1946 the government had decreed that it had 'not got the heart' to ask pilots to fly faster than sound, and cancelled the Miles M.52 supersonic research aircraft that was being built to the E.24/43 specification. But, far from feeling relieved, the pilots appeared to think supersonic flight an important uncharted realm to explore, and Chuck Yeager's demonstration of it in October 1947 merely helped shift the centre of activity to the United States. By the end of 1946 Petter was studying possible supersonic aircraft, and early in the following year he was having discussions with the MoS at Thames House regarding the practicality and value of building a manned aircraft to explore this unknown region beyond Mach 1 which seemed to be likely to become the exclusive preserve of the Americans. In May 1947 he won English Electric a study contract for a Mach 1.5 aircraft to meet the E.R.103 (experimental research) specification. In May 1948 Beamont temporarily got out of the cockpit mock-up of the A.1 bomber and made a valuable visit to Wright Field and Lake Muroc (Edwards), where he talked with his American opposite numbers and flew the B-45 jet bomber, the F-80, F-84 and F-86. The last-named, of course, had swept wings and in just a few seconds of a steep dive could make a splendid sonic bang—which was then a completely new phenomenon causing much puzzlement in Los Angeles. Bee did all he could in the brief time available to investigate the behaviour of the F-86 at Mach numbers up to about 1.01, becoming the first non-American (so far as I can discover) to fly faster than sound.

In June 1948 he returned to Warton and immediately found himself in the centre of enthusiastic discussions with the E.R.103 design team. The F-86 conformed to the predictions of swept wings, it exhibited no unpleasant or irregular characteristics in the transonic region, and recovery from the dive to lower speeds and level flight was straightforward. A few weeks later John Derry reached about Mach 1.04 with the third, modified D.H.108, but this tailless aircraft was a bit of a handful and the first example had earlier shown it could suffer sudden catastrophic disintegration at about Mach 0.89. Bee reported that the more conventional F-86 behaved perfectly, and in no time the Warton drawing boards were littered with all sorts of likely and unlikely supersonic shapes. Why not a supersonic fighter?

At first Petter maintained a conservative, almost dour attitude; there was no official requirement, and supersonic aeroplanes were still taboo. Then, around November 1948, he suddenly seemed to swing right behind the idea and enthusiastically led the studies out of the 'back of an envelope' stage and into that of a full company project. In December he took a g.a. drawing of something recognisable as an ancestor of the Lightning up to

London, and early in 1949 English Electric received one of the first design contracts ever signed for a military aeroplane to fly faster than sound. In view of Britain's earlier view that supersonic flight was something to be investigated by using models this is remarkable. The only room for argument lies in how far the F.23/49 requirement was 'military'. Its purpose was 'to investigate the practicality of supersonic speed for military aircraft'. It could be said that this is only research, but the document specified 'guns and a sighting system', and called for fighter characteristics and design factors (7g). The requirement was not put out to general tender, so far as I can determine. On 1 April 1950 English Electric received a contract for two flight prototypes and one static-test airframe.

English Electric called the new aircraft the P.1, the letter signifying merely Project and not Petter, Page or pursuit. By the time I was creeping round the works hoping for a glimpse of something the configuration had been decided upon. It abounded in odd features. In those days new British jets had straight, moderately swept or triangular (delta) wings, and were frequently tailless, yet the P.1 had an almost untapered wing that was swept back like an arrowhead at 60°, roughly twice the sweep angle of other high-speed aircraft at that time. This meant that the trailing edge was sharply swept as well, which was unique; and the ailerons were placed transversely so that they joined the leading and trailing edges and formed the tips—or rather rearwards extremities—of the wing. The two turbojet engines were installed in a most unusual way. One was mounted high in the rear fuselage, removable through a large door on top, while the other was mounted low in the forward fuselage, removable through a similar door underneath. The two jet-pipes were superimposed, and the engines were staggered to reduce frontal area. Beneath the lower jet-pipe was installed the power unit driving the tailplane, which was a second 60° arrowhead made as a single slab.

This configuration has been used in only one other type of aircraft, the Grognard prototypes flown in 1950–51 by the French Sud-Est group. Their grizzled test pilot Pierre Nadot told me these were superb performers and cried out for development beyond Mach 1 (the first had the bold wing sweep of 47°), but the important point is not the use of superimposed engines but the low tailplane. Several other French fighter prototypes of this era had low tailplanes, and most of them behaved extremely well at the highest speeds they could reach. The French, like the English Electric team, had discovered that a low tailplane can overcome the problem of transonic 'pitch-up' which was sorely afflicting British machines with tailplanes in mid or high positions. Putting the tailplane as low as possible was one of the basic design breakthroughs of the late 1940s, and it was a significant factor in the success of the Lightning and several other aircraft in this book.

Yet some communications blockage must have existed within the Ministry of Supply, because, despite the evidence of the French programmes and of the impressive tunnel results at Warton, English Electric were instructed in 1950 to redesign the P.1 with a high T-tail. Petter, who had abandoned a T-tail in 1949, read the instruction, handed it to Page and departed to Folland. Page had the temerity to argue with the officials. He reminded them that earlier in the year Dai Ellis had managed to complete the first slotted-throat transonic wind tunnel in the British industry, that it had shown the P.1 to behave perfectly well at all speeds and Mach numbers up to the initial design figure of Mach 1.2, and that in the disputed low-speed, high-incidence regime the low tail worked beautifully. He was told that it couldn't, because the boffins at Farnborough said it couldn't. The RAE aerodynamicists were predicting the most dire stability and control problems, with catastrophic pitch-up. Page and his own aerodynamicists went back and did all their tests and sums again. Their results were just the opposite: the P.1 would behave beautifully.

Head-on controversies such as this are fortunately very rare indeed. Unlike such subjects as politics and football teams, which—being emotional rather than numerical—can keep arguments raging for years, this controversy was about hard, measurable fact. Admittedly, in those days tunnel turbulence, choking throats and other ills were prone to turn measurable fact into unmeasurable errors, but the RAE's sustained disbelief of the work done at Warton appears to me curious, to say the least. English Electric demonstrated how the P.1 behaved in the tunnel, and produced books full of test data. But the RAE were so insistent that, in the end, the MoS decided to get a special research aircraft built to try to settle the issue before the P.1 flew. The one good thing about the whole affair was that they allowed Page to go on building the P.1 with a low tailplane. Meanwhile, Short Brothers at Belfast were contracted to design a rather dissimilar parody of the P.1, with the designation S.B.5, to serve as a low-speed research aircraft in general and as a vehicle to show English Electric the error of their ways in particular. The S.B.5 had a box-like fuselage containing a Derwent engine, fed at the nose and exhausting at the tail, and a wing centre-section to which could be attached three sets of wings with sweep angles of 50°, 60° and 69°. Likewise there were two complete tail units, one having a delta T-tail perched on the fin and the other having a rather different tailplane low on the rear fuselage. It almost goes without saying that the shapes and system dynamics bore only the most superficial resemblance to the P.1, and also that flight trials in the P.1 configuration were left till last.

The British government has a long heritage of trying to delude the public. The official view seems to be that the landlady in Wigan is not supposed either to know anything about where a tailplane ought to be put or have any interest in the matter, but such a view must (I hope) give way to the more enlightened policy of the government telling taxpayers as much as it can, short of recklessly endangering the nation, of what it is doing with their money. When Tom Brooke-Smith flew the S.B.5, WG 768, on 2 December 1952, there was no public hint of any controversy over the shape of the P.1. Indeed one was not even supposed to link the two aircraft at all, though every schoolboy knew better! My own ferreting only succeeded in uncovering the fact that there was a link between the P.1 and S.B.5, though I had better not dare to say so in print, and that it was all to do with 'research at full-scale Reynolds numbers'. So Brookie flew first with the wing at a modest 50° and a T-tail, because that was what the boffins said would be safest. It wasn't very nice, and it was some time before Short's chief test pilot cared to explore the whole ± 10° range of tailplane movement even over a restricted range of airspeeds. Well into 1953 he set forth again with the wing at the daring 60° of the English Electric fighter. On 10 January 1954 Brookie began the third series of tests, the really dangerous ones with the tailplane in the wicked low position. To the discomfiture of Farnborough, which promptly tried to forget the whole thing, the S.B.5 flew better than before at all angles of attack. This was actually rather remarkable because, to improve matters, the S.B.5 had been given huge down-sloping inner leading-edge sections, rather like the big 'gloves' of an F-111; previously the S.B.5 had had full-span narrow-chord droop. This was because Farnborough also refused to believe Petter and Page when they insisted that the P.1 did not need slats, droops or any other movable leading-edge surface.

I am sorry to have to record all this, because Farnborough is probably the most hallowed name in aeronautical engineering. Anyone who studies the history of aircraft structures, engines, instruments or any other pioneer aviation art will learn that in an extraordinary number of cases Farnborough did it first, and showed other people where the path to the future lay. But in World War 2 the RAE, like the rest of the nation, began perceptibly to slip behind in important areas of technology. Since then the slippage has accelerated and the breadth of slipping subjects has widened. The inability correctly to predict the stability and control behaviour of the P.1 was one of the first big instances of this deep, long-term problem. In the ultimate it all boils down to hard cash. No matter how experienced or dedicated people are, or how far they think they have some native genius that rival nations lack, they are going to make mistakes if they do not have all the research tools they need. Today the RAE has some splendid facilities, but the period 1945–55 is one they would probably rather forget.

Later the S.B.5 was flown with an Orpheus engine and the even bolder 69° wing, and its relevance to the P.1 became increasingly hard to detect.

Indeed, in true British fashion, the timing of this research aircraft was such that the results obtained with it could not do very much to help the P.1. If the behaviour with the low tailplane had indeed proved as frightful as Farnborough predicted the P.1 would have to be rebuilt, because by the time these results were coming in the first P.1, WG 760, was virtually complete. In May 1954 it was put on a long trailer and taken to the AAEE at Boscombe Down. Here, like so many vital prototypes before and since, it was erected by manufacturer's personnel, exhaustively checked and tested and readied for flight.

It is difficult to exaggerate the importance of this aircraft. Ever since 1945 British policy towards pushing out the frontiers of aviation had been, to put it very mildly indeed, confused. Great emphasis was laid on laminar-flow wings, tailless configurations, deltas with no tailplane, deltas with high tailplanes, colossal lumbering landplanes, colossal lumbering flying boats, and an interminable succession of research aircraft and half-baked 'fighter prototypes' not quite up to the standard of the F-86 and Mig-15 which had been in squadron service for years. In 1950–51 the Americans had begun to build supersonic fighters; though nobody in Britain knew it, so had the Russians. When the first P.1 was being checked in its hangar at Boscombe the F-100 (p.138) and Mig-19 were already in production, and by 1955 both were in service in hundreds. Bee, as he walked across the dewy grass from The Pheasant inn soon after dawn each morning, appreciated the situation only too well. He knew the F-100, and how fast that programme was moving. In contrast he had just a single P.1, with a second hand-built flight prototype slowly taking shape back in Lancashire. Behind them there were only pieces of paper. After years of inaction Britain was at last trying to go supersonic. But, whereas the Americans and Russians had the benefit of very extensive supersonic flight research during those years, Britain had deliberately chosen to do nothing—except with ineffectual pilotless models. Bee's sleek P.1 had to make up alone for all the lost time. Moreover, it was not only the nation's first supersonic research aircraft but also the only prototype that could lead to a future fighter for the RAF. Later in 1954 Fairey took the first F.D.2 to Boscombe and flew it on 6 October. It is merely a reflection of official policy that this was planned as a subsonic aircraft. It took quite a time for Fairey to get across the fact that it could easily be supersonic, and might be more useful that way. It is small thanks to the customers in the MoS and RAE that, in March 1956, Peter Twiss was able to set a world speed record in the FD.2 at 1,132 mph, 310 mph faster than the best that could be done by the F-100. As soon as British industry was permitted to do anything about supersonic flight it beat the world, but the prevailing official view continued to be that it was difficult, dangerous and best put off until some other time. The successive governments which held this view were those that dictated what the industry could do, yet by the 1960s the industry was being castigated by ministers for being 'featherbedded' and pouring the public's money down the drain in 'prestige projects'.

Believe it or not, in 1954 there were people in high places—especially the Air Staff—who considered the P.1 a prestige project. While accepting jets as the essential successors to piston engines, they questioned the need for supersonic performance, pointed out all sorts of reasons why this might be a retrograde step and generally fostered the notion that, if a fighter was to emerge at all from the P.1, it would not do so for a very long time. They adduced, in highly secret documents, complex arguments concerning gun and missile armament, the nature of the airborne target, range and endurance, field length, cost and other factors to question whether supersonic aircraft were either practical or wanted. To a considerable degree it was 1935 all over again; one remembered the heated arguments of the fighter experts that good fighters had open cockpits, fabric covered biplane wings and the ability to turn in a few times their own length and slip into any old grass field. Fortunately, even though the RAF was still waiting for its first Gladiator biplane in April 1937, there were just enough monoplanes to cope with the Battle of Britain. But in the perilous 1950s British aircraft took far longer to develop. They were very much more complicated, and it was blindingly obvious that a lot of aircraft ought to be used to clear the engine, flight controls, systems, avionics, armament and other items. What on Earth could Bee hope to accomplish in a reasonable time with WG 760?

On 23 July 1954 he returned to Samlesbury for a day to make the maiden flight of the Canberra B(I).8. He was often up at Warton 'flying' the P.1 flight-controls rig, which was very nearly the first airborne-system rig in Europe. There was never any doubt of its value, and in subsequent advanced-aircraft programmes static systems rigs have become increasingly taken for granted. The day after he flew the Mk 8 Canberra Bee began the P.1 taxying programme, and streamed the braking parachute. On 26 July he lifted off the runway briefly and the rakish machine felt fine. On 4 August he made one of the most enjoyable first flights that any test pilot could imagine. This is a good place at which to break off the story and discuss the aircraft itself, but one must record another scarcely credible fact. It is over 20 years since that flight took place. Since then there has not been a single first flight by any completely new all-British aeroplane designed for the RAF that subsequently reached the RAF. This fantastic gap of 20 years will, I hope, have been ended by the maiden flight of the first Hawk before this volume appears.

Altogether the P.1 was a strange mixture. In its basic design it was extremely advanced, far bolder in concept than the F-100, Mig-19 or any of the other supersonic aircraft of the time, even though Petter had first roughed out the configuration in 1947. Later it was to prove itself an absolute winner from the point of view of stability and control, and it was also developed to have outstanding flight performance; but on the other hand the P.1 was quite a long way from being a fighter. The good features were the basic layout, and especially the wing and tailplane which contrived to combine a conventional section profile and structure with good supersonic performance. The engine installation was odd. Today two engines are invariably placed side-by-side, and this facilitates the breathing through the inlet ducts and often makes room for a large internal fuel capacity, whereas the P.1 had no fuselage fuel at all and just a 2,500 lb integral tank in each wing. This seemed by far the most serious shortcoming, and to continue a long tradition of RAF fighters being short on range that one would have thought would have died out after the countless harsh lessons of World War 2. On top of this the main gears were long and heavy, and folded into a big wing bay which might otherwise have housed fuel; the two Armstrong Siddeley Sapphire 5 engines were rather crude non-reheat installations; the pilot had a flat windscreen yet no rear view; and there was very little room in the box-like body for avionics and weapons.

One didn't know quite what to make of WG 760. As Britain's first supersonic aircraft it was clearly very welcome and long overdue, but I harboured a worrying suspicion that it was a bit too much of a limited-endurance research machine which seemed even to lack any obvious place to hang an external tank. Of armament one could only surmise, because none was yet fitted. Secrecy forbade any disclosure of dimensions or weights, but one could always do a little quiet sleuthing in those exciting times when there were lots of secret aeroplanes. An impressive exhibit on the British Messier stand at the 1954 SBAC show was a steel forging for an unmentionable main landing gear. It was obviously for the P.1. Resting against its lower end was a finished wheel and tyre. I looked up the tyre in the Dunlop catalogue and was staggered to see that the inflation pressure was no less than 280 lb/sq in, then an incredible figure. The catalogue helpfully matched the tyre to a limiting aircraft weight of 39,220 lb, and gave several other details, but to publish all this would have led to dire trouble with the officials. One wondered whether it would have served any useful purpose to tell the same officials how silly all the security, or rather non-security, really was. Years later I was able to confirm that the tyre displayed in 1954, and the entry in the catalogue, were both correct; previously I had harboured a suspicion they had been cleverly falsified, to lead the baddies astray.

Nobody had ever seen anything that looked like the P.1, and *Flight*'s then assistant editor, Rex King (who began his career as an artist), wrote that it had 'all the shapeliness of a suitcase'. In fact this odd shape was the one thing that was totally new. It had to be, for obvious aerodynamic reasons, because in the late 1940s a modern 3.5% wing would have been quite beyond the structural art. But in every other respect Petter deliberately tried to make the P.1 as ordinary as possible. His philosophy, like Dassault's, was 'optimise current knowledge, use proven methods and stick your neck out as little as possible'. This explained the two dry engines, which were available off-the-shelf, the crude pitot nose inlet through which they breathed, the simple nozzles and many other rather surprising features. Petter's main objective was to create a supersonic aircraft which could be easily flown by any RAF fighter pilot, and which would have fighter-like rates of roll, control response and g characteristics. I think he was entirely right, and when he departed Freddie Page took over the basis for an outstanding interceptor; but it must not be forgotten that there are at least two sides to most decisions and Petter was able to plan the P.1 in this way only because the customer was in no hurry. The F.23/49 specification had a research ring to it, and did not spell out in numerical terms an acknowledged gap in the RAF's order of battle. If English Electric had been told about the F-100 and Mig-19 and instructed to achieve parity in timing—which would have been impossible—I suspect the result would have come out somewhat different.

In fact, while the two flight articles were being built in 1953, Page's team had taken the development process so far down the road that they could see very clearly how to build a P.1-derived fighter, and it meant a lot of redesign. After all, at that time the aeronautical art was galloping ahead faster than at any other time in history, and in the six years since the E.R.103 concept was drafted it had gone a long way. Both E.R.103 and F.23/49 had stipulated a maximum level speed of Mach 1.2, which at the time was a challenge enough. But by September 1953 Don Horsfield and his project staff at Warton kept finding themselves looking at curves of thrust and drag which did not cross until Mach 2 or even 2.2. In those days this was almost like flying to the Moon, except that the evidence was there in the form of clear lines plotted on a graph. Admittedly the last part of the curves before the crossover point suggested that the excess of thrust over drag would be small, but it was there nevertheless. What was indisputable was that one could build a fighter with sparkling acceleration even at Mach 1.5, which was way beyond the design performance of the P.1.

At Mach numbers of this order one needed a two-shock centrebody intake and a proper reheat (afterburner) system with a variable propelling nozzle; ideally the intake also should be variable, and the nozzle ought to be of the convergent/divergent type, but in 1953 this seemed rather a tall order in Britain (though not to GE in the United States, who in that year first ran the J79 engine that was to drive the B-58 supersonic bomber). What made the thrust curve stay above the drag curve to beyond Mach 2 was the promise that both the Sapphire and the Rolls-Royce Avon would become available with very much greater thrust, the rating with full reheat being roughly double that of the 7,500 lb Sapphire 5. In turn this meant not only a new front end but also an enlarged duct cross-section and bigger nozzles. The nose gear was redesigned, it was logical to raise the cockpit to give a good all-round view, and there seemed to be a possibility of putting the necessary radar scanner inside the new intake centrebody. By the end of 1953 the fighter had crystallised as the P.1B, so that the original aircraft, which was still not yet complete, began to be referred to as the P.1A.

In 1954 English Electric were awarded a contract for the princely total of three P.1B aircraft, the first to fly early in 1957. These were to be prototypes of an operational RAF fighter, still to the original F.23/49 specification but fully armed. For long-range attacks each was to carry two of the Blue Jay heat-homing air-to-air missiles then well advanced in development by de Havilland Propellers Ltd. For close-in fighting they were to carry two 30 mm Aden guns and 48 2-inch FFARs. Ferranti were to develop the vital new AI-23 radar and pilot attack sight. The sole purpose of the aircraft was to be interception over short ranges, without the pilot acquiring the target visually. No thought was given to any long-range role, to surface attack or even at that time to any form of collision-course interception. The whole burden was placed on the traditional stern chase, even though from 1942 onwards all the evidence had indicated that this was just one—and not necessarily the most important one—of several ways of shooting down enemy aircraft. Indeed since 1949 the US Air Force had devoted most of its interception energies towards the development of automatically guided, missile-armed machines which could attack from any direction (see F-102, p. 166).

As that chapter makes clear, the US Air Force considered at that time that there was no justification in carrying a human navigator or radar operator in such aircraft. In the ultimate progress along this path the human pilot was discarded as well, resulting in an expendable surface-to-air missile or a non-expendable RPV. Retaining the pilot appeared logical in a fighter carrying separate weapons, but it was equally sensible—thought the USAF staff—to try to make the aircraft as automatic as possible so that the pilot should be cast increasingly in the role of system manager serving in a passive monitoring function. Thus it mattered little whether the interception mission was flown in good or bad weather; it would make little difference to the 'black boxes', and the man on board would not need to see the target. The only occasion when he might need to break into the control loop would be the landing, and even here a link between the ILS beam and the autopilot might serve instead, as it had in many automatic landings by aircraft up to the size of the C-54 (DC-4) since 1946. Yet in Britain the Air Staff continued to adhere to the view that 'night and all-weather' fighters demanded a second crew-member. I discussed the topic with everyone I could get hold of and formed the view that this belief was a vague one. Some said the second man was needed solely for navigation, some said he was needed to handle the work-load of the radar and convert indistinct blips into crisp steering commands, while a few even thought his second pair of eyes would help in seeing the target! It was only after three years of argument that it was finally agreed by the Air Staff that the P.1 might be able to operate at night or in bad weather while still being a single-seater. This obviously made a very great difference to the operational value of what was inevitably to be the RAF's most expensive fighter in history, especially as enemy bombers would be unlikely to attack Britain only in good weather.

English Electric had enough to do without arguing too much with the customer. Taking on the task of developing the original P.1 had been a giant task, but now the still quite modest team at Warton were faced with turning it into a fully equipped Mach 1.5–2.0 fighter, whilst simultaneously bearing a heavy burden with a dozen marks of Canberra. It was natural that there was a big expansion, the engineering staff growing from about 200 to more than 600 in a matter of two years. If the P.1 had been unsound even this would not have been enough; what made it all almost enjoyable was that from the very beginning the P.1 was an unbelievably wonderful aeroplane.

On its first flight, on 4 August 1954, there was no malfunction, no handling problem and 100% clearance of test objectives. Bee retracted the gear, climbed to 15,000 feet and explored handling to the agreed limits of 450 knots and Mach 0.75. The behaviour couldn't have been better. Then he came in at the planned 160 kt, faster than necessary but a prudent figure avoiding any low-speed difficulties. No such difficulties were expected, and Bee found the whole flight a pleasant introduction to an aeroplane that was already taut and responsive.

One must to some degree thank the S.B.5 for this, even though it was due to something the Men from the Ministry never thought of when the S.B.5 was ordered. Both Brookie, who cleared the S.B.5 in its original configuration, and Bee, who from June 1954 flew it 17 times, were keenly aware of the powerful vortex generated at the leading edge of its highly swept wing, which grew swiftly in intensity and spanwise extent at increasing angles of attack. As the vortex rolled off the wing it crossed the ends of the ailerons, and these manually driven surfaces responded. The S.B.5 pilot felt what the reports would describe as 'variations in aileron hinge moment' but which the layman would call 'a sudden lumpiness' in the lateral control, with incipient wing-dropping and the stick shaking from side to side. The airflow was mapped out and palliatives considered. Ever helpful, Farnborough shouted eagerly for fences to be fitted, but these cause high drag. Comrade Mikoyan fixed six on every Mig-17, thereby cutting about Mach 0.05 off that fighter's performance. Page and his team wanted to keep the splendid P.1 aloof from such things. Turning a deaf ear to the RAE aerodynamics department they cut a deep axial slot in the leading edge of the S.B.5 well outboard, aligned close to the mid-point of the ailerons. The inner wall of the channel was opened to serve as a simulated inwards-vent valve for the P.1 wing tanks (there weren't any in the S.B.5). It was calculated that this fore-and-aft groove, a thing never before seen on a wing, would act as a fence in arresting the burbling spanwise vortex flow but without adding the fence's drag or being so susceptible to damage. It worked perfectly first time. Such a cut, with a real tank vent, was on the P.1 on its first take-off. It is still there, and a more or less similar cut can be seen on every Lightning. To verify its value Warton later back-tracked and filled the slot in on WG 760. At once Bee felt the unpleasant lurching due to air breaking away from the tips in huge vortices (though the P.1's powered controls prevented feedback through the ailerons to the stick). He very quickly had the saw-cuts opened up again.

The only criticism Bee could make on the first flight was that at speeds above 340 kt the aileron control was if anything too sensitive, and he had to take care to avoid causing PIOs (pilot-induced oscillations). There was no real problem, because if an oscillation did develop he merely had to relax his grip on the stick, but it was a clear case for a change in aileron gearing. But this could wait. There was great eagerness to get on with the flying, partly because of the excellent first flight and partly so that 10 hours could be logged to qualify the P.1 for participation in the 1954 SBAC Show at Farnborough. On Flight 3, on 11 August, Bee was cleared to 30,000 feet, and to do a 'maximum dry run' at more than Mach 0.9. Bee worked up to an indicated 0.98; then the needle seemed reluctant to go any further, and Bee was not surprised because even with the P.1 this was well into the drag-rise region and with completely fixed-geometry dry engines 0.98 was all he could expect. Next morning he found Don Horsfield wreathed in smiles; after an all-night session with the project aerodynamicists and instrumentation engineers he said 'We reckon you did Mach 1 yesterday.'

In those days nobody fully understood how to make a good pitot/static system that would work through the transonic region, and the P.1 was experiencing unpredictable variable position error as the shockwaves played up and down the pitot head. Horsfield said 'If you had had enough fuel to hold full power for 30 seconds longer we think the needle would probably have jumped up to at least Mach 1'. There had been no snags and WG 760 was ready, so Bee straight away planned a longer 'maximum dry run'. After the expected thrilling fast climb he reached the tropopause at 38,000 ft off Swanage, turned left at Mach 0.9 levelling out, kept full power and watched the Isle of Wight pass under the nose. He planned either to reach Mach 1 by Selsey Bill or cancel. The Machmeter fairly steadily went round to 0.985 and then hesitated, as before. Then there seemed to be a barely perceptible shudder, and the ASI and altimeter readings suddenly changed slightly—and there was 1.02 showing on the Machmeter. The P.1 was rock steady, there was no trim change, and cautious control 'nibbles' showed crisp responses, not quite so well damped in pitch but still very good about all axes. Bee turned to port and reduced power, and in the course of this turn became probably the first British pilot to experience the slight nose-up trim change as a supersonic aircraft transitions back to subsonic flight. On course for Boscombe he could see the airfield far ahead and could not resist once again opening the throttles, this time in a slight dive, and giving them the good news with a terrific bang.

In the first month WG 760 flew 14 times, and 32 times by the end of September, though by the start of 'Farnborough week' it had just missed its tenth hour and so was barred from taking part—though Bee was often high overhead during the show and could easily have joined in (the real reason was surely the Ministry security experts). A little later the company was asked to put on a demonstration for Prince Bernhardt, and when Bee landed he was angrily rebuked by the accompanying UK Minister of Defence for 'dangerously risking the aircraft' (which, I hardly need add, test pilots do not do). Later the company received official confirmation of the minister's displeasure, and was forbidden to do any demonstration flying—until the next call for a VIP show three weeks later when the ban was suddenly forgotten. Can you wonder that some people question the British tradition of government by 'cultured amateurs'?

When Phase I at Boscombe had been completed, including system tests and landing measurements (one of the areas of previous uncertainty), the aircraft had flown 21 hours in 27 flights and amply fulfilled all expectations. On 23 September Bee flew it back to Warton, making a fine bang on his arrival for the assembled work-force but sadly having to tell the tower he was forbidden to do the requested flight demonstration. From then until 1957 Bee, later joined by Desmond de Villiers and Peter Hillwood, worked through a vast programme of P.1 flight development that was made easy by the superb flying qualities and high serviceability of the aircraft and difficult by almost everything else—especially the input from the customer. Throughout, lack of fuel remained an annoying and limiting restriction. As I commented earlier, this was a prized British tradition for fighters, but from 1955 Bee constantly campaigned for the fuel capacity to be increased. The total of 5,000 lb was less than the minimum normal for recovery on the Canberra!

In November 1955 WG 760 was re-engined with Sapphire 5R engines with primitive reheat and fixed-area nozzles giving a maximum sea-level thrust of about 9,200 lb. It was a real hairy experimental installation, because without reheat the crude big nozzles reduced thrust to barely 5,500 lb, which was grossly inefficient and gave no single-engine safety. But the reheat, if it lit properly, enabled the speed in level flight gradually to be worked up to 1.53. The aircraft could have gone faster, but directional stability was becoming marginal and fuel was inadequate. There was just enough for a single run to about Mach 1.5 and then a direct descent to Warton to arrive overhead with enough fuel for one spare circuit (assuming the whole flight plan had been flown with precision). In 1956 Peter Twiss showed me the flight recorder trace for his world record with the FD.2. The velocity and Mach number rose steadily from the beginning of each run to the end. The average was about Mach 1.73, but if the little delta had had more fuel he could probably have exceeded Mach 2, enabling Britain to set a 1,500 mph mark that would have been even harder to beat. I think the trouble is simply that living in a small island gives people rather restricted minds. I mean this quite literally. It was fundamental to the P.1 that the eventual fighter was supposed to release its brakes, scoot up to 35,000 ft, intercept something (right first time) and then dive straight back to base. The only people who thought that it might get lost in bad weather, or have to intercept two targets in one sortie, or fly a different kind of mission, or be ferried overseas, or operate in a bigger country, were people outside the Air Staff.

So a typical P.1 flight was planned very carefully so that a first-class pilot could just squeeze in the required test. Many of the tests in 1955 were rudder jerks to test yaw damping, which was observed chiefly in terms of the decay of the roll oscillation induced by the yaw. As explained on p. 155, the test pilots at North American learned in the hardest possible way about inertia coupling between roll and yaw, but this potentially very catastrophic regime was thoroughly explored by the P.1 without incident. What was obvious was that the fin would have to be bigger on the P.1B, if that aircraft was safely to reach Mach 2. A happy discovery was that the plot of cross-section areas of the P.1 approximated closely to the optimum according to the NACA Area Rule, which was disclosed in 1954 (p. 178). In sharp contrast to such machines as the Hunter, Javelin, Sea Vixen and Scimitar, which were doomed to stay subsonic, the P.1 conformed to the required plot of area distribution as a result of the axial length of the wing and the long parallel section of body. From 1955 project studies took this rule carefully into account in planning shapes and locations for the excrescences which were later added for various reasons. But at no time did area ruling appear obvious, as was the case with some of the American fighters of the mid-1950s.

By 1954 the government had become distinctly tetchy over the very slow rate of development and production of new aircraft for the RAF, especially swept-wing (but subsonic) fighters. This was due in part to a late start, to timid step-by-step introduction of any new aerodynamics, and to extreme industrial weakness in terms of numbers of engineers and availability of wind tunnels and other research tools. It was accentuated by the fact that all the development, right up to clearance for service, was supposed to be done with two or three prototypes. When, as often happened, at least one of these was written off, the programme was significantly delayed still further. Duncan Sandys, Minister of Supply, wrung his hands and sagely observed (in September 1953) 'If only we had sufficient prototypes and pre-production aircraft we might have got the Swift and Hunter into service a year earlier'. His former Parliamentary Secretary, Toby Low, had an absolute brainwave: why not order more? This suggestion was hailed by Sandys as a British triumph, and he called a press conference to explain how wonderful it was. I naughtily tried to find out if he had heard of the Cook–Craigie plan (p. 173); someone in RAF uniform came to his aid with 'That's American Sir', and I was told that Britain had 'studied the US method, but the new policy is better for our purpose'. One simply dared not pursue the matter and ask why. At least the tangible result emerged that there were to be 20 P.1B development aircraft. Much later I discovered that the exact situation was that there would be three hand-built P.1B prototypes, five P.1Bs built in production jigs and a third batch (added at the time of the press conference) for a further 15. The intention was that when the last of these came off the line it would be immediately succeeded by the first true production fighter. It seemed reasonable to assume that some of the 20 production-built aircraft might later be brought up to CA Release standard and issued to Fighter Command, but I eventually received a letter stating '. . . this information cannot be disclosed . . .'. One took it that the matter had not been decided, so it was made secret.

The second P.1A, WG 763, flew at Warton on 18 July 1955. It was built with an Aden 30 mm gun on each side of the cockpit, a permanently attached 250-gal fuel tank faired into the belly aft of the wing—the first bit of area-rule in-filling—and instead of split flaps had plain flaps which in later aircraft might be sealed to serve as integral tanks. In September 1955 this aircraft flew impressively at the SBAC show, Bee pulling sustained very tight turns in a way that was probably best appreciated by the American pilots who were familiar with the USAF's Century-series aircraft. Later, in January 1957, WG 760 appeared with a noticeably modified wing. Following similar modifications by many other supersonic and subsonic fighters, the wing had reduced sweep on the outer leading edge beyond the saw-cut, giving a broader tip with reduced thickness/chord ratio and slight camber to curve the leading edge downwards. The aileron was terminated short of the tip and the saw-cut was modified. The resulting wing had better lift at high angles, lower subsonic drag and a better high-altitude buffet boundary. In other words it was just what was needed for a future heavier version, and also increased the range appreciably. It was so obvious an improvement that I was genuinely surprised when it was not seen again for seven years. The Treasury had discovered it would add about 0.01% to the price of each aircraft, and the RAF were quite happy to stay with the old wing with less lift and more drag.

In January 1956 Bee gave a Royal Aeronautical Society 'young people's' lecture in which he explained how hard he tried not to make bangs on populated areas. I suspect most of his audience would have loved a few juicy bangs, and they were always a great attraction at Farnborough shows in the early 1950s, but by this time the environmental lobby was just beginning to awaken and make itself felt. Trying not to cause a nuisance, said the test pilot, 'adds considerably to the workload'. In the following year he and his growing team were confined to a small area of the Irish Sea where they could, with precise flying, just fit in a 60 second run at over Mach 1, sometimes at extremely low level (but they could not get near the maximum speed because of lack of fuel). Simultaneously the MoS sternly decreed that 'Valuable prototypes must not be flown over the sea'. While this nonsense was sorted out there remained the problem that there was no proper navigation system, which could be a crucial problem with such a ridiculously small fuel supply, and that—as one test pilot said—'you can never get a chase aircraft unless something has already gone wrong'. Not too much went wrong with either P.1A, apart from the difficulties with the undeveloped reheat and nozzle system of the engines, though I must record that in August 1956 the canopy came off in flight for the third time in less than a year. I remember engineers at Republic Aviation in New York being staggered at this; their attitude was 'anything can happen once, but nothing—but nothing—ever happens three times'.

This habit of losing canopies was odd, because Martin–Baker's ejection devices are nothing if not reliable (which means that they do not go off by themselves) and the canopy itself was unusually rigid, being in the form of a massive light-alloy hood with left and right inserted transparencies instead of the more common single blown transparency with a metal frame. But, so long as nobody gets hurt, this kind of history is merely embarrassing. What about the programme as a whole? Elsewhere more than a dozen other supersonic fighters were being developed—most of them are in this book—and by 1957 at least seven were in operational service. All had been started later than the English Electric programme, and by any yardstick they had moved at a cracking pace (several established a time of approximately two years from first flight to operational service). The general idea seemed to be that supersonic fighters were things that nations needed for their self-protection in an unpredictable world, and the sooner the better. Nobody could tell what the British policy was—apart, I suppose, from the CAS and maybe two or three people in the Cabinet—but one inevitably formed the view that official policy was that all this sort of thing was terribly difficult and so was going to take ages. In a companion volume on 'Bombers of the West' I recalled how, when the British V-bombers were still on paper, the only thing that ministers publicly emphasised was that they were going to take very many years to develop. In the same way, the very notion of a supersonic fighter seemed so 'futuristic' to the British planners that it appeared to escape their notice that the timing might be important.

Moreover, there seemed to be a vague yet powerful feeling in British official circles that developing a supersonic fighter was bold to the point of rashness. So, while three types of V-bombers were solemnly put into production, each as an insurance against 'failure' of the others, the English Electric fighter (which posed much higher technical risks) remained a solitary programme with no fall-back insurance. In contrast, by the time it entered production the US Air Force had six types of supersonic fighter in service, and the US Navy had three.

One of the national handicaps seemed to be that it was considered inevitable to reach a final design via a series of plodding intermediate stages. Thus, the Hunter and Swift were preceded by interminable fiddling research programmes, many of which kept being bogged down by development problems on items which were not used in the final fighter at all. Nobody seemed to notice that the first F-86 Sabre to fly, several valuable years earlier, was merely the first off the production line. In the same way, while the first F-100 was merely the first off the line, the first P.1 was as much like a fighter as chalk is like cheese. One cannot blame Petter, who produced exactly what the customer ordered. Likewise Armstrong Siddeley and Rolls produced what the customer ordered, though I think the prolonged lag in British reheat systems must reflect to some degree on the engine firms. Altogether the result was that time from first flight to squadron service was not two years but six—one year late on a 10-year programme.

I must emphasise that this timing was set by the customer, not by the contractor. They don't come much better than the team at Warton, and I believe that if their customer had been the Russians or the Americans the P.1B would have been in service by late 1956 (four years earlier than the achieved date). The cost saving would have been considerable, because time costs money. There was no evident reason why there could not have been three or four P.1Bs in 1954 and at least 20 the following year. I could find nobody at Armstrong Siddeley, Rolls-Royce, Ferranti, Elliott or elsewhere who was prepared to say he could not have met such a schedule if the pressure had really been on. If the PERT technique had been used it would have shown up the DH Propellers missile as pacing item; extra effort could have been put on to this, while the first squadrons could have formed in 1956–57 without it. I once had a chat along these lines with Mr Page himself; rather drily he commented that he didn't know if such a fast programme was possible because nobody had asked.

But the P.1 was such a splendid aeroplane it made up for the muddled, plodding customer. I briefly visited XA 847, the first of the hand-built P.1Bs, in March 1957 shortly before first flight. Apart from the wing it was a near-redesign, and looked marvellous. I was impressed by the profusion of numbered access hatches, almost all of them added since the P.1A, which appeared to cover about two-thirds of the lower part of the lofty fuselage. To my surprise it had not only a pair of Rolls-Royce Avons, but also a completely different airbrake geometry and several other unexpected features, but I was politely told not to be daft when I asked about armament and radar (which was still absent). Bee flew XA 847 on 4 April 1957. On the very same day the government published its classic *Defence—an Outline of Future Policy*, which is colloquially known as The Sandystorm (our Duncan was now wearing a different hat). He put his signature to some startling statements, one of which, having lately dealt with surface-to-air missiles, continued 'In view of the good progress already made, the Government have come to the conclusion that the RAF are unlikely to have a requirement for fighter aircraft of types more advanced than the supersonic P.1 and work on such projects will stop'. The die was henceforth cast. Though the P.1 programme was going to survive, by the skin of its teeth, the view was going to be 'It's only an aeroplane, so it's a temporary expedient until we get missiles, and we're certainly not going to spend money improving it'. In the MoS one found a wonderful new confidence. At last the future could be seen with clarity. Though almost everyone was agreed that the P.1 was needed, as a temporary stop-gap, nobody though it would be in service more than two or three years. The Controller, Aircraft, said to me 'It does seem a pity that, having worked so hard to perfect this fine fighter, it is clearly going to have a very short operational career.' He would not be drawn on just how short, but another expert promised me the last fighter would be gone 'well before 1964' though there might be some need for a few overseas beyond that time. The important thing was that now there was at last a firm policy, even though a few misguided people appeared to be trying to prove it faulty.

This made life even more difficult for the Warton team, and so far as I can tell did little to help the DH Propellers missile team either—Guy Gardiner, Dr George Hough, John Mullin, Chalky White *et al.*—whose odd complaint was that the first batch of Blue Jay missiles with full guidance all worked perfectly, and thus taught them nothing. Later Blue Jay missiles did succeed in misbehaving, which I suppose in a way made them happier. Meanwhile the Ferranti team in Edinburgh got AI-23 flying in a Canberra, created a super attack sight and then tied the two together in Airpass, a singularly happy acronym formed from 'Airborne Interception Radar, Pilot Attack Sight System'. Parts of Airpass, and the airborne part of the Blue Jay system, were built into the next two aircraft, XA 835 and 856. By this time the two P.1As had almost become irrelevant, apart from proving the cambered wing until 1958, but the pace of P.1B flying stepped up sharply. Bee flew 847 no fewer than 32 times in the first month, despite the interim engines with a peak reheat rating of about 13,000 lb. He reached Mach 1.2 on the first flight, soon explored behaviour out to the initial CA Release figure of 1.7 (everything fine, bags of power in reserve) and finally, in a wonderful flight on 25 November 1958, that was chancing his arm just a little, crossed the Lake District from the Irish Sea at Mach 2—and then cancelled reheat, turned to starboard and at Mach 1.8 sharply closed the throttles to prove the intake stability. The P.1B behaved perfectly, and this was a very big step forward indeed.

The previous month the CAS, Sir Dermot Boyle (who later became deputy chairman of BAC), performed a pleasant ceremony at which he named the P.1B the Lightning. It is worth recalling that, in 1942, the first British jet fighter, the Gloster F.9/40, was about to be named Thunderbolt when this name was chosen for the Republic P-47 (so the British fighter became the Meteor). By 1958 the Thunderbolt's partner, the Lockheed P-38 Lightning, was no longer in service so this time there was no conflict. As the 20 production-built development aircraft had been coming off the line since April 1958 the Lightning's development really got under way with a vengeance in that year, with Wg Cdr Jimmy Dell arriving from Fighter Command to help clear the operational aircraft. I telephoned Alan Brothers, the helpful PR man for English Electric, when I heard that six Lightnings had flown. I was after a sensational picture and asked 'Can you get them all in the air together?' His classic response was 'Cripes, mate, we can't even get them all on the ground together!'

Materials, jigs and tools for production had been ordered in November 1955, the first production order for 50 Lightning F.1 aircraft was placed in November 1956, and a bigger order, for what became the Lightning F.2 and T.4, followed in April 1958. This was a sound basis for a sound programme, but it continued to be based solely on the short-range, short-sighted mission of Fighter Command in the point defence of East Coast V-bomber bases and 2nd TAF airfields in Germany. The first of the 20 development aircraft, XG 307, was virtually a Lightning F.1, though it first flew—on 3 April 1958—with the original size of fin which had been judged smaller than ideal in view of the obvious possibility of the ultimate aircraft exceeding Mach 2. It had AI-23 in the intake cone, the full Airpass system, two Adens above and a quickly-fitted pack below containing either two more Adens or the missile pylons and airborne missile interface equipment. The missile itself, which in 1958 went into initial production with the new name of Firestreak, was carried clipped to neat pylons projecting on each side of the lower pack. Under the rear fuselage was the standard 250 gal tank, and the engine was an Avon 201 (RA.24R) with reheat which came in in four steps and at the top step gave about 14,430 lb, or almost double the thrust of the original P.1. With 7,500 lb of fuel there was just enough for a climb to 35,000 ft, acceleration to 1.5, a one-pass stern interception and return to base with 1,600 lb fuel on landing.

English Electric had in early 1958 prepared a detailed design for an improved and more flexible Lightning which appeared virtually certain to win large export sales. It had the kinked and cambered wing, which had been flying for two years. It had a much bigger, fully area-ruled ventral tank which actually had slightly lower drag, as well as fuel in the flaps and an option of jettisonable external tanks above the wings. A further option was a wide range of surface-attack or reconnaissance stores in place of fuel in part or all of the big belly fairing. Compared with the Lightning F.1 this offered 40% more range and a multi-role capability, with no penalty in flight performance. There were several obvious customers, of whom by far the most important was Federal Germany. Her Majesty's Government (HMG) replied that the Lightning was too expensive already, was only a stop-gap until Fighter Command used nothing but missiles, and that it had no intention of funding any Lightning development that the RAF had not asked for. As for Germany, HMG was going to sell that country the SR.177 (p. 63), and would English Electric kindly go away and get on with the RAF's F.1s. As English Electric had for years been financing export versions of the Canberra it could not afford to fund this obvious development of the Lightning, but it did make a habit of never letting too many months go by without writing a formal memo on what ought to be done.

Although the Germans were intensely interested in the SR.177, they regarded a multi-role Lightning as worthy of full evaluation, and made a number of inquiries of HMG and English Electric before finally deciding the British were mad. Ultimately the only possible answer seemed to be the Lockheed F-104G (p. 200), which thereby picked up European sales exceeding 1,000. It appeared not to have occurred to anyone in HMG that the modifications that needed to be done to the Lightning to meet the German requirements were not as extensive as those needed by the F-104. And the huge NATO market would have been approximately equalled by potential sales for an optimised Lightning in 14 other countries. But English Electric simply could not find the money to do it unaided, and the idea of a long-range multi-role Lightning seemed to give the RAF a pain.

Before the F.1 was cleared for service there were one of two other interesting developments that came to nothing. One was rocket boost. As the SR.177 chapter makes clear, although the turbojet with reheat is great for supersonic propulsion, its thrust falls away with altitude, and above about 36,000 feet it falls away very sharply indeed. As the margin of thrust over drag at supersonic speeds is in any case small, it follows that fighters can easily run out of fuel trying to accelerate to maximum speed. Even quite a small rocket can make a dramatic difference to the margin of thrust over drag, and this margin increases enormously at increasing altitudes high in the stratosphere. The Armstrong Siddeley Screamer and de Havilland Spectre were available off the shelf, but the top men of English Electric, Sir George Nelson and his son (dare I mention that the latter was, inevitably, Half Nelson?) were also top men of D. Napier & Son Ltd., proud makers of aero engines. In no time they had secured a contract for the very neat Double Scorpion HTP/kerosene rocket which thrust a Canberra to a world record altitude of 70,310 feet on 28 August 1957 in the skilled and patient hands of Napier c.t.p. Mike Randrup and test engineer Walter Shirley. This was a period when dear old HMG was trying to fit rockets to V-bombers, fighters and almost anything with wings. In February 1958 it was officially announced 'The Double Scorpion will be fitted to the production P.1B aircraft'; but of course it wasn't, any more than the other rockets were fitted to all the other types of aircraft. How could we waste money on things with men in them? We needed rockets for the marvellous missiles, which were suddenly going to inherit the Earth.

Another promising scheme was itself based on one of the marvellous missiles, although this one unfortunately still needed an aircraft to carry it within range of its target. It was the American air-to-air rocket now called Genie. Really it was not a very clever missile because it had no guidance, but it more than made up for this by having a nuclear warhead. Quite early in its development, when it was still known only by its code-name of Ding Dong, it was considered sufficiently interesting to the RAF for English Electric to receive a paid study contract for a Genie-armed Lightning. The obvious way to carry the rocket would have appeared to be two extra pylons, either above the wing or below the fuselage, but the scheme finally chosen was a semi-recessed installation of one Genie on the centreline ahead of a shortened belly tank. Development reached the hardware stage, with one aircraft conversion and missiles earmarked for a UK trials programme, before the RAF decided to drop their requirement in view of what Mr Sandys had said about manned fighters (odd, because what Mr Sandys said was supposed to *reflect* the view of the Service, not influence it).

I spent a lot of time with the Lightnings in the final stages of their clearance for service, and it was a time unique in history. Everyone knew the aircraft was potentially an absolute winner, and the great manufacturing industry of hundreds of companies that lay behind it had fully recovered from its desperate weakness of 1945–53 and had almost all the people and equipment and raw material it needed to sustain a good programme. But that silly piece of paper of April 1957 exerted such a powerful and far-flung effect that decisions were frequently wrong; on the occasions when they were right, they were half-hearted and late. There was hardly a single item in the Lightning F.1, or missing from it, that was not thus affected. To pick an example at random, the need for a steerable nosewheel had been under discussion since about 1955, but persistently deferred. English Electric developed a nosewheel steering system, fitted it, flew it and cleared it for service use. Then in 1958 it was cancelled, so the RAF pilots had to wend their way along aprons and perimeter tracks by using the rudder pedals to make the brakes on the main wheels work differentially. It was widely felt that this was a mistake, just as it would be a mistake to fit acetylene lamps to a modern Rolls-Royce car, but any long-term objective view of the situation was impossible. The Lightning F.1 was supposed to be the last manned fighter. There was no point in developing any new equipment for it when it was only going to be a stop-gap; it was too expensive already—and as for this perpetual complaint by its maker that it ought to carry more fuel, this was just preposterous!

So, although English Electric, and increasingly the RAF as well, could see all the things that needed to be done to make it a really useful aircraft, the Lightning F.1 was the most basic short-range interceptor that could be devised. It was given CA Release (at Mach numbers to 1.5, English Electric having cleared 1.9) in December 1959, by which time four production machines (XM 129 *et seq*) had flown, the first on 29 October 1959. Deliveries began in December to CFE, and in July 1960 a flood of aircraft were sent to 74 Sqn at Coltishall. At last the RAF was in the supersonic business, and with a home-grown aircraft. To say it was a time of relief is an understatement, though one had to temper one's enthusiasm with the knowledge that what had looked like a 'flood' actually numbered a mere eight, and the rest were coming along at the rate of about one a week, with no possibility of any speed-up in output. Any expression of continuing anxiety to a minister tended to be met with the retort that a Lightning 'cost as much as $59\frac{3}{4}$ Spitfires' (some such daft sum was actually worked out, and almost got into an MoA press release) and that one could not expect to see large numbers of such aircraft—and of course surface-to-air guided weapons would soon replace them anyway.

Coltishall, in the flat Norfolk Broads country, was in 1960 one of the most exciting stations in the RAF. To get there one drove past Horsham St Faith, one of the most famous fighter airfields, which in 1960 was being swallowed by the expanding city of Norwich. Housing estates were already being built across the grass hallowed by the take-offs of RAF fighters from

Hunters back to S.E.5as. Such bases were no longer tenable, not only on the score of field length but also because of noise in the increasing urban environment. Coltishall represented the future, in so far as manned aircraft were thought to have one. The main runway was 8,000 feet long, paved with concrete and fitted with ILS. Millions had been spent on new buildings and facilities, including such things as underground storage and ready rooms for the Firestreak missiles. CFE had lately moved in from West Raynham, and 74 were displaying their Tiger badge, and yellow/black fang-like markings, with justified one-upmanship. Their pilots had to search quite hard to find features in the Lightning to complain of, and there has never been a supersonic aeroplane with fewer vices or pilot problems, apart from early snags with avionics and reheat. Despite its cleared speed in excess of 1,500 mph the Lightning could be landed at under 150 knots, and flown to 115 knots before stalling, so that its speed range was remarkable. Pilot view was excellent, the take-off and climb breathtaking, and the Airpass, Adens and Firestreaks worked very well. In theory the Firestreak pack could in about an hour be replaced by a pack containing two more Adens and their ammunition, or by yet a third pack with flip-out launchers for 48 2-inch FFARs, but the Air Staff did not seem very interested in these options. The rockets were considered 'lousy except at point-blank range' and it was heresy even to think of the Lightning performing any surface-attack role where FFARs are more effective.

One could easily have gone away from Coltishall feeling wholly elated, with vivid mental pictures of a squadron working up into the supersonic age with its overtones of high technology and livid gold shock-diamonds thundering from superimposed nozzles. But when one dug a little deeper it was clear that the RAF had a very long way to go. It only needed a single question, such as 'What is the target for maintenance man-hours per flight hour?' to cool the atmosphere sharply. This particular question brought forth an instant series of sidesteps and passed bucks, until the Station Engineering Officer sought guidance—and possibly for authority to give me an unhelpful reply. After quite a long discussion with a rather worried-looking group of chaps, and solemn promises on my part to print nothing, I was given a pretty complete picture. Even today someone might complain if I quoted numbers, and it would serve no useful purpose, but I am referring to it because in my view the RAF had made inadequate preparation for the Lightning and would have been very hard pressed indeed if there had been a sudden real emergency. The MMH/FH figures were almost staggeringly bad, and so was the achieved flying rate, yet nobody could accuse the Lightning of being a 'can of worms' or even difficult to look after (a lot of people did, but they were merely looking for an excuse). Many years later the view was put to me that the RAF has a long heritage of problems with each new aeroplane. 'For the first few years they call it a heap of old rubbish, because they can't maintain it . . . they go off on week-end stand-down from Thursday to Tuesday, and take a week's leave a month, and knock any new hardware because it's too difficult for them.'

One began to feel a course on internal and external relations might be a useful exercise—not to make people say everything was falsely wonderful, but to control the 'knockers' for whom nothing was any good until it had been around for years and was part of the accepted scene. Perhaps a very good result of using foreign or collaborative aircraft, such as the Phantom and Jaguar, has been to make the RAF realise that other people may have been getting better results with the same hardware which they abuse with such gusto. So when the Lightning at last went into service it had to take its place with all the other no-good difficult-to-maintain horrors that really reflected the user's incompetence. And it wasn't only a matter of talk; the inadequate ground support practically neutered the true operational strength of Fighter Command.

What made the poor old RAF's task harder was that they had to keep learning new marks of Lightning. After making 20 F.1s production switched to 28 designated F.1A, with a horrid flight-refuelling probe which could be clipped on beneath the port wing like a huge jousting lance and then unbolted before flying a combat mission. It would have been so much better if a neat folding probe had been included at the start, as it was on the Crusader (p. 234). The 1A also introduced a uhf radio and had rearranged equipment, with a long external cable duct along the left side of the fuselage below the wing. Then followed the F.2 and T.4. The latter was virtually a side-by-side two-seat version of the 1A, with a cockpit nearly a foot wider, and controls, instrument panels, radar scopes and sights, but with only one Aden gun. Work on the English Electric P.11, as it was first known, began in June 1957 to provide an aircraft for conversion training and proficiency checks, and the RAF batch of 20 called Lightning T.4 were ordered in April 1958. Two prototypes were built, the first (XL 628) flying on 6 May 1959; the first production aircraft (XM 966) flew on 15 July 1960 and deliveries to 226 OCU at Coltishall began in June 1962. The F.2, of which 44 were ordered at the same time, introduced Avon 210s with four-stage reheat, a liquid-oxygen breathing system, a completely revised 'integrated' instrument panel, improved avionics and other changes. The first, XN 723, flew on 11 July 1961, and 65 were built for 19 and 92 Sqns, entering service with these units in 1963 at Leconfield and in 1965 moving with them to the hot spot at Gütersloh where we shall meet them again.

In 1958 the F.2 had been a rather annoying but so obviously better kind of Lightning that it was judged marginally worth having as an insurance against delays with the marvellous missiles. But by 1960 the position had changed dramatically. By this time the Sandystorm was something ministers were trying to forget, and with TSR.2 under contract for delivery in 1967 the manned combat aeroplane was no longer an unmentionable idea and even had to be re-accepted by the Treasury, which in 1959 had still been resisting any improvement to the Lightning whatsoever. During 1960 the RAF succeeded in establishing a case for a complete 'second-generation Lightning', both to supplement earlier marks and to replace them, because it was now agreed that it would be 'unwise to predict, or attempt to predict, when manned fighters will finally go out of use'. Perhaps the government was influenced by the huge European production plan for the F-104G Starfighter, and by America's mighty scheme to replace its Century-series fighters with the TFX. And delta-winged Migs and Sukhois, all with seats for a human pilot, were obviously pouring off the lines by the hundred. So when the F.2 became hardware it was not the ultimate, but only an interim machine pending a completely new ultimate, the F.3.

All this time English Electric, which in February 1960 merged its Aviation company into the new British Aircraft Corporation (BAC), kept pecking patiently away with the need for twice the fuel capacity, and someone was politely acknowledging the memos and pigeon-holing them. But the RAF were not interested, and instead wished the F.3 to incorporate a new radar, new missiles and new engines. So I had better go back to the question of flight performance, and how it was used.

All Lightnings so far had been planned to meet the 1949 specification calling for a curve-of-pursuit stern chase. After hearing about the US Air Force's collision-course technique from 1948 onwards the RAF decided after ten years there must be something in it. DH Propellers had from the start of a programme called Firestreak 4, in 1956, sought to produce an improved air-to-air missile that could home on to infra-red radiation from enemy aircraft even from head-on, or from any other direction, and by 1960 this was well advanced in development under a new name: Red Top. Compared with Firestreak it is bigger, has a hemispherical seeker head instead of one looking like a sharp pencil, and has the seemingly more logical layout of a warhead at the front (instead of wrapped round the rocket blast pipe) and control actuators near the controls (instead of at the other end, driving through long push/pull rods). Red Top is still partly classified but can do a much greater interception job than Firestreak. Unfortunately it was incompatible with the original Firestreak airborne equipment and avionics, so it really needed a new Lightning to carry it. The Lightning F.3 was in fact planned with a new Airpass system and a versatile missile pack which could be armed with either Firestreak or Red Top. Lots of Firestreaks were in use, and Fighter Command did not wish to junk them when the new Lightning arrived—though in 1961 an unfortunate erk caused two Firestreaks to fall off the pylons of a parked F.1 and they were written off at a cost of (the MoD said) £20,500. I considered it would be more sensible for these missiles to have been stripped and repaired, but trying to discover what happened, and why, was like hitting one's head on a brick wall. I would still like to know—and so might other taxpayers—and I doubt if the knowledge would endanger the kingdom.

All Lightnings had ample performance, but Rolls-Royce not only kept improving the Avon's reheat system (which was very necessary) but also made the basic Avon more powerful (which was a bonus). For the F.3 the RB.146 was developed, and put into production as the Mk 301 Avon at 12,690 lb dry and 16,300 lb with reheat. A Swedish-built version, with even greater thrust, powers the Draken (p. 106). Thus we have a most interesting situation in which there are two excellent Mach 2 interceptors, one having a single RB.146 and the other having two. By this time the Avon had a properly developed reheat system, so at air displays one had to abandon the pastime of frantic betting on the winking eyes one would see from the rear. Moreover, whereas in 1957 Rolls had predicted the Avon's 1g surge line at well under Mach 2, in fact the RA.24R family behaved very well, so that the Lightning test pilots began exploring surge under g loadings and eventually plotted a boundary which, though having the shape the Derby company expected, was really quite far away from most normal flight manoeuvres. In practice it meant you could work a Lightning up to Mach 2, slam the throttles closed and then pull a 5g turn—something that could not be done in any other fighter until the F-14 and F-15.

This marvellous propulsion system, though terribly long in the tooth (the Avon dates from 1945), gives the Lightning a thrust/weight ratio close to unity, which for an aeroplane to a 1949 Spec. is not bad. This is most valuable for fast acceleration from brakes-release, fast climb, and sustained manoeuvres without losing speed. It was so good, you will recall, that the promised rocket was judged not needed, and thrown away. In parallel, the basic aeroplane was so right first time that no aerodynamic change was made at all, apart from clearing the added 250-gal tank with its narrow central fin. With the Lightning F.1 and F.2 there was need for nothing more than fine tuning of the flight controls by attending to gear ratios and artificial feel, but for the F.3 it was judged prudent to add a further 15% to the area of the fin. The original big fin, introduced on the P.1B, was needed as soon as it was clear that Mach 2 could be reached. But the yaw/roll damping with the F.3 in full-power turns at maximum speed again looked, on paper, to be marginal, so a new square-topped fin was adopted and flown on one of the several F.2 and P.1B aircraft used for F.3 development (it was XG310, flown on 9 January 1962). This new fin was especially welcome when the missiles were Red Tops, with their bigger areas fastened well forward of the c.g. A further major aerodynamic, structural and systems development, which the company had wanted to do for a long time, was to clear the use of two 260-gal ferry tanks on overwing pylons, with powered ejectors. One might have thought this would lead to all sorts of trouble, but the unusual installation worked like a charm. The RAF, of course, showed no interest, and bought 63 F.3s in 1961 without it. Even more unbelievably, it also bought them without guns, because the Air Staff finally thought these were not worth having.

At this point I must mention the Auto-Attack System, which was placed under contract with Ferranti, English Electric, Elliott and other companies in 1958. Whereas in 1949 the concept of a radar-equipped single-seat supersonic all-weather fighter seemed a formidable challenge, by 1958 it was clear that the US Air Force had moved even faster. The near-automaticity of the F-102 (p. 166) had led to the totally automatic F-106 in which the pilot could in theory fly the entire mission as a passive observer, ready to break into the control loop only if something went wrong. By adding a computer and a precise air-data system, and redesigning major modules in the avionics, it was possible to do the same thing with the Lightning. By 1960 one of the 20 development aircraft was flying with the whole Auto-Attack System in operable condition. Although some of the 20 P.1B development aircraft had unearthed major systems problems, all the development programmes ran very well to timetable, and this one, the most advanced of the lot, was actually particularly trouble-free. Automatic flight trials against other Lightnings went like clockwork, and Boscombe wrote a highly encouraging report, after exactly the planned number of tests with no contingency time. Then came the parrot-cry of 'No more money for Lightnings' echoing down the Ministry corridors, and the MoA suddenly said the RAF didn't actually have a requirement. And, in any case, RAF chaps were judged very good at poling fighters round the sky manually. So the system was junked; and, in true British fashion, it was first announced when it was cancelled.

Fortunately the Lightning is a marvellous aeroplane to pole around the sky. Anyone still unsure of this can put himself in the position of Wg Cdr Jimmy Dell, who in May 1961 was one of the BAC test pilots assigned to the Paris air show. The Le Bourget controllers were finding life hard, and Dell found himself caught in a 45-minute stack, bumping about through the low clouds with his fuel gauges unwinding alarmingly. Eventually he had no alternative but to divert to Boscombe. Having shut everything down, and seen the bowser coupled up, he went and phoned Le Bourget. A crisp French voice said "What a pity you're not still standing by; we've got a gap coming up in 15 minutes." Dell politely thanked the controller, sprinted back to the Lightning and made it into the show with 60 seconds to spare.

From 1961 BAC were constantly discussing export Lightnings with a range of overseas nations, but continued to be frustrated by the disinterest of HMG in funding a new fuel system. Had this been done I think BAC could have found the money to develop all sorts of surface-attack systems and weapons such as those they wistfully exhibited in model form at that year's SBAC show, in defiance of the RAF—though an inertial navigation system might have been beyond them. South Africa, Israel, Brazil, India, Finland, Greece—the list of potential customers prepared to stand up and be counted was impressive, but in Whitehall the cry 'No more money for Lightnings' had become almost a clarion call. Even though it was now admitted that manned fighters were not quite dead after all, BAC were doing the TSR.2 and ought to stop their tiresome campaign about exporting the Lightning. Even the kinked/cambered wing, flown in 1956, was left off the F.3 to save paying a bit extra for it. Yet when contracts were signed for 22 T.5 trainers, the dual version of the F.3, nobody minded paying quite a lot extra to have this mark developed and built at Filton, which was a part of BAC that badly needed work. XM 967, the first T.5, was flown by Jimmy Dell at Bristol on 29 March 1962. Production T.5s, beginning with XS 418, were delivered to CFE, which moved to Binbrook, to the Lightning OCU (No 226) at Coltishall and to all Lightning squadrons (5, 11, 19, 23, 29, 56, 74, 92 and 111). Production F.3s, from Warton, began with XP 693 on 16 June 1962, and this mark gradually replaced earlier Lightnings in all squadrons except 19 and 92 in Germany.

It was while F.3s were rolling off the line in 1963 that something happened that must have made people at Warton take a firm grip on their chairs to avoid keeling over in a dead faint. The MoA formally told BAC that it had been decided that, as the Lighting was deficient in range and could not easily be flown out to reinforce overseas theatres, a development contract would be issued for a modified fuel system of very much greater capacity. Moreover, the new fuel system, when developed, would be built into all the existing F.3 aircraft as a costly modification. I don't think there were any red faces in Whitehall; the experts who had obstructed this development for six years seemed to have retired, or gone into hiding.

BAC took the fifth F.3, XP 697, and spent more than a year rebuilding it, and when it finally flew on 17 April 1964 it was so different it had a new mark number, F.6. The most obvious change was that the whole underside of the fuselage was a smoothly curved area-ruled bulge, which actually had slightly less drag than the original 250-gal tank but housed 600 Imp gal of fuel. To preserve yaw/roll behaviour at over Mach 2 this tank had twin inclined ventral fins at the rear, bigger than the original centreline fin yet having slightly better ground clearance. The new (or should I say old) kinky wing was at last fitted, giving extra lift to carry the much greater take-off weight, and the flaps were filled with fuel. Several other changes were made, including the addition of an airfield arrester hook. With more than 10,000 lb of internal fuel the F.6 was a completely new aircraft. Around it BAC were able to wrap all the stores options they had so long wished for. I cannot list them all here, but they include various reconnaissance packs, retarded bombs blown off the overwing pylons, and a twin pylon under each wing for four 1,000 lb bombs, 144 rockets or an unmentionable but large quantity of fuel. And, after endless argument and muddle, the RAF were finally persuaded that guns were no more obsolete than manned fighters, and a pair of Adens were installed in a pack in the front of the belly fairing.

The resulting Lightning F.6 had roughly 40% more range, quite apart from a completely new multi-role capability. So when the first F.3 to be delivered, XP 693, reached CFE in January 1964 it was no more the ultimate Lightning than the 1A or 2 had been. The fact that the F.6 was originally called Mk 3A, and that almost all the F.3s were eventually brought up to F.6 standard is slightly confusing. In 1965, for example, the RAF was receiving F.3s at F.6 standard, while the first of 62 aircraft actually bought as an F.6 (XR 752) flew on 16 June 1965. In those days the numbers of RAF Lightnings were as secret as accident rates (incidentally the *Guardian* newspaper did a well-researched review of Lightning accidents compared with those of F-104Gs on 13 June 1968), but the totals were allowed to be published in 1973. The Lightning procurement for RAF squadrons was 259, the last F.6 being delivered in August 1967. And to show I have not forgotten 19 and 92 Sqns in Germany, these painted the upper surfaces of their old F.2s olive green, to make them less conspicuous from the air, and progressively had 30 rebuilt by BAC almost up to F.6 standard with the misleading designation of F.2A—misleading, because they are quite unlike an F.2. An F.2A or F.6 turns the scales at 39,000 lb clean, and over 45,000 lb with maximum external load, compared with 26,000 lb gross for the original P.1A. Yet it still retains a sparkling performance and sweet handling, unlike some fighters which became rather unpleasant with the over-weight problems of advancing years. Indeed an F.6 can touch down at 140 knots in routine flying, which is the same as the landing speed of the old P.1 at about half the weight.

On 25 April 1968 all the UK-based Lightning units contributed to an impeccable formation fly-past at RAF Bentley Priory on the occasion of the stand-down of Fighter Command. Next day they were all back in business with Strike Command, and instead of smartly being replaced with Phantoms some of these Lightnings may soldier on wearing RAF roundels until almost 1980, racing up to take a peek at Zombies—Soviet reconnaissance aircraft on 20 hour missions. I do not blame the Air Staff for declining all the marvellous new sorts of Lightning BAC offered them as possible Mk 7 versions—with powerful look-down radars, lateral intakes, semi-recessed missiles, inertial guidance and reheat Spey engines—but I am surprised the RAF never equipped their existing Lightnings with an IR scanner nor with the radar-guided Sparrow or Falcon to give a 'mix' of weapons. The latter appeared to be highly cost/effective additions that were made to all the other all-weather fighters in this volume.

Even with just Airpass, IR missiles and Aden guns a Lightning is not a bad thing to have, and when the RAF finally decides to phase out its Lightnings it ought to get a good price for them. Indeed, as soon as the Lightning was allowed to have an adequate fuel capacity it found overseas customers for new aircraft, while at least two other air forces said, figuratively 'Blast, if only we'd waited'. BAC still had to find substantial cash sums to meet the full requirements of these customers, but the contract placed by the first of them, Saudi Arabia, in 1965, was the biggest single export deal ever gained by Britain at that time. I was amused to see that, predictably, whoever happened to be incumbent minister at the time—it was Tony Wedgwood Benn—took the credit for the deal on behalf of the government, claiming that the US had 'stood aside' because of Britain's offset deal connected with the purchase of the Phantom, F-111 and other US defence hardware. This merely made everyone think that the Saudis bought the Lightning (the Mk 53 fighter and Mk 55 trainer) because of some UK/US political deal. In fact they bought it because it was the best buy, as they will tell anyone who asks them, but 1965 was a time when the British government was determined not to let anyone think that anything good could come out of the British aircraft industry.

Later a batch of fighters and trainers were bought by Kuwait, and all these aircraft were delivered from December 1967, having conveniently followed the RAF Lightnings on the production line. On 29 August 1967 Bee made the first test of the first Saudi Mk 55. Then he hung up his bone-dome after a test-flying career which began with the Hurricane in 1941 and included the entire early development of the Canberra, Lightning and TSR.2. No better combat aeroplanes have ever been built, and it is hardly BAC's fault that all three programmes were badly hurt (lethally in the case of TSR.2) by lack of foresight and common sense on the part of the customer. This is no more than the British industry expects, and people in that industry very seldom say anything about this in public (because, as *Flight*'s Roger Bacon has pointed out, even though Ministry of Planes officials let your tyres down and throw grenades through your office window, you must never, never offend them). So I was quite unprepared when, in 1967, A. F. Atkin, BAC Lightning project manager, unburdened himself in forthright terms, 'The RAF must be the only air force with a single type of supersonic aircraft. This is a discredit to the administration, a discredit to the Air Staff and a discredit to industry . . . It is a truly great aircraft which has exceeded its specification in every significant detail . . .

but if only we had set about developing it in 1957 we should have had a very versatile aircraft . . . and saved a lot of foreign exchange on American aircraft. I for one regret that the Air Staff requirements policy was so inwards-looking . . . BAC has had to use its own money to develop the versatile export versions. We have even been charged for the use of ranges on which to carry out ground-attack trials.' I would reply 'Good on yer, Alex!' I did not realise there was anyone left in the industry prepared to say such things.

But I do not wish to end on a carping note. There is no question in my mind but that the Lightning programme, begun in 1947, yielded the aircraft that flew more excitingly yet more forgivingly than any other fighter of its generation. Young Saudis who four years ago were desert Arabs are now experienced multi-role exponents of the Lightning. They have no doubt this aeroplane is the best fighter in the world. The RAF think so too, and have a string of wins of the NATO Hudleston Trophy (top fighter unit competition against all comers) to prove it. Today the Lightning squadrons of Strike Command and 2ATAF have learned to operate a wee bit more intensively than in 1960. Let's go with *Flight International*'s photographer, Tom Hamill, to RAF Gutersloh, W Germany, to see how the 'front line' outfits are coping:

'Two Lightnings, separated by perhaps 15 seconds, appear over the inevitable German trees, put themselves accurately and somewhat unceremoniously on the centreline, spurting quick little clouds of blue smoke, and disappear smartly from view behind bobbing tail chutes. It's the calm before the storm in the revetment—20-odd ground crew, unrecognisable behind gas masks and inside full NBC (nuclear, biological, chemical) kit, stand by their respective equipment ready to swing into the routine where every man has a job to do which has to be done absolutely right, but the deadline was two minutes ago.

As the aircraft taxi in, one of the walking gasmasks greets them with a radiation check; a quick thumbs-up and the hoses play—not too much down that intake—sending off great swirling mists of steam and spray from the hot end. Into the revetment proper (tight turning for two Lightnings), inspection hatches come open, fuel hoses are attached. Houchins plugged in, Firestreaks trolleyed up and winched, Adens re-armed and cocked with that peculiarly thudding hiss, Avpin tanks topped up, tail chutes replaced. Chief Technician Jack Abbott mounts one ladder, Chief Technician 'Monty' Mountford the other; check lists displayed to and approved by the still-insulated pilots. Everyone moves clear for the eardrum-piercing self-starts and the aircraft are rolling again.'

It's all go chaps. When they're in the air they don't just fly straight and level either.

Saunders-Roe SR.53 and SR.177

During the 1950s the British aircraft industry was curiously ambivalent. On the one hand, the nation had an across-the-board lead in advanced engines that nobody could dispute, and this provided an essential foundation for a seemingly endless succession of superior types of aircraft. The man in the street—not only in Britain but almost everywhere else except, perhaps, the United States—took it for granted that British aircraft 'led the world'. But there was another side to the coin. Anyone who really knew the industry appreciated that the available talent was spread very thinly, so that while each programme imposed a bigger burden of engineering development than its predecessor, the number of engineers available remained far too small; thus, by simple mathematics, the amount of time needed for each programme grew. Coupled with the fact that the officials who specified the nation's civil and military aircraft had yet to learn that they could not keep asking for new designs at the rate of 12 to 15 per year, the result was inevitable. Though the industry was immensely talented, it launched a range of successful (ie, mass-produced) aircraft which could be counted on the fingers, plus a range of unsuccessful ones which could not be counted on the legs of a millipede.

There was not necessarily anything wrong with the unsuccessful aircraft. Technically they were generally good, and in isolation could have launched successful programmes. But there were two crippling handicaps. One was that they took far too long, for the reason given above, and so tended to be overtaken by events. The second was that Britain had gradually relapsed into a frame of mind in which a terminated aircraft programme had become a perfectly normal thing. So many aircraft had been launched and then cancelled, from the earliest days of government-supported aircraft procurement, that nobody shouted from the roof-tops that a cancelled programme really ought to be an extremely rare event, an extraordinary blot on the landscape and a cause for a searching inquiry into the reasons. By the late 1950s the strategic planning of British aviation (if there was any at all) had gone so far adrift that cancellation seemed to be the natural fate of any

British project. Out of 121 major British projects in the decade 1948–58, 113 were either quietly dropped or noisily and publicly cancelled. It was the second fate which befell the SR.53 and SR.177.

This chapter describes how extremely advanced supersonic fighters were planned by the little firm of Saunders-Roe Ltd (Saro), at East Cowes, Isle of Wight. With the benefit of hindsight one can perhaps see, even more clearly than one could see at the time, that Mach 2 fighters armed with guided missiles and propelled by both turbojets and rockets ought to be tackled by a very big organisation with vast resources. At Cowes there were hardly any resources, other than about 200 very good design and development engineers. What did this little company do? It earned its bread and butter making wings for Viscounts and pressure cabins for Valiant bombers. It single-handedly ran the programme for the gigantic ten-turboprop Princess flying boat. It developed the unique SR.A1 jet-fighter flying boat. It took over Cierva and developed that firm's Skeeter and P.531 helicopters. It completed a project study for the six-jet Duchess flying boat, and an ocean-patrol boat with Nomad compound engines, and then wondered whether it ought not instead to build a far bigger flying boat with 24 Conway turbofan engines. It also got into the supersonic fighter business, and as well as the aircraft described in this chapter carried out a project for a bigger fighter with one Gyron and one Spectre rocket, and a monster long-range interceptor with two Gyrons and four Spectres! Fortunately at this time manned space exploration did not occur to them. (I have left out several non-aviation activities at Cowes, such as the development of strain-gauge technology.)

One critic said the trouble with the British industry was that there were 'too many channels for too little water'. What he meant was that there were too many companies in the airframe business, and certainly the 1960s took care of that problem! But the number of companies was an unimportant side-issue. Competing factories in Britain could collaborate on a programme at least as well if they each kept their traditional proud identity as if they were all made to call themselves by the same name. The real problem was numbers of programmes. 'Too many cooks spoil the broth' is emphatically untrue where aerospace is concerned. What the nation wanted to arrange was thousands of cooks efficiently organised to produce a few good broths in a short time. What it had was thousands of cooks getting ulcers trying to produce scores of different broths. It was probably inevitable that reshaping the industry should be painful. In any case, before the process of mergers and take-overs began, the Minister of Defence did his bit by wildly swinging a great axe which chopped most of the biggest programmes, including those of this chapter, to pieces. The fact that he did it for totally irrelevant reasons is, in the context of history, unimportant. At the time it seemed a disaster, and of all the programmes he chopped up the one I was personally most upset about was the Saunders-Roe SR.177.

Perhaps it bears out my argument to recall that Saro got into the business of supersonic fighters because none of its numerous existing programmes seemed likely to lead to a commercial product! In 1950 BOAC had made it quite clear it did not intend to order the Princess, the SR/A1 was a terminated programme, the RAF looked askance at the big patrol boat, and the proposed six-jet Duchess was just a set of drawings which had interested Tasman Empire Airways. Rather than pour further company money into 24-engined flying boats, Saunders-Roe began to cast around for a new line of business that appeared likely to lead to useful orders. Chief designer Henry Knowler asked his deputy, Maurice J. Brennan, to study the problem. As I have emphasised, in 1950 small British teams were prepared to tackle anything; the Americans, with their huge engineering staffs, were simply thought to be recklessly extravagant. The answer Brennan came up with was a fighter capable of flying at 100,000 ft and intercepting a supersonic bomber (when such a bomber was built). This appeared to be the kind of job which could be done by a rocket aeroplane, and nobody in Britain seemed to be looking at such a thing. His immediate proposal was quite naive and limited, and merely suggested a study programme costing a small sum. The company's board gave its assent in December 1951.

In fact there were other people in Britain looking at rocket interceptors. Though enthusiasm for the giant task of developing supersonic aircraft was conspicuously absent, the RAE Project Office had begun a study of target-defence interceptors of the 'manned missile' kind in 1946. To provide propulsion support and a new national capability Armstrong Siddeley Motors was awarded a contract for the design and prototype development of a small liquid-propellant rocket engine, drawing partly on the experience of the German Walther firm. On their own initiative de Havilland Engines also got into the act, but to get some funds their first project was a simple ATO (assisted take-off) motor for the Comet I airliner.

The first operational rocket-propelled interceptor in history, the Walther-powered Me 163, had an endurance under power of barely eight minutes. Brennan's study had hardly begun before he decided there were compelling advantages for the 'mixed-power' aircraft, which could fly normally on a turbojet yet also had a rocket for use during take-off, supersonic acceleration, and for high performance at extreme altitudes. It is one of the fundamental shortcomings of any air-breathing engine that its power falls away roughly in proportion to the density of the surrounding atmosphere. At 45,000 ft a typical turbojet gives a maximum thrust only about one-fifth as great as at sea level. The rocket, on the other hand, gives increasing thrust as it climbs into thinner air because the falling back-pressure on its combustion chamber means the propulsive jet can accelerate to a higher velocity. Thus, even quite a small rocket can make a dramatic difference to the performance of an aeroplane at great heights. It can cut 70, 80 or 90 per cent off the time to reach a given high altitude, or to accelerate from Mach 0.8 to Mach 2. It can raise the service ceiling from 50,000 to perhaps 90,000 feet, and at great heights it can multiply the power of manoeuvre by five or ten times. And, of course, the higher you go, the greater the rocket's advantage. Brennan wanted a turbojet as well merely to overcome the tendency of all-rocket aircraft to run out of fuel. With a turbojet he could plan an aircraft that could take off and land conventionally and fly for at least half an hour in between. This was not a new idea; probably the earliest mixed-power fighter in history was a version of the Me 262 of 1944.

Unfortunately, adding a long-duration rocket necessitates also adding a separate rocket-propellant system, and the choice of the best propellant(s) was clearly fundamental to the success of a mixed-power aircraft. Brennan went to talk to the embryonic British teams that had begun to work on aircraft rockets. At de Havilland Engines at Stag Lane, Edgware, he sought the opinion of Val Cleaver, whose Sprite was the motor intended to boost the take-off of the Comet. The Sprite operated by the rapid decomposition of HTP (high-test hydrogen peroxide) to form a jet of steam and oxygen, using a fine mesh of silver as a catalyst. As no combustion took place the Sprite was called a 'cold' rocket, but decomposing HTP is not stuff to be trifled with; it gets hot enough to roast a steak, and the original liquid is corrosive to human skin. Cleaver told Brennan of his project for a Super Sprite, in which kerosene would be injected into the decomposing HTP. It would ignite instantly, converting the 'cold' jet of hot oxygen and superheated steam into an indisputably hot one with a brilliant gold flame. As described in the companion book *Bombers of the West* the Super Sprite became the ATO motor for the Valiant bomber. Beyond it Cleaver was planning a pump-fed fighter engine of greater thrust, the Spectre, for which Brennan appeared to be a potential customer. Brennan learned all he could of this exciting new technology and then went to see Sid Allen at Ansty, near Coventry.

Allen led the team at Armstrong Siddeley Motors. Though part of the giant Hawker Siddeley Group they were backwoodsmen working in a way reminiscent of Whittle in 1937, doing something obviously rather dangerous and thus consigned to scattered huts and test beds where the odd fire or explosion would do no harm (except to Allen & Co). Their main brew looked like being kerosene and liquid oxygen (lox), though in place of kerosene they had been using methyl alcohol. The great V-2 of World War 2 had run on liquid oxygen and alcohol, and in 1944 the German Army was getting through lox at the rate of some 100 tons a day. But in 1950 in England it was still a laboratory curiosity. Though Allen had been there since the company received its original rocket contract in

1946 there was still no need for more than experimental quantities, and if any visitors came they had to be shown a bucket of the stuff (even worse than HTP if knocked over, because intense cold can burn at least as badly as intense heat). When I first visited Allen's team I was fascinated to see how items such as rubber balls or rose petals became hard and brittle after immersion in the bucket, so that they could be shattered into sharp splinters by a blow from a hammer. I have no doubt Brennan was introduced to lox in the same way, but he wanted to learn about engines for fighters. The 2,000 lb thrust lox/alcohol Snarler had successfully (with a few hiccups!) flown in the Hawker P.1072, and Allen's team had begun development of the much more powerful lox/kerosene Screamer. Allen was delighted to see Brennan. Whereas the 1946 contract had been orientated mainly towards take-off and climb boost, he judged that the rocket could serve as the main propulsion for fighters in the thin air at great heights where turbojets ran short of breath. At 30,000 ft the little Snarler multiplied the rate of climb of the Hawker jet by five.

Back on the Isle of Wight Brennan plotted curves of rocket specific impulse, propellant consumptions, engines-plus-fuel weights for dozens of fighter missions, and various other parameters. It is in such studies, often made by a single man, that aviation makes its central thread of progress. By early 1952 Brennan had acquired a 'feel' for mixed-power aircraft and could assess parametric studies with the skill born of experience. He was told as much by Cleaver, who then asked 'Aren't you going in for this high-altitude interceptor? You've done more in this field than anybody else.' But Saunders-Roe was not judged to be a fighter firm. The SR/A1 was regarded as an odd freak, and the authorities had taken little interest in the company's unexpected research into the field of supersonic mixed-power fighters. So they had not even asked the company to tender for the marvellous new specification F.124D which had been dreamed up by the Air Staff—and which most people thought would be won by Doc Russell's team at Bristol. Brennan sought audience with Dr Duncan Cameron, then Assistant Director R&D (Projects) at the MoS. Cameron would not allow Brennan to take a copy of the document away. Undaunted, the designer persuaded his chief executive, Sir Arthur Gouge, to put in a formal request to tender to the new spec. The official response was 'OK, but you won't be paid', which I suppose is interpretable as 'The British aviation scene is a closed shop, and nobody moves out of his proper place. Your place is flying boats.' Be that as it may, Saunders-Roe were reluctantly allowed to see the F.124D specification.

The basic idea seemed to be that the Air Staff had become impressed by the Me 163 kind of interceptor, which climbs steeply up to protect a particular vital surface target and then, having fired its guns or missiles, promptly swoops or glides down again. This kind of thinking permeated the Air Staff for years, as is evident from the chapter on the Lightning. Indeed I think the officials of that vintage year 1952 would have considered the Lightning a cissy aeroplane because, after one smart firing pass at the enemy, its pilot could arrive back at base with almost enough fuel for a spare circuit!

F.124D, like many post-1945 specifications, passed through various paper forms. At the outset it really did call for a manned missile. Obviously impressed not only by the Me 163 but even more deeply by the Bachem Ba 349 *Natter* (Viper), it was decided that what the RAF wanted was a pure-rocket interceptor fired at an inclination of about 80° by one or more big boost rockets. It would then climb to about 50,000 feet in fewer than 50 seconds, instantly annihilate the enemy and then glide home. The cool pilot would either slide along his home airfield and pull up at the right dispersal, or, if he found this a bit difficult, would try to set down in one piece on the nearest level ground. A large and extremely elaborate recovery vehicle would then do its best to collect the pieces and bring them back to base, the eager pilot just itching to do it again. RAE studied this concept in great depth, and got Fairey to build a rocket-powered, radio-controlled test aircraft with initial control by twin swivelling nozzles. Later Fairey built the rather hot little manned delta, the FD.1, which—fortunately for Grp Capt Gordon Slade—was allowed to begin its flight-test programme in March 1951 operating in the conventional mode from a runway.

By the time it got to Brennan F.124D had an optional landing gear of the normal kind, though zero-length launch seemed to be the official favourite. It was still a pure rocket fighter, though there were dark mutterings at St Giles Court that some of the chief designers seemed to think a small turbojet essential, to give sustained electric and hydraulic system power and help stretch the recovery glide until it reached the home runway. The mutterings were dark because this ran counter to the beautifully stark original scheme of a very cheap, simple, rocket interceptor. The officials reluctantly began to write in a paragraph about the Turboméca Palas, with a rated thrust of a mere 330 lb.

At that time the RAF/MoS procurement team were sure of only a very few things, but one was that they wanted a tiny, cheap fighter. This to them meant all-rocket, but the propulsion staff at the RAE—perhaps having listened to industry—had swung round to favour a small rocket backed up by a big turbojet. They wanted the new turbopump-fed engine(s) for the F.124D to be sized to a sea-level thrust of 2,000 lb. Then they decided 4,000 lb would be better, and this was the target thrust level for Sid Allen's team when they designed the Screamer. But Cleaver, who did his own sums, insisted on 8,000 lb for his Spectre. Doc Cawood wrote to Cleaver's boss, Major Frank Halford, to see if de Havilland's rocket man could be made to see reason. But Bob Weir, MoS Director-General of Engine R&D, thought Cleaver might even be right. So the Spectre was ordered at 8,000 lb, and soon Allen's engineers were having their arms twisted to promise the same thrust. Of course, before long everyone was shouting for 10,000 lb, including not only Brennan but also the RAE!

What about the choice of propellants? One of the best-loved British aviation people, W. G. A. (Bill) Perring, then Director of the RAE, was firmly of the opinion that 'Oxygen is what you want, in large quantities, so why not lox? You can make it cheaply from the air!' He was quite right, in one way. Unlike lox, most of the alternative oxidants (US = oxidizer) were expensive liquids necessitating new and often very tricky production plants. There was one important exception; nitric acid, which had been in tonnage production for well over a century (and which figures in the next chapter). It takes both knowledge and courage to hold out for what may superficially seem to be an unpopular minority decision. Cleaver had both qualities and stuck fast to HTP, even though it was available only in laboratory test quantities, and therefore was fiendishly expensive. To him only HTP promised to meet all the requirements, not only for fighter rocket engines but also to provide energy for high-altitude accessory power systems. Lox, on the other hand, boils at −183°C; this means a lox-filled fighter cannot be kept at readiness for a quick scramble without the liquid having to be pumped in at frequent intervals to top up the tanks and compensate for the boil-off. Furthermore, the mechanical systems in the aircraft have to be kept warm to protect them from freezing solid, and this in turn increases the boil-off loss. A third problem is that a lox fire is extremely frightening. It has the unnerving quality of the broom in 'l'Apprenti Sorcier'—the more you try to put it out, the worse it gets! Allen's team bought the lox argument, and used it for the Screamer, but—though he nearly succumbed to nitric acid—Cleaver adamantly held out for HTP. Brennan sided with Cleaver.

In November 1952 Brennan completed his F.124D submission and took it to the Ministry. Knowing how the official mind works he did not for a moment question the spec. Probably 95% of his carefully worked out brochure was devoted to a proposal for meeting F.124D in every detail (which alone was more than some of his rivals could do). The odd 5% was a little addendum casually tucked in at the back, 'for interest'. The addendum was a detailed proposal for a completely different sort of animal. It was an ordinary fighter, with conventional landing gear, to be powered by an Armstrong Siddeley Viper turbojet of 1,640 lb thrust and a de Havilland Spectre rocket of 8,000 lb thrust. It had not only staggering performance but quite long flight endurance with the rocket shut down (on a mere 500 lb of jet fuel), and it landed and taxied-in in the usual way.

Brennan drily pointed out that this aircraft would be smaller and cheaper than the requested VTO type, quite apart from saving the cost of the zero-length rockets and complicated retrieval systems. He backed up his proposal by an almost indecent mass of data and performance curves, and also explained in detail why lox should not be used in manned aircraft, and certainly not in a fighter.

It should be obvious that I dislike official minds (not, I emphasise, the officials themselves but the way they are constrained to think). This *tour de force* of Brennan's brought me huge delight. One conjured up pictures of how the immediate reaction would be offhand questions among the officials about the addendum. Those few pages, demurely lying in wait yet incapable of being completely overlooked (even in the dark-horse and almost improper submission from those flying-boat people) must gradually have sown the seeds of flaming arguments. The maddening thing was that it was so reasonable. Whereas almost all the officials had gone along with the uniformed Air Staff and become mesmerised by the manned missile idea, here was Saunders-Roe demonstrating with a mass of graphs and figures that you could do a better job with an ordinary aeroplane. If you didn't like it the only way to fight it was to say 'It doesn't meet the F.124D requirement, so there is nothing more to be said'. And, of course, in the back of everyone's mind was the feeling 'How could we possibly give this challenging supersonic fighter to Saunders-Roe, of all people?' Steam must have been issuing from every crevice in St Giles Court in November 1952, when Saunders-Roe were told they had won the development contract. Two weeks later they received a laconic instruction that they were to proceed with their addendum aircraft. I don't know whether they then got paid for their study, as their rivals had been.

Of course this triggered off a further flaming row among some of the rivals. How dare the job go to Saunders-Roe!! Dobbie (Sir Roy Dobson, Managing Director of A. V. Roe & Co) was especially niggled, and before long he had thumped so many Ministry desks that he managed to get a contract too, as I shall relate. And the Fairey FD.1 ceased to be terribly useful because its original purpose of research into zero-length take-off had ceased to be relevant. Today, of course, we have the V/STOL Harrier, but this is a totally different kind of animal for totally different reasons concerned with the vulnerability of airfields. It is also a fact that the very latest fighters have sea-level engine thrust greater than their weight, but this is solely in order to increase their combat manoeuvrability. Not one is designed to stand on its tail to take off.

In December 1952 Saunders-Roe were awarded a contract for three prototype aircraft designated SR.53 (conforming to the firm's tradition of using the last two figures of the year when detail design started), to meet the completely new F.138D specification that had been written around the company's addendum. Brennan was appointed chief designer, with Lew Rosenthal his deputy, Knowler becoming technical director. F.138D spelt out pretty clearly what the SR.53 would be like—because Saunders-Roe had already spelt it out in their addendum—the only new item being provision for carrying two Blue Jay guided weapons (the IR-homing air-to-air missile later called Firestreak). Unfortunately there was one area of total vagueness, and it was just as vague at this time on the programme to specification F.23 which gave birth to the Lightning. Nobody on the Air Staff seemed able to make up his mind just how the new interceptor would be used. Back in the war there had been 'day fighters' which were flown visually, and 'night fighters' with which the interception was accomplished entirely with the aid of AI (airborne interception) radar. This had carried over into the first jets, the only change being that the AI-equipped machines were now called 'all-weather', although in practice this was very much an exaggeration. But what was to be done with these proposed supersonic machines?

Common sense surely ought to have dictated that a fighter that could be used only in broad daylight and good visibility was unlikely to be of much use, because enemy bombers might choose to come at some other time. Moreover, as supersonic fighters looked like costing as much as a whole squadron of Meteors, it did not seem (to me, at least) very sensible to buy even a single one that was incapable of operating at the times when it was most likely to be needed. F.138D said nothing about operation at night or in bad weather, but merely specified 'radar' in the nose. The strong inference was that the Air Staff were thinking only of simple, low-power gunlaying radar of the kind fitted to the Hunter. Indeed, at this distance in time I do not think it an unwarranted slur on their thought-processes to suggest that they did not know what they were about. Reaching early decisions on difficult technical questions was apparently possible in the United States (see later chapters) but not even attempted in the RAF. So Saunders-Roe started mild enquiries on precisely what was meant by 'radar', and meanwhile got on with an SR.53 mock-up.

It was an impressive mock-up, and it could be hoisted up into various flight attitudes. Not the least of the things that history might judge important was that Brennan's team were so inexperienced in the design of supersonic aircraft that they just went straight ahead and did it, completely failing to be diverted into consideration of all sorts of tailless designs or unconventional wing shapes. If you look at the wings of today's fighters they either have variable sweep (if they are multi-role) or else, apart from the Viggen, a very ordinary planform shape which, apart from being of low aspect ratio (ie, short and broad), would not have looked unusual in World War 2. I rate the wing of the SR.53 a major break-through, because of its very ordinariness. Johnson's F-104 could not claim to be ordinary, because though it had a similar planform it was fantastically thin and had a sharp leading edge. Brennan's wing was a full 6% thick and had a round, drooping leading edge that lifted well at low speeds, yet the SR.53 was designed for Mach 2.

Moreover, it offered flight performance which was good at low altitudes, far surpassed everything else at medium altitudes and at high altitudes was staggering. Even in comparison with modern fighters of two decades later, such as the F-15 Eagle, the little SR.53 shows up very well and at heights above 35,000 ft still cannot be equalled. For example it could climb to 50,000 ft in just over 2 minutes and then accelerate from Mach 0.9 to 1.6 in 73 seconds whilst in a turn with a radius of 9,600 ft! One can imagine how this compared with the RAF's fighters of 1953! Brennan spent a lot of time attending RAF exercises, and learned exactly how the ground controllers operated (at Sopley Radar, for example) and what were the problems and limitations of the Meteor and Vampire squadrons. At that time the Hunter, which had yet to reach the RAF, had been presented to the public as the last word in modern fighters. Though nobody then knew how long a life the Hunter would have as an outstanding ground-attack aircraft—a role virtually ignored at the time of its design—the fact was that as a 'fighter' it was extremely hard pressed even to shoot down a Canberra. No controller could handle more than two fighters at a time—a fact which seemed to make a nonsense of Teddy Petter's wish to produce swarms of baby Gnats—yet, despite this intense individual attention, the team of controller and fighter pilot needed consummate skill to achieve success. The fighter had to attack in a traditional curve of pursuit, and had to begin its turn at exactly the right place and time. Looking over the controllers' shoulders in the darkened caravans not only gave Brennan the ability to 'speak the language' but afforded a valuable insight into how the existing system worked. The importance of tremendous high-altitude performance became obvious, and so did the need not only for guided-weapon armament but also for powerful AI radar. It was also evident that any method of interception demanding a curve-of-pursuit attack was subject to severe fundamental shortcomings. Did not the US Air Force already have a collision-course system in service?

As outlined in the story of the F-102 (p. 166), the collision-course system escapes from the limitations of the curve of pursuit. By carrying a few more kilowatts of radar power and an airborne computer the collision-course fire-control system allows the fighter to attack the enemy from any direction, aiming its weapons at a point in the sky which a few seconds later will be reached by the target and the weapons simultaneously. For a reason which I have never been able to discover, the British Air Staff appeared to affect a total lack of interest in the new technology of the American fighters. They emphatically held the view that a night and all-weather fighter had a crew of two, and crept up behind its quarry in the traditional curve of pursuit like a Beaufighter in 1940. This was the philosophy behind the Javelin, which did not reach the RAF until 1956. Whenever I asked senior RAF officers or civilian officials, from Ministers downwards, I was always assured that the Javelin concept was (to quote a Minister) 'the only practical answer for British conditions'. Indeed, the RAF always claimed it had to operate 'in conditions different from any other country or Service'. I never discovered just what these conditions were. One vaguely concluded it was a reference to the weather. If it was, there must have been a different kind of weather peculiar to the region around Manston, in Kent, where in the early 1950s were based two squadrons of the US Air Force's 406th Fighter Interceptor Wing, equipped with the F-86D. Though the 'Dogship Sabre' had only one man in it he seemed to find no difficulty whatever in locking-on to Canberras or any other traffic, at ranges up to 30 miles and not only in curve of pursuit but also from any other direction as well. I visited them twice and found them slightly peeved that the British host government appeared to be schizophrenic, saying on the one hand, 'Welcome, you're doing a great job', and on the other proclaiming, in so many words, 'The F-86D is impossible and cannot work.'

I have no doubt that the Saunders-Roe designers would have been most interested to compare notes with the pilots of the Dogships, because by mid-1953 they had become deeply troubled at the apparent lack of understanding by the Air Staff of what sort of fighter ought to be built. I have brought the F-86D into the story because here was the essential radar and fire-control system for a totally new sort of fighter already in operational service, though packaged into an old airframe. Its pilot did not need to acquire his targets visually (which is the technical jargon for saying that he did not need to see them). Of course, if an enemy bomber is leaving a dense contrail this can usually be seen from a great distance, but in the stratosphere it is often surprisingly difficult to see anything outside the cockpit. You feel remote, locked in your snug little world, and the only obvious visual cues are your instruments and controls which are picked out in the most brilliant sunlight in unnaturally sharp focus. If you look through the windscreen you see the reflections of the hard light-and-dark scene inside the cockpit. The slightest film of dust looks like an opaque screen. To search for a distant target you desperately try to focus your eyes on infinity; but, as there is probably nothing to focus on, this is likely to prove impossible. If you are young and supple you may be able to screw your head round and look at your wing or drop tank, but with swept wings and long noses this can be a surprisingly tiring task! Having thus refocussed on something more than three feet away you may then be able to go on and extend the focussing process to infinity. But with a featureless dark vault above and featureless 'clag' underneath you are likely to find that your eyes simply snap back to focus on those reflections and grains of dust. When this sort of thing is combined with constant vigilance whilst listening to the brief and distorted transmissions of the ground controller, and the enervating effect of pulling high g in manoeuvres, the net result is rather frustrating and extremely tiring.

This old-fashioned technique was fine in the Battle of Britain, though even then visual acquisition was often far from being a 'piece of cake'. For the SR.53, boring in at Mach 2 at 75,000 ft, it seemed to be utter nonsense. The simple gunlaying radar which the SR.53 was to carry in its nose was no help whatever. It was useful only out to about 1,000 ft in front—less than half a second's travel—and was fitted to help the pilot get the range right before firing his guns. It would have been nice for a Sopwith Camel, but seemed to have no use at all in the SR.53. Had not guns been officially pronounced unnecessary? By mid-1953 the sole armament of the SR.53 had been decided upon: two Blue Jay missiles. These were for use at ranges of the order of several miles and were thus incompatible with the feeble radar. The whole situation was a farce, and I suspect this was appreciated even by the Air Staff.

What made it all doubly distressing was that the profusion of British planemakers kept pouring out a profusion of good ideas, and the poor old RAF just couldn't make up its mind. This one looked nice, and that one was terribly interesting, and this other one was too good to turn down and that other one might prove the best of the lot. I suspect a few of the more senior people whose job it was to take the big decisions found it increasingly hard to take those decisions merely on the basis of brochures and slick curves plotted on graphs. Without calling anyone a liar, how could they be sure these curves were right? Perhaps, after the marvellous new fighter was built, it would be discovered that the figures were all wrong. How much easier it was in those glorious days at Martlesham when you could put four rival prototypes into the sky and take actual measurements—and get the chaps in the squadrons to fly them and offer criticism (which is just what the Americans have been trying to do since 1970). It was a trifle shattering when Grp Capt Broadbent came down to Cowes on an official visit, had a good look at the SR.53 mock-up, and said 'Well, of course, we won't know if we want it until we fly it'.

This sounded like an instant return to the dark ages. The idea of a mixed-power fighter had been started largely because Saunders-Roe were fed up with prototypes and wanted to create something that the RAF undoubtedly needed and would buy in quantity. Now here was the customer saying, in effect, 'I know this is what we asked for, and that you are committed to building expensive prototypes, but we might not want it at all.' This raised the fundamental question of what the customer needs in order to take his decisions. Today, as I commented above, the Americans have had such unhappy experiences with some of their most important aircraft that they have reverted, wherever possible, to the old formula of waiting until they can evaluate real aeroplanes in the air. But this is not quite the same problem. What the US Air Force tries to do today is to say 'Here are two (or more) rival designs. When we have had our fly-off competition we will know which is the one to pick for the inventory.' In contrast the RAF's problem back in 1953 seemed to be 'This SR.53 is just one of heaps of new fighter prototypes and projects. We're a bit mixed up at the moment and we haven't any idea which, if any, we ought to go for.' To Brennan this seemed unreasonable. His argument was 'I, like my rivals, can tell you what my fighter will do. You can look over my shoulder and see how it works, and check our costings. What more do you need to take a decision?' (Broadbent might have replied 'Experience on visual acquisition at great heights'.)

Brennan telephoned the CFE and asked the Commandant to come and have a look. Air Cdre Geoffrey Stephenson knew the fighter situation in the RAF intimately, and of course was also familiar with the problems of visual acquisition at high altitudes. Late in 1953 he came down to Cowes and, after a most valuable discussion, left the company in no doubt on two vital points. The first was that the mixed-power interceptor made sense, was urgently needed, and excited the RAF very much. The second was that visual acquisition and mere gunlaying radar was all rubbish; a modern AI radar was essential. Stephenson was right behind the Saunders-Roe team, but within a year he had been killed in an F-100 (p. 138).

Brennan at last could see what to do, but his doing of it was hampered by the fact that his company had no information on AI radars. Accordingly he telephoned the RRE at Malvern, to discover that this pleasant establishment shared none of the confusion of the Air Staff but was possessed of scientists and engineers who were not only brilliant at electronic circuitry but were also very closely in touch with the operation of modern fighters. Saunders-Roe were astonished to learn that RRE had for a very long period taken it for granted that mere gunlaying radar was 'out'. There could no longer be any such thing as a 'day fighter'; to be of much use, any aircraft intended for future air-to-air combat had to have a modern AI radar. What were these modern AI radars? There was the spiral-scan set by E. K. Cole designated AI Mk22 and the more advanced Ferranti AI-23. The latter was the one to go for. Though too late for the Javelin, it looked as if it would be available for the definitive fighter expected from English Electric. RRE and Saunders-Roe bent over a drawing board and soon established the fact that even the neatly packaged AI-23 would not fit into the SR.53. Brennan could still see what to do, and it was going to be a bigger job than he had thought. Swiftly he prepared a brochure for a new fighter based as closely as possible upon the SR.53 but with a much bigger body and gross weight increased by 10,000 lb to about 28,500 lb, and fully equipped with AI-23 and a modern fire-control system for blind interception. He strongly recommended collision-course rather than the curve-of-pursuit method. He submitted this to the Air Staff, and it was accepted without the slightest argument!! Specification F.177D was written around it.

Accordingly, early in 1954, Saunders-Roe began a company-funded programme to develop this new and much more sensible fighter, which had the company designation of SR.177. This was in addition to the SR.53, and it was not long before the company was also working on the fantastic 2 Gyron plus 4 Spectre fighter I mentioned earlier to try to meet the F.155 specification. But would any of this lead to a solid production programme? Though all the officials were making increasingly encouraging noises, Saunders-Roe might still be doing no more than building a succession of prototypes. From the start parts of the RAF had shown intense interest in what was sometimes called the 'P.177', but Saunders-Roe were still not a recognised fighter company and apart from Stephenson the uniformed RAF seemed scared to get involved. There was also intense interest on the part of the Royal Navy, but this had yet to reach the stage of writing a specification. And there was also much more than passing interest in the United States. The British government applied for an 'offshore procurement' award for the SR.177, because this appeared to be a suitable project for support by the MWDP and production financing by the Defense Department. The immediate result of this was that full briefings had to be given to visiting evaluation teams from the US Air Force and Navy. Unlike almost every other programme in Europe the SR.177 had no counterpart in the United States, and no American project could come anywhere near it in high-altitude performance. The interest was therefore genuine, and—unlike the situation with such pedestrian things as the Javelin and Mystère IV—the evaluation teams were concerned to feed everything back as soon as possible to the United States.

The mid-1950s were a time of unparalleled R&D activity in British aerospace. The industry had by frantic efforts greatly increased its engineering strength from the dangerously low ebb reached in 1950, and production capacity—in terms of both facilities and materials—had likewise been greatly augmented. But this increased strength had, as I have emphasised, been diluted by being spread across literally dozens of challenging projects. Even in the field of mixed-power fighters there were now three aircraft programmes. To the two at Saunders-Roe could be added the Avro 720, to meet Specification F.137D, which had been started early in 1953 largely because of the blistering fight put up by Dobbie ever since Saunders-Roe had won their first contract for the SR.53. Despite the obvious hazards of lox as a propellant for manned aircraft, the 720 was committed to this fluid—largely, as far as I could see, because the Hawker Siddeley Group's engine firm could offer only the Screamer. Cynically, one could also suggest that the Avro fighter could be justified only if it was quite different from the SR.53, and it thus had to use a different propellant combination. Design and construction of the 720, under the leadership of Roy Ewans, went ahead at Manchester very fast. It was a simple mid-wing machine with pure delta wings and tail. Whereas Brennan had elected to put his rocket underneath his turbojet, Ewans put the Screamer on top, the air-breathing Viper being fed from a small fixed-geometry chin intake. Like several supersonic Avro projects of the period, the 720 had an external surface constructed almost entirely from honey-comb-core sandwich. What it did not have was anything like a proper radar fire-control system.

Another of the profusion of British aerospace projects was a series of more formidable air-to-air guided weapons. Though the Blue Jay appeared to be a thoroughly well designed missile, into which de Havilland Propellers were putting quite remarkable expertise in the technology of IR homing and fuzing, there had for a long time been a need for alternatives. Blue Jay's obvious shortcoming was that it could home on to its target only from astern and so could not make a collision-course interception. Fairey's beam-riding missile called Blue Sky had been judged only an interim weapon, and with the new name of Fireflash it served only in a development and training role with the Swift 7 in 1957. Vickers-Armstrongs (Aircraft) were very busy with a far more formidable weapon with microwave homing guidance and a mighty warhead, the Vickers Type 888, which had the splendid code-name of Red Dean (a reference to the left-wing Dean of Canterbury of the day). Red Deans were specified as primary armament for several projected RAF fighters of this period, including the monsters to F.155 specification, but were too large for the small mixed-power interceptors. To meet their needs a much improved Blue Jay, the Mk 4, was placed under contract at de Havilland Propellers. Later it was to change out of all recognition, and be given a new name, but from the outset it was planned to have a completely new IR homing head capable of detecting and locking-on to the very small thermal radiation emitted by an enemy bomber in its forward hemisphere, so that the missile could make collision-course attacks from any direction. This was exactly what was wanted for the SR.177.

During 1955, while the SR.53 was painfully slowly translated into flight hardware, Saunders-Roe worked to make the SR.177 the basis for a firm programme. They had little help from the RAF Air Staff. Though it was by now beyond dispute that the SR.53, with its concept of visual acquisition, could not possibly lead to a production programme, the Air Staff could not come to any conclusion about the 177. Superimposed on a general wish to make haste slowly and totter from one indecision to the next, the Air Staff appeared to be wondering whether or not the traditional aeroplane was obsolete, and to regard guided missiles as not so much complementary to aeroplanes as replacements for them. By the end of 1956 this belief was all too obvious, and anyone who has read the preceding chapter in this book will have an idea of the magnitude of the upset this notion caused in British military aviation. Only in one place could one find procurement thinking that was forward-looking, well-informed and enthusiastic. This was in the Admiralty.

Leaders of this thinking were Lewis Boddington, Director of RN Aircraft R&D; Capt (later Vice-Admiral) F. H. E. Hopkins, DNAW; and Capt (later Vice-Admiral) J. A. Ievers, DDAW. It was my privilege to know all three, and no Service ever had a better team to lead its aircraft procurement. One of their accomplishments was the NA.39 specification, which led to the Buccaneer as described in the companion volume *Attack Aircraft of the West.* In an age when specifying the right combat aircraft in Britain seemed to be just too difficult, NA.39 was precisely correct in almost every detail. Naturally the Air Staff scorned the Buccaneer in vitriolic terms when it was suggested the RAF might operate it, and thus can take little credit for the excellent job this aircraft does in today's RAF. When the trio descended on Cowes in 1955 they had gone far towards preparing an equally good spec for a carrier-based mixed-power interceptor, complete with AI-23 and armed with two Blue Jay Mk 4s. The only major error seemed to be that they wanted to use lox/kerosene, because whereas HTP had to be bought at a high price from such people as Laporte Chemicals it was possible for an aircraft carrier to produce its own lox by liquefying oxygen from the atmosphere. It was a nice concept, but Brennan asked 'Have you ever seen a liquid-oxygen fire?' I don't recommend readers to play with lox fires, because they are likely to misjudge what constitutes a safe quantity.

For the next visit of the men from the Admiralty Brennan had ready a detailed brochure on an SR.177 with a lox/kerosene Screamer. Ever ready to oblige the customer, he had bulged the fuselage to maintain rocket endurance, because lox has a specific gravity of only 1.13 (much the same as water) while HTP is 1.35 and thus fits into a smaller space. He had also added a tank of cooling water for injection into the combustion chamber, because in those days trying to run a long-duration aircraft rocket engine on a stoichiometric mixture of lox/kerosene would have melted the combustion chamber. When he glanced at the brochure Boddington said 'Oh, we haven't come down to see that, we've gone right off lox . . .' What the Navy wanted was a navalised SR.177 with Brennan's own choice of engines. This was a de Havilland Spectre 5A in the upper position and a de Havilland Gyron Junior of the new PS.50 type (DGJ. 10R), with fully variable reheat and con-di nozzle, in the lower position, fed by a double-wedge chin intake.

The Gyron Junior was potentially an outstanding little engine. A two-fifths scale of the big Gyron, it first materialised as the PS.43 (PS = project study), which was finally put into production at 7,100 lb thrust for the Buccaneer. The PS.50 had a zero-stage on the compressor, and an afterburner which on paper seemed a notable advance on the primitive reheat systems built elsewhere in Britain. It also had variable compressor stators, and wrought turbine rotor blades with cooling-air passages formed during an extrusion operation. With full reheat it had a rating at sea level of more than 11,000 lb, yet its weight and frontal area were not much more than half the values for an Avon. If DH Engines had had the 4,000 development staff of Rolls-Royce, instead of a mere 400, the Gyron Junior could have made a major impact on supersonic aviation. As for the Spectre, this was a tiny package yet it was self-starting, fully controllable (idling to full power in about 1 sec) and very highly developed. The first flight-development Spectre flew in a Canberra in 1956. The Spectre was a topping-cycle engine, with a high combustion pressure for its day and the largest range of thrust-throttling ever attempted from a single chamber. Later marks were the smallest and neatest aircraft engines of their thrust ever constructed, and despite the company's limited resources they were developed fast. At the same time de Havilland Engines quite logically and remarkably quickly developed a range of on-board accessory power systems running on HTP. An HTP turbine was a well-understood creature, because one drove the propellant pumps in the Spectre. The great advantage of HTP-driven accessories was that full power was at once available at all altitudes. For this reason HTP-driven accessories were used very successfully in a production missile, the big Blue Steel 'stand-off bomb'. Altogether I found this burgeoning HTP technology as convincing, in the strictly military context, as it was exciting.

So did the Navy. That evening the Admiralty delegation took back to their Cowes hotel copies of a new brochure for the navalised HTP SR.177 which had been prepared during the day and made up and stapled in the late afternoon. Next morning Brennan accompanied the delegation back to London by train. Ievers asked for an estimate of the possible timing. Brennan, like every designer I have met, thinks in terms of graphical plots. As a reply he sketched out the classical curve of a programme against time, with years as the horizontal axis and either man-hours or money as the vertical. He pointed out that, no matter what you do, in the early phases you can only put a small number of men on the job. Thus, 'If you made up your mind now, you could begin with a £25,000 design study. This would get the programme away and take it a long way along the curve and save time in the end.' The reply was 'That's great, we have immediate funds for that sort of thing.' On 18 May 1955 Saunders-Roe had their study contract, which enabled them to go ahead with the design and work out the details of the structure, power plant, tankage, systems and weapons (which by this time included two 24 × 2 in FFAR launchers and later added under-wing attack stores). This was the beginning of what looked like being an outstandingly successful fighter programme. Then, out of the blue came a second £25,000 study contract for a land-based SR.177 for the RAF! The outcasts at Cowes had won their spurs so convincingly that the new requirement was never put out to tender. When he heard about it Sir Sydney Camm was livid (but very proud of his pupil, Brennan). Dobbie was unprintable.

It didn't help the latter's blood pressure when, in January 1956, the Avro 720 was cancelled. The sole prototype, XD 696, did not really make sense, though technically it was filled with interest. The remarkable thing is that it lasted as long as it did, because not only is a single aircraft hardly a viable programme but lox/kerosene was at last judged to be dangerous. Switching to HTP would almost duplicate the SR.53, and a fly-off comparison with the SR.53 was hardly warranted because even that had been overtaken by the 177. So at the same time the third SR.53 also got the chop, which was no great loss. Saunders-Roe had frankly been dragging their feet with the SR.53. The first, XD 145, had been in the jigs in 1954 and structurally complete before the end of the year. But it took no less than three further years to get all the bits of equipment together and clip them on. If one wanted to make excuses one could point out that the small and densely packed SR.53 was not the easiest thing to work on, but I think a more important reason for the slow progress was that the company had utterly inadequate resources and were more eager to go flat out earning their daily bread helping make Valiants and Viscounts and did not apply sufficient shop-floor effort to completing the two remaining SR.53s.

The red-letter day in the SR.177 programme was 4 September 1956, when Saunders-Roe received an order for 27 aircraft, split into nine each for basic development, RAF development and RN development. For what I believe to have been the first time in history a word was coined to describe the process of trying to make aircraft for different customers differ as little as possible. The word, if you can take it without wincing, was 'commonization', which slips off the tongue even more excruciatingly than the 'commonality' which was later a central feature of the American TFX (F-111) programme. In fact commonization was no trouble at all to the SR.177. The RAF stipulated at the start that on no account were penalties to be incurred by their version as a result of meeting RN requirements, and it is remarkable that such penalties were always held close to zero. Of course the carrier-based machine had a landing gear stressed for a higher rate of descent, an arrester hook, towing catapult hooks and special naval equipment, but the two versions were identical to a remarkable degree.

This accomplishment is worth emphasising. Such a thing had never before happened at the Requirement stage, not even when the Air Staff ran the Fleet Air Arm. The remarkable ability of DNAW and ACAS(OR) to agree a near-common specification for two unpenalised versions of this supersonic multi-role fighter was a marvellous thing which was not accomplished with the later P.1154 nor with the American TFX, despite sustained efforts to do so with both.

Saunders-Roe understandably put a bomb under almost every department at Cowes, whipped young Dick Stanton-Jones back from California—where he wasn't terribly happy anyway—to head the aerodynamics team, arranged for SR.177 wings to be made by Marshall's at Cambridge, and negotiated with Armstrong Whitworth for 'productionization' (there's no other word, I'm afraid) of the final design, and for handling the major part of production assembly and flight test. The potential of the programme was very big. Not only were the Royal Navy planning to buy 150, with at least as big a number considered likely for the RAF, but the reborn Luftwaffe was shopping for a completely new supersonic fighter to replace the F-84 and F-86 which could be built at least partly in Germany and would be the subject of an order for something in excess of 600. It did not seem inconceivable that other NATO countries might come in on the programme, taking the total procurement far into four figures. In July 1956 Saro sales director Robert V. Perfect went to tickle up the Germans and found his reception far more than mere polite interest. Generals Kammhuber and Steinhoff, respectively Chief of Staff and C-in-C Fighters, were very soon sold completely on the mixed-power concept. Two enormous German delegations came to Cowes, the talk moved from the basic briefing level to the one of detailed standard of build and production planning, and it began to look almost as if the SR.177 was the only thing in sight.

By 1957 the whole programme was going flat out. While detailed talks went ahead with the Germans, which now included the Kriegsmarine as well as the Luftwaffe, the Royal Navy and the RAF sat in on each other's progress meetings and everyone seemed delighted. One can imagine the shock felt by everyone, not least by the RAF project staff, when the RAF order for nine was suddenly cancelled. The Minister of Defence, in his *Defence—an outline of future policy*, published on 4 April 1957, had spelt out the belief of the RAF that it would be 'unlikely to require' any fighters or bombers beyond the P.1B and V-bombers. I almost have to pinch myself to confirm that I am not dreaming and that it really happened. Of course we shall never know how far this is really what the Air Staff told the Minister and how far it was the Minister's own reading of the situation. Later in this chapter it will be abundantly clear that Mr Sandys had an almighty bee in his bonnet that, in general terms, combat aeroplanes were obsolete, and took decisions that bore no relation whatever to what the fighting services wished. For the moment we can picture the sheepish feeling of redundancy of the RAF team assigned to the SR.177, and take comfort in Lewis Boddington's retort 'So what? The Royal Navy needs the 177 and there is no reason why our programme should not continue.' So work went ahead on the remaining 18 development aircraft, plans were drawn up for the full run of 150 for the Fleet Air Arm, and discussions continued with the just-a-teeny-bit-shaken Germans.

Saunders-Roe began to wonder whether there had been any ulterior motive in giving them the job of making the Black Knight. This simple ballistic rocket was wanted to fly the re-entry vehicle intended for the Blue Streak long-range ballistic missile which was planned to become the prime carrier of the British deterrent after the V-bombers were obsolete. Sir George Gardner, director of the RAE, had one ear to the political ground and so said that, while he could not see Saunders-Roe getting a production contract for their fighter—not for quite a long time, anyway—the company might be interested in a missile contract. John E. Serby, Director-General, Guided Weapons, had been thinking of giving Black Knight to Boulton Paul, but was interested in Saunders-Roe's experience with HTP—though a ballistic research rocket is one of the few applications where HTP does not show to advantage. In May 1956 the company were awarded the contract, under the design authority of the RAE, but it was peanuts compared with the SR.177. Black Knight was just a big cylindrical tank, riding on a battery of little rocket chambers from Armstrong Siddeley Motors which burned, as if you hadn't guessed, not lox but HTP. Now that the Defence Minister had got the idea that fighters were obsolete, the company almost wished it had never heard of Black Knight. It began to look like a sort of very poor *quid pro quo*.

Early in 1957 the first SR.53 at last left Cowes under a tarpaulin, and made the tortuous journey by ferry-boat and road to Boscombe. There it was put together and carefully inspected. It is probably unhelpful to recall that in 1945 the M.B.5 fighter was dismantled in the morning, trucked to an airfield 40 miles away, put together, fully inspected and cleared for flight, and then flown in the afternoon (and I do mean of the same day!). The same job with the SR.53 took more than two months. Finally chief test pilot John Booth made a very satisfactory maiden flight on 16 May 1957. I will break the story here to take a deeper look at the SR.53.

Painted glossy white, XD 145 looked very nice. It was slightly smaller than a Hunter or Sabre, had an almost unswept square-tipped wing with a conventional laminar 8% section with no special high-lift devices, a rather deep but finely streamlined and area-ruled fuselage and a very low-aspect-ratio fin carrying a slab tailplane on top. This tailplane had trimming elevators which could be moved manually in the event of hydraulic failure. The Viper, rated at about 1,750 lb thrust and thus not powerful enough to fly the aircraft alone, was fed through a split duct from simple intakes high on each side behind the cockpit canopy. By the 1957 SBAC show at Farnborough Booth had reached Mach 1.33 and demonstrated rates of climb in excess of 50,000 ft/min, but still had a very long way to go in exploring the flight envelope. It was during that show that I had a discussion far into the night with Dave Anderton, one of the finest American aerospace writers, who triggered off a heated argument by insisting that you can often tell shortcomings in an aircraft just by looking at it. 'For example, the SR.53 needs more fin area . . .' I do not subscribe to the old saw about 'If it looks right, it is right' (or was it the other way round?). I can point to many ugly monstrosities that were world-beaters, and to many beautiful aeroplanes that were disasters. The SR.53 looked all right to me, and never had its fin enlarged.

It is perhaps important to emphasise that the SR.53 was not, as many people seemed to think, a research aircraft. It was the prototype of a fighter, and though the concept of such a fighter was outmoded it could still have gone to war. From the first it could carry Blue Jays (by 1957 called Firestreaks) on the wing tips, and if you had a top-notch ground controller you could have done a very effective interception job with this little aeroplane.

The bigger SR.177 was, however, a very different kettle of fish. This was not only a lethal and self-sufficient interceptor but it could also carry a wide range of offensive stores for surface attack, reconnaissance and other missions, and it had provision for the right black boxes. Its immensely strong structure, almost entirely of aluminium alloy, was planned by chief structural designer Alec Prickett to be largely machined from the solid in the way that had by then become popular in Britain. The 6% wing was built around four massive spars which terminated at the inboard end in a row of tapering roots. Each spar was pinned at the thickest point to four fuselage frames carved from DTD.683 alloy and prevented from hingeing upwards by being securely butted underneath at the aircraft centreline. One advantage of this was that by pulling out the four pins it was possible to put on a wing of different design or material. There was at this time a requirement for a research aeroplane that could soak at Mach 2.2 for 10 minutes, and thus underpin a future SST. For some reason that I have yet to understand—and I have been trying for 17 years—E. T. Jones, then Director-General of Technical Development (Air), wanted this to be a steel aircraft. He scorned the SR.177 because it had light-alloy wings, and seemed rather less than delighted to be told it could have steel ones any time he liked. This particular steel airframe programme seemed to be intended solely to give the structures men at Bristol Aircraft, Firth-Vickers, and a lot of other places, many long years growing ulcers in trying to fashion the T.188. Nobody was ever able to tell me what the T.188 could do that the SR.177 could not do, but it was obviously a sacred cow with the top Ministry officials. As a research aircraft it made a good gunnery target at Shoeburyness. The T.188 did, incidentally, have two of the same engines as the SR.177, but no rocket.

The 177's row of strong bulkheads were machined by Cramic profilers, polished smooth and then just bolted together. Massive structure of this kind hardly needs jigging, apart from an erection fixture to hold it in place. The upper part of the fuselage of the SR.177 was given over to HTP and kerosene, and there was jet fuel under the inlet duct and in the wings to give an outstanding range when flying on the turbojet alone, in dry thrust. A neat folding FR probe was hinged to the left side of the fuselage, a thing I had previously seen only on American aircraft. The nose was faintly reminiscent of a Crusader, with a shapely radome, double-shock variable chin intake and completely new vee windscreen and clamshell canopy. On the wing tips were two of the formidable Blue Jay Mk 4 missiles, which were shortly to be renamed Red Top. There were various other armament options; indeed the Naval Staff were by no means convinced that it was wise to stop fitting guns, though they had gone along with this idea with the Sea Vixen. Officially the SR.177 was called a long-range strike fighter as well as a high-altitude interceptor. Maximum Mach number was limited by the light-alloy structure to 2.35, but altitude performance was all anyone could ever have wanted. The HTP accessory systems could, I was assured, function reliably at the 1g ceiling of 94,000 ft. At 80,000 ft it was possible to accelerate from the top-of-climb speed of Mach 1.4 to Mach 2 in 66 seconds, and the level turn radii were superior to anything known to be on anyone's drawing-board. At 50,000 ft it could accelerate from Mach 0.9 to Mach 1.6 in 70 seconds *in a five-mile-radius turn.* The Lightning, which is no slouch, takes 200 sec flying straight at a lower height; if it must turn, it cannot pull round less than about 15 miles radius if the speed is not to fall away. Abundant power at great heights was something totally new and very welcome.

At the 1957 SBAC show John Booth, having been asked how the 177 was coming along, likened it to one of the wonderful missiles that were supposed to be replacing fighters: 'The 177 flies faster, and it flies further. Usually it gets back home; and its guidance system weighs 200 pounds and drinks gin.' A little later the MoA took the surprising step of releasing for publication a picture of an SR.177 model, well before first flight. It was printed in *Flight* for 18 October 1957, and the editorial staff were wickedly delighted to see that the model was wearing a pair of Red Tops, which were then highly secret and could not even be mentioned. The caption writer, after a lot of head-scratching, admitted that the missiles did not look like Firestreaks though, he demurely suggested, 'this fact may have little or no significance'. When the neddies at the Ministry make a breach of security it often needs careful thinking to try to minimise the consequences. In fact this was the second obvious security flaw in the programme. When the original official photograph of XD 145, taken at Boscombe on a sunny day, was released for publication it was decreed that the shadow must be air-brushed out to protect the shape of the wing. Someone forgot to do this, though I don't think this was as important as it was made out to be at the time.

By the summer of 1957 the SR.177 had given rise to a family of related aircraft projects which differed mainly in the way their rocket and jet thrust was split. The RN aircraft continued with the Gyron Junior DGJ.10R and Spectre 5A because this had minimum installed weight and gave a good compromise between peak flight performance and turbojet-only endurance. For the Germans the DGJ.10R was replaced in one proposal by an Avon RA.24R, which was a more highly developed engine of greater thrust. The missions of the Luftwaffe indicated a need for greater thrust, and the ideal answer seemed to be a 10,000 lb (sea level) Spectre plus the Avon giving about 14,500 lb with full reheat. The third variant, again enjoying very high 'commonality', was a single-engined fighter with (probably) an advanced reheat Avon and much greater kerosene tankage gained by removing the Spectre and its HTP. This showed to advantage in many missions where performance at high altitude was less important.

Early in August 1957, when the naval SR.177 programme was going at full speed, the indefatigable Sandys suddenly announced that it too had been cancelled. He then departed to see his beloved Weapons Research Establishment at Woomera, S Australia, where nobody could get hold of him. It all seemed like Alice in Wonderland. I came to the conclusion that his attitude was 'I know I'm right, but a lot of less gifted people may wish to argue, so instead of terminating this programme openly and meeting people round a table, I'll have to make myself scarce and hope that in the course of time they'll realise I was right.' The termination was complete and absolute. As Defence Minister he had, I thought, a duty to try to reflect the wishes of the leaders of the armed forces in his procurement (or anti-procurement) decisions. He had been careful to present things in this light in his great round of RAF cuts earlier in the year. But now he had chopped away the most vital aircraft programme from the Fleet Air Arm without even consulting them! (I heard, in fact, that he did consult, disagreed, and ignored the Navy's views, which is even more difficult to comprehend.) Certainly the Navy team were absolutely shattered. Lewis Boddington took the considered view that, had he known the Minister wanted to cancel a naval programme he would have let him destroy the NA.39 (Buccaneer) and would have kept the 177. The whole thing seemed utterly unbelievable, inexplicable and indefensible. Nobody in the government could even be bothered to think of a reason, to explain the cancellation to the public—or perhaps it was thought that, by this time, cancellation of a major programme might be judged as quite natural. Much later an official document said the SR.177 was cancelled 'in a government economy campaign'. I suppose this will do if you can't think of anything else.

Immediately the new Minister of Supply, Aubrey Jones, was on the receiving end of frantic signals from Air Cdre Skelton, the UK Military Air Attaché in Bonn, who described the cancellation as DISASTROUS. It comes all in capitals in the signal and looks better that way. Jones had been over-ridden by Sandys and was rather unhappy at the situation. He knew the 177 was the front runner in the big and extremely important evaluation to re-equip the Luftwaffe and Kriegsmarine. It was first choice on technical and operational merit. One imagines this fact was also known to Sandys; one imagines Sandys had some interest in the British aircraft being chosen; one can only imagine that he thought cancelling it would not hurt its chances, but this supposition is unbelievable. Jones came down to Cowes to try to make the best of an impossible job, and after a lot of discussion agreed to fund five SR.177 aircraft up to Christmas 1957 provided that Saunders-Roe would accept a more sudden run-down afterwards. In early December 1957 the Germans sadly came to the company and said 'You know, with the best will in the world, we cannot see our way to funding this programme while your own government shows no interest. We are afraid we must very reluctantly exclude this outstanding aircraft from our list for evaluation.' Privately they thought we were a little insane.

Of course, the eventual winner in Germany was also not wanted by its own government. But Saro was less than one-tenth as big as Lockheed and was utterly incapable of carrying on with the SR.177 alone; and, of course, there was far more to do. It seemed typical of the times that, whereas the crassly inept cancellation of both the RAF and RN programmes by the Minister had evoked not a murmur of comment from the British press, the elimination of the 'P.177' from the candidate list of the Luftwaffe caused howls of dismay. The general argument seemed to be 'Nasty rotten Americans, they've fiddled things so that we won't get the order'. Now I would be the last to suggest that Lockheed was backward in coming forward, but in this case their most dangerous rival was simply rubbed out by its own government. The noisy radio and newspaper commentators appeared not to have spent two seconds calmly asking themselves 'How could a cancelled programme win?' But in those days aerospace seemed to be just too difficult for the British to understand. From 1956 until 1965 the whole scene was a manager's nightmare.

Six SR.177s, almost completed, were cut up for scrap in October 1957, but Mr Sandys spared the two SR.53s, the flight development of which had been remarkably fast and free from trouble. Several experts had predicted all kinds of difficulties and disasters which the little Saunders-Roe team overcame or avoided. The flight-trials staff, under R. B. (Dick) Stratton, worked miracles in turning a potentially problem-ridden prototype into the basis for a thoroughly practical piece of military kit. As far as possible they tried to simulate operational conditions, to think of difficulties in advance and find the answers. The biggest advances were made in HTP fuelling and de-fuelling. Protective clothing was reduced and simplified, but constantly backed up by strict procedures and immediately available water douches in the event of splashing or spillage. Stratton masterminded a hydrant fuelling scheme, which the Ministry experts had predicted would blow up half the countryside, and made it a reliable operational system with HTP purer than when it arrived in the tank-car (and by 1957 HTP did arrive in tank cars, at 3% of the price of ten years earlier). Trials were held with HTP in the aircraft tanks over the week-end, in all cases keeping the fighter at readiness just as if it was on active service. In the first year of flight trials more than 50,000 gallons of HTP were used, and every conceivable kind of maintenance performed in all conditions (for example, the vital copious water supply could never be allowed to freeze).

A different kind of problem showed up on paper when deep stalling was to be investigated. It looked as if the T-tail might be ineffectual at extreme angles of attack, so to avoid trouble Saunders-Roe got hold of two reliable solid rocket motors—actually of the type used to carry Royal Marines scaling ropes to the tops of cliffs—and fitted them in the rear fuselage with 90° nozzles pointing straight down. I mention this because five years later two different T-tailed British jet airliners suffered fatal crashes during deep-stall trials, because such a method of pushing the nose down had been overlooked. After each crash the lethal 'locked-in stall' with a T-tail was regarded as if it were a completely new problem!

Saunders-Roe's chief test pilot had for many years been Geoff Tyson, a great aerobatics wizard and former captain of the huge Princess flying boat. But he retired in February 1956 and his successor was Sq Ldr John Booth, whom we met earlier. Booth had to do all the early flying single-handed. His assistant had, not unnaturally, been gained from the Royal Navy. Lt-Cdr J. R. S. Overbury was a brilliant engineering test pilot, and as soon as he arrived at Cowes in 1956 he started training strongly. Unfortunately he put himself in hospital flying a Turbulent at a rally at Sandown, and had not properly got back in action when he was back in hospital after a farm cart had emerged directly in front of his speeding Jaguar car. Accidents were untypical of Overbury, but that did not help poor Booth. After the second mishap Saunders-Roe hired another pilot, Peter 'Sheepy' Lamb (since renowned as No 1 hovercraft trials driver). But Lamb did not arrive until well into 1958. Booth continued to fly the entire SR.53 programme, though he was long overdue for leave. On 5 June 1958 he was flying the second aircraft, XD 151, and had to take off from the short north/south runway at Boscombe. As he became airborne he exclaimed 'Panic stations—come and get me'! The rocket flame died, the white fighter continued unchecked—on and on, until it sped off the end of the runway and plunged down the grassy slope beyond. Owing to the slope, the concrete poles of the approach lighting got taller and stronger. After passing several, the fighter hit a mighty pole fair and square. The concrete broke in three parts, and the top portion fell straight on the cockpit, killing Booth instantly.

To this day this accident, which brings the mixed-power story to a close, remains a mystery. Booth's brief message did not really indicate panic at all, but merely showed that something had gone wrong and that he was coping in a perfectly cool way. It is a fact that the Spectre suffered no malfunction, but was shut down by a movement of the power lever well short of the end of the runway. Booth did not apply the wheel brakes, open the speed brakes, retract the gear or stream the parachute; but he did deploy the chute much later, as he went off the end. The SR.53 was designed for recovery at 9,000 lb, and its wheel brakes were not up to an emergency stop on a short strip at 18,400 lb. Indeed, this particular take-off seemed to me hazardous, when you pause to think about it, especially with such lethal lighting poles. Suffice to say that every one of the searching tests done on the wreckage showed a fully serviceable aircraft at the time of take-off. Perhaps the main positive outcome of this tragic event was proof of the way the steam from the HTP, spilling on to a barley field from the ruptured tanks, completely smothered and extinguished the intense kerosene fire.

It was indeed ironic that Booth, the very personification of the handsome, debonair test pilot, should have met his death in such circumstances at a time when the programme he had worked for so tirelessly had been thrown on the scrap heap. I have never ceased to be certain that terminating the SR.177 programme, either for the RAF or RN, was a monumental error. Admittedly today performance at 90,000 feet is less important, because one is more likely to find enemy aircraft about 89,800 feet lower down, where rocket engines are hard to justify. But this is a side-issue. The central fact is that the Saunders-Roe SR.177 was potentially the basis for the greatest family of multi-role tactical aeroplanes of the period 1960–1975, and for many of its missions it would not have used a rocket at all. There is very little that can be done by the Mirage, F-104G or any other tactical combat aircraft of the pre-1960 era that could not have been done better or more economically by derivatives of the SR.177, yet Mr Sandys threw the whole programme away. And he was merely reflecting the inability of the Air Staff to make up their minds on manned fighters. Later, when they counted the F-104Gs and Mirages, and watched the supersonic armadas at Tushino, they no longer had any doubt. By then it was a bit late.

Dassault Mirage III and 5

Aviation is full of paradoxes. While, as Rabbie Burns commented 'The best laid schemes o' mice and men, gang aft agley' (which, if you are not a Burns buff, means that carefully planned schemes often come unstuck), there are plenty of examples of aeroplanes which were never really planned at all and yet which became smashing success stories. In the latter category, nothing can surpass the Mirage III and its derivatives. It was never through any master-plan of Dassault (though they would very much like to think it was) that this highly motivated French private company scooped up practically the entire world market for first-generation supersonic fighters, outside the great powers (and it almost sold some of them, too). The Mirage delta fighters are really a happy marriage of various bits which happened to become available in the same time-scale. Even when put together the result is really a very ordinary aircraft, which many critics could say was 'hot' on landing, deficient in range and lacking some of the clever devices that are needed to fly modern missions in bad weather. It just so happens that the Mirage has fitted the needs of a score of air forces better than anything else. The continued death of competition has, at the time of writing, given Dassault export sales exceeding 1,000 aircraft. This is about 950 more than the export sales of the West European supersonic fighter in the No 2 position.

Nobody can be neutral about Dassault—either the man or the company. You either love and admire or you get aggravated. In my case it's a bit of both. Nobody can fail to admire such engineering expertise, commercial success and ruthless determination. At the same time, Dassault can be terribly tiresome. I do not believe companies operating in advanced realms of technology can be guided by a personal relationship between the top man and a cadre of top executives whom he has 'taught to think exactly as I would think myself'. I believe Dassault are mistaken when they pour scorn on the way other companies do things. The Dassault tradition is that with a few brilliant men they can accomplish more than rivals can achieve with hordes, and that decisions are taken in seconds—with the occasional sketch on the back of an envelope—while less gifted companies have to have interminable boring meetings and do costly research to get the answer. I'm afraid I have always regarded the Dassault combination of magic, mystique and alchemy as a very good sales line to feed to a non-technical audience, but something that in the harsh real world was going to become increasingly hard to sustain. In effect, the company has been trying to preserve the methods of the past. In the early days of aviation entrepreneurs gathered a very small and devoted staff who worked impossibly long hours and took decisions on the basis of hunches, and on what looked nice and which they knew from their own experience would work. But today, what now goes under the rather clumsy name of Avions Marcel Dassault/Breguet Aviation has to use hundreds of engineers, powerful computers and lots of expensive research tools just like ordinary mortals. And I think none the less of them for doing so.

When you skim off the veneer of arrogant superiority you find that, underneath, Dassault is very like any other successful aviation company, with the possible exception that its people tend to work harder and stay with the firm longer. The proud belief of Dassault that they have to be right every time (because, unlike their rivals wallowing in lush government contracts, they cannot afford to be wrong) is just another bit of mythology which is sustained by hiding away the one-offs before they are noticed. Likewise another bit of the credo, that 'we never innovate; we merely improve on what we already have' is difficult to uphold as something peculiar to Dassault. If you accept it with limitations, it is just what other companies try to do. If you take it literally it is nonsense. I would be the first to admit that Dassault have done very well by copying successful features in the aircraft of others, and in trying never to stick out their neck in a way that could lead to it being chopped off; but it is unrealistic to pretend that this firm alone has a kind of divine key which unlocks the doors to the successful future while others grope in the dark. The furthest I would go is to admit that Dassault does have the ability to take decisions fast, and to build or modify prototypes quicker than any other West European company in the same supersonic class. As time is to be equated with money, this really does mean Dassault can accomplish many things cheaper than their rivals. It is still possible for Dassault to make mistakes, take a long time to solve problems, build ugly aeroplanes, and take big technical risks trying something quite new; but in the main they do just the opposite, and do it extremely well.

In his early days Marcel Bloch (as he then was) had no need to avoid doing new things; new aircraft designs could be churned out for a sum that today looks like peanuts. During World War 2 his equally eminent brother, General Paul Bloch, adopted the Resistance code-name of d'Assault (assault tank, a grim reminder of his fight to try to get the French army equipped with armour equal to the German Panzers) and in 1946 both brothers adopted Dassault as their family surname. Marcel finished the war a very sick man in the concentration camp at Buchenwald, and by the skin of his teeth avoided being hanged; but he gradually got well again, gathered his great team—such men as Henri and Paul Deplante, Jean Cabrière, Benno Vallières and a few skilled fitters (*mécaniciens*) who had been with him since about 1930—and got back in the planemaking business. By far the most important of his new products was the MD.450 Ouragan (hurricane), a straightforward jet fighter roughly in the class of the Attacker or F-84 which flew in February 1949. With 30° of sweep the Ouragan became the Mystère which in 1952 was—to Dassault's delight—dived faster than sound by an American evaluation pilot looking for subjects for aid programmes. A switch to the home-grown Atar axial engine (home-grown by a team almost entirely composed of former German BMW engineers) resulted in the Mystère IIC, flown in June 1954 and the first all-French post-war combat aircraft to go into production. By following the lead of North American Aviation—then undoubtedly the world pace-maker with swept-wing fighters, because the Russians did not disclose the state of the art at the MiG bureau—the IIC's wing was reduced in thickness from 9% to 7.5%, necessitating a big investment in skin mills and stretch-wrap presses—over £3 million-worth given free by US aid—and increased in sweep to 38°. The result eventually became a new production fighter, the Mystère IVA, quite a few of which are still to be found doing odd jobs in India and Israel, often bearing honourable scars from aerial combat. The IVA was good, but to set it in perspective it was the first fighter on the continent to reach the 40° sweep and 8% of young Voigt's wings in the Messerschmitt works at Oberammergau a full ten years earlier! Still following North American's lead, the obvious next step was a 6% wing swept at 45°, which was thrust by a more powerful Atar with reheat to beyond Mach 1 on the level. This machine was the Super Mystère B.2.

One could easily fault the SMB.2 by pointing out that if it had been designed for Mach 0.9 instead of 1.125 it would have been able to carry heavier ordnance loads and so would have done a better job in its eventual prime mission of ground attack (as good a job as the Hunter, in fact). But the SMB.2 will always remain a considerable achievement. It was the first supersonic military aircraft to be developed outside the USA and Soviet Union. Unlike North American Aviation, the Dassault designers managed to use outboard ailerons and a tailplane in the same mid-high position as on all their fighters right back to the Ouragan. The last SMB.2 will probably not be replaced by a French Jaguar or Israeli Phantom until after this book appears. In any case its importance in this story is that it gave Dassault the capability of making aircraft in the general class of the F-100, with tapered and machined skins, and forgings so big they were squeezed out by Société Imphy on a 20,000-tonne press. It also gave

SNECMA, the maker of the simple and effective Atar engine, valuable experience with a supersonic afterburner when Britain was still fiddling with crude systems on subsonic machines.

Dassault didn't know it at the time, but this was the end of a big and lucrative family. They sketched developments of the SMB.2 with more powerful engines, and with twin engines. They planned a scaled-down version, called the Etendard (the French standard, or national flag), to meet both national and NATO requirements for light fighters. They had already built a very small delta prototype to try to meet a much earlier Armée de l'Air specification for a target-defence interceptor, but this looked as if it had no future. They bought a manufacturing licence for the long-life manned-aircraft version of the little British Viper jet engine, and began to develop an improved Viper of their own called the R.7 Farandole (a lively Provençale dance). Then they examined the market for an executive jet, which in 1955 was a very new idea, and roughed out the Méditerranée with two Farandoles. And out of this profusion of possibilities nothing looked very attractive except the trim Etendard.

Certainly the little delta interceptor, the MD.550 Mirage, seemed to have been a waste of money. Dassault had built it mainly as a private-venture research aircraft which he hoped would lead to the winner of one of the most significant combat-aircraft specifications ever to be formulated. In 1950–51 the Armée de l'Air was one of the leaders of the school of thought which professed to be horrified at how big, complicated and expensive military aircraft had become. Countless arguments were advanced and erudite papers written to show that before long the typical NATO combat aeroplane would be so complicated it could not afford to be bought, would be so weighed down with clever devices it would have a sluggish performance, and would have so much to go wrong that short-service conscripts could never learn how to keep it serviceable. In contrast, it seemed, the hordes in the Communist countries were armed to the teeth with simple and effective aircraft which would dominate the sky over any future battlefield. A lot of people were deeply concerned at the prospect. Some designers, notably Teddy Petter in Britain and Kelly Johnson and Ed Heinemann in the USA, were thrust into the role of a Messiah as a result of their heretic willingness to see what could be done to make aircraft smaller and simpler. But the British and US air staffs did not quite buy the argument. They pointed out that the limiting factor was highly trained pilots, and that it was pointless to give the modern jet pilot anything short of a 100% aeroplane. The US Air Force pointed to the alleged kill rate of $12\frac{1}{2}$:1 established by the rather complicated F-86 over the simpler MiG-15, and as nobody could disprove this it was as convincing as the combat claims made by Allied aircrew in World War 2. Long and fierce the battle raged, and it was with a slightly supercilious air that the British and Americans helped to draft NATO requirements for simple, light, cheap aeroplanes which they had no intention of using themselves.

The French went for the 'light fighter' concept in a big way. In 1952 they wrote their classic *Intercepteur Léger* requirement. The Etat-Major of the Armée de l'Air merely laid down some basic guidelines and a very few numerical values—such as the ability to climb to 65,600 feet in six minutes—and authorised limited funding to buy competing prototypes. The amazing thing was that very few firms showed interest, and I gathered that this was because only four design teams considered themselves capable of creating a supersonic fighter—even a small one. On the other hand, plenty of French companies were making supersonic research aircraft. Furthest advanced was the SO.9000 Trident by the Sud-Ouest national group. The Trident had actually begun life in 1948 as a rocket interceptor, but was wisely built as a pure research machine. It was a bold design. The 46-foot fuselage was of almost perfect streamline form, with a needle nose, circular cross-section and no excrescence save the small canopy. At the rear end were two of the first slab tailplanes ever built, sloping sharply downwards, and an SEPR (Société d'Etude de la Propulsion par Réaction) Type 251 rocket engine. Mounted well above the mid position, the tiny 99 sq ft unswept wing carried an 880 lb-thrust Turboméca Marboré turbojet on each tip. It was a very 'hairy' creation indeed. Jacques Guignard flew it on 2 March 1953, before the rocket had been cleared for flight, and needed the whole of the Istres runway even when operating at very light weight. In September 1953 the second aircraft crashed on its first flight, putting Guignard in hospital for months. Not until September 1954 did the first Trident fly with its rocket.

SEPR had decided to use RFNA (red fuming nitric acid) as the oxidant in their liquid-propellant aircraft engines. RFNA was cheap and readily available, though every schoolboy is made aware of the need to treat 'conc. nitric' with extreme respect. SEPR's test crews looked like deep-sea divers, and a special inhibitor had to be used to prevent the acid from attacking the stainless-steel piping and valves. The fuel was called Furaline, a patented mix that was about 99% aniline. When mixed together the two liquids combined hypergolically, so no ignition system was needed. The Trident installation filled the entire centre fuselage with rocket propellant. There were three thrust chambers, and though each could run only at full thrust they could be cut in and out individually, to give sea-level thrusts of 2,755 lb × 1, 2 or 3. Perhaps the dominant problem of the Trident was that the endurance at full thrust was a mere 4.5 minutes. At full power, with both turbojets and all three rocket barrels blasting, the total thrust was 10,025 lb; this was very close to the gross weight, and the design Mach number was 1.6.

Out of the SO.9000 was planned to arise the SO.9050 Trident II to meet the interceptor specification. It would have had more powerful wing-tip engines and rudimentary combat equipment, the main weapon being a guided air-to-air missile carried beneath the fuselage (no such missile was available, but the SO.9000 flew carrying a dummy). Ten SO.9050 Trident IIs were ordered in 1953.

Among the other French supersonic research aircraft of the period an outstanding example was the SFECMAS 1402 Gerfaut (gerfalcon). This was the smallest aeroplane that SFECMAS, the former Arsenal organisation, could design around an Atar turbojet. It was a trim little delta, with a tiny all-moving tailplane, flown in January 1954 with a 6,170 lb Atar 101C. On 3 August 1954 it became the first aircraft in the world to exceed Mach 1 on the level with no afterburner, rocket or any other propulsion boost. Again it was intended to lead to a light interceptor, in this case the plan being to build the SFECMAS 1501 powered by an Atar 101G giving 9,260 lb with full reheat. SFECMAS kept an open mind on armament, and expected to use guns as well as some form of missile.

Nord, which later took over SFECMAS, and Leduc slowly pressed ahead with the development of ambitious ramjet and turbo-ramjet aircraft which in the fullness of time were hoped to lead to highly supersonic military aircraft, but neither company tendered for the light-fighter order. One firm which was very keen, however, was the powerful Sud-Est group. After a lot of paper studies, which delayed their start date but put them very much on the right track, they decided to go straight to the optimised fighter and to use a big afterburning turbojet and a small boost rocket. The result was the SE.212 Durandal (the sword of Roland), tailless delta powered by an Atar 101G and a single-barrel SEPR rocket. Two prototypes were ordered, the first flying on 20 May 1956. Both were at the Paris Show in 1957.

Dassault, of course, were in at the start of the light-fighter contest in 1952 but took some time to decide on the best formula. The preferred configuration seemed to be an extension of the traditional Mystère configuration with more than 50° of sweep and a thin wing, and fitting an Atar 101G appeared likely to give a speed close to Mach 2. But there were problems. One was that the Armée de l'Air were strongly in favour of using two small turbojets in the thrust range 2,200–3,300 lb, and took the supremely mistaken decision to fund three competing engines: the SNECMA Vesta, the Hispano R.800 and the Turboméca Gabizo. A second problem was that the maximum thickness of the wing came out to about four inches, which made it practically solid metal—hard to make, very heavy and of little use as a fuel tank. After a lot of heart-searching, and many looks at the Convair XF-92A/F-102 programme (p. 166), Dassault took what was for him the very bold step of adopting the delta configuration without a tailplane. (The story goes that his senior designers were delighted, because Dassault had previously paid endless attention to tailplanes and found fault with them day and night.) As none of the little French engines was ready Dassault stole a march on his rivals by using the British Viper. Two ASV.7 Vipers were fitted to the prototype MD.550 Mirage I, a neat little delta which also differed from most Dassault jets in having a needle nose and lateral intakes, though such intakes had been used on the Mystère III prototype night fighter. Another feature was a huge, highly swept fin mounted a surprisingly long way forward. The little MD.550, a one-off, weighed only just over 7,000 lb unladen; gross weight was about 11,000 lb, half as much as a Mystère.

Dassault's chief test pilot, the great Vladimir Rozanoff, kept in intimate touch with the little delta and was looking forward to its flight programme. It was one of Dassault's toughest knocks when Rozanoff was killed giving an aerobatic display in an SMB.2, seemingly as the result of a low-speed stall. Into his shoes stepped an equally outstanding man, Roland Glavany, on five years' leave from the Armée de l'Air, and he made the maiden flight of the first Mirage on 25 June 1955. It handled very well, and showed remarkable performance considering that it had a mere 3,280 lb thrust from its two unaugmented Vipers. A little later Glavany reached Mach 1.15 in a 20° dive, which is something Armstrong Siddeley never expected when the Viper was designed. There was little doubt the tiny delta ought eventually to go well beyond Mach 1.5. Meanwhile, Dassault's project staff at St Cloud completed the design of the definitive interceptor, the Mirage II, with the Vipers replaced by two Turboméca Gabizos rated at 2,645 lb each dry or 3,300 lb with afterburning. This was to be a scaled-up aircraft, with a gross weight of 17,600 lb. It seemed as good as its various rivals; but Dassault had become disenchanted with the whole programme.

For one thing, there was no evident way of producing a Mirage II markedly superior to, say, a Durandal. The completely undeveloped little Turboméca engines were not what Dassault himself would have chosen for his supersonic delta, and in any case their combined thrust was appreciably less than that of an afterburning Atar G. Most important of all, Dassault's staff had increasingly come to doubt the validity of the whole light-fighter concept. From the start this type of aircraft had been tailored to the defence of point targets in France, and possibly other NATO countries in Western Europe. It had been assumed that the aircraft would carry only rudimentary communications radio, IFF and a radar gunsight, and that it would rely completely on ground controllers for vectoring on to its target and for navigation during recovery back to base. Range was to be short, and any question of an export market was ignored. Dassault increasingly wished to build a more versatile and less restricted kind of fighter, able to operate without such reliance on ground guidance, and with longer range and if possible a greater and more variable weapon load.

Hardly had the company begun to think along these lines when, in 1955, SHAPE concocted a completely new military philosophy for the defence of Western Europe. Only too keenly aware of the enormous numerical superiority in most conventional armaments of the Warsaw Pact powers, the Western generals and John Foster Dulles decided the only thing to do was adopt a policy of 'Massive Retaliation': the moment a Red soldier stuck one foot over his own frontier all hell would break loose in the form of scores of nuclear weapons—the only arms in which the NATO forces were predominant. As a policy it may have made sense, though I do not think many readers would consider it a socially acceptable one today. In 1955, however, the popular view was 'better dead than Red' and the public thought 'Massive Retaliation' a jolly good thing, if they bothered to think about it at all. To Dassault, however, it seemed to be the final nail in the coffin of the light fighter. In a nuclear environment the first few minutes of war would mark the obliteration of all known fixed installations, such as runways and ground radars. So the light fighter would be unable to operate. What the Armée de l'Air really wanted was a more flexible high-performance fighter and ground-attack machine able to operate from dispersed airstrips and carrying its own search radar so that it ceased to depend on ground vectoring.

The crunch came to a head in October 1955. By this time the Armée de l'Air Etat-Major considered privately that the original *Intercepteur Léger* formula would be unlikely to lead to a production aircraft, and the decision had been taken to concentrate on light ground-attack machines for dispersed operation in a nuclear scenario. Dassault stopped work on the Mirage II and decided to conduct an internal competition by swiftly building two private-venture machines and seeing which looked the best bet. One was a new version of the Etendard, with an Atar G with afterburner. It seemed to offer a good combination of flight performance, heavy offensive load and short-field performance, and to pose virtually no technical risk. The other was a derivative of the Mirage II called Mirage III, also powered by the Atar G. This promised to be much faster, but to need longer airstrips and to carry less load. The Atar-Etendard was earlier in timing, but in March 1956 something happened that had a profound effect on Dassault himself. In October 1954 Fairey had flown the FD.2 research aircraft. Dassault thought it looked good, and—worried at his own lack of delta knowledge—proposed a programme of technical collaboration between the two firms which was accepted, subject to the agreement of the MoS, whose property the FD.2 was. It was with Dassault's collaboration that the FD.2 hastened its flight programme at sunny Cazaux, on the Bay of Biscay. Then, on 18 March 1956, Peter Twiss set a world speed record in the FD.2 of 1,132 mph, beating the existing F-100 figure by a staggering 310 mph. From that moment on, Dassault could think of nothing but slender deltas. Though he did not drop the Etendard he reshaped it as a subsonic ground-attack machine with the non-afterburning Atar E3 as a rival to the NATO-preferred version with the British Orpheus engine, which was called Etendard VI. As far as Dassault was concerned the flashing performance of the FD.2 had shown him the way to the future.

On 23 July 1956 the first Etendard, the II, flew on its pair of little Gabizo engines. On the following day the Atar-powered Etendard IV flew; and, much later, this led to the carrier-based Etendard IVM and IVP and thence to the Super Etendard of 1974. The Orpheus-powered Etendard VI flew early in 1957; it was unpressurised, had the US-sponsored armament of four 0.5in guns and did not interest Monsieur Dassault very much. He was totally committed to the Atar-powered machines (having dropped the twin-Gabizo Etendard after the first programme of handling trials). At the 1957 Paris Show the company was still working hard on multi-role rough-field Etendard IVs for the Armée de l'Air, and for the Aéronavale, which was fast showing itself a likely customer, but by this time a lot of steam had gone out of the Etendard programme. Though it was still only a one-off company-funded prototype, built merely for comparative purposes against the Atar-Etendard, the Mirage III had consolidated its position as the most likely starting point for the company's next major family of combat aircraft. It wasn't planned that way.

Glavany flew Mirage III-001 at Melun-Villaroche on the evening of 17 November 1956, at the height of the Suez crisis. Apart from a malfunctioning main-wheel door the flight was very encouraging. The new delta looked very like the Mirage I, though it was about 20% bigger in linear dimensions, twice as heavy and more than twice as powerful. The top line of the fat fuselage was straight, the bottom was a smooth curve and the huge reheat system projected far behind the tall vertical tail. Like the Mirage I the wing had a leading-edge sweep of 60° and thickness of only 5%, but the increased size raised the maximum depth to about one foot, making it worth using as an integral fuel tank. Though space and weight provision was made for military equipment, 001 was a very simple aeroplane, carrying little but a communications radio. The inlet ducts were fed by plain holes, and there was no provision for a radar or external stores. On the other hand the main wheels carried remarkably big tyres able to operate at pressures down to about 85 lb/sq in—half the pressure of an SMB.2—and thus were suitable for unpaved strips. The trailing edge of each wing was a single elevon, driven by two Dassault hydraulic power units housed in prominent fairings on the underside, with spring feel. A braking parachute was stowed in a box above the jet pipe.

By this time the original Mirage I was flying at full power, with afterburning Vipers and an SEPR 66 rocket engine with a single chamber developed from those of the old Trident. With about 2,200 lb coming from each turbojet and 3,300 lb from the rocket, the Mirage I reached Mach 1.3 in level flight on 17 December 1956. But this was overshadowed in importance by the performance shown by the new Mirage III. In early 1957 it was moved to the good weather and less cluttered airspace over Istres, and on 30 January Glavany was at last able to try a maximum level run. He reached Mach 1.52 at about 40,000 feet, and the needle was still moving; to conserve fuel and speed things up he then went into a 20° dive and quickly confirmed Mach 1.6. This was a remarkable performance, with the early type of Atar fed by plain pitot intakes. Later in 1957 Mirage III-001 was fitted with a more powerful Atar 101G2 fed by reprofiled intakes fitted with sliding half-cone centre-bodies which could be manually screwed forwards at supersonic speeds. This attained Mach 1.66 on the level, and at the end of 1957 the single-barrel SEPR.66 pack was added and a level Mach number of nearly 1.9 was recorded.

At the 1957 Paris Show my colleague Mark Lambert chatted at length with Glavany, who emphasised that the big thing about the Mirage III was that, unlike other deltas, it had ample power. Previous slender deltas could easily get 'on the back of the drag curve'—a state in which reducing speed actually increases drag, because the nose comes up very steeply if you are not to lose height—and the only way to recover is stuff the nose down, if you have enough elevon power to do so. Whatever happens, you will lose a lot of height, so going too slow on the approach in such aircraft is guaranteed to be lethal. In contrast, with the Mirage III the afterburning Atar could get you out of trouble, even at very high angles of attack at well below the minimum-drag speed. Other Dassault men were eager to describe how the Mirage III production version, which they were sure the Armée de l'Air would buy, would have a completely new type of Atar engine and a clip-on two-barrel rocket pack giving 6,600 lb thrust to allow the aircraft to dog-fight at heights up to 82,000 feet. It would have two 30mm DEFA guns or an air-to-air missile, though c.g. problems would make it impossible to carry both. The nose would house one of the Dassault radars, such as Aida or Antigone. Nobody had any information on external loads for use in attack missions, though Glavany insisted the Mirage III would be able to fly such missions. The internal fuel capacity of 572 gallons was not impressive, and my own opinion at this time was that the new prototype was a bit marginal in lots of ways. The body, for example, fitted the engine so tightly that the sculptured frames that picked up the wing spars actually formed the external profile, the skin panels being fastened on between them. The one thing that did impress me was the new Atar 8 and 9, disclosed at that Paris Show. The Atar 8 introduced a new two-stage turbine and a compressor with a zero-stage and better blading, and this was combined with many other improvements to yield a thrust of about 9,700 lb, or as much as an Atar 101G with full augmentation. The 9 was the 8 with an afterburner of completely new design, and even in its first form, which SNECMA assured me was temporary, the rating promised was 13,230 lb. The Atar 9 could obviously work wonders, both for the future of the Atar—which I had not previously taken very seriously, except in a French context—and for the Mirage.

In fact the Mirage was about to change dramatically, much more than was externally obvious. Though the fact was not made public, the Armée de l'Air were engaged in deep conversation with Dassault several weeks before the 1957 Paris Show, and by July Dassault had an order for a *pré-série* batch of ten aircraft designated Mirage IIIA. As the standard of build was refined it became obvious that there would be little of the original aircraft left, apart from the landing gear. The fuselage was completely redesigned, with different structure, different cross-section, a much more capacious nose, a straighter bottom line, a new back-end and new intakes with more efficient translating half-cones. The fin was in a different place and not only restressed but a different shape with reduced height, a square top and a big dorsal extension. The wing was even more completely redesigned, with area increased from 312 to 366 sq ft and thickness reduced to a mere 4.5% at the root and 3.5% at the tip, making it the thinnest wing in Europe. The whole aircraft had been area ruled, which the original III had not been. And, of course, the engine was also new: an Atar 9B, giving the promised thrust.

The first Mirage IIIA flew on 12 May 1958. The new Atar behaved very well and the general performance was outstanding, being higher than that of either the I or the III, despite the further increase in size and weight. In fact the IIIA was able to fly in light condition with a thrust/weight ratio close to unity, and there was never any doubt that the greatly augmented thrust of the slim and cheap Atar was the main key to success with this rather 'hot' little delta, with its very thin wing completely devoid of high-lift devices (which are difficult to fit to tailless deltas). In the course of 1958 subsequent IIIAs introduced a succession of further changes and military equipment, notable features being a wing with conical camber (p. 177) and a saw-cut in the leading edge (p. 177), an SEPR 841 rocket pack, a 1,000 lb attachment under the centreline and under each wing, a CSF Cyrano radar (much to the surprise of some Dassault people who had expected to see their Super Aida chosen) and two 30mm DEFA 5-52 guns with 125 rounds each. The new rocket pack had only one barrel instead of the expected two, and it was rated at two thrust levels: 1,500 lb (sea level) for 160 seconds or 3,000 lb for 80 seconds. The package, weighing about 500 lb in all, incorporated the RFNA tank; the special tank for

Furaline (called TX2 by the Armée de l'Air) had to take the place of the guns and their ammunition. It was a neat installation, clipped in place just under the Atar, from which a power take-off shaft drove the rocket propellant pumps. When it was removed, an extra kerosene tank could be installed. In emergency the whole thing could be jettisoned, because, unlike HTP, these particular propellants are most undesirable in a forced landing or runway overrun.

From the fifth pre-production IIIA the standard of build was virtually identical to the first production version, the Mirage IIIC, of which 95 were ordered late in 1958. By this time the Mirage was known to be one of the select band of Mach 2 fighters, the first IIIA having just exceeded this speed on 24 October 1958 without the rocket installed. When Glavany did this, at 41,000 ft on a test from Istres, no fighter outside the USA and Soviet Union had accomplished the feat and the number of types of Mach 2 fighter known to exist could be counted on the fingers. On 18 June 1959 Gérard Muselli used a IIIA to take the 100 km (62.1-mile) circuit record at 1,109 mph, and he also held Mach 2.05 for four minutes. By 1960 the IIIC was in full production for the 1er Catac (Fighter Command), production machines flying from 9 October of that year and entering service with the 2nd *Cicogne* (stork) squadron in December. They were used as all-weather fighters, usually with the rocket pack in place of guns and fitted with the Cyrano 1bis radar. A pair of Sidewinders, bought from the United States in advance of similar missiles being available from European NATO sources, were usually carried under the wings. On the centreline pylon was often seen a Matra R.511, the twist-and-steer canard missile with passive optical or semi-active radar guidance which served in the indoctrination and training role with the Armée de l'Air just as the even more rudimentary Blue Sky (Fireflash) did with the RAF.

By this time Dassault had received a very favourable response from the Armée de l'Air to his proposal that he should build a range of Mirage IIIs each tailored to a given task. He predictably disliked versatile multi-role aircraft, believing—unlike me—that a jack of all trades cannot be master of any of them. Yet he was concerned at the price of the Mirage III, which did not appear likely to fall below about £450,000 and which in 1960 seemed to him very expensive! His answer was to use a common basic aircraft for several variants, and proposed: the IIIC all-weather interceptor; the IIIB tandem-seat dual-control conversion trainer, normally to be offered without radar or armament but with various possible armament options; the IIIE, with augmented radar and avionic equipment, originally intended primarily for the nuclear strike role; and the IIIR photo-reconnaissance version, without radar but again with various armament options. All were initially ordered by the Armée de l'Air, but at first only in quite small numbers. The first IIIB was on view inside the main hall at the 1959 Paris Show but did not fly until four months later, on 21 October. The first IIIE, which succeeded the IIIC in production, flew on 5 April 1961. This has a fuselage about a foot longer, bringing the rear of the clamshell canopy just ahead of the intakes, thus increasing the internal fuel capacity to a more useful 733 gallons. The engine is the Atar 9C, with a steel compressor, improved afterburner and an automatic device allowing the rpm to overspeed at Mach numbers above 1.4 to give greater thrust at high supersonic speeds, raising the level speed at the tropopause to about Mach 2.2 or 1,460 mph. Under the nose is a bulged radome for the Marconi doppler, the forward radar is the Cyrano IIbis, there is a navigation computer (fed with any of 12 plastic punch-cards to enter into the core-store the co-ordinates of any 12 selected waypoints or targets), a bombing computer, automatic gunsight and several other clever devices. Dassault allowed the maximum weight to rise to a startling 29,760 lb, about 10,000 lb more than the clean gross weight, needing a take-off ground run longer than 5,500 feet. The first IIIR, a converted IIIA with a battery of OMERA cameras, flew on 31 October 1961.

This looked like a winning team—at least it does in retrospect. At the time, around 1960, Dassault himself knew the Mirage III to be a technical success, thought it the most beautiful aeroplane his company had ever created, and hoped it would find export sales. But there were big problems. It seemed very expensive to a man used to selling fighters at around £35,000 a time, and who had tried to hold the price of even the Mystère IV at £100,000. The size of the Mirage III programme seemed likely to be small in terms of numbers of aircraft, and nothing like the Ouragan and Mystère totals. On the only occasion when I was able to have a discussion with Marcel Dassault himself—and by 1959 he had become a recluse, as far as the press was concerned—he said he hoped to build as many as 200 Mirages, but he was obviously doubtful. There was only one really big potential market and this was the new West German Luftwaffe. But before Dassault's salesmen began to visit Bonn, a customer came to visit them.

The best export purchaser of Dassault's early jets had been the infant air force of Israel. In those desperate days before the Suez campaign the Israelis had grasped at anything available with which to defend themselves. By 1957, however, they could take stock in the sure knowledge that they would not be attacked by an Arab state for a year or two at least. But taking stock was a very limited process because few arms were available. The US and British had jointly placed an embargo on sales to Israel, and the Russians were pouring supplies into Israel's enemies. The Mirage III seemed to be almost the only horse in the race, though General Ezer Weizman, Israeli Air Force C-in-C, insisted on a thorough evaluation. Young Colonel Danny Shapira began this on Mirage IIIA-001 in 1958, when the Mirage had been flown by only a handful of test pilots from Dassault and the Armée de l'Air. Shapira was soon an enthusiastic convert to the little delta, but high-level diplomacy concerned with France, the Arabs and Israel, consumed many months and it was not until June 1960 that Dassault was allowed to sign a contract to supply the Israelis with 72 Mirage IIICJ aircraft. These were identical to the C but had no rocket packs; at the time I was told they had no missile armament either, but later events showed that they had. It is extremely difficult to try to keep secret the fact that you are supplying someone with military aircraft, especially when their purchase is an obvious foregone conclusion. I do not remember how or when the fact leaked out that Israel had bought the Mirage, but it was before the first batch was delivered in 1961.

This Israeli purchase, the first Mirage export sale, was heavily overshadowed by the political overtones, and it is common knowledge that during the 1960s the French government—by which I mean de Gaulle himself—gradually became 100% pro-Arab. Dassault was increasingly put in a difficult position, because the Israelis had been his only consistent overseas buyer and appeared likely eventually to come back for more Mirages, perhaps in even larger numbers, despite the heavy financial burden. It also seemed to me odd that the Israeli aircraft should be designated CJ, the J standing for Jew! But nobody could take exception to the designation of the Mirages for the next customer—though some would take exception to the customer. With the IIICZ, Z stood for Zuid-Afrika, the Republic of South Africa. Here again the big battalions in Britain and the USA had ruled themselves out of court, through dislike of *apartheid*, and France had begun to fill the arms gap in a very profitable way which, as I write, is still doing very nicely, thank you. Despite the United Nations embargo on arms for the RSA, France has supplied tanks, armoured cars, helicopters, submarines, guided missiles and practically every other weapon you can think of, without the angry protesters seeming to notice. The first RSA Mirage sale was for 16 IIICZ aircraft configured for the ground-attack role, carrying Nord AS.20 and AS.30 guided missiles. Later, many more Mirages were supplied (Dassault will not disclose how many), among which are some fine-looking IIIRZs fitted with doppler radar. A little-known fact is that many have the new 9K-50 engine.

As described in the chapter on the F-104 (p. 184) Dassault lost the fight to equip the Luftwaffe—and with it about two-thirds of all NATO fighter strength, as several other big customers were waiting to follow the German lead. The French did not play this part of the game very well; instead of either remaining aloof, or going in determined to win, they went in very half-heartedly, and practically handed everything to Lockheed on a plate. Dassault himself behaved like a prima donna and resisted any attempt to convert his 'fighter' into an all-weather tactical nuclear strike aircraft. The French had a reputation for being intransigent, especially with their NATO allies, and upset a lot of friends. I received a letter from a Canadian—nay, a French-Canadian—dated 19 January 1960 pointing out that the Belgians' decision (not then announced) to come in on the F-104G programme 'removes one of the last possible markets for the Mirage'. Little did he guess that the Mirage programme had barely begun, and that one of the many later buyers would be Belgium!

After Israel and the RSA the first country to evince strong interest in the Mirage was Australia. Despite a 1958 decision to 'integrate American equipment throughout the Australian armed forces', the Mirage III had by the end of 1959 become front-runner in the long search by the RAAF for a replacement for the trusty CA-27 Sabre. This surprised even the Aussies, because they had not got used to the idea of France as a place from which to buy major defence hardware. The crucial decison to adopt the Mirage was announced on 15 December 1960. Defence Minister Athol Townley rather weakly said 'We will try to make it compatible with US equipment as far as possible'. Apart from transferring some Sidewinder missiles from Sabres I don't think this wish for American 'commonality' amounted to much. If the Aussies had really wanted to, they could have done some interesting things; for example they could have made quite an aeroplane by fitting the J79 engine, as did the Israelis much later. Instead, the only major engineering changes they investigated were both British. Ferranti, who hate to miss a trick, pointed out the very considerable superiority of Airpass 2 multi-mode radar over the rather dated Cyrano. Rolls, who were working with Dassault on VTOL, fitted a Mirage with an Avon 67 in the hope it would appeal to the RAAF who had Avons of much earlier vintage in their Sabres. To my surprise Dassault frankly admitted that the Avon-Mirage was a superior aircraft. From its first flight, at Melun on 13 February 1961, it went like the proverbial bomb and demonstrated markedly faster and steeper climb, higher ceiling (the gun-firing ceiling was increased by over 10,000 feet), shorter field-length, much better combat manoeuvrability at all altitudes, and roughly 20% longer range. But on 17 May Senator Harrie Wade, Air Minister, said the RAAF preferred the Atar, which was cheaper 'and we have been promised the more powerful Atar 9K later'. The final contract, signed in June 1961, was all-French, with the Cyrano radar as well.

Knowing the sense of humour of Bernard Wacquet, Dassault's renowned Mirage salesman, I do not doubt that it was he who suggested the designation Mirage IIIO, the O standing for Orstralia. The deal was for Dassault to supply the first two as pattern aircraft, and for the rest to be built with an increasing proportion of Australian parts. Commonwealth Aircraft, which called the Mirage the CA-29, assisted the prime contractor, the Government Aircraft Factories at Fishermen's Bend, Melbourne, the chief locally produced items being the Atar 9C engine (they never got the 9K), the wing, fin and rudder, rear fuselage, and many doors and panels. Poor Aussies! After having bent over backwards to ignore significant improvements in order to avoid engineering problems—like those they found so irksome when they put a very early Avon in the Sabre—they suffered such difficulties that by mid-1965 the programme was running close to a year late. Even the trivial changes the RAAF had sanctioned, such as the Sperry twin-gyro platform, took months to clear for production, and the effort needed to build the very ordinary, simple structure of the Mirage airframe was almost too much for a country whose aircraft industry was desperately short of skilled labour and couldn't even hang on to the men it did have, but—said Minister for Supply David Fairhall—suffered a 'terribly high turnover of what there is'. Eventually, in December 1968, the RAAF received its 110th and last Mirage, made up of the two trials aircraft, 48 IIIOF interceptor fighters with Cyrano IIA, 50 IIIOA attack fighters with doppler, Cyrano IIB, radar altimeter and a few other extras, and 10 IIID trainers. In 1967 the RAAF became upset over the fact that without supplies from France, usually shipped by boat, they could not operate (for example, in 1966 they had spent A$519,000 on 30mm DEFA ammunition), and the French could take a poor view of their involvement in Viet-Nam and cut them off just as they had cut off Israel. In Canberra Senator McClelland said 'I doubt we could produce this ammunition even if we had a licence. . . . Australia produces only 3.8% of the ammunition needed by the RAAF'. All most odd, because there was no problem over 30mm ammunition for the Aden guns of the Sabres, which could have replaced the French guns. What was odder still, when the RAAF later wanted to buy six more trainers it bought them complete from Dassault—who had always been grateful to the Australians for producing the IIID trainer version of the long-range IIIE which has now been sold to 12 foreign customers and to the Armée de l'Air, who call it the Mirage IIIBE.

Today the RAAF have camouflaged their Mirage force and turned almost all the OFs into OAs, as anyone could have predicted who had read the preface to this book. For the past five years they have been very busy trying to think what the Mirage replacement ought to be, and looked extremely hard at the Mirage F1; but Gough Whitlam's government has temporarily taken most of the steam out of this little exercise, and also disbanded one existing Mirage squadron. Perhaps the most instructive feature of the Australian Mirage story is the way big defence procurement deals have become more and more involved with the purchaser's national economy, so that before selecting a Mirage-replacement you have to discuss the most detailed offset deals involving raw materials, products and services that have nothing whatever to do with aviation. Fighter procurement is today a difficult business, calling for men with skill and experience in both the engineering and fiscal fields if the needs of the customer air force are to be economically met.

If you do not possess this double skill and experience the programme is likely to 'gang aft agley' rather badly. This is what happened to the next Mirage customer, which announced its choice in the same month as the RAAF, on 28 December 1960. For three years the Swiss had been looking for a nice supersonic fighter to replace the last Vampires, and augment, and later replace, the Hunters and Venoms. With ample money and time, they meant the procurement of their new fighter to serve as a text-book example of how the job ought to be done. The plan was to choose the best aircraft from a list of ten possible types and make 100 of them in Switzerland, together with the engine, major systems components and even some of the electronics. The predicted cost was put at SwFr 850 million at first, but was soon refined to 871 m, or about £72.5 m.

By the autumn of 1960 the laborious process of elimination had whittled the list of candidates down to two, and the Mirage was finally chosen over the Saab 35H (Helvetia) Draken because it seemed to be 'a more highly developed weapon system'. The Swiss wanted to use their new fighter from short strips serving underground bases, and though the Mirage needed a longer run than the Draken it was still within the stipulated 2,000 metres (which is a heck of a 'short' field length); and as it was marginally smaller they could 'accommodate a greater quantity on the same floor area'. I am quoting Paul Chaudet, head of the Military Department, who went on to announce the choice of the Atar over the RB.146 (Avon 67) on 31 January 1961 by explaining that the British engine was 'more expensive and would cause delay'. It seemed to me strange to announce a choice of engine by giving only one side of the argument. If such considerations were valid there would never be any new aircraft or engine types at all! What one has to do is balance the minuses against the pluses, and if the Swiss had waited until the Avon-Mirage flew two weeks later they would have discovered just how great were the advantages of using the British engine. There was no reason to suspect any delay on this score because the conversion had already been completed, and the Swiss industry—principally Sulzer—had long experience of making British turbojets but none of making French ones. At the time nobody in Derby, or in the British MoA, had any concept of how big the Mirage export programme was going to be. With the benefit of hindsight it would have paid to use the Swiss, or the Australians, as a 'loss leader' to get the Avon established. It is hard to say how many other customers would have followed suit, but as more than half of them already used the Avon (and none the Atar) the prospects were bright. And the reheat Spey, even more powerful and economical, would have fitted later Mirages like a glove;

but no engine ever failed to be adopted for so many fighters as the reheat Spey in the 1960s.

The precipitate decision of the Swiss to choose the Atar immediately before the start of flight trials of the Avon-Mirage did not prepare me for what happened next. Stressing how much they wished to keep out of technical trouble, the Swiss spent the rest of 1961 thinking of how they could change their Mirages in all the ways most likely to cause really major problems. It was perhaps predictable that the DEFA guns should have been thrown out in favour of the Swiss Oerlikon 302—though, as I hinted earlier, the Australians stuck to the DEFA, with its imported ammunition, when they already used the almost identical British Aden. What was absolutely staggering was that the final standard of build of the Mirage IIIS, as the Swiss fighter was called, specified the Hughes Taran fire-control system and Hughes Falcon missile! The Taran (Tactical Radar and Navigation) is an attractive fighter fire-control by the firm I rate as No 1 in the air-to-air field in the world. It is of advanced design (for 1960–61) and neatly packaged, and offers a wide range of options in air-to-air and air-to-ground operations; it is also extremely complicated and totally different from anything ever fitted to a Mirage before. The Falcon missile chosen was the HM-55, the big conventional-warhead weapon earlier adopted by Sweden and made by Saab. This was as much like the French Matra missiles as chalk is like cheese. The crowning irony was that the Swiss had done their best to convert the Mirage into something resembling the Draken Filip, even to the extent of buying their missiles from Saab, having earlier rejected the Draken itself!! They also asked for lots of minor engineering changes, including a stronger landing gear, longer nose leg and an arrester hook.

Anybody who wanted to make easy money could have done so by betting the Swiss they would have severe trouble with the Mirage IIIS programme. The government aircraft establishment, which has titles in German, French and Italian but in English is called Federal Aircraft Factory, has a pleasant little manufacturing facility at Emmen, near Lucerne. They were able to tool up and start making Mirage IIIS airframes, because these had not been significantly altered. But the rest of the aircraft was a nightmare, and even Dassault were unable to produce a combat-ready IIIS but instead delivered their two pattern aircraft in 1963–64 as close as possible to the Swiss standard as they could manage. The first IIIS did not fly at Emmen until October 1965. By this time the problems could no longer be hidden —for one thing the timing had slipped by two years!—and in May 1964 a hint of the fiscal disaster had surfaced when it was discovered that the estimated bill for 100 aircraft had escalated from SwFr 871m to 1,447m. The government thought this 'a great surprise', though in fact it was nothing like the whole story. In September 1964 the number of aircraft was cut to 57 (later one extra was added), only 36 of them being of the costly IIIS type; the rest are IIIBS trainers and IIIRS photographic machines without Taran or missile armament. I do not know the total R&D bill, which eventually had to pay for 300 hours of extremely costly flight development in the US in 1967 to try to get Taran to work reliably without problems either within its own circuitry or at the interfaces with the Mirage. Suffice to say the Swiss paid twice as much for half as many aircraft; and a lot of Swiss heads bit the dust, including that of the commander of the Air Force, and the saga has strongly influenced Swiss military procurement ever since. I believe they are now re-considering the Me 109.

At this point I must mention one or two side branches to the main story which cannot be ignored. In 1956 Dassault had schemed a considerably scaled-up Mirage with two Atar engines to serve as a long-range night and all-weather fighter. As described in the companion volume *Bombers of the West* this stillborn project was later used as the basis of the Mirage IVA strategic nuclear bomber. The engineering development needed to produce the Mirage IVA exceeded that of the original Mirage fighter, yet an even greater effort went into a totally different programme which eventually came to nothing.

In 1960 the NATO Military Committee formulated a requirement—NATO Basic Military Requirement 3 or NBMR-3—for a V/STOL tactical strike fighter. It was conceived partly to replace the Fiat G 91—which had angered the French because it was not French—and partly because the Massive Retaliation policy had never been rescinded and seemed to rule out reliance on any aircraft needing proper airfields. The specification called for a field length so short as to demand VTOL capability, as well as a mission radius at low level of 250 nautical miles and a speed of at least Mach 0.92. Two aircraft were already active programmes in the field of military jet lift: the Hawker P.1127 and German VJ 101. But military aircraft were an almost unmentionable idea in Britain, and it was the team of de Gaulle and Dassault that moved fastest and farthest. Usually decisions on Dassault aircraft were taken by Dassault alone, but early in 1961 he agreed to investigate the possibility of producing a jet-lift Mirage III as Rolls-Royce had suggested. Drawings of such things had littered offices at Derby for three years, and the Short SC.1 had shown that the Rolls-Royce formula of installing a battery of purpose-designed lift jets was sound. Rolls had no share in the P.1127, and the Mirage was one of the obvious opportunities (another was the F-104, p. 184).

The upshot was a major programme to develop the Mirage IIIV (= *verticale*) for the Armée de l'Air and, hopefully, most other NATO air forces. The first 'back of an envelope' sketches showed that it would have to be considerably bigger than the Mirage III. It finally came out weighing between 30,500 lb (VTOL) and 46,000 lb, and the engines were a big SNECMA/Pratt & Whitney TF 106 for propulsion and eight Rolls-Royce RB.162-31 lift jets in the fuselage. The IIIV demanded a very big development programme, almost entirely funded by the French government. To prove the general principle, the original Mirage III-001 was rebuilt with a smaller (Bristol Siddeley Orpheus) propulsion engine and ducting, eight RB.108 lift jets, and a bleed-air reaction control system for use in hovering flight. The 001 had always been nicknamed the Balzac within the company, because of the 'Balzac 001' telephone number of an advertising agency that was incessantly flashed on French cinema screens. The converted VTOL machine was officially called by this name, with the result that Dassault received a nice letter from the Honoré de Balzac literary society expressing thanks and gratification that the Dassault jet should have been named after the great French writer!

Unfortunately the Balzac eventually crashed, killing its pilot, was rebuilt, and then crashed again, killing a second pilot (a sad record which surely few other aircraft have accomplished?). Meanwhile Dassault worked fast to build two prototypes of the much bigger Mirage IIIV, which was to combine jet V/STOL capability with at least Mach 2 speed. By this time the old Mach 0.92 figure had been forgotten in the excitement of VTOL Mach 2, which for undisclosed and mainly emotional reasons had to be attained. The only serious rival, and a potentially deadly one, was the British Hawker Siddeley P.1154. Dassault missed no opportunity of knocking this single-engined vectored-thrust design. Henri Deplante cunningly pointed out that Dassault had 'investigated two schemes: one, a high-wing vectored-thrust design was abandoned after the French Air Ministry had favoured the greater safety, versatility and development potential of the Mirage IIIV layout'. (He said this, incidentally, at Brough, Yorkshire, where there is a Hawker Siddeley factory!) Not to be outdone, Benno Vallières said the rivalry with the P.1154 was 'mainly a question of timing; the Mirage IIIV is the only aircraft which could be in service by 1966—show me a BS.100 engine or a P.1154 airframe with a proven Mach 2 capability'. (He omitted to mention that the airframe and engines of the IIIV would likewise be totally new.) One outfit that was either sold on Dassault's arguments or else just had to jump on this bandwagon, because they could hardly join their rival Hawker Siddeley, was the Military Aircraft Division of BAC, where by November 1961 a team under Freddie Page was collaborating on a Mirage IIIV version for the RAF and Royal Navy. Even more remarkably, Boeing-Wichita also got into the act, partly to learn all they could about this kind of aeroplane but also in a genuine bid to sell it, made under licence in Wichita, to the US Air Force. Now you see my comment at the start of this chapter that the Mirage was nearly bought by some of the great powers.

One obvious snag was cost. In November 1963 Defence Minister Pierre Messmer said 'Each IIIV will cost $8 million, six times as much as a Mirage IIIC, so we shall not be building many'. (Earlier, at the start of the programme, Dassault had thought there was a 1,200-aircraft market just waiting to be picked up.) Indeed by September 1962 the original NBMR-3 requirement had been shelved, and the programme to hold a NATO competition abandoned, because it was obvious that any procurement would be on a national basis. Everyone in NATO is glad to collaborate in common weapons programmes, providing their own design is chosen. A little later the P.1154 was declared 'technical winner'; but Dassault was so sensitive he announced in 1964 that the Mirage IIIV was 'equal technical winner' of the supposed contest, which I think made the French feel a bit better. Dassault even refused to admit that BAC, the company's partner on the AFVG programme (and on the IIIV), had design leadership on the airframe as the two governments had agreed, and in June 1967 that programme collapsed, as related in *Attack Aircraft of the West.* Dassault find genuine collaboration, where you share the design work, almost impossible.

René Bigand began free hovering trials with the first Mirage IIIV on 17 February 1965. This was a very difficult time for Western European aerospace, when large sums were being frittered away on programmes that were grossly mismanaged. The Mirage IIIV was one of the biggest technical challenges in the history of aviation, yet the essential back-up programmes were either skimped or not done at all, because the government attitude in London and Paris was one of horror at escalating cost. When Bigand opened up the eight RB.162 lift jets he was flying them for the very first time, and even the TF 104 propulsion engine was devoid of any significant background of ground or flight testing. The TF 104 was a SNECMA modification of the Pratt & Whitney JTF10A subsonic civil turbofan. The difficulties experienced with the TF 104 and the supersonic afterburning TF 106 were such that SNECMA abandoned these engines and switched to the TF 306 based on Mr Pratt's TF30, the engine of the American F-111, which a little later became a household word as a supposed 'can of worms' itself. Even the basic idea of a jet-lift V/STOL was by 1965 being called into question. One man well able to offer an opinion, Gen Bruce K. Holloway, told me 'I think I can say the opinion of the US Air Force is that there are severe operational problems and that VTOL has been oversold'. Even Dassault himself had begun to lose interest, but the IIIV kept going, and on 25 March 1966, at Istres, made a successful transition from hover to wing-supported flight and back again. Mirage IIIV-002 was flown by Jean-Marie Saget on 22 June 1966, and on its 11th flight, on 12 September, reached Mach 2.4, roughly twice as fast as any other VTOL aircraft. But termination of the programme was inescapable, and it was made somewhat easier by the loss of IIIV-002 on 28 November 1966, Col Garrigues of the CEV ejecting safely.

The Mirage IIIV was a very big and challenging programme. It would not be correct to claim that Dassault regretted it, but it serves as a copybook example of something that 'seemed to be a good idea at the time'. In the long term it was valuable—though, as is often the case in the difficult discipline of aviation, this was for quite unexpected reasons. In 1962 Dassault secured funds for a third IIIV airframe to be completed swiftly without lift jets or reaction controls to serve as a test bed for the troublesome TF 106 engine. This machine, called the Mirage IIIT, was flown by Jean Coureau with a TF 104 engine on 4 June 1964. Predictably, Dassault took a hard look at the IIIT and decided it could form the start of a new family of non-VTOL aircraft much bigger and more powerful than the Mirage III series. As early as 1962 Dassault had begun to worry about the future and look for a successor to his little delta. He considered it inadvisable to gamble on the Mirage III programme continuing beyond 1965, and in any case the Armée de l'Air were thinking about a successor too. In March 1964 Dassault received a design contract for a next-generation aircraft, and after extensive parametric studies the company decided on a straightforward development of the IIIT. The test-bed was redesignated IIIT1 and the new combat aircraft was designated Mirage IIIT2, which seemed very clumsy as it was not a 'III' at all. It was a tandem-seat attack fighter in the 40,000 lb-class to be powered by the big TF 106 reheat turbofan engine. The only thing that really worried Dassault was that by 1964 the rather crude delta wing looked somewhat dated. Though air forces were becoming less enchanted by VTOL they still wanted to carry big loads out of short unpaved strips, and this was just what the Mirage III-type wing was hard-pressed to do. Though the Mirage III had always been able to use soft ground, thanks to its generous tyres, it took off and landed very fast indeed, and with a heavy load of armament it seemed that any tailless delta would need an airstrip longer than 1,000 metres (3,300 ft).

This problem caused a lot of head-scratching. Dassault had, not unnaturally, been deeply interested in the TFX (F-111) programme, and had since 1961 had a few engineers looking at swing-wings. By 1964 he was almost back to 1955, so great were the number of possible options. His new-generation fighter might have a delta wing—or a kinky double-delta, because the IIIV and IIIT had a wing plan almost like a Concorde, largely in order to increase the root thickness sufficiently to accommodate the dual-wheel main gears. It might have a variable-sweep swing-wing, plus a tailplane. It might have a conventional fixed wing and tailplane. The propulsion might be provided by a TF 106 or by two Atars; or there might be a case for scaling everything back again to Mirage III size with a single Atar, or with a projected new Super Atar of similar size but more thrust. By 1965, with the inspiration of the Viggen, Dassault were looking at the practicability of adding a flapped foreplane ahead of the existing delta wing, either with or without high-lift trailing-edge flaps.

Late in 1964 Dassault took the bold decision to erase the Mirage IIIV from future planning and to build four contrasting non-VTOL prototypes. Certainly no other manufacturer in the West (or anywhere else) could have dreamed of such a thing. One would be the IIIT2. One would be a swing-wing aircraft, called Mirage G. The third would have a very thin fixed wing, with high-lift devices, plus a tailplane, and would be designated Mirage F2. Finally there would be a small Mirage III-size version of the F2 called Mirage F1. As far as possible these aircraft would use common parts, to minimise cost. The most urgent was considered to be the F2, which was needed for the low-speed flight development of the TF 106 which was still, on paper, lagging behind the required flight programme for the Mirage IIIV. Construction of the Mirage F2 went ahead with top priority. There was a fine model of it at the Paris Show in 1965. The British TSR.2 had lately been cancelled, and Dassault salesmen were eager to tell me they called the F2 their 'TSR.1'. They considered it not greatly inferior in capability to the defunct British aircraft, though I privately considered it would be more like the Hawker P.1121. Understandably, the Dassault men were arrogant and condescending towards a mere Briton, whose country seemed content to leave the field to Dassault. Round the edge of the Dassault stand were models of the other new projects, notably single-engined (TF 106) and twin-engined (Atar) versions of the ambitious swing-wing Mirage G, one of them in Aéronavale markings, and land and carrier versions of the F1. There was no model of the T2, the straightforward big delta, and I learned it had been abandoned. It was at the same Salon that I learned of SNECMA's severe difficulties with the TF 106, and of their plan to replace it with the TF 306 as the engine of the Mirage F2 and G. Predictably, SNECMA today insist the Americans developed the TF 30 from their TF 306, instead of the other way round.

I hope this profusion of new aircraft and engines is not too confusing. British politicians may care to recall that this was at the time that military aircraft development in Britain had virtually come to a standstill and been replaced by rather unhappy collaborative projects and purchases from the United States. To assist the bargaining posture of its collaborative negotiators the British government announced it would never build a British combat aeroplane again. In contrast, all the Dassault programmes were all-French. When Dassault had a potentially huge collaborative programme handed to him on a plate (AFVG), his engineers worked hard enough but the senior management showed not the slightest enthusiasm and eventually managed to get French funds transferred to the Mirage F1.

This killed the big AFVG programme stone-dead, and Dassault rubbed his hands with glee and got on with the little F1.

This excellent fighter serves to underline the inadequacy of the old tailless delta, because with the same size of aircraft (in fact, with only two-thirds as much wing area) and only very slightly more thrust, from an engine of the same size and weight, the Mirage F1 is faster than the Mirage III, can loiter before an interception for three times as long, carry a much greater offensive load, fly ground-attack missions over almost twice the radius of action, pull much greater g in manoeuvres, roll faster, and cut 20% off the approach speed and landing run. The F1, and its many derivatives (F1A, F1B, F1C, F1E and the International with the new M53 engine) may eventually form a story as big and as interesting as that of the Mirage III. So too will the Mirage G, which waggled its swing-wings 'in the wings' as the AFVG died in 1967, and its offshoots the twin-engined G8 and fixed-wing ACF (Avion de Combat Futur) which promises outstanding performance in the period after 1977. But these aircraft hardly justify inclusion in a book on 'first-generation' supersonic fighters. Their story must wait for another time, and the rest of this chapter continues the history of the little Mirage delta which, instead of fading out by 1965, has since gone from strength to strength.

One of the lesser-known bits of the long Mirage III tale is that Boeing was interested in not only the IIIV but also in the smaller non-VTOL fighter. During 1962 the US Air Force was in the process of dotting the i's and crossing the t's on a big contract for the Northrop N-156F Freedom Fighter as a standard warplane for minor allies. While doing so it kept evaluating various proposals put up by Northrop's rivals. Boeing's Wichita division had tried very hard to win the giant TFX programme—indeed, many said they should have won—and when they lost the future looked bleak. An Americanised Mirage III seemed an outside possibility to knock out the Northrop fighter, because it appeared to offer equal capability in defensive and offensive roles (its flight performance was much higher) for a cost that might even be less. Wacquet talked to Ed Wells, Boeing senior vice-president, and the deal was on. The Mirage IIIW (W for Wichita) was similar to the Swiss aircraft in having the Hughes Taran radar and the option of Falcon missiles. Pratt & Whitney, who were already in partnership with SNECMA (whom they partly owned, despite the fact the French firm is a nationalised one), said they would act as a US source for Atar engines in the event of a US Mirage programme—though they were so heavily extended at the time that I do not think they could have taken on much additional manufacturing. The US Air Force was interested, and studied the proposal in depth; one of the evaluation pilots was Lt-Col James McDivitt, the astronaut. But I think it is only realistic to say the IIIW was a non-starter.

By the mid-1960s sales of the Mirage III had dropped to a trickle. This happens with big civil transports too, and it is often hard to determine whether this is the end of the programme or just a temporary 'bathtub'. Dassault thought it could well be the end, hence his concentration on the profusion of follow-on projects. But there was a new ground-attack version which was potentially of some importance. In 1964 the Israeli Air Force made a formal proposal to Dassault concerning a simplified Mirage III tailored mainly to the ground-attack role in the blue skies and near-perfect visibility of the Middle East. If VMC weather is not merely prevalent but absolutely predictable, and if you are not bothered about defensive fire and can make multiple passes over your target, then a simple VMC attack fighter makes all the sense in the world. Removal of the Cyrano radar, and most of the other elements of the navigation, fire-control and weapon-delivery system, saved roughly 1,000 lb and £100,000. In place of these black boxes Dassault put in 110 gallons more fuel and provision for a much heavier external load. For example two 1,000 lb bombs can be carried on the centreline, two 500 lb bombs can be carried on the inner wing just behind the main gears, four pairs of 500 lb bombs can be carried on long 2 × 2 racks under the outer wings and two more 500 lb bombs on pylons close to the tips. The effect is startling, because there is hardly any wing visible from the underside, just a mass of bombs. Thus laden the safe field length is over 6,000 feet (more in the tropics), but if you can accept this the idea is obviously highly cost/effective.

By this time Dassault had used up most of the available suffix letters for the Mirage III so this simplified version was called the Mirage V, which since 1968 has been written Mirage 5. As it was their own invention the Israelis were the first customer, placing an order in September 1966 for 50. Though it is externally similar to the IIIE, apart from having a slim, pointed nose, the Mirage 5 incorporates more than 70 engineering changes as a result of the feedback of not only arduous front-line service but also a large number of air combats against Russian-built Egyptian and Syrian fighters armed with cannon and guided missiles. From 1963 onwards this invaluable combat experience had been fed back to Dassault, and though some of it was used to improve the IIIC and IIIE, the main beneficiary was the Mirage 5 which has been carefully planned for maximum serviceability, minimal maintenance and greater survivability in battle. The Mirage 5 is a fine example of 'product-improvement' which, like that performed on the Boeing 727, has lifted a great programme out of the doldrums and made it a smashing best-seller.

Unfortunately the tale now becomes deeply intertwined with politics with a capital P. One of the factors was Charles de Gaulle. Another was the eventual decision of the French to give up Algeria, after a terribly long and brutal war, thus marking the completion of the process which turned

France's African colonies into independent Arab states. Whatever the reasons, and I do not profess to be informed on the matter, de Gaulle—but by no means all of his ministers—chose to espouse the Arab cause, which automatically meant ceasing to be friendly with Israel. I do not know if de Gaulle ever discussed the change in policy with his faithful friend Dassault, but the planemaker was obviously put in an extraordinarily difficult position. As early as 1965 Dassault or the French government were discussing the supply of Mirages to several Arab nations including Saudi Arabia, the Lebanon and Jordan. Despite various snags the Lebanese signed for 24, but later cut their purchase by half. Negotiations were also opened with other Arab countries, but these were interrupted by the swift boil-up of a major Arab-Israeli crisis in May 1967. Triggered off by Nasser's eviction of the UN peacekeeping force, and his subsequent closure of the Red Sea to Israeli shipping, the crisis escalated daily whilst Western diplomats reached out with tweezers to release tiny drops of soothing oil on the cauldron. De Gaulle was made of sterner stuff. He ordered an embargo on the shipment of arms to Israel. His main purpose appeared to be to spite Israel for some private reason, rather than to prevent war. In fact he helped to spark it off: realising it was cut off from its chief source of spares, the Israeli Air Force carried out the pre-emptive strike against Arab air power (notably Egyptian, Syrian and Jordanian) which opened the Six-Day War on 5 June 1967 and which has ever since been studied by military tacticians as the most brilliant operation of its kind.

De Gaulle, who appeared to make some monumental blunders in his handling of the situation, never released the force of 50 Mirage 5J aircraft which the Israelis paid for in full over the three years they were being made. At various times assorted French ministers issued encouraging statements to Israel, and it may be too early to explain what the French policy really was. Superficially it seems that the objective of de Gaulle was just to deprive the Israelis of arms, because assurances of eventual delivery of the fleet of Mirage 5Js were redoubled as soon as it looked as if the Americans might fill the gap with Phantoms (as, of course, they did). The first 5J, which was also the first Mirage 5, flew just before the war on 19 May 1967. During the summer of 1967 5Js began to litter the apron at Bordeaux-Mérignac, and were test flown with almost empty tanks by Israeli officers. Delivery was due in November. The Israelis tried every subterfuge to get at least some of the aircraft they had paid for, and even secured permission to continue training in Corsica during the winter, but de Gaulle petulantly ordered that the aircraft should be partly dismantled and put into guarded storage. There were lots of behind-the-scenes machinations, as well as highly public visits by the Israeli Defence Minister General Zvi Tsur to Paris (where, the papers reported, he met a stone wall, and told his hosts he was thinking of sueing them in the International Court at The Hague for breach of contract). Finally the Israelis were persuaded to accept a fait accompli, and the French 're-purchased' the aircraft, completed them in 1972–73 to a slightly different standard as M5Fs and—so I am assured—put them into service with the Armée de l'Air.

What a saga this bit of the tale is! As I do not wish to be found floating in a dark canal I have never tried to ferret out all the things that did not get into the papers, but I hope some bright chap will eventually tell all. It is extremely unusual for a formidable lot of defence hardware to be impounded by the vendor in peace-time, in the full glare of publicity, and eventually to put the weapons into his own inventory. Probably 99 out of every 100 people outside the Arab world thought the Israelis had been shabbily treated (though their anger was soon to be sharply intensified), and wondered if Israel would be able to cope with her great, big, belligerent neighbours. After the Israeli Commando raid on Beirut airport on 28 December 1968—itself a reprisal for Arab hijackings of El Al airliners—de Gaulle angrily cut off every kind of military supplies from Israel, including such things as spare springs and washers. The outcome was predictable. In February 1969 Israel Aircraft Industries said it had not only 'introduced further valuable modifications' to the old Mirage IIICJs as a result of combat experience in the Six-Day War, but 'we are also tooling up to make spares'. Asher Ben Yosef, deputy managing director, said 'We can fully cope with the situation', and Prof Moshe Arens, deputy general manager (engineering) said 'The only penalty will be suffered by the French aircraft industry'.

What they did not disclose, but which stood out a mile as a natural thing for the Israelis to do, was that IAI appeared to be prepared to test its potential to build the Mirage from scratch, with a more powerful engine. In early October 1970 an unconfirmed news report from Tel Aviv claimed that an Israeli 'Super Mirage', powered by a GE J79-17 engine (the same engine as fitted to the Israeli Phantoms), had made a successful maiden flight at Lod. Subsequently one heard tales of a mystery fighter called the Black Curtain, and these finally gave way late in 1972 to a more detailed report of the J79-powered Mirage, which is actually called the Barak (Lightning). There were said to have been 'development difficulties' which had been successfully overcome, and it was expected a squadron of 24 Baraks would be in service by 1973. The Barak was said to reach Mach 2.5, carry a '4–6 tonne payload' and have 'STOL capabilities'. As for the question of Israeli production of the Barak from scratch, it would be interesting to discover if the Swiss or Australians have sold any Mirage tooling. In any event, Dassault has lost his oldest and best overseas buyer.

Dassault did not need to worry overmuch about this, nor over the harm done to his prospects elsewhere by the curt embargo placed on his customer. The scintillating performance of the Mirage IIICJs in the Six-Day War was the finest, most immediate and most widely broadcast publicity any maker of war material has ever had. Both in air-to-ground and air-to-air operations the quite old Mirages performed wonders in the hands of their extremely professional and desperately eager pilots, and there are reports of Mirages flying up to 12 missions in a single day under rough and ready war conditions. It is hard to give a credible numerical result to the air fighting in this amazing war, but the Mirage force probably achieved a figure close to 10:1 in its favour, some four-fifths of the Arab aircraft losses being on the ground. To bring the Israeli tale up to date both the IIICJ and the Barak, carrying the Shafrir (Sidewinder-type) missile, were engaged in the renewed hostilities in the autumn of 1973, though this time the Israeli Air Force had plenty of American jets to help bear the load. Barak technical problems remain considerable.

Before the Six-Day War, in February 1967, Peru was suddenly named as shopping for the Mirage 5. The news caused the US State Department almost to explode. No supersonic aeroplane existed in Latin America, and in any case this was a traditional US preserve which the big American aircraft industry was prepared to defend by violent lobbying in Washington. There were immediate rather heated talks, which in October 1967 resulted in the US government offering Peru the Northrop F-5 instead of the Mirage, which showed that the Americans' objective was not to prevent a South American arms race but to keep the area hooked on US products. A lot of people got very cross, including the British whose sale to Peru of well-used but completely reconditioned Canberras was likewise blocked by the State Department, which claimed (incorrectly) that the aircraft had originally been built with the aid of US offshore-procurement funds. The angry Americans were on a loser, in both cases. In April 1968 Premier Rebagliatti said in Lima his air force would receive 12 Mirage 5Ps and two two-seaters, as well as the Canberras. Later Peru bought more Mirages, including six in 1973. Just to keep the State Department busy, Argentina, Brazil, Venezuela and Colombia have now also placed substantial orders for the Mirage. I think that almost wraps up Latin America, apart from Ecuador which has professed interest in both the Mirage and Jaguar [sale announced September 1974], so Dassault cannot lose.

On 16 February 1968 the Belgians were having a grand crisis, shouting rude things at each other in both their tongues and trying to elect a new government. As almost its final act the outgoing administration of Van den Boeynants at last said which aircraft was to be adopted as the replacement for the F-84F and RF-84F. For over two years the argument had raged—quite separate from the main political crisis—and there was obviously a case for either having more F-104Gs or following the example of the Netherlands and going for the F-5 and RF-5. These Northrop aircraft, in production by Canadian and Dutch companies, were quietly pressed on the Belgians by the US government, but this may have put them off. Anyway the choice fell on the Mirage 5. I was surprised at this, as many of my memories of Belgium are of low clag and drizzle, but it later transpired that the Belgians did want a 'more advanced navigation system' than the basic VMC aircraft, which for much of the time would be almost useless in Northern Europe. Today the Belgian air force has its force of 106 Mirage BA, BD (two-seat) and BR (recce) aircraft, all assembled by SABCA, with major contributions by Fairey SA, who will also make rear fuselages for the whole production run of Mirage F1 fighters and can participate in other Dassault military programmes including the Mirage G8 or ACF. So the Belgians have done very well out of the Mirage, which they were sensible enough to accept almost exactly 'as is', and the only possible regret is that its adoption is one more nail in the coffin of NATO commonality and a break in a 20-year tradition of integration with the Dutch. As I write, it remains to be seen whether the clever Dassault 'give away' of the Mirage F1 rear fuselage will get Belgium hooked on this as well, or whether they will buy the considerably more useful Jaguar (which, as they did not design it, never seems to be recognised by Dassault as their most important product). By mid-1974 they had tried to choose a common aircraft with the Netherlands, Norway and Denmark to replace the F-104 (p. 184). They want a nice flashy 'fighter' that is cheap, even if not very useful.

Dassault's mounting success with the Mirage seemed invariably to be gained at the cost of violent reactions, either within the customary country, or by a rival, or by almost everyone. None of these eruptions quite equalled that which followed the sale to Libya. In April 1968 BAC had announced a large order for purely defensive guided weapons for the Kingdom of Libya, in the form of a five-year contract for Thunderbird, Rapier and a lot of training and supporting equipment. But in 1969 King Idris was ousted by a revolutionary coup, and it was soon clear that the new administration of young Col Khadaffi was dedicated to bellicose sabre-rattling against Israel. I would have thought the two British missile systems extremely potent things to have in any future conflict with Israel, but Khadaffi told the RAF and USAF to get out of Libya, tore up the agreement and went to see Dassault. As is so often the case, there were all sorts of complicating factors. The French had a very bad adverse trade balance with Libya, almost entirely on account of the huge one-way traffic in petroleum. There was a rebellion in the African territory of the Chad, with the French trying to help the local government smash the rebels and the Libyans giving the rebels all the help it could.

And, of course, there were the 50 Mirages that could not be delivered to Israel.

The French will now frankly admit they rather mis-played the public-relations side of this affair. It would have been better to come clean and say 'In view of the factors listed above it serves our purpose to sell lots of Mirages to Libya, and this is just what we are going to do'. This would have been what Harold Wilson would call pragmatic. Instead the French funked the storm they knew must come. Though Khadaffi had insisted on maximum publicity, the French tried to keep everything dark. This was foolish; I suppose the Israeli intelligence knew what had been said by each side within 24 hours. Eventually, just before Christmas 1969, the Israelis rather naughtily tipped off the US State Department (which didn't know a thing). The Americans were very angry indeed, mainly because the Libyans had been toying with the same old Northrop F-5, even managing to crash three, and had been thought a possible big customer. The Israelis intimated the deal might be for all 50 of 'their' Mirages. The embarrassed French said the negotiations involved 'only about 15 aircraft, to be delivered from Armée de l'Air stocks'. Ouch!!! In January the figure had climbed to 100, and the following month the true figure of 110 was disclosed. France's name was vilified from Marseilles to Manhattan (where poor President Pompidou had just arrived, to face a disastrous series of hostile press conferences). In Paris there were near-riots.

At first the arguments had centred around the way the French had welshed on the contract with Israel—indeed, they had the effrontery at one point to send the Israelis a bill for storage of their paid-for Mirages!—and then proposed to sell an even bigger number of Mirages to the other side. But the more thoughtful observers asked what on earth Libya wanted with 110 Mirages? It was all very nice for France to get over £63 million in revenue from oily Libya, thus helping put the screws on the oil producers in Algeria, and simultaneously give the French aircraft industry its biggest-ever sale; but Libya had hardly any pilots or bases and seemed quite unable to operate such a big force of supersonic aircraft. Dassault was obviously very unhappy about the whole affair, felt his honour was to some degree at risk, and insisted on a clause in the contract prohibiting the use of the aircraft by any third party (especially, by Egypt or other Arab state involved in the Six-Day War). Before 1970 was out I was tired of reading hair-raising magazine articles describing how the Libyans would merely pass on the powerful force to Egypt (or the Soviet Union), and would in any case find out all about 'the latest French and British electronics' (which were not fitted). Certainly the scare-stories had some effect, because in January 1971 French Premier Jacques Chaban-Delmas announced that 'if it appeared that any of these Mirages was changing its destination . . . then the following one would be placed immediately under an embargo'. What aggravated the situation was the formation by Egypt, Syria and Libya of the Union of Arab Republics. I wondered if some of the Mirages, by now designated 5D, 5DD, 5DE and 5DR, would have to suffer the indignity of being embargoed twice, once on each side—surely a new event in the history of arms traffic!

Of course, in a situation like this you can be certain that somebody, somewhere, will report that (1) the Libyan Mirages are being flown and maintained by Egyptians/Russians/Chinese, (2) some or all have been sent to Egypt/Russia/China (or wherever else is considered to make people aggravated) or (3) they are being used to bash the Chad government/Chad rebels/any other rather remote place that might stir up trouble. In the event this sort of thing has burst into print about once a week, but the only credible story is that in March and April 1973 there was a large-scale airlift, by Egyptian An-12s, between Egypt and Libya. There were several 'confirmed reports' or 'it subsequently became clear' type stories that the main purpose of the lift was to carry some or all of the Mirage support equipment to Egypt. On 20 April Gen Elazar, the Israeli Chief of Staff, stated that it was known that one squadron of Mirages had already been supplied to Egypt; the French government said it had not. When the war broke out in full violence, Israeli pilots reported on several occasions encountering hostile Mirages, and the Israelis eventually claimed 'irrefutable evidence', including camera-gun film showing that two of the Mirages had been shot down. The French, who had eventually stopped deliveries after the 60th aircraft without explaining why, asked the Libyans if the Israeli reports were true. The Libyans said they were not, and asked the price of the Mirage F1.

This nonsense could well fill the rest of the book, so I'll turn to a very fine air force which, believe it or not, operates Mirages from France, Lockheed F-104 Starfighters from the USA and Russian Mig-19s bought from China. The country is Pakistan, and its purchase of a force of Mirage IIIEP night and all-weather fighters plugged an important gap in its inventory which showed badly in the war with India in September 1965. It is significant that Pakistan was given its F-104s, and bought the extremely useful Mig-19s at a very low price indeed, whereas the Mirage IIIEP and DP force cost a sum which to Pakistan was considerable. In 1972 they came back for a batch of Mirage 5-PAs. Other recent customers include Abu Dhabi, Zaïre and Saudi Arabia, who began their Mirage purchases with a single whopping contract for 38 (and they already have Lightnings).

If I were asked what the Mirage III/Mirage 5 is most in need of I would say 'not to be a delta'. The crude triangular wing was a good choice in 1955 when there seemed no other way of making it big enough, light enough and still not thicker than $4\frac{1}{2}\%$, but this is no longer the case; indeed the Crusader suggests that it never was, and that perhaps deltas ought never to have been born except in the very special case of supersonic-cruise aeroplanes such as the SSTs. Obviously the Mirage F1 is a vast improvement, but earlier I listed the various wing options studied in 1964 and mentioned the flapped foreplane à la Viggen. Dassault never built this, though simple tunnel models were tested. But in 1966 work began on a most interesting concept: the 'moustache'. Even without a customer this would probably have happened eventually, but the immediate need for it was in order to make a Mirage 5 meet the specification of the Swiss Air Force for a close-support attack aircraft to replace the trusty Venoms. The Dassault management must have steeled their nerves to work a second time with the Swiss, but in fact the proposal of a modified Mirage 5 was well received. The moustache concept was schemed by Dassault, but developed in partnership with the Federal Aircraft Factory at Emmen. It comprises a pair of slender high-lift aerofoils which can be either retracted into the nose or, by means of an electric screwjack, extended on each side. The single-slotted moustache surfaces have only 1.7% of the area of the wing, but their great advantage is that their strong nose-up force (which, for longitudinal stability, is sensibly constant over a wide range of angles of attack of the basic aircraft) is countered by slight downward deflection of the main elevons, thus increasing lift. With the ordinary tailless delta, take-off or landing demands a strong upward elevon deflection, destroying lift when it is most wanted. I have always considered we ought to have fewer tailplanes and more foreplanes, because the concept of pushing up the front instead of pushing down the back seems blindingly obvious.

A Milan (kite, the bird) was produced by borrowing a Mirage IIIE from the Armée de l'Air and fitting it with the tiny swing-wing moustaches, which added a mere 44 lb. The gains were startling. They included take-off 25 knots slower in 2,000 ft shorter run, rate of climb at Mach 0.8 raised by 3,700 ft/min (13%), ability to turn at 300 knots round a circle of 30.5% smaller radius, and a landing 30 knots slower and 460 ft shorter. To clinch the deal with the Swiss, Dassault added the new Atar 9K-50 engine of 15,875 lb thrust, the nav/attack system of the Jaguar A, an airframe fitted and stressed to carry an external load of 14,000 lb and a string of customer options. The Swiss still did not buy the Milan. They did not buy the A-7G Corsair either, which they quite rightly thought a superior tactical delivery system, but instead settled for some second-hand rebuilt Hunters so that they could go away and think some more. Dassault had spent their own money on the Milan, and had little to show for it. They even had to give back the Mirage IIIE, after degrading it back to its original Armée de l'Air standard.

So far nobody has bought the little moustaches, which are quite cheap and can be had as a locally fitted mod. I am sure the penny will drop and that Dassault will make some eventually. As for the Swiss, they are nothing if not unpredictable. In mid-1974 they at last decided their ideal, cheap tactical fighter was the Northrop F-5E Tiger II. Within days someone 'discovered' some surplus bits of Mirage III-S, supposedly left over when the order was cut back (what nonsense!), Dassault made a cut-price bid with offsets, and the old delta was back in the running.

It seems to me remarkable that the little delta Mirage, which as I said at the beginning is quite an ordinary aeroplane, should have swept the world market for first-generation supersonic fighters. It makes an extremely interesting comparison with the Mig-21, which is of the same vintage, fractionally smaller and has the same layout, plus a tailplane. The Mig-21 has likewise developed though a long series of variants, and it has a splendid flight performance and is sweet to handle; but it has never aspired to do a proper ground-attack job, and Western or 'neutral' nations have never chosen to buy it, despite its lower price, in preference to the Mirage. As China may supply her version of the Mig-21 to Pakistan we may soon have an opportunity to compare under identical conditions the most widely used fighters in the world.

How good is the Mirage III or 5 today? One answer is that it depends what you want. If you think you are likely to find your aircraft spending most of their time clobbering ground targets, then the Mirage is deficient in range, load and, except in good weather, in sensing and weapon-delivery systems. If you are odd enough to think you need an air-superiority fighter then it shows up reasonably well, except in comparison with more modern aircraft. In all cases the runway requirement at full load is marginal or, in tropical conditions, often unavailable except at a very restricted number of major airfields. Indeed, all over the world there are air forces equipped with the Mirage which can use them with a full warload only from their main national airport and, in some cases, one other base. This could easily lead the superficial observer to conclude that the Mirage has been bought as the easiest way to display a modern high-speed shape in the sky wearing the local air force markings—in other words, that it is no more than a PR exercise. But I am sure such a view would be mistaken.

Perhaps the acid test of a fighter's worth is how it copes when it is fighting, and it is worth noting that the nations that have had to defend their homeland by force in recent years have tended to buy Mirages; indeed, it looks as if the Arabs like them too, echoing Adolf Galland's famous suggestion to Hermann Goering that he wouldn't mind a squadron of Spitfires! As I write, ten years after Dassault's expected run-down of the production line in 1965, production of the Mirage III and Mirage 5 is running at a record 13 a month, and it has been that way for three years.

Marcel Dassault is quite right to spurn Britain and say 'You could have built the Mirage'. Indeed we could, and what a fighter it would have been with first a reheat Avon and then a reheat Spey! But two famous British firms looked at such a thing in 1954 and 1955 and dropped the idea smartly. There was no market for it.

Saab-35 Draken

There are barely eight million Swedes, and their defence budgets are proportionately limited. Yet they have a deep desire to be strictly neutral and 'do their own thing' in defence. Close partnership between the Royal Swedish Air Board and their airframe contractor, now called Saab-Scania, has made Sweden virtually self-sufficient in military aircraft. Far more than this, the successive families of Saab jets have been among the world's best, and in an unforgiving game where one error could mean Sweden was out in the cold forever—on purely financial grounds, if for no other reason—the Swedes can look back on five outstandingly successful examples of how the procurement process ought to work in an ideal world. Of these five programmes my own favourite is the one that brought forth the Draken. I have often wondered whether the design of the Draken was a matter of luck, utter brilliance, or divine guidance. In a world where most fighter designers were timidly progressing in tiny, halting steps—and often falling flat on their faces—the Swedes took a leap so great yet so totally successful that the Draken will still be in service 30 years after the leap was taken.

Only Erik Bratt and his little team at Linköping hit on the basic method of designing a supersonic fighter by sorting out the items that have to go into it and then seeing how these can best be arranged for minimum supersonic drag (whilst simultaneously thinking about how to taxi at high speed along forest roads, how a conscript with six months' service wearing fur mitts to keep out the cold can best change a fuse, and how a thousand and one other things can be made to yield a reliable, efficient and economic weapon system). In my opinion they really were very clever and perceptive. The only other team that tried anything like the same configuration was Heinemann's, with the Skyray (p. 215), and they adopted a more conventional approach which limited the possibilities. It was this basic, yet marvellous, realisation, that in a supersonic fighter project you start by arranging the packaging, that provided the foundation for one of the most perfect fighter programmes in history. But it was only the foundation. The Swedes still had to choose the right engine, start off with a fairly simple fighter to get early experience and then gradually fit in all the clever things they had seen in 1949, and made allowances for in the original design, in order to see a run of more than 600 aircraft and keenly contested export sales almost a quarter-century later.

Admittedly the number of Drakens exported is very small in comparison with the number of Mirages. This may be because the French are better salesmen. It may be because the Mirage is relatively a cheap fighter/bomber, whereas the Draken is an extremely advanced all-weather machine integrated into a computerised airspace over Sweden. It may be because not until 1967 did Saab, spurred by the Danes, offer a Draken tailored for the export market. Whatever the reason, the Swedes can still point to the Draken as a perfect copy-book lesson in how a supersonic fighter should be planned. Like most great aircraft you could say the Saab 35 is an example of family planning. There are different members of the family for different tasks, and all of them justify their changes. The latest of the fighters, the 'Filip' in the Swedish phonetic alphabet, is a sheer joy to anyone who likes good aircraft engineering. It could not even be dimly discerned in 1949, but it was the sound foundation in the basic airframe that has made it possible.

What could be seen clearly in 1949 was that the normal speed for bombers over hostile territory would soon be about Mach 0.9, and that subsonic fighters were going to be finding life very difficult indeed. Accordingly the Air Board in Stockholm issued a draft specification, called Project 1250, for a fighter capable of Mach 1.4 to 1.5, capable of operating from existing Swedish runways and of fulfilling a number of other severe requirements including numerical values for rate of climb, ceiling, radius of action and maintenance burden. Saab looked hard at what everyone else was doing, and found little inspiration. By the end of the year Convair and Avro had flown deltas and run into trouble. The Bell X-1 and Douglas Skyrocket were supersonic aircraft in being, but neither was remotely like a fighter. Other companies were seeming to find supersonic fighters either difficult long-term projects or else too hard even to contemplate. But as soon as Saab stopped looking at their rivals and began to consider the possible solutions independently everything fell into place quite quickly. It is really rather odd that no other company managed to achieve the same result. Most of the early supersonic fighters in the West are in this book, and they are pedestrian by comparison or else severely hampered by inherent shortcomings. I do not know of any early supersonic fighter in the Soviet Union that can rival the Draken in timing, flight performance and effectiveness in its designated roles. Though some aircraft, notably the Crusader, came very close, no other aeroplane in the Draken's timescale achieved such a good all-round result.

In a nutshell I think this was because Bratt's project staff stood right back from the problem and just put the pieces together and waited to see how the assemblage came out. Other design teams began by thinking of a shape. The way the Swedish study worked is important. The Air Board did not suggest a configuration, nor did Saab have any preconceived ideas. The main thread of development that led to the answer to Project 1250 really did begin with pencil drawings of engine(s), inlet ducts, cockpit, tanks, landing gear and similar items all packaged and re-packaged without drawing in the outline. Other designers, and I have talked to most of them, began with the outline. When they had explored all possible alternatives Saab arrived at two optimised configurations. One was what you might call 'conventional'—though Lockheed's PR people certainly did not present it as such when they launched the F-104 (p. 184)—in that almost everything was in a big, long fuselage, carried by a tiny, thin wing with clever high-lift devices, and stabilised in pitch by a tailplane. The alternative was a truly radical layout. Even though Saab wanted to use a wing of no more than 5% thickness/chord ratio, or less than half as thick as the wing of the excellent J29 Tunnen (Barrel) then going into production, it was possible to make the wing quite thick if it started at the extreme nose of the aircraft and finished at the tail. The packaging problem could then be solved in a new way by putting many items, such as fuel and main gears, inside this wing. Of course other aircraft, such as the contemporary P.1, put the fuel and main gears inside the wing. Where Saab differed was that the wing did not run in the usual direction but from front to back. Thus the fuel could be housed in triangular-section tanks, thick at the roots and thin outboard, arranged in a long row from nose to tail, with a gap at one point for the wheels. Most of the systems-management responsibilities devolved upon chief engineer Hans Olof Palme.

At first Saab drew a shape around this arrangement in the form of a pure delta, with the amazing sweep angle of 70°, starting with a nose intake like that of an F-100. It was rather like some Lippisch projects, though I am assured this was incidental. Then, because it did not seem likely to fly nicely, the leading edge sweep of the outer wings was reduced and the inner part extended forwards to get the c.g. and c.p. in the right places. Thus the wing was finally made in the form of a double-delta, with an inboard portion having tremendous chord but hardly any span, and a sweep of no less than 76° on the leading edge (which actually faces outboard rather than ahead), and outer wings of conventional delta form. As the single engine was inescapably on the centreline it meant there would have to be long ducts passing on each side of the cockpit. By 1950 it had been decided to add a pointed nose ahead of the cockpit to house the eventual radar, though the armament had always been expected to be in the inner wings. This split the inlets into left and right portions, the ducts joining aft of the cockpit. From the start there was a big swept fin, but the fact that the wing extended to the extreme tail seemed to make a tailplane superfluous. Thus, to a considerable degree the Saab proposal was an all-wing aircraft. The pilot and engine did, however, necessitate a central fuselage, though this was always envisaged as integral with the inner wing and designed to be made with it in a single entity 4.4 metres (14 ft 5 in) across. For minimum interference drag the wing was placed at the mid position; indeed, bearing in mind the wing extended from nose to tail it could hardly go anywhere else.

By the spring of 1950 Bratt's team had a three-view drawing that seemed to make sense. It was unlike any previous fighter. Whereas a previous all-wing fighter, the Northrop XP-79, had disposed everything across the span, the Swedish proposal had everything arranged from front to rear in a unique body/wing structure. The outer wings were empty. The estimated gross weight was 15,000 lb, and the engine was to be an axial giving 10,000 lb thrust with afterburner, the most likely choice being the Rolls-Royce Avon. A quarter-century ago this was a very high—I think, unprecedented—ratio of thrust to gross weight for a fighter. Saab thought that, in conjunction with their design's very big wing area and apparently minimal supersonic drag, they ought to be able to create a fighter of outstanding flight performance that could still operate from not only existing RSAF runways but even from the emergency roadways and other paved strips that formed part of the dispersed 'wartime base system' then being planned throughout the country's vast areas of farmland and forest. The one thing they didn't know was whether it was going to work.

There was a small 12-inch supersonic tunnel at the Royal University of Technology in Stockholm, but though this was used for basic tests on different configurations it was too hampered by choking, turbulence and Reynolds scale problems to give the kind of results needed. So in May 1950 Saab began to build a much more useful transonic tunnel, the first in a vast inventory of costly research and testing tools the company have since made or purchased for their supersonic programmes. In the same month design began on a half-scale research aircraft to explore the novel configuration at low speeds. This machine, the Saab 210, was powered by an Armstrong Siddeley Adder, the 1,050 lb-thrust turbojet that resulted from removing the reduction gear and propeller drive from a Mamba. This thrust was only just enough to make the 210 useful, but Bengt Olow, chief test pilot, told me much later that he had little real trouble and never got 'on the back of the drag curve' on the approach—when the Adder would not have been powerful enough to avoid a landing short of the runway. The 210 was ready in December 1951, but deep snow kept it from flying until 21 January 1952. Saab did a fantastic amount with the little 16-foot-span 210. Though it had manual controls it did a great deal to verify or modify the control system of the fighter, the landing gear could be adjusted to change the ground angle, and c.g. could be changed in flight by pumping water from nose to tail or vice versa. Eventually the intakes were cut right back in line with the cockpit windshield, leaving a proper fuselage and nose. From that time on the 'all-wing' appearance evaporated. Altogether the 210, built for the equivalent of £50,000, made more than 1,000 test flights and provided an essential foundation of knowledge on low-speed behaviour—which, incidentally, was generally admirable and was gradually made well-nigh perfect.

Detail design of the fighter began in December 1951, in advance of contract cover. In March 1952 the specification for the fighter was finalised and a mock-up authorised. The type was to be called Type 35 Draken. This name, which means Dragon, was also applied to the Type 210, when it was said to mean 'kite' in allusion to the dragon-like kites used by the Chinese. I don't know how this misunderstanding arose, but it was repeated for years afterwards. Data on the Saab-35 began to flow from three American transonic tunnels in May 1952 and from Saab's own tunnel a month later. In August 1953 the Air Board placed a contract for three prototypes, three pre-production aircraft and a forward fuselage for a tandem-seat trainer version. Though Saab had chosen the 200-series Avon, no afterburner had been developed for it and in 1955 Svenska Flygmotor supplied an RM 5A (RA.7R), one of the old 100-series engines, with a crude on/off afterburner exhausting through left and right eyelid shutters. Similar engines were used on the speed-record Hunter prototype and Swift F.4, and at least were considered fully developed (though I rate this a matter of opinion). The Swedes were building this engine for the excellent Lansen attack machine, having given up their own Dovern axial engine in early 1949. Very soon it was replaced in the prototype Draken by a non-afterburning Avon 200-series.

Olow flew the first Saab-35 prototype on 25 October 1955. Though he found the powered controls rather sensitive, many aspects of the handling were delightful and the landing was easy. On 26 January 1956 Mach 1 was exceeded easily in level flight, and I think it fair to point out that Olow did not have to watch his fuel state quite so twitchily as Beamont did with the P.1 as he had half as many engines and 50% more fuel. Second and third prototypes joined in in March and June 1956, and the first pre-production machine followed in February 1958. Throughout, the flight behaviour had been very encouraging, and it is particularly worth noting that drag was below prediction over the whole speed range down to 170 knots, lift coefficient at extreme angles of attack was outstanding (and much above prediction), take-off and landing runs were shorter and supersonic manoeuvrability better. The only major problem that persisted was control in pitch at high speed in dense air, and I shall return to this later.

The main change introduced with the pre-production machine was to use the definitive engine. I have always been puzzled at the fumbling attempts Britain made to produce good afterburners and variable nozzles. I think the trouble was that many experts thought 'reheat' a crude and brutish way of getting extra thrust, and took a poor view of the jump in fuel consumption, so as a nation we dragged our feet. This left the Lightning with a pretty indifferent lot of engines, until some real effort was applied to the problem. The Swedes were frankly fed up with the situation, and way back in 1951 began to develop their own afterburner for the Ghost for later versions of the J 29. In 1953 they accepted the RA.7R complete with its rudimentary reheat system and nozzle, but got down to developing a proper afterburner, called Type 65, for the much better 200-series Avon, the 10,000 lb dry engine with the Sapphire compressor, and had this qualified in time for the night-fighter version of the Lansen. This engine they called the RM 6A, and it was rated at 14,200 lb. For the Draken it was modified in detail, re-rated at 14,400 lb (about the same as the empty weight of the aircraft) and put into production as the RM 6B. It seems to me an indictment of British reheat policy that the Swedes developed a better afterburner for the 200-series Avon than the British did and got it into production, and into service, much earlier. The fault, of course, lay not in Derby but at Rolls-Royce's dreadful customers in Whitehall.

There was a second major advance in the pre-production Draken. Its structure was considerably refined for greater efficiency and easier manufacture and maintenance. The inner and outer wing joints were strengthened, the fin mounting was changed from shear to set-bolt fastenings, the fuselage was subdivided not just into front and rear but into six portions, the frames were simplified and the rear tank doors were changed from riveted corrugations to bonded honeycomb. Elevon and rudder moments were increased. Even in the 1950s the Swedes were very concerned at the prospect of having an air force (and navy and army) consisting mainly of short-service conscripts, and the Draken, as by far their most sophisticated aircraft, posed very large difficulties in training ground crews to achieve quick turn-rounds. Some of the modifications introduced with the first pre-production (or, as it was later regarded, first production) Draken were intended to make it especially simple to look after. Others introduced newer processes and materials, but there were hardly any parts made of titanium, or chem-milled or integrally stiffened. Owing to its unusual geometry the Draken—especially in early versions—is made in traditional ways, with thin skins held by flush rivets or bonding. The fact it can pull an 8 g turn (an acceleration frequently exceeded in combat training) is due to the profusion of wing spars and the wide diffusion of stresses, much of the lift being provided by the inboard 'wing' right forward to the intakes.

An order for the Flygvapnet (RSAF) inventory, with the designation

J 35A ('Adam'), was placed in August 1956. These aircraft were at first used to speed development and service clearance, the total test fleet at one time numbering 20. By the end of 1959 a large number of service pilots had flown the Draken. This is the point where I must mention the problem of PIOs (pilot-induced oscillations). At high speed in dense air, where the Draken like almost all other combat aircraft increasingly has found itself operating, the original Draken flying-control system gave near-instant response. In the pitching plane, where a mistake can cause structural failure or put you into the ground, it was found exceedingly difficult to handle the J 35A with the three-axis autostabilisation switched off. Flying in this 'raw' mode, a pilot inexperienced on the type always (bar none!) built up a phugoid oscillation which gave him a violently uncomfortable ride. Almost all pilots found the response so fast that they were unable to correct properly; instead they got in phase with the PIO and instead of damping it out they augmented it. Several inexperienced pilots injured themselves slightly, and it is a matter of great credit to the Draken that no structural failure occurred. Gradually the word went round that it was vital, to avoid breaking the aircraft, never to attempt to correct pitch oscillations when flying 'raw'; instead you must just let go of the stick, and wait for the motion to damp out. With autostabilisation on there was no problem, though pitch control was pretty sensitive. This is one of the basic problems in the design of high-speed aircraft, which the control system designer tries to solve with his autostabilisation and 'q-feel' black boxes, which, among other things, curb the response at high speed at low altitude.

By the end of 1959 both the J 35A and its RM 6B engine were completely developed and in production in Sweden, and the various bits of equipment were likewise either available off foreign shelves (in the case of the gun and a very small number of other items) or in Swedish production. On 8 March 1960 deliveries were made to the F 13 group, the Bravalla *Flygflottilj* based conveniently close to Saab at Nörrkoping. F 13 found few major difficulties, though it took until just a year later to complete conversion from the J 29. It was a matter of deliberate policy to introduce the Draken in a simple basic form. The J 35A did all the J 29 did, so nothing seemed to be retrograde, but it lacked the clever equipment that was planned for later versions. This allowed quite a high flying rate to be sustained from the start, so the bugs were worked out quickly, nobody poured scorn on the Draken as 'a can of worms' and there were no harassed National Service ground crew unable to cope. The lesson here for the RAF is perhaps significant.

From the start the Type 35 had been planned as the most versatile all-weather fighter possible, but the J 35A was an interim machine. It did have something better than mere gun-ranging radar, the set being one of

After years of struggle against the Air Staff, who wanted a small fuel capacity, and the Minister of Supply, who thought manned fighters were obsolete and a waste of money, English Electric (later BAC) ultimately succeeded in convincing both that the Lightning ought to be developed into a useful aeroplane. The result was the Mk 6, shown here, which BAC then further developed, still in the teeth of official opposition, into a multi-role aircraft which could be sold abroad

Had its development been pressed ahead much faster, by a bigger team, the Saunders-Roe SR.53 (above) could have provided a valuable foundation of operating experience in the right time-frame for the far more important SR.177 (below). The latter was planned in several versions for the RAF, Royal Navy, West Germany and other potential customers, and could have been a global best-seller. Unfortunately it came to fruition just at the time the British government decided manned fighters were all being replaced by missiles

In 1955 the baby MD.550 Mirage had no visible market. Excited by Britain's FD.2, Dassault developed it into the Mirage III, which sold over 1,300 in 18 countries, and then produced the simplified Mirage 5 (pictured here) which by 1975 had added a further 460 for 11 countries

Swedish proficiency in advanced aviation is emphasised by the sure and successful design of the radical J35 Draken before any other supersonic fighter had appeared. This Mach 2 interceptor was later developed through several versions, culminating in the semi-automatic J35F 'Filip' illustrated

Canada's success with the CF-100 made it seem natural to design a supersonic successor as a national project. The resulting CF-105 Arrow was by a wide margin the biggest and most advanced interceptor of its day, and despite formidable difficulties promised to be a complete technical success. But the escalation of its costs seemed excessive, and, after bitter political acrimony, it was curtly cancelled and replaced by missile and second-hand fighters from the United States

To create the F-102 Delta Dagger, Hughes designed an unprecedented system of integrated radar, autopilot and air-to-air missiles, around which Convair then wrapped a supersonic aircraft. As this action picture shows, the F-102 was the first fighter in which, instead of guns, there was a large internal weapon bay like a heavy bomber

Though it missed the Korean War the F-100 Super Sabre spent its twilight years in Vietnam, where it showed itself to be good at both offence and defence. At one time this pioneer of supersonic military aviation equipped the 'Thunderbirds' aerobatic team (top), while other examples were blasted out of bombproof shelters in a startling technique called Zell (zero-length launching, below)

U.S. AIR FORCE

The F-104A was revealed publicly with masked intakes and a pilot wearing one of the new pressure suits. This 'missile with a man in it' excited the mass media more than it did the customer, but Lockheed later achieved the feat of selling the F-104G to many major countries whilst failing to sell it in the United States

Derived from the 1944 proposals of Lippisch, the Skyray was probably the first supersonic fighter design in the world. The first XF4D-1 would have been supersonic had it had more thrust, and another became the first naval aircraft ever to gain a world absolute speed record. As the F-6A this stubby tailless fighter remained in combat service well into the 1960s

Designed with great rapidity, the splendid Crusader outperformed land-based fighters of its day and supported a long production run followed by a major rebuild programme. The first F-8E(FN) for the Aéronavale (shown here), the ultimate version built as new aircraft the early Cyrano series by the French CSF company, made in Sweden by L. M. Ericsson. A typical AI radar, it provided only for search, lock-on and breakaway modes, with no fire-control link and no provision for ground control. The Saab S 6 fire-control was a simple radar-only lead-pursuit sight, and the Lear autopilot was again a basic attitude-holding lead-pursuit unit. Armament comprised a pair of Aden M/55 30 mm guns, one in the edge of each inner wing with a 90-round magazine extending inboard to the root rib. Internal fuel capacity was 493 gal, and this could be supplemented by four 66-gal drop tanks carried on outer-wing racks and ferry tanks in lieu of the gun/ammunition installation. Gross weight was about 20,000 lb, and performance was quite spectacular, the initial rate of climb being close to 40,000 ft/min and the level speed at 36,000 ft being Mach 1.8 despite the plain fixed air inlets. Simple, and relatively cheap, the Adam flew a lot of valuable combat training missions.

Later in 1960 Svenska Flygmotor switched to the Type 66 afterburner. As this was almost three feet longer it meant a new rear fuselage, and this projected far behind the wing, with a long brake-parachute box on top. To prevent scraping the tail Saab added a retractable twin-wheel gear in place of the original fixed bumper. This back end became standard. J 35As from No 63 had it at first-build, and most of the first 62 were later modified (the main exceptions being those turned into Sk 35C trainers). During 1961 the Flygvapnet introduced the Sidewinder air-to-air missile, made in Sweden as the RB 24 and RB 324, examples of which had undergone compatibility trials with a Draken the previous year. The J 35A was the first carrier of these IR-seeking weapons, with four single wing racks. The S 6 sight was replaced by the S 6B, with added IR fire-control.

During the first half of the 1960s nearly all the J 35As were relegated to trials and hack work, or used at the OCU at Uppsala, converted to Sk 35Cs or converted to become J 35Bs. The B (Bertil) is identical to the later Adam except for improvements to the fire-control and a new weapon option. During the 1950s the Swedes had planned a national air-defence control system which I can only describe as a much neater version of the American SAGE (p. 180). Called STRIL 60, it involved a similar mix of radars, data links, automatic data-processing and human monitors/operators, and it likewise filled the sky with a carefully coded electronic environment. The Bertil was tailored to slot into this system, and the S 7 fire control was fully integrated from the start with STRIL 60, whereas with the J 35A the only possible link was voice R/T transmissions. S 7 also marked a big improvement in that it incorporated an airborne computing facility for making collision-course interceptions, using guns or Sidewinders or the new weapon option: two pods housing 19 Bofors 75 mm rockets. Further external loads could comprise twelve 135 mm air-to-ground rockets, four 550 lb bombs or nine 220 lb. The first J 35B flew on 29 November 1959. The inventory models were partly new and partly rebuilt Adams, and they equipped F 16 at Uppsala, which had briefly had Adams, and F 18 at Tullinge, which was operational by late 1962. Earlier, in 1958, a modified Bertil had been a contender in the big Luftwaffe competition, but it was unable to meet the German requirements for all-weather nuclear delivery.

The next variant, the Sk 35C (Caesar), warrants only passing mention as it is not a fighter but a tandem-seat dual-control trainer. It proved to be one of the happier conversions, largely because of the customer's foresight in ordering the new front fuselage at the same time as the original prototypes. The instructor sits high and to the rear and has a periscope. There is no radar, though full weapons capability is otherwise retained. The single canopy is remarkably large, though still hinged upwards as a clamshell, and flight performance is virtually identical with that of an Adam. Most Caesars are Adam-rebuilds, and none was built as a trainer from scratch.

With the J 35D (David) Saab made a major advance in flight performance. This seldom happens, because most aircraft just get heavier and heavier and end up in their old age not half as sprightly as in their lightweight youth; but when the engines come from Rolls-Royce they have a tendency to grow in thrust even faster than the airframe can put on weight. In 1954 Rolls had planned an advanced development of the Avon designated RB.146, and by 1958 this was fully qualified and ready for production. Though its original afterburners weren't so hot, the Avon was a splendid gas turbine to have as a basic engine. The RB.146 introduced the zero-stage on the compressor used on the civil Avons for the Comet and Caravelle, giving higher mass flow and pressure-ratio. It also at last came with an adequate British afterburner, with infinitely variable multipetal nozzle and reliable hot-streak ignition. As the Avon 301 it went into production for the Lightning F.3. An export version, the Mk 60, was adopted for licence-production by Svenska Flygmotor, and matched with a fine new Swedish afterburner derived from the Type 66 which gave even more augmentation than the Rolls one. As the RM 6C this became the standard power-plant for all subsequent Drakens, with a guaranteed rating of 17,650 lb and an average rating often close to 18,000 lb.

This boosted the level speed of the David to Mach 2, or fractionally higher, despite the continued use of plain air inlets. The inlet ducts were redesigned and lengthened, and it became handy to sit on the left intake to talk to the man in the cockpit. Internal fuel capacity was also appreciably increased, to 680 gallons, but despite the clean gross weight rising to more than 24,600 lb the rate of climb at low level rose to almost 50,000 ft/min—which, say Saab, is superior to all other fighters in the same timescale except for the Lightning, which has the same type of engine but twice as many. The David's time to any given high altitude is considerably less than half the figure stipulated in the original 1250 Requirement! The rest of the aircraft is much like a Bertil, except for the further improved S 7A fire-control system, the PS-ø3 radar and the completely different Saab FH 5 autopilot. The first J 35D, a much-converted J 35A, flew on 27 December 1960. Production machines were delivered from December 1963 to F 13 and to F 10 at Angelholm. By this time F 13 were old hands, and with their powerful Davids they broke a lot of new ground (figuratively, that is!) and really got down to the business of operating from dispersed emergency (road) bases. The nose gear steers beautifully, and chaps found they could taxi at nearly 100 mph in dry conditions and had no trouble even in wet or icy weather landing on roads no more than 33 feet wide. The brake chute is used as routine in such work, holding the roll to well below 2,000 ft or about half the limit for reasonable brake life without it.

The Draken has always used Saab ejection seats. Saab were one of the original pioneers of ejection seats, because in 1943 there was no other evident way of getting the pilot safely out of a stricken J 21A, the twin-boom fighter powered by a pusher DB 605. It took until 1945 to perfect the ejection seat for this aircraft, and Saab then promptly junked the German piston-engine and fitted a de Havilland Goblin jet, but the ejection seat remained. Saab seats were fitted to the J 29 and J 32, and were also adapted by Folland for the Gnat (and the Saab-Folland seat is still in production in India for the Hindustan-built Gnats). Early Drakens had a seat similar to the proven type used in the Lansen, but in the David the largely redesigned 73SE-F seat was introduced with rocket boost to confer ground-level capability (but not 'zero/zero', because aircraft speed must not be less than 62 mph). Like earlier Saab seats it uses a GQ parachute system. Several older Drakens have been given this rocket seat as a retroactive mod.

The next version, the S 35E, Erik (when I first wrote this I instinctively put 'Emil', thinking of the old Me 109E), comes outside the scope of this book for it is used purely for reconnaissance. It is a David with a new nose housing a battery of vertical and oblique cameras bought from OMERA in France. It was deliberate policy again to make the Erik simple instead of a multi-sensor machine so that the large number built could shake down in trouble-free service and get lots of hours in. Not until 1973, almost nine years after the start of operational service, did the Flygvapnet order some new externally carried pods equipped with British Vinten cameras for night and low-level missions giving 120° coverage at 330 feet at 630 knots—which is fast enough for me! I know of no plans to buy SLAR, linescan or LLTV, which in a negative way is very interesting.

Next comes by far the most important of the Swedish Drakens, the

J 35F, Filip. Though it is basically similar to a David it is really a completely new aircraft; it is a complete weapon system, and the whole package was designed around the weapons. The fact that the metal skin round the outside is the same shape as that of earlier Drakens merely made the design task very much more difficult. In fact I rate the Filip one of the truly outstanding achievements of the fighter designer's art. Where the J 35A was crude and basic, the J 35F is extremely sophisticated and capable; yet, though the two aircraft are the same size, the Filip actually has a bigger engine and much greater fuel capacity. I once looked hard at an old Adam to see where the empty space was, and found none. This is what you can do by what is called 'development', though the results are seldom so outstanding.

Starting at the front, the Filip's radar is the Ericsson PS-ø1 (or-ø1/A) which is very much more powerful than the PS-03 and can acquire targets at a range which I must not disclose but which I believe exceeds that for any other operational fighter designed in Western Europe (and I have talked to all the rivals). Under the nose is a Hughes IR sensor, with a range of over 15 miles in clear air, which is an especially valuable target-seeker in an environment of intense hostile countermeasures. Both sensors feed to the S 7B fire-control, which can handle guns, rockets and—the new armament—guided weapons of two types. The weapon, chosen in 1958, is the Hughes Falcon family of air-to-air missiles. In March 1959 a big plan was conceived for making two versions of this missile in Sweden and designing the completely new Filip around them.

Hughes engineers at Tucson told me how they at first regarded the Swedes as country yokels, and wondered why they wanted such clever little things as Falcons. This feeling wore off very soon indeed! Before long Hughes were having to work hard to stop feeling that it was they who were the country cousins, and two years later the Arizona plant was introducing to its own production for the US Air Force improvements originated by the Robotavdelningen and Saab which the Swedes thought up when they drew attention to deficiencies in the American detail design. The two Falcons are really alike only in name. RB 27, as it is called in Sweden (RB = robot), is a fat (262 lb) radar homer, with a semi-active seeker in the nose capable of homing from a distance of about six miles at Mach 3. Two are carried under the Filip's fuselage and work very well at high altitudes. RB 28 is a slim (134 lb) IR-homer, the descendant of the original Hughes Falcon of 1950. The Filip carries two of these on pylons near the kink of the wing, for use at low levels or under intense ECM. The weapon mix has been demonstrated to be extremely lethal against all kinds of targets attacked under every conceivable conditions or from any direction (including from tens of thousands of feet below). Neither Falcon has any US counterpart; the only one remotely like an RB 27 is the AIM-

26A with nuclear warhead. I can also report that the Filip remains 'very highly supersonic' with the four missiles on board.

Going back inside the airframe, there have been major improvements to the navigation, autopilot, fire-control, air-data and data-link systems, and the pilot has new instruments, a bigger clear-vision canopy and a zero/zero seat. One of the Aden guns has been replaced by an electronics package, but the Swedes were rightly anxious to retain the other; indeed they have been talking ever since about fitting more guns, either internally or in pods. In addition, the Filip is the first multi-role Draken, with a very much augmented capability in the strike or attack role. There are no fewer than eleven stores pylons, four under each wing and three on the fuselage, the five inner stations being stressed for 1,100 lb loads and the rest for 220 lb. All this adds up to quite a package, but, amazingly enough—and it is here that the 'quart in a pint pot' procedure seems to have entered the realm of utter fantasy—Saab-Scania were able to add 30% to the internal fuel capacity and almost double the bomb load in a still later version!

Developing the Filip has been described to me as a task at least equal to that of the original development of the Draken. After he had said this, Dr Lars Brising, who was then Saab's director of engineering, added 'No—it was a bigger task'. It was the only part of the Draken programme that slipped in timing, and even then the slippage was small. Two 'prototypes', which were earlier versions converted to fire RB 27 and RB 28 missiles but lacking almost all the other advances, began flight development in 1963. It had been hoped to clear Filip for service in 1965, but at that time flight development was still going ahead at an even faster rate. Aircraft 48—an Adam converted to a David and then given Filip features for use in missile trials—launched 44 Falcons during this period, nearly all of them with guidance and a live warhead. Altogether more than 80 missiles were fired before the Filip was cleared for service, though on the whole things went with remarkable smoothness. With a weapon system of this class the final year or two of development is so much like operational service it is hard to say where one begins and the other ends. Probably it is fair to put the service-entry of the Filip as 1966–67. By this time a large number had been made, and production continued until 1971. The total number of Filips is appreciably larger than that of all other Flygvapnet Drakens added together, the total of all versions amounting to 550. The price of a Filip is roughly double that of an Adam, but is still unbelievably low by American or British standards. A rough approximation is SwKr 6 million, or about £420,000. I won't be unhelpful by pointing out how much of an F-14 or F-15 you could buy with this sum.

Since 1969 the Flygvapnet has been steadily covering up its shiny polished Drakens with camouflage paint: olive drab and dark blue-grey on top and pale blue-grey underneath. This seems pretty obvious, but in fact it was preceded by long study to decide the colours, the specification of the paint and many other factors. Anyone with memories of trying to paint gorgeous unit markings on such relatively slow fighters as Sabres and Meteors twenty years ago will recall that the physical strength and sticking power of the paint left much to be desired. Today it is no problem at all, and hailstones that damage modern polyurethane paint will also damage the aircraft if you are unlucky enough to encounter any at over Mach 1. On top of the big problem of getting the paint to stay on, supersonic fighters also need a smooth exterior, and, ideally, very smooth paint. Yet the need for surface smoothness is less important than it seemed in the old biplane days. A close look at most modern fighters, especially around the stores pylons, will emphasise that a lot of their performance comes from brute power rather than finesse.

From the start of this chapter it will be evident that I like the Swedes, who have consistently demonstrated correct military aircraft procurement, competent development and highly effective operational deployment, and whose adult approach to the problem of security maintains strict protection over the few things that matter whilst freely disclosing such things as how many aircraft they buy, what they pay for them and how often they crash. For example in 1969, when I would have been put under arrest for disclosing such information about the Lightning, the Flygvapnet reported they had lost five Davids, and introduced several modifications including the rocket zero/zero seat and a bird-proof windscreen. Other improvements and updating programmes were in hand on other Swedish variants. In addition, Saab were in production with an export version.

I had been consistently surprised at how often potential customers for the Draken had decided to buy the Mirage III instead. Even the Swiss, who did wish to make some pretence at having an all-weather defence, eventually turned down the proposed Saab 35H (Helvetia) and bought a non-existent version of the Mirage matched with the Hughes Taran radar and Falcon missile and found the problems and costs of making it so severe that there was a storm in the Swiss parliament (p. 89). Several Swedes, not all from Saab, have told me they have long felt they lack experience in international aerospace marketing, and are pretty thin on the ground in terms of manpower. I know other countries who think the same thing, but the difference with the Swedes is that with the Draken they really did have a highly saleable product (and, in the Viggen, they have another). But they never managed to clinch a Draken sale until 1968, when Denmark signed for 20 of a new single-seat version called the XD, as well as three two-seaters. Later that year the Danes bought a total of 46 aircraft in three versions, the F-35 fighter, RF-35 reconnaissance and TF-35 trainer versions to back up their F-100s and replace the RF-84F. In 1973 they added five more TFs at an un-inflated price.

The Danes drove a hard bargain. Not only was the price very low—the first 23 aircraft cost £13.8 million, which is cheaper than a Mirage III or an F-5—but the deal included substantial long-term offsets, mainly concerned with Danish support to the Saab-Scania car factories, and in addition the XD was a more potent multi-role aircraft even than the Filip. Export customers often want everything, and then a bit extra, and Saab were able to find this bit extra. They redesigned the entire wing to accommodate 30% more fuel, and to bear the loads of nine weapon pylons (three under each wing and three under the fuselage) each stressed to 1,000 lb. It is possible to take off in 4,030 ft with nine 1,000 lb bombs, or to fly with 14 at 500 lb, or two 1,000 lb bombs plus two 280-gal drop tanks and two of 110 gal. Ferry range with four 280-gal drop tanks (1,980 usable out of 2,000 gallons) is 2,020 miles. Both guns are installed, and there is an arrester hook compatible with the NATO cable system. The only bits lacking from the X (export) model are the weapon fits for the Falcon missiles and links with the STRIL 60 air-defence system. A similar Draken has been evaluated by Austria, a long-time user of Saab jets.

In April 1970 Finland bought one squadron of 12 aircraft designated J 35XS (export Suomi = Finland). These are a specially equipped all-weather interceptor version, again without Falcon and STRIL 60 equipment, which will replace the Gnat in the 21st Sqn of the Finnish Air Force. These aircraft, which bring the Draken programme to 606 in all, are being assembled in Finland by Valmet Oy to help provide an offset and maintain a Finnish capability in advanced aircraft. The Finns could have chosen any Soviet fighter in operational use, and in fact did evaluate several including the Mig-25 (Foxbat), but considered the Draken easier to assimilate, cheaper to operate and at least as good in the all-weather role, and an ideal partner to their Mig-21 day interceptors. Financially the deal was good, the ceiling price for all hardware needed to build, arm and support the squadron up to 1975 being FMk 196 million (about £20.5 million), and the Finns securing a general-industry offset worth SKr 100 million (about £9 million). Valmet Oy had run down after licence-building CM170 Magister trainers, and the Finns were delighted at keeping the works in being. To bridge the gap before portions of J 35XS arrived in 1973 the Finnish government leased six aircraft designated Draken 35BS at the rate of 100 hours a year for pilot familiarisation. They are old Bertils, flown to Valmet's works and there rebuilt as simplified (VMC only) trainers, giving Valmet useful manufacturing experience in the process. Even when the Finns have finished with them these old Drakens will still have no fatigue worry and be almost as good as new. I would rate any Draken a very good investment. No other aircraft on Earth gives you such a range of options at such a low price.

Avro CF-105 Arrow

Twenty years ago a British company in Canada was a world leader in long-range all-weather fighters. Its project staff were well advanced with the successor to the CF-100, the fine machine which filled the humming production shops. The next generation, the CF-105, was being very carefully planned to meet the demanding needs of the Royal Canadian Air Force, and it was taking shape as no mean fighter. In 1958, when the first CF-105 flew, it was by a wide margin the most advanced fighter in the world. In its airframe, avionics, weapons and—by no means least—flight performance it set standards which nothing else actually built in the West could rival until today's F-14 and F-15 (except for Kelly Johnson's Blackbird YF-12A which is not so much a fighter as a research aircraft). The thunderous white Arrows were in 1958 the only aeroplanes, military or civil, under development anywhere in the British Commonwealth that appeared to be indisputably better than the opposition. But they were unfortunately born at the worst possible time. Within a year of first flight the entire programme was stopped dead, the company's work-force was dismissed, the completed Arrows were cut up for scrap, and the only survivor was a five-cent commemorative postage stamp that continued in circulation. The drama of this unprecedented occasion was heightened by an extraordinarily intense conflict of personalities, notably between the head of the firm and the Canadian Prime Minister. For those who were there, reading on will be quite an ordeal.

Canada is much bigger even than the United States. The Canadian people and the Canadian weather often show sharp and clashing contrasts, and trying to render the great Dominion secure against air attack during the Cold War posed giant problems. Canadians are ever watchful that their manufacturing industry should not become wholly owned by such American groups as General Motors, General Electric and General Dynamics, all ultimately directed from south of the 49th parallel. These three giants have long owned very large slices of Canadian industry, but at the end of World War 2 the biggest aircraft plant was bought from the Canadian government by a British company. Victory Aircraft, at Malton, Toronto, had been building Lancasters at a commendable rate, and it seemed a good move when in June 1945 it was bought by Hawker Siddeley and renamed Avro Canada. It seemed even better when the powerful British group set up an aggressive design staff at Malton, and still better when in 1949 the home-grown C-102 Jetliner emerged and flew. This 60-seat short-haul jet would suit the market quite nicely today if it had a pair of M45 fan engines, but in 1949 it was far ahead of its time and the customers were afraid to discard the devil they knew with juddering piston engines. But no problem; in parallel with the Jetliner the new team had also planned the CF-100 to meet the RCAF need for a fighter to defend Canada. The black-painted prototype flew over the deep snow in January 1950.

The CF-100 was a significant thing for Canada, both industrially and militarily. Judged merely as a fighter it combined high speed and fast climb with extremely long range to cover the vast distances of its homeland, plus near-STOL performance (in comparison with other jets) to enable it to operate from 4,000 foot strips in all kinds of weather. Though it looked like a caricature of how not to conform to the Area Rule, it could exceed Mach 1 in a shallow dive. It was strong, formidably armed and equipped by Hughes Aircraft Inc with as good a radar fire-control system as any fighter in the world. Successively improved versions kept the big plant busy until 1958, when the 692nd and last (it was the 53rd of a batch for Belgium) came off the line. Taking a broader view, the CF-100 put Canada firmly in the harsh business of not merely making advanced aeroplanes but also of designing them to meet challenging requirements and developing them to make them work properly and stay abreast of the competition during a ten-year programme. This even extended to advanced jet engines, because the production CF-100 also had Orenda engines designed and made by another division of the same firm. Canada had never seen anything like the industrial success of Avro Canada, which in its first ten years sold CF-100s and Orenda engines worth more than a billion dollars.

Of course a similar result might have been achieved merely by making Canadian versions of other people's aircraft, as did giant American-owned Canadair at Montreal. But the fact that the Malton plant was wholly self-sufficient was judged a very great national asset. The obvious validity of the CF-100 and Orenda programmes were such that there was no difficulty in gathering a technical staff of 1,200 top-flight engineers and scientists, of whom 40% came from Britain, 25% from Canada and 15% chose Toronto instead of their native USA. Avro Canada had been created almost single-handedly by the drive of Sir Roy Dobson of the parent group, but Dobbie was usually elsewhere. A mainspring of the Malton effort was Crawford Gordon, the dynamic young president appointed in 1951. Fred T. Smye was vice-president and general manager; the original chief engineer was E. H. Atkin; and the leader of the design team was Jim Floyd, who became v-p engineering in 1952 having earlier headed the team that created the Jetliner. The technical staff at Malton were rather special, and one could not help sensing this on one's first visit. I was not surprised to hear that Gen Lauris Norstad of the US Air Force considered them 'just about the best team anywhere'.

Long before the CF-100 flew, projects existed for advanced versions, such as the swept-wing C-100S of July 1948 with two Turbo Research (later Avro) TR9 engines. By July 1949 the main project was the supersonic C-100D, which like Teddy Petter's E.R.103 of chapter 1 had its TR9s arranged one above the other. A year later there were two fresh ideas: the C-104 with twin TR9s, crew of two and cannon; and the C-105 with the contrasting approach of a lox/kerosene rocket to thrust a tiny 20,000 lb, 600 sq ft machine to fast interceptions within a radius of 120 nautical miles. The small rocket project stayed during 1951 and acquired an APG-37 radar fire control, but the customer RCAF had yet to decide what they would want for a decade hence and could only suggest a scramble time of one minute from a readiness hangar at an airfield altitude of 2,500 feet, which is not terribly helpful. Floyd, with his Chief Technician Jim Chamberlin, stuck his neck out and started again, using the C-104 as a basis, and by June 1952 had drawn the C-104/1, a superb delta. The wing had a span of only 32 ft 6 in but an area of 1,200 sq ft, the long chord reducing the thickness/chord ratio to a new low at 3.5 per cent. The 58 ft 10 in fuselage was mounted under the wing to give good accessibility to the two TR9 engines (or Sapphire 4s plus a rocket) and the weapon box of six Sparrow air-to-air guided missiles. This high-wing project seemed a very good basis on which to build.

Early in 1953, while the first CF-100 squadron was forming, the RCAF suddenly emerged with Air 7-3, a detailed specification to meet OR 1/1-63 for a supersonic all-weather fighter for use in the period from 1960. The Air Staff in Ottawa, under CAS Air Marshal Roy Slemon, had at last come to the conclusion that in any future nuclear war Canada would be 'the first line of defence'. Their new specification appeared to call for more of everything than any previous document in any country. They wanted a fighter which would operate from a 6,000 ft runway, have a mission radius of 600 nautical miles (including five minutes at Mach 1.5), would have two seats and an unprecedented nav/attack system for operations in a harsh environment outside any ground control, and which, in addition to many other things, could pull 2g at 50,000 feet! An incidental was that, to meet the stipulated flight performance while carrying the full weapon load, the fighter had to have an internal missile bay bigger than the bomb bay of a B-29.

Altogether 7-3 was one of the greatest challenges ever set down in the form of an aircraft specification. It quantified in hard numerical terms just what the RCAF needed from its next fighter in order to protect the nation. The contrast between 7-3 for Canada and the contemporary F.23/49 for Britain was staggering, though I suppose the two staffs judged that they had done their homework properly and come up with reasonable answers. Certainly the fact that Britain wanted a relatively primitive interceptor with hardly any range or endurance made it impossible for the two nations to get together with their first supersonic fighters, and the prevailing mood in Ottawa was that nothing but the best would do. Time after time the history of military aircraft procurement has recorded a programme that could have delivered 99% of the requirement within timescale and budget but which escalated away out of reach in a fruitless chase after the missing 1%. In January 1954 I was able to spend six hours discussing 7-3 with Air Vice-Marshal John L. Plant, RCAF, as we waited for fog to clear at Gros Tenquin in France. Around us were scores of Canadian Sabres, but 7-3 had no immediate relevance to the European theatre. Plant confided that, deep down, he too had a slightly uneasy feeling that 7-3 might turn out to be too much for the nation through trying for the last percentage point.

To be fair, Slemon did not idly commit Canada to this enormous and perhaps impossible task. His staff discussed the requirement with the RAF (heaven knows what useful comment they could have made!) and with the USAF and embryonic Norad team at Colorado Springs (whence Slemon himself went later, as deputy to General Norstad whom I mentioned earlier). He sent a powerful evaluation team, headed by Wg Cdr Ray Foottit, to shop around all the obvious aircraft companies that might have something useful on the drawing board. It is ironic that, in the course of this searching tour, the team looked at a fighter in St Louis, the F-101 Voodoo, which missed meeting their requirement by miles. They did not spend very long with it, though they were more interested in a preliminary project for a much later fighter that the same firm were planning for the US Marine Corps and Navy. They had not the slightest inkling that the aircraft planned for the US Air Force, which fell so far short of the Canadian need, would turn out to be the one the RCAF would finally get.

Foottit's team had especially long talks with Floyd and Chamberlin, because Avro Aircraft (as it was now called) seemed the most likely firm to build the new fighter. Indeed C-104/1 and its variants appeared to be commendably close to the requirement—though a study was also made of a spectrum of six aircraft down to a single-engined single-seater carrying four Sparrows internally which weighed just half the 60,000-odd lb of the 7-3 machine. Throughout the gestation of the design in 1953 the customer favoured the big aircraft that fully met 7-3. It also gradually became apparent that the RCAF were hardening on their demands and becoming increasingly unwilling to consider tradeoffs that would reduce time and cost. It seemed odd to me that, while one could predict with assurance that the Aussie air staff in Canberra would always pick the known hardware off the shelf (not the latest model but the generation before) because it would be cheap and give no trouble, their opposite numbers in Ottawa went out of their way not to demean themselves by using anything off the shelf at all.

For example, by the end of 1953, when Avro had a design contract and looked like being sole prime contractor, the major unknowns were the fire control and weapons package and the engines. In both, the RCAF showed a positive aversion to existing hardware, or systems already under development. There were plenty of possible engines: while the baseline for parametric studies remained the TR9 with Solar afterburner, alternatives included the Rolls RA.17 and RB.106, the Bristol Olympus 3 and 4 and its Americanised version designated Wright J67, the de Havilland Gyron and the Pratt & Whitney J75. A little later reheat Conways would also have been attractive. As for weaponry, Avro were afraid that the RCAF might cry for the moon and get the whole programme into deep trouble. The staff in Ottawa had no experience of this kind of big-league management of advanced and totally new systems. Compared with this the CF-100 had been peanuts, and it had used missiles, FFARs, guns and FC-1 fire control all available off the shelf. Avro strongly recommended that, at least for a start, the RCAF should settle for the existing Hughes radar fire-control and Falcon missiles, but this combination was judged 'inadequate' by the Air Staff. Avro had young and aggressive management, but they were scared stiff of offending their only customer.

Hindsight is simple, but I suppose Dobbie and Crawford Gordon might at this point in 1953 have put their heads together and tried a little forecasting of the range of possible futures—in plain language, gazing into crystal balls. While the CF-100 would last until about 1958, the company's trading position beyond that date appeared to depend totally upon the supersonic successor. If its development was delayed, there would be what the Americans call a 'bathtub'—an empty space that has to be filled by grabbing fresh work. If its development was halted there would be no company. Perhaps such a possibility simply never occurred to the Avro management in the booming days of 1953, but I can't help thinking the company ought to have got a second string to its bow even if it was only making bathtubs.

Nothing was done to provide any kind of back-up programme, and the Avro technical staff had their work cut out creating an interceptor which, as I have said, was far in advance of anything else. The broad parameters were settled in July 1953, with the new designation CF-105. It was essentially a scaled-up 104/2 with a span of 50 ft and length of 73 ft 2 in. The requirement called for Mach 1.5 with internal armament of six Falcons and 24 FFARs or Mach 1.2 with external armament of bigger missiles. Originally the latter were planned to be two 600 lb Meteors or four 300 lb Velvet Gloves, under development in Canada by teams led by Gerry Bull at NRC and Johnny Green at CARDE—the Canadian Armament Research and Development Establishment, at Valcartier—but in 1954 the RCAF decided these infra-red missiles were insufficiently sophisticated. They were judged incapable of licking the problems posed by clouds, the sun and enemy IR decoys—though doubtless the RCAF knew that Britain was pressing on with the IR-homing Firestreak. Attention switched to the formidable microwave-guided Red Dean (p. 39) under development at Vickers, Weybridge, whereupon the British government promptly cancelled it. (The Red Dean was cancelled because its carrier aircraft, the Gloster G.50 'thin-wing Javelin', powered by two reheat Olympus engines, was also cancelled. At the time, in 1956, I thought this cancellation a monumental error for many not very obvious reasons. I still do, and I very nearly put a G.50 chapter into this book.)

By mid-1953 the CF-105 had pretty well settled down. The aircraft had a vee windshield, fixed lateral engine inlets with large ramps and boundary-layer bleeds, fuel capacity of almost 20,000 lb in two large fuselage bladders and 12 integral cells occupying almost the entire wing, tandem-wheel main gears retracting inwards into the very shallow wing, control by fully powered rudder and elevons, with an extremely advanced autopilot system and duplex stability augmentation for use above 40,000 ft. The only unknowns were that nobody had decided what engines would occupy the great powerplant bays, nor which missiles would fit the huge weapon bay, nor which radar fire-control system would fill the nose and spread its tentacles throughout the aircraft. Where weapons were concerned the one factor never in doubt was that guns were obsolete, the RCAF remaining quite uninterested even in the new GE 'Gatling' which in 1953 was highly audible on the butts at Burlington, Vermont.

Running true to form, the Air Staff heartily agreed with the NRC that Canada ought to stay in the engine business with a second-generation turbojet for the CF-105. Avro's engine division was renamed Orenda Engines—resulting in its first product thenceforth being clumsily called the Orenda Orenda—and the TR9 was developed into one of the most impressive engines I ever met, the PS13 Iroquois. A century earlier the Iroquois had been probably the most powerful group of Indian tribes in the entire eastern part of the US and Canada, and Orenda is an Iroquois word for magical power. Pure-blooded Iroquois used to clock-in to help make the PS13, which was an outstandingly 'clean' two-spool engine sized to a mass flow of 300 lb/sec. It was very advanced in design and construction. With two spools and a 1,750°C afterburner it still had fewer component parts than the much smaller Orenda with one shaft and no afterburner. And it was largely made of magnesium casings and titanium blades, Canadian Steel Improvement Ltd—another of Dobbie's jewels to stick in the Hawker crown—having discovered how to make perfect precision-cast blades even in the largest sizes in what had previously been regarded as impossibly difficult titanium alloys. The specially developed fuel control system and accessories were packaged in a ventilated box along the underside of the engine where they could be kept cool in the hurricane airflow that surrounded the engine in supersonic flight regimes. A shrewd move was that, while the engine for the CF-105 was wholly uncompromised, a less radical Iroquois was planned with 'state of the art' US accessories in case the engine found a second application in an American aircraft, and this became the subject of a US licence agreement.

Orenda did miracles to get the first Iroquois running on one of their mighty new test beds as early as 15 December 1954. In 1956 a B-47B was transformed by Canadair into the CL-52 to fly an Iroquois, without reheat, in a huge pod on the right side of the rear fuselage. The big bomber could have flown quite nicely with its six original engines removed! But from the start of the CF-105 programme it had been accepted that the native engine would probably not be ready in time for the first CF-105, and in any case a proven engine—even if of lower power—was judged a prudent choice for the first two prototypes, to avoid the risk of flying such an advanced new airframe with a new engine. Avro looked very hard at Rolls and Bristol, but Britain lagged badly with afterburners (as I remarked in the first chapter) and had nothing suitable to offer. The otherwise impressive Gyron was too fat. The best bet seemed to be the Wright J67, but the inability of Wright to develop this engine gradually became inescapable. By April 1954, when Avro signed the first contract for hardware, there was only one possible choice. Mr Pratt's reheat J75 was of typically conservative design, with a thrust/weight ratio not much more than half that of the Iroquois, but it happened to be available when nothing else was.

So in April 1954 Crawford Gordon committed Avro to four prototype CF-105s, the first two with the J75-P-3 giving 18,500 lb dry thrust and 24,500 lb with full afterburner for an engine weight of about 5,900 lb. The third and fourth aircraft were to have the Iroquois rated at 19,250 lb dry and 27,000 lb with full afterburner for an engine weight of about 4,100 lb. Avro had received an ITP the previous January, which meant that the Department of Defense Production began funding the programme. Until that time the Hawker Siddeley Group had funded the work, having agreed on the go-ahead in October 1953. As the weapon and radar fit was still uncertain it was impossible to attempt an accurate costing, and the best estimate Avro and the DDP could contrive in June 1953 had been $22,925,000 to the second prototype in August 1957. In November 1953 the engineering 'total cost of the programme' was put at $22,664,513. In July 1955 the estimated programme cost to fly the 5th aircraft (then ordered) was $40,574,625. These costs seemed eminently reasonable. Costs invariably do in the early stages of a programme.

The plan was to use Cook–Craigie procedure (p. 173), with full production tooling. Indeed airframes in this class cannot be 'hand-built' in the traditional prototype manner even if anyone wanted to. For example, Avro contracted with Kearney & Trecker for a skin mill with tables measuring 28 ft by 9 ft, built to their own specification to machine CF-105 wing panels. K&T spent over $1 million on this machine, charged Avro $350,000 and recovered several times their original investment selling a run of these huge mills at $600,000. The magnitude of the R&D effort to produce the Arrow was staggering in the context of the 1950s. The burden was borne not only by the Canadian Defense Research Board, National Research Council and National Aeronautical Establishment, but also by the US Air Force and Navy, NACA Langley and Lewis Laboratories and Cornell University. Many of the techniques and design features had to surpass anything done in the United States; for example, while the F-102 (p. 166) took three seconds to open its missile-bay doors and salvo its load, the CF-105's weapon doors, which were larger, had to open and shut within 300 milliseconds. I would love to go into much greater length on the splendid profusion of engineering problems posed by this huge fighter, and on how they were solved, but anyone interested can refer to *Flight International* for 4 October 1957 in which I was able to report these things in surprising detail.

Of course the Avro team leaned on other people when they could. As early as November 1954 they had picked up NACA's conical camber over an extended outer leading edge, and English Electric's use of a leading-edge 'sawcut' notch instead of a fence, giving the CF-105 a 5.0% notch, six inches wide, at 50% semi-span. This was perhaps a better British import than Dobbie's belief, expressed two months earlier, that 'By 1959 every high-altitude interceptor will be fitted with a rocket as well as a gas turbine' (as the second chapter in this book makes clear, this seemed a safe prediction at the time) which caused the Avro team to ponder on rocket boost a little deeper than they might otherwise have done. But by far the biggest reliance on a foreign country was that the technical underpinning of the radar, weapon and fire-control system was obviously going to lie in the United States.

From the early days of the old CF-100 the Avro team had been closely linked with Hughes Aircraft, who I suppose are as good as they come on fighter fire-control systems (in terms of track record nobody could touch them in the mid-50s, and today they appear to be even further ahead). Avro would have liked to dump the whole thing in Hughes' lap, as they had done with the CF-100, but I have already mentioned the wish of the Canadian Air Staff to have 'the very best'—whatever that might be. Air Staffs traditionally want the mostest, and in the 1950s did not seem to learn in their staff college days the results of this policy as shown by the chequered history of weapon procurement. What made things harder was that in the first half of the 1950s Hughes could offer only the rather pedestrian E-9 (MG-3) fire-control used in the F-102, which the Air Staff in Ottawa predictably scorned. The fully automatic MX-1179 system, to be compatible with the SAGE (Semi-Automatic Ground Environment) defence system, was far from fully developed, though it was planned for the F-102B. The choice of system exerted fairly profound effects on the CF-105 itself; for example, with the MX-1179 installed the second member of the crew could be left out, though provision would have to be made for a much bigger radar scanner in the nose.

In July 1953 it was reluctantly agreed by the Air Staff that the first CF-105 would be planned to have the existing E-9 fire control, provided that full provision was made for replacing it with the MX-1179 in production aircraft. This meant the aircraft design could go ahead on the basis of two seats, a small ($23\frac{1}{2}$ in) scanner and six Falcon missiles in the weapon bay. But in parallel with this the customer wanted to use a bigger missile for interception at much longer ranges, and after studying the Meteor, Velvet Glove and Red Dean, came to the conclusion that the best bet was to produce a new version of the Sparrow. The original US Navy Sparrow, by Sperry, was a primitive beam-riding missile that became operational in 1956 on the McDonnell Demon. In the United States it was later redesigned by Raytheon to turn it into the very successful family of Sparrow missiles of today. But the Canadian Air Staff chose to take it under their own wing and plan a completely new version with fully-active microwave homing guidance as the long-range armament of the CF-105. The savants in Ottawa also solemnly decided that it would be nice if Canada could develop a marvellous new fire-control system custom-built for the CF-105 and much better than anything else.

I suppose if you are spending a lot of money on a new fighter weighing more than a Lancaster but capable of Mach 2, it makes sense to spend a little more on the traditional 'ha'porth of tar' without which you spoil the ship. But old proverbs may not be relevant to avionic systems with a packing density of a thousand components per cubic inch. Indeed, in this challenging field the simplest way to be sure what to do seems to be to wait until the errors are only too obvious. Throughout 1956 and 1957 Avro were sure the customer had made a major error in trying to fit the CF-105 with a completely new fire control and completely new missile, but were unable to bring any convincing arguments to bear. By 1958 the customer could see the difficulties for himself.

The new missile was called Sparrow 2. Though relying on Sparrow 1 aerodynamics and structure to a major degree, Sparrow 2 had totally new guidance and also differed greatly in flight control, propulsion, warhead and in other ways. Prime contractor was Douglas Aircraft, but a complete team was built up in the US and Canada to create this new and sophisticated weapon which was hoped to be usable over long ranges in all environmental conditions, especially those that the Canadians were sure would defeat any missile that relied upon IR-homing. The CF-105 was to be capable of carrying Sparrow 2 both internally (the number depending on how many Falcons were also on board) and on four wing pylons. On any mission the big fighter was to carry not fewer than three of the radar-homing Sparrows, all of them capable of supersonic release at all heights up to 60,000 ft. In addition there were to be eight Falcons, four IR-homing and four radar-guided, all capable of being fired on a single pass.

The new, optimised fire control was called Astra I. Major contractors were RCA-Victor, the Montreal associate of the giant RCA which unfortunately had little experience of avionics for fighters, Honeywell Controls and Computing Devices of Canada. Astra I was planned as an all-can-do system of extreme sophistication. One could even agree that it ought to be better than anything else, if it ever came to fruition, but from the very beginning Avro Aircraft were cast under a cloud of gloom. It was obvious that they could no longer control the programme costs, and the potential costs of Astra I were enormous (before long the CF-105 team wryly suggested that the system's name was short for 'astronomically expensive'). In 1956 Avro formally recommended the use of an improved Hughes system, but again found it difficult to marshal convincing arguments because the Astra I system was highly classified and had yet to overrun its budget or timing in a serious way. On paper Astra offered new digital computer technology, better accuracy in the navigation and interception attack modes, and better integration with other on-board equipment. So Avro continued to shrink from having a major dispute with the customer on whom they depended for their entire income.

Earlier, in 1953, Avro had been requested to try to accommodate successively, a $23\frac{1}{2}$ in radar aerial, a 28 in, a 32 in and then a 38 in. At one time a 42 in dish was studied, before 38 in was chosen for the baseline nose radome. This size of scanner was significant, because each new size meant a bigger vertical tail to keep the aircraft directionally stable. In September 1954 Hughes announced a two-year delay with the MX-1179 system, deferring prototype flight trials (in an F-102 and in what was by then the F-106) until 1957, with production expected in 1958. One of the main causes of the delay was the radar aerial, which at a final size of 40 in

I believe was then the biggest mechanically scanned fighter radar; there was also a severe problem with the critical damping system. By 1957, while Avro had done the expected miracles in building the CF-105 (which had by then been named Arrow), political problems had been encountered with the Sparrow 2 and the Hughes MX-1179. While the first might have been expected, difficulty with Hughes was a shock. It was caused by a formal directive by the US Air Force that Hughes Aircraft was drastically to restrict all its work other than that for the USAF, because the Americans urgently wanted improved fire controls themselves. And, while RCA headquarters had no difficulty talking to RCA Victor Ltd, there were terrible security and communications snarl-ups with Sparrow 2 because no official channel existed to allow Avro, Hughes or Douglas to speak to each other!

In the presence of such adversity the vital radar fire-control programme lagged badly, but the Arrow itself did not. Avro succeeded in building the first of these giant fighters in 28 months, measured from release of first drawings in June 1955 to ceremonial roll-out on 4 October 1957. The first CF-105 Arrow Mk 1, serial 25201, was painted gleaming white because it was judged this would keep it cool and minimise thermal fatigue due to sustained supersonic speed. The Mach 3 XB-70 was painted the same colour, whereas the Lockheed A-11/YF-12/SR-71 family and the hypersonic X-15s (as originally built) were respectively very dark blue and jet black, because further research showed that supersonic aircraft are cooler if they are black because that is the best colour for radiating thermal energy. I think the truth is that white is best unless you can soak at above Mach 3. In any case it doesn't make very much difference, and before long the Arrows were given big patches of Day-glo scarlet so that they would show up better if one had to make a forced landing on snow.

How close to being a fighter was 25201? I think it is fair to say it was amazingly close to the production machine, apart from having instrumentation instead of the fire-control system (and, of course, it had J75 engines). Fuel capacity was 19,561 lb (2,508 gal), plus 3,900 lb in a ventral drop tank for ferrying, giving a normal gross weight of 62,431 lb. There were air-turbine starters, twin 30 kVA constant-speed alternators with ram-air cooling, duplicated 4,000 lb/sq in hydraulics (a pressure then still almost unknown in North America) with emergency ram-air turbines, and —so far as I could discover—no absentee anywhere among the formidable inventory of systems and equipment. If I had to select anything for a special bouquet it would be the landing gear. The main gears were by Dowty in Ajax near Toronto, while the nose unit came from Jarry Hydraulics in the French part of Montreal, and in an age when advanced designs of undercarriage were ten-a-penny I can think of nothing—not even the B-58 gear—that could equal these for beautiful engineering.

Despite a long history of grand ship launches, Britain does not have roll-out ceremonies for aircraft, because for the people who pay for advanced British aircraft to be allowed to judge their size would imperil the security of the nation (anyway, it's usually raining). But the Canadian Arrow emerged to a splendid ceremony. Various people spoke. Slemon's successor, Air Marshal Hugh Campbell, dwelt at length on the NATO alliance, and never commented on the fact that Canada was doing this huge project alone. Or, at least, almost alone; he went on: 'In acknowledging the assistance given by American agencies, I can but express the hope that . . . the Arrow will be the success that we expect it to be, and that it will be accepted by them as a significant contribution to the defence of North America.' This could have been interpreted as a suggestion the US might adopt the Arrow for its own inventory. This is what the RCAF increasingly wished could come to pass. Dobbie then came to his feet and confused me by describing the aircraft as 'half an era ahead of anything else in the Western world' as if a whole era was too much to claim! But he gave the wholly credible information that the man-hours per pound needed to construct 25201 worked out to only '80 per cent of the average for projects of similar size and complexity throughout North America'. One also discovered that Avro had in 1956 been given an order for 13 development aircraft, plus long-lead parts and materials for the first 37 Mk 2 Arrows for RCAF service from early 1961. Ostensibly the 13 Mk 1s would all be identical, powered by the Iroquois, though even when the contract was signed it was obvious there would have to be some more with the J75 and in the final outcome the first to have the Canadian engine slipped from No 3 to No 7. The Mk 2 was the Iroquois-powered machine for inventory service. By 1958 Avro had schemed a Mk 2A, with more fuel, fully variable engine inlets and con-di nozzles, and also the very long range Mk 3, with the uprated Iroquois 3 fed by even more advanced inlets (superficially resembling those of an F-105) and supersonic afterburner, additional fuel, and a thermally insulated structure for soaking the exposed parts at about 200°C. It was whilst doing this that the company became increasingly aware of the escalating cost of the programme, and of the possibility of not merely hitting severe storms but even of running aground. In view of the conspicuous absence of other work it was a frightening thought.

But the management had a welcome uplift on 25 March 1958, when 25201 was at last cleared for flight. Avro had two great Poles in the flight-test team. At the helm on the first flight was Janusz 'Zura' Zurakowski, whose fabulous display flying will be impressed in the memory of countless readers; flying chase in a CF-100 was 'Spud' Potocki. The CF-105 pilot team also included Peter Cope at Avro and Jack Woodman of the RCAF. Mike Cooper–Slipper and Len Hobbs looked after the Iroquois CL-52.

For the first flight the entire Malton workforce was released a few minutes beforehand, and thousands were soon watching. I doubt that any other large manufacturing industry, save perhaps shipbuilding, gets everyone so intensely and personally involved with the product. Nowhere is this so apparent as at first flight, and that is partly why I regret the traditional British policy of carting all the prototypes away to the backwoods at Boscombe. For 14,000 Toronto people 25 March 1958 was an unforgettable day. Zura, who flew precisely according to the book, had an excellent first flight. But on 11 June a hairy situation arose when one main gear resolutely stayed at the 30° outwards inclination at which it extends, and failed to line up fore-and-aft; the high-pressure tyres burst and before long the leg broke, yet the aircraft was quite quickly repairable. Apart from a few things of this kind, flight development went very well indeed. All the stability, control and performance points were logged on schedule, and technically there seemed no doubt the Arrow would be a world-beating success. But, though early in 1958 I doubt that anyone can have fully realised the fact, the stage was set for what some would call a tragedy, some a farce and some perhaps even a comedy; but nobody could fail to call it drama in the fullest meaning of the word.

Apart from the fact that the programme was enormously costly, by previous standards, the storms ahead had nothing directly to do with the Arrow itself. The underlying difficulty was that during the 1950s various kinds of missile programmes had made tremendous progress. Surface-to-air defensive guided weapons had reached operational service, and promised to be so much more effective than manned fighters (so the British announced) that the RAF did not expect to require any more fighter aircraft beyond the original Mk 1 Lightning and would instead use nothing but missiles. In the United States there were nine quite different families of surface-to-air missile, one of them—the mighty IM-99 Bomarc—being as big as a fighter and needing a launch base rather like an underground city. In view of all this, although the US Air Force was careful not to say anything about not wanting any more fighters, it did in fact curtail the buy of the F-106 interceptor and only very grudgingly contracted with North American for the F-108 Rapier mainly to keep its options open. Quite apart from this, the US Air Force had long-range bombardment missiles: by 1957 both the Thor and the Atlas ballistic missiles were flying, and the man in the street became an instant expert who could see for himself that in a few years all the enemy bombers would have been rendered obsolete by ballistic missiles that not even the Arrow would be able to shoot down. Was not this huge and costly fighter a great mistake?

Today, of course, we can see that all these slick assumptions and obvious conclusions were really illusions, and that in the real world the role of the manned air-superiority fighter would continue to be valid. As I write, in 1973, I could easily be tempted to suggest that the air combats of the future will be fought by RPVs. Just as the jet-engine afterburner can be as hot as you like, because it is not subject to the limitation of turbine blades, so can the RPV pull as many g as it needs because it is freed from the limitation of having a fragile human on board. Yet this also is a trite and incomplete conclusion. There is no visible end to the story of the manned fighter, and I am astonished that supposed experts in the 1950s could have been so misled. Not everyone was misled, but many politicians unfortunately had a large axe to grind and did not want National views. Throwing away manned fighters appeared to be a possible route to massive savings in defence expenditure, and in Canada such savings were being urgently sought. They always are, of course, in almost every country, but Canada in 1957 was exceptional.

In that year the Canadians had elected a new Conservative Prime Minister, John George Diefenbaker. He was described by an opponent as 'a small-time Prairie lawyer', and while this is unkind it does give a fair idea of his background. 'Dief' neither knew nor cared much about semi-active guidance and air-cooled turbine blading. He had swept into office on a tide of electoral promises, most of which were aimed at his homeland where you can fly a lightplane over rolling golden wheat for an hour and still not reach the edge of the field. How could Dief make good on his battle-cry that his administration would give the farmers more dough? There seemed to be only one simple way and that was to cancel a major existing project. Long before he came to office the Arrow had been standing out like a sore thumb. Dief had spent a lot of time from 1956 trying to find out how vital it was to the RCAF. The fairly sudden emergence of the missile as a sort of 'replacement' was manna from Heaven, and when Britain's Duncan Sandys published his Defence White Paper in April 1957 Dief's joy knew no bounds. All he needed now was for something to go sour in the Arrow programme.

It would be wrong to portray Dief as a casual or destructive man capable of capriciously junking a weapon vital to the security of the nation. He was as patriotic as any other Canadian. Had he been for one moment convinced that the Arrow really was essential I am certain he would have done his best to hasten its development and cast about for other sources of funds for agriculture. But who in 1957–58 was prepared to stick his neck out and assert that the manned fighter was NOT finished? Nobody could do it and then slip away quietly. Such an opinion would have meant a thundering argument, and most of the people Dief talked to had careers to think of. I suspect that, whatever the chaps may have believed deep down, almost everyone took the easy way out and sided with the majority which said 'Manned fighters seem to be on the way out. The Arrow is a terribly costly programme. It looks as if we'd be better off buying some missiles.' This is what Dief wanted to hear.

Nobody had to feel embarrassed about it; the programme had taken shape years earlier, when the missiles could not be regarded as a viable alternative. Now, as 1958 saw thousands of dollars being poured into the Arrow programme each day, the ultimate conclusion appeared inescapable. Dief asked the British, and their answer can be guessed. He asked the Americans, and their astute salesmen smelt nice missile business in the air. He also asked his Defence Minister. General George Pearkes had served Canada loyally for a very long time indeed. His training had been concerned with such things as choosing the best fodder for your horse, and when it came to semi-active guidance and air-cooled turbine blading Dief in comparison with Pearkes was an expert. As I said, the stage was set. All it needed for the final touch was a nice injection of personal bitterness. This was provided in lavish abundance by Diefenbaker and Crawford Gordon. Not to put too fine a point on it, they hated each other's guts.

Crawford soon found himself drafting formal memoranda on possible ways of saving cost on the Arrow programme. Two obvious answers were to abandon the Astra system and try to get away with fewer than 13 flight-development aircraft, though the latter could only be a short-term gain because there was meant to be continuing production afterwards. In July 1958 Pearkes told the public the costs were high because of the small number of aircraft, and that to bring down the unit price he was inviting the United States to consider buying the Arrow. This suggested to me that there must have been faulty communications between the Pentagon and Ottawa, because—though the staff at Norad were intensely interested in the Arrow—the Washington view was that it was doubtful they would go all the way with their own F-108, which was even more of a mouthful than the Arrow. I have no doubt Pearkes was merely laying the groundwork for cancellation, and would have been greatly displeased if the Americans had said they wanted to buy Arrows. A little later he announced that so far $220 million had been spent on the programme (which appeared to be getting on for ten times the first estimate to this point, though such comparisons are usually found not to be comparing like with like), and that each Mk 2 of the initial production batch of 37 would cost $6.1 million. In full production it was hoped later aircraft might be a little cheaper. This undoubtedly had the calculated effect of spreading a combination of gloom and outrage among the Canadian population, but in 1975 an Arrow 2 for $6.1 million would be positively cheap.

Temperatures, tensions and tempers mounted steadily that hot summer of 1958 until on 24 September—which I believe was Yom Kippur, the Jewish Day of Atonement—Dief announced an immediate order for the US Air Force's IM-99 Bomarc anti-aircraft missile. He said some bits would be made by Canadair in Montreal, and that the whole force would be tied in with the SAGE system and be operational with the RCAF by 1961. The Arrow would meanwhile continue, but the programmes for the Astra fire-control system and the Sparrow 2 missile had been terminated (a decision conveyed to the prime contractors in confidential telegrams at 5 pm the previous day). RCA Victor promptly laid off 2,000 people, and many other contractors, including even Douglas, could think of no better answer. As for the Arrow, said Dief, this programme had so far consumed $303 million, 'and completion of development and production of 100 for the RCAF will cost about another $1,250 million'. He promised that the programme would be reviewed again on 31 March 1959—'when', bravely said Dobbie in London, 'we are convinced the Arrow will be ordered into production'. Hawker Siddeley were perhaps beginning to go off clever aeroplanes. Less than a year earlier they had had to stop building the Hawker P.1121, which had been funded entirely with company money (not all of it Hawker, either), and now they could see the prospect of losing the biggest programme in the entire Group.

A month later, in October 1958, Jim Floyd said in a lecture to the Royal Aeronautical Society 'The whole programme is in the shop window, and every setback becomes almost a national calamity. This can be quite embarrassing from an engineering point of view, especially superimposed on the added pressures of attempting to meet what was probably the most advanced contemporary fighter requirement'. In fact I think Jim suffered the lesser of the available evils, in that the development programme continued to go remarkably well, so that the mass media were reduced to all sorts of banal trivialities in trying to give the public the impression it wasn't. By this time missile-firing trials were taking place with the third aircraft at over 1,000 mph, and not one major snag had reared its head. Many people had come to see Avro and gone away staggered at what had already been accomplished. The company tried to see if there was any interest in the programme by the RAF, but though the CAS—Tom Pike—said 'We must look at this', the official angle was that the RAF had said it would be unlikely to require any more fighters and Avro was politely told not to rock the boat.

So Avro waited for the coming 31 March feeling rather like a convict in Death Row. Nobody was prepared for the electrifying announcement, by Dief himself, in a radio broadcast on 20 February, of 'immediate termination' of the whole programme. In the course of an emotional statement he let it be known 'The cost per unit for 100 could have been reduced from $12.5 million to $7.8 million . . . but the aircraft could not economically be used by the United States and could not be in service before mid-1962 . . . when the missile seems likely to be the major threat'. Everyone at Malton was stunned, and I can use the word quite accurately.

People went around as if in a dream. Work simply stopped. Some people talked quietly; thousands just stared in front of them. Within minutes Crawford Gordon came on the public-address system and announced that, with the exception of a skeleton staff of security personnel to man the gates, the entire workforce of more than 13,800 at Avro Aircraft and Orenda Engines was dismissed 'pending a full assessment of the Prime Minister's statement'. I cannot think of anything like it in modern history.

I must leave the reader to judge the wisdom of having a very large industrial enterprise more than 95% dependent upon a single programme of extreme political vulnerability. To me it seemed undesirable, to put it mildly; and in any case Avro Aircraft and Orenda Engines were not isolated, but units of the diverse Hawker Siddeley Group. As to Crawford's instant dismissal of the employees, this was widely criticised as a petulant and cruel act, performed with the express objective of hitting Diefenbaker; but I do not think he had any alternative. Whether or not the company could have got more strings to its bow—and Heaven knows, it had had long enough warning—the fact was that on 20 February, henceforth called Black Friday, it had nothing to speak of. Crawford could not personally have afforded to pay one day's salaries for his workers. In any case, there was nothing for them to do.

Not even those close to Diefenbaker expected him to jump his own gun like this, nor to let the company learn of his decision in a public radio broadcast. Poor Crawford downed an amazing quantity of hard liquor during the rest of Black Friday. Finally, after midnight, he telephoned the Prime Minister, got him out of bed and told him exactly what he thought of him, describing the manner of the cancellation as 'scandalous' —and describing a great deal more besides. Nobody would believe it if it was staged on TV. Next day Dief tried to take him apart, publicly. In his dismissal statement Crawford Gordon had said 'We have no alternative, since the company received no prior notice of this decision and therefore we were unable to plan an adjustment'. But according to Dief 'The company had hidden from its employees . . . the knowledge that the government was serious in its intention to discard the Arrow program. It engaged in a high-pressure campaign of lobbying and influence in an attempt to force the government to change its decision. It immediately dismissed the 14,000 employees in an attempt to embarrass the government and arouse public resentment. It had not used the period of grace provided since the warning of cancellation last September to obtain new contracts . . . The company had failed to advance a single serious proposal of alternative work . . . '

In London an unhappy Dobbie denied it all and tried to pour a few drops of oil on the distant storm. Meanwhile Crawford was not by any means the only Avro man to hit the bottle; but on 2 July Dobbie sent him a memo mentioning 'a difference of opinion on matters of policy' which brought not only Crawford's resignation but also that of John L. Plant, the company's president (yes, the RCAF air marshal I had chatted to so long before), and Fred T. Smye, the executive vice-president. By this time there was nothing left of the once splendid modern industry at Malton, nor of 'just about the best team anywhere'. More than half the Canadian aircraft industry practically evaporated, and ever since Canada has been unable to consider tackling any big home-grown military programme.

As for the Arrow, there is nothing left of this either. Five aircraft had flown, and flown superbly, but to Dief the Arrow was symbolic of Crawford Gordon and he issued instructions that the aircraft should be 'melted down'. US General Electric announced that they could use an Arrow from the flight-test programme, and would be prepared to pay a substantial price for it, and spares, in a straight commercial deal; Dief said 'melt it down'. The National Aviation Museum at Ottawa said that, as the Arrow was by far the most advanced aircraft ever produced in Canada, and a mighty tribute to Canadian industry, one of the first batch ought to be part of the national heritage exhibited at the museum; Dief said 'melt it down'. One began to think the Prime Minister had been sticking pins in toy Arrows for months past.

As for the RCAF, who kept well clear of the in-fighting, they duly received their Bomarc missiles. To intercept an enemy attack all they had to do was set in train a perfectly clear-cut sequence of communications between the President of the United States, the Prime Minister of Canada, the C-in-C of Norad, the US officer on duty at the SAGE control centre and a designated Canadian officer. After all this had been done—and it couldn't have taken more than half an hour or so—an American key and a Canadian key could be taken from a carefully guarded hiding place and turned in two locks. Hopefully the locks worked, allowing the missiles then to be activated and launched. Of course, once they had been fired—from North Bay, Ontario, or La Macaza, Quebec, which I suppose enemies would have avoided going near—that was that; they couldn't be fired a second time. Dief also degraded the lethality of the RCAF missiles by insisting that they had conventional warheads, instead of nuclear ones. I wonder if he noticed that, in the 1960 Budget Statement to the US Congress, Bomarc was described as 'a very questionable weapon system . . . it is considered inadvisable to place any reliance at this time upon such a weapon'. So money was taken from the tail-end of the US Air Force Bomarc programme and put into—surprise, surprise!—more manned fighters.

Eventually the unfortunate RCAF was allowed some manned fighters too. In June 1961 it took delivery of 66 McDonnell F-101B Voodoos. They were virtually the same fighter that Ray Foottit's team had rejected in 1953. What's more, they were second-hand.

North American F-100 Super Sabre

Though we in the West do not know the exact date when Mikoyan's bureau first flew the Mig-19, nor when the initial version was cleared for service, I think I am on good ground in describing the F-100 as the first fighter in history to fly faster than sound in level flight. Though it was started later than English Electric's P.1 it yielded a production aeroplane no less than six years earlier! It was certainly in service ahead of the Skyray, though this was partly because of the Skyray's long wait for engine and radar. North American Aviation (NAA) were, at the time in question, indisputably the most powerful fighter firm on Earth. They acquired combat experience with swept-wing fighters significantly earlier than any other organisation apart from the Mig bureau, they had strong and aggressive leadership, and they were able to plan their first supersonic design as a fairly direct extrapolation of the well-proven F-86. By no means least, they worked throughout for a customer endowed with immense expertise, ample funds and an overwhelming sense of urgency.

When the first F-86 (then XP-86) Sabre made its maiden flight on 1 October 1947 it did so on the 3,750 lb thrust of one of the first American axial turbojets to be cleared for flight. Though this engine was later refined into the mass-produced J47 rated at thrusts exceeding 6,000 lb with water injection, NAA calculated that significantly greater thrust still would be needed to exceed the speed of sound in level flight. How was such thrust to be obtained? One could add a rocket; use a bigger engine, such as the giant XJ53 being developed by General Electric specifically for supersonic flight; use afterburning, to boost thrust of existing engines; use more than one engine; or just use the most powerful engine available. Cutting a very long story short, NAA's project team chose two immediate courses of action. On the one hand the use of the D-series J47 with afterburner was expected to result in a useful increase in performance of the NA-165, later called F-86D, a radar-equipped Sabre which gained a world speed record at 715 mph. On the other the Pratt & Whitney J48 was selected as the engine for the NA-157, later called F-86C and still later F-93A, which was intended as a 'long-range fighter' to launch a new family of much enhanced performance. The NA-157 was totally new apart from having superficially similar wings and tail, and had such advanced features as twin-wheel main gears and NACA flush side inlets, to leave the nose free for radar. The fat body was profiled for an afterburning engine, which would have given 8,300 lb thrust, but the stumbling block was that the J48 was a centrifugal engine, with double-sided compressor, in the classic Whittle/Rover/Rolls tradition. NAA's vice-president engineering, Raymond H. Rice, never expected to use a J48 in a supersonic Sabre, and the NA-157 was quickly dropped.

By 1948 Rice had reached three important conclusions. The first was that a project for a supersonic fighter was valid and capable of attainment. The second was that it would have to be a totally new design. The third was that it would have to be based on a completely new axial engine, and there were promising candidate engines under development. Rice's staff briefly toyed with various unconventional shapes, but the mainstream of development never wavered from a low-wing fighter with single afterburning axial engine and swept wings and tailplane. By June 1948 the optimum angle of sweep had been fixed at 45° on the leading edge, and thenceforth the project was popularly known as the Sabre 45 despite the obvious indication that the future fighter would be very different from the Sabre and also significantly larger.

Had the Korean war broken out in 1948 I believe there is a chance that NAA might have elected to go ahead with a very big fighter indeed powered by the J53, which later gave over 23,000 lb thrust with afterburner. As it was, this engine always looked too big for the immediate market, as did the very similar Gyron in Britain. NAA thought the most likely engine would be the Westinghouse J40, a Navy engine, which in 1946 had beaten a rival proposal by Pratt & Whitney Aircraft (PWA) and promised to give a thrust of 7,500 lb dry and over 10,000 lb with afterburner. But PWA was determined to become pre-eminent in the new field of gas turbines. Its T&R (Technical and Research) organisation, headed by Perry W. Pratt (no relation to the original Pratt!), had hit on the idea of making what we variously call a two-shaft, dual-rotor, two-spool or split-compressor engine: the air is compressed first by a low-pressure compressor, driven by the LP turbine, and then by a high-pressure one driven round much faster by a separate HP turbine on a tubular shaft surrounding the inner LP shaft. Though it sounded complicated it promised greater compression ratio without incurring such penalties as compressor stall, bad handling and inadequate surge margins. High compression meant better fuel economy, and to some degree higher power. The original idea had been to make the PT4 turboprop for the XB-52, but in March 1948 the Air Force agreed with PWA that a turbojet would be more useful, even for a long-range bomber, so work began on the JT3.

The JT3 is perhaps the most significant gas turbine since Whittle's W1.

Ultimately it led to production of more than 21,200 engines, not only for fighters and bombers but also for the 707 and DC-8 and many other aircraft. The initial thrust target was 8,750 lb, but Luke Hobbs, PWA vice-president engineering, pushed relentlessly for 10,000 lb in order both to meet the needs of the B-52 and to keep ahead of the opposition. It is very significant that, had NAA talked to Armstrong Siddeley and Rolls-Royce, they would have discovered that both the British companies could see 10,000 lb dry thrust coming fairly soon from both the Sapphire and the Avon; and Bristol's BE.10, later called Olympus, was a two-spool engine identical in form to the JT3, which ran in the same year (1949) and though at least as powerful was significantly lighter. The only criticism one could level at the JT3 was that, true to the Connecticut company's conservative traditions, it was big and heavy in the belief that reliability mattered more than slick brochure figures. By mid-1948 the J57, the military JT3, had become No 1 future engine in the minds of the procurement engineers of the US Air Force. Air Cdre Rod Banks, who in those days used to make periodic visits to see what the Americans were doing, formed the view that the J57 was being regarded almost as a wonder-engine, largely on account of its high compression (a ratio of 12.5:1) which was becoming looked upon as an answer to almost everything. In fact it might have been true that one could have built a better fighter around a lighter and smaller engine—such as a late Sapphire or Avon with a proper afterburner—but the giant, beefy J57 gradually assumed a dominant position at many plants, including NAA down in Inglewood, California, on the south side of LA International Airport.

The studies to make a completely new fighter that could fly faster than sound received the approval of the Air Force early in 1949, and were launched as a full company programme on 3 February. The first detailed three-view was finished on 14 September 1949. It still looked remarkably like an F-86, though all surfaces were swept at 45° and the size was bigger, the engine being an unspecified engine of 9,000 lb thrust dry and 12,000 lb with full afterburner. During 1950, however, the design changed considerably as a result of extensive tunnel testing and engineering refinement. In April 1949 NAA commissioned their first supersonic tunnel. It was a 16 in-square blow-down installation based on the German wartime Kochel pattern, with a sphere of dry air exhausting through the working section into a vacuum chamber, the peak Mach number attainable being 5.25. I remember an eminent British fighter designer proclaiming 'They've got money to burn'; but then he never produced a supersonic fighter!

An important landmark was definite selection of a version of the J57, the J57-P-7 with a long afterburner and complex variable nozzle. In sharp contrast to the philosophy in Britain, which held that afterburning (reheat) was a nasty and inefficient way of boosting thrust, PWA and other American engine firms were by 1950 working on advanced afterburners and variable nozzles which by 1954 had yielded good supersonic engines as reliable as those used in earlier fighters. Whereas the Lightning, and subsonic Javelin, suffered from poorly developed and relatively primitive reheat which either worked or didn't, the P-7 was by 1953 already an advanced and reliable engine which, when put into afterburning operation, unfailingly jumped in sea-level thrust from 9,250 lb to 14,000 lb. There was no intermediate position. Having reached 9,250 lb at full rpm the extra 4,750 lb came in with a noise rather like a clap of thunder. The suddenly opened nozzle spouted a long flame, which at night scintillated in brilliant mixtures of gold and lilac, punctuated with glowing 'shock diamonds' where the internal shock-waves crossed and re-crossed the supersonic flame as they were reflected from its turbulent periphery. The noise was fantastic. As for the pilot, if he had his parking brake off (or if he was already in the air), going into afterburner meant that his seat hit him a blow on the spine and he felt a surge of power as if he had suddenly got an extra engine—as, in a way, he had.

This promise of 14,000 lb of thrust removed any doubt from Rice's mind that he could make the Sabre 45 supersonic. Though the J57-P-7 was well over 20 ft long and weighed more than 5,000 lb, it was nowhere more than 42 inches in diameter; and, above all, it looked like being wholly reliable both as an engine and as a programme. During 1950 the decision was taken to use a plain air inlet in the nose instead of a chin inlet or flush inlets on the fuselage sides. This was because the Air Force had decided that, for the present, the Sabre 45 should be a day fighter, with secondary capability as a fighter-bomber, without all-weather radar. The wing was made broader in chord to reduce the thickness/chord ratio to 6%, the area and aspect ratio being chosen to optimise ceiling and the t/c ratio being thought the best compromise between low drag and the structural and weight penalties of thin wings. After extensive research it was decided to use inboard ailerons. Several other Air Force prototype aircraft of 1949–52 suffered from progressive loss in roll control as indicated airspeed increased, due to the fact that the ailerons were merely twisting the wing (in one or two cases it was possible to get complete aileron reversal, so that putting the stick hard right caused a roll to the left!). Though the Sabre 45's wing was very strong and rigid, the Air Force heartily concurred with the belief that inboard ailerons would avoid trouble. In the event, very large two-piece ailerons were fitted, occupying most of the trailing edge and leaving so little room for flaps that none were fitted. This left the wing with no high-lift device save full-span automatic slats—a most unusual thing which often tended to make pilots unfamiliar with the aircraft regard it as slightly 'hot'. It was a compromise, and today a designer would use spoilers, outboard ailerons or tailerons, but the important thing is that it worked.

On 19 January 1951 the Air Force completed a detailed review of the proposed design and gave NAA clear indication that it expected to place a contract. For those who believe that the US industry is 'featherbedded' I should emphasise that up to this time the whole programme had been funded almost entirely by NAA, the only Air Force investment so far being in the J57 engine. But the identification of some gleaming silver arrowheads encountered—from November 1950—high over the Yalu river in Korea as a new species of Russian jet fighter caused the Air Force to accelerate its own fighter plans, and think about a supersonic fighter a little sooner than it might otherwise have done. It also loosened the purse-strings of the US Congress. On 1 November 1951 NAA received an order for two prototypes, designated YF-100A, and 110 production F-100 fighters for delivery beginning in 1954. North American called the aircraft the NA-180. It was perhaps almost a foregone conclusion that it should be named Super Sabre.

In 1952, while preparations for production of the F-100 and J57-7 went ahead side-by-side with urgent completion of engineering development, the whole project still looked something of a gamble. The choice of the USAF fighter type-number of 100 was purely fortuitous, partly because the Hughes Falcon air-to-air missile and Boeing Bomarc surface-to-air missile had been allotted the numbers XF-98 and XF-99 as 'pilotless fighters'. Nobody then knew that the F-100 would be the first of a big family of fighter and attack aircraft known for obvious reasons as the US Air Force 'Century series'. I would like briefly to break off from the F-100 story and take a wider look at some of the things that had to be done to make supersonic military aviation, as exemplified by the Century series, a reality.

Any new advanced aircraft calls for long and sustained engineering effort, but the four crowded years 1951 to 1954 were quite exceptional. The effort then expended on supersonic fighters in the United States was prodigious, because these aircraft, mostly described in this book, called for advances in structures, materials and techniques, propulsion, systems, and above all in aerodynamics that transcended everything done earlier. Frequently there were sharp discontinuities; it was no longer possible to push a well-established method a little further, and instead a completely new answer had to be found. The bill for aerodynamic research alone for the first generation of American supersonic fighters exceeded \$360 million, including the cost of such research aircraft as the X-1 family, the X-2, X-3 and Skyrocket. The cost of research into advanced propulsion systems for supersonic flight, including that performed by engine manufacturers, exceeded \$280 million; about half of this was spent by the NACA and

AEDC, and a great deal of work was done by Navy facilities, universities and other organisations. Between 1950 and 1954 the US Air Force spent $397 million on a heavy-press programme, the main burden of which was borne by the Wyman–Gordon and Alcoa companies, for squeezing to shape large light-alloy forgings which would otherwise have had to be fabricated from many separate parts or else sculptured from a solid slab in the process colloquially called 'hogging'. The heavy-press programme was a long-term national investment which represented a logical extrapolation of German work in World War 2. Britain had nothing like it, other than a single 12,000-ton press at High Duty Alloys which was small beer in comparison.

The sum devoted to improved and often radically new machine tools is impossible to calculate, because who is to say which tools should be included? But certainly more than $180 million was spent on giant machines from such companies as Cincinnati, Kearney & Trecker, Giddings & Lewis and Onsrud for removing vast amounts of metal at unprecedented rates and with extreme precision, and with such suppliers as Hufford and Sheridan for enormous stretch-presses and similar machines for forming complex double-curvatures in thick plate in a matter of seconds. Automatic precision machinery for drilling, countersinking, dimpling, riveting, reaming, bolting and sealing, often doing five or six operations in sequence, were created for new US aircraft and later percolated down into other industries and other countries. This manufacturing effort was paralleled by the work needed to set up a completely new industry to supply titanium at the rate of 500–600 tons of wrought metal per month. All the supersonic fighters used this metal, often in considerable amounts, because it offered a valuable compromise between light alloys and high-strength steels. In addition, many hundreds of millions of dollars were spent, mostly by the US Air Force, in the development of electrical and hydraulic systems that could reliably function after soaking at up to 300°C, and a range of miniaturised yet high-temperature avionic devices (and this was before the great breakthrough into solid-state electronics based on semiconductors). Not much of this high-temperature research was relevant to the F-100, nor was it accomplished early enough, but it was needed to underpin the Mach 2 fighters that came later.

To a very rough approximation I think the research and manufacturing expenditure in the United States in 1950–55 in merely acquiring the capability of producing supersonic fighters exceeded $2,000 million. This vast national effort seldom got into the papers; trying to make progress in the United States is not really news. But the effort was a capital investment by no means concerned only with making supersonic fighters which might soon go to the scrap-heap. The effort made sense, in the first place, because of the numbers of fighters needed, and the rapid rate at which they had to be built. Except in the Soviet Union no other nation could plan any comparable programme. In the long term the result is that, ever since, if a British planemaker wants a new piece of accessory system, or a giant machine tool, or large quantities of tapered sheet in an advanced aerospace alloy, he either has to wait while a struggling manufacturer tries to meet the demand or else he just buys it off the shelf in the United States. There are certain areas—such as ejection seats and fighter nav/attack systems—where individual British companies have hung on grimly with such persistence that today they even sell to the United States; but they are the exceptions. The fact that Britain, in particular, had no counterpart to the Century series, with its enormous R&D effort prior to 1955, must be counted a factor of some significance in assessing the subsequent performance of many branches of British industry.

But this is quite incidental to the F-100. Though it was the first of the Century series, this fighter needed less research underpinning than most, and what new technology was needed was to a remarkable degree generated by NAA themselves. I will later describe some of these engineering advances. In 1952 the design of the F-100 had still not been completed. Continuing tunnel tests were even bringing about continual refinement of the shape, and four times in 1952 quite major changes were introduced. Two were concerned with the basic profile of the fuselage in both longitudinal shape and cross-section, the main result being a lengthening of the nose to a fish-like gaping mouth of characteristically broad form. Backing up this refinement was a redesign of the cockpit canopy to a longer and more streamlined profile, merging at the rear into a dorsal spine. Most important change of all was a gross redesign of the tail to reposition the slab tailplane at the extreme bottom of the fuselage instead of on the fin. NACA carefully investigated this novel arrangement and confirmed that it gave improved stability and control at operational angles of attack and airspeed. So, unlike what happened with the P.1 programme (p. 13), nobody called for a research aircraft to prove that the F-100 would fly.

All the design changes were incorporated in the mock-up which was approved by the Air Force on 26 August 1952. From that date, construction of the first YF-100 (52-5754) went on around the clock. The date for completion was scheduled as 26 June 1953, but 754 was actually ready on 24 April. Taken by road to the AFFTC at Edwards AFB it was then carefully instrumented and inspected and readied for flight almost two months ahead of the planned date of 20 July. Senior engineering test pilot George Welch had a bet with Lt-Col Frank K. 'Pete' Everest, chief of flight test at the AFFTC, that the F-100 *would* go faster than sound. For days beforehand Welch's world had been dominated not so much by the mere thought of flying the pugnacious brute as by the fact that it was designed to go faster than sound in level flight. No aircraft had ever done this, apart from purpose-built rocket research machines, but with the F-100 the curves of drag and thrust did not cross at the tropopause until some way beyond Mach 1. So the breathless question around Rogers Dry Lake was 'Will she or won't she?' Hence Welch's wager, as he started the big J57 under a cloudless sky soon after dawn on 25 May 1953, that he would buy his chase pilot two beers if the answer was affirmative. Everest took off in his F-86D and then formated with the 'hunnert'—years later contracted to Hun—on its very first take-off, after only a single fast taxi run. In no time he was through to afterburner himself, and found the sleek 'Dogship' quite unable to keep up until Welch came out of afterburner. Then, with the YF-100 in cold thrust and the F-86D still in afterburner they climbed together to 35,000 ft. Welch then quietly said 'Hang on, here we go'. The brilliant jet of shock diamonds re-appeared, the great Super Sabre lunged forward and within two minutes Everest was looking forward to the two beers due from his long-vanished colleague. Later on the same day Welch did it again. It was a pretty decisive start to the era of supersonic military aviation.

Welch looked about 25, but in fact 12 years earlier he had been one of the two American fighter pilots to make it into the air at Pearl Harbor, when he notched up the first four of his 18½ wartime victims. Like all senior test pilots he was cool and disciplined, and it was no sudden impulse that made him lift 754 right off and fly without the expected prior 'hop'. From the first the serviceability of both the aircraft and its engine was outstanding. The 100th hour of flight was logged within six weeks, and by this time Welch and his colleagues had explored a substantial part of the flight envelope and completed a great deal of the systems testing. They were also engaged in stability and control evaluation, but long before Phase I (contractor) testing was finished the Air Force were getting into the act. Everest got his hands on the first machine within two weeks, and throughout the summer of 1953 other AFFTC pilots were busy with their own unofficial evaluations. Never, since the service had begun to do its own test flying after World War 2, had its pilots been so excited and eager to fly a new prototype still in a manufacturer's hands. Meanwhile the Los Angeles plant was finishing not only the second YF-100 but also the preparations to build the 110 F-100As which were following directly behind it. The programme was, to use a more recent expression 'going like a bomb'. On 17 September 1953 the Air Force completed Phase II flight testing in 19 hr 42 min, to which I shall refer again. On 28 September the first production F-100A, 52-5756, was completed (the scheduled date, unbelievably, was Christmas Day—NAA *did* have holidays, even during the Korean War). On 14 October Welch made the first flight of the second YF-100, on 19 October the new fighter was publicly unveiled, on

20 October the first F-100A was accepted by the Air Force, and on 29 October Welch flew the first F-100A while Col Everest flew old 754 to set a world speed record. As this pace is rather breathtaking, I will break off for a moment to look at the F-100A itself.

Although it was big enough and different enough from all earlier fighters to be deeply impressive, one of the most remarkable things about the F-100 was its conventionality. Superficially it was even more straightforward than Petter's P.1; almost all the differences between the NA-192 (F-100A) and earlier fighters were merely ones of degree. It was bigger, heavier, more powerful, had higher tyre pressures and took off and landed faster, but there was hardly anything quite new in concept. Despite the huge industrial and research-lab effort needed by Century-series fighters, it was strictly evolution rather than revolution. For example the F-86 had introduced the use of tapered sheet, for the top and bottom skins of the wing box. With the F-100 the sheets were not merely tapered but machined into the first one-piece integrally stiffened upper and lower skins used on any fighter, the material thickness at the root being 1.75 in. Each side of the fuselage was a single sheet of light alloy, formed in one operation in a giant stretch-press. Compared with an F-86D the first F-100 used more than six times as much titanium, and in 1953–54 NAA bought 80% of all titanium alloy sheet produced in the United States. NAA even said that 'tolerances required on the F-100 are so small that normal temperature changes in the plant in the course of a day cause tool and material dimensions to change to such an extent that tolerances could not be held without special handling'. It's a good story. I'd rather believe Adrian Sorrells, who in those days was editor of the company magazine *Skyline*, that the daytime temperature was maintained at night when they switched on the 200-foot neon sign on the roof saying HOME OF THE SABRE JET.

Manufacturing the F-100 was peanuts compared with the later B-70 programme (described in the companion book *Bombers of the West*), though the Air Force wanted the F-100 in such a hurry that, as I shall relate, NAA had to open a second-source plant to reach a monthly output in excess of 60 aircraft. Why did the Air Force want the big fighter so urgently? I think it was a mixture of prestige-type thinking, of fear of supersonic developments of the Mig-15, and of belief in the basic fighter's multi-role potential. In fact, I am not personally convinced that the F-100 was markedly superior to what could be done much more cheaply with development of the F-86 as far as air-superiority dogfighting was concerned. I have been unable to discover if a dogfight ever took place between an F-100 and a late-model naval Fury, such as an FJ-4B (the ultimate F-86 development), but my money would be on the Fury. In air combat supersonic speed is far less important than it was reckoned to be 20 years ago, with the sole exception that the slower fighter cannot avoid being caught (though it can be slippery as an eel, witness the Harrier) and cannot elect to break off the fight. I hope this chapter will leave the thousands of 'jocks' who later flew the beloved 'Hun' in no doubt that I will always regard this aeroplane as one of the truly great fighters of all time, but it is a fact that, if I had to do battle with any sort of Mig, I would choose a subsonic FJ-4B Fury in preference to the F-100A.

The F-100A had little in the way of navaids or attack systems; it was cleared for service in the days when a pilot made do with communications radio and a case of maps. The radar gunsight (APX-6) was little different from that of an early F-86; indeed the second major production model of the F-100, the C model, actually reverted to the identical A-4 (APG-30) sight carried by the F-86A-7, E and F. As in the F-86, the waveguide led to an aerial in the 12 o'clock position in the lip of the nose inlet, but the installation was complicated by the fact that the F-100 had the most constricted nose of any fighter. The inlet periphery had a sharp lip, with no auxiliary suck-in doors such as would certainly be used today, and I am sure the only reason it worked at all is because the long duct smoothed out the airflow before it reached the engine. Its characteristic subtle profile seemed to defeat a remarkable number of artists—even those who prepared three-view drawings. The air duct at first ran along the underside of the forward fuselage before rising to clear the bay of the rearward-retracting dual nosewheels and then arch around the wing and change to circular section to mate with the engine. Ahead of the instrument panel there was room for not only the meagre avionics of the A model but also for the more extensive array of 'black boxes' of later types, but in the extreme nose the duct wall was amazingly shallow and by no means simple to construct. The gunsight aerial, a mere five inches deep, caused a marked bulge in the upper wall of the duct.

In contrast to the primitive nav/attack systems, the F-100A did have something completely new in the way of guns. During World War 2 it was indisputable that the front-runner in aircraft guns was Germany, and the finest of the German guns was the radically new MG-213 by the Mauser company. By feeding its ammunition via a rotating cylinder somewhat akin to that of a revolver the MG-213 could fire much faster than previous weapons of comparable hitting power, and after the war it was used as a starting point by almost every country that considered it needed a new fixed gun for use by fighters. Britain chose to adopt the big calibre of 30 mm and a rather modest rate of fire and muzzle velocity. The USAF, on the other hand, finally plumped for a gun of only 20 mm calibre but with very high muzzle velocity and rate of fire. In 1953 this gun, the M-39, went into production by the Pontiac division of General

Motors, and the F-100 was designed around four of them, under the cockpit, with 200 rounds per gun. The M-39E, as used on most F-100s, is a fine gun, but it was used on only a few other types of fighter of the same vintage (notably the F-86H and F-101A) as well as the later F-5 which never received the multi-barrel M-61 'Gatling'. The Air Force looked hard at equipping later F-100s with the Gatling but on each occasion judged four M-39Es an adequate punch in what had by then become primarily a ground-attack role.

As well as these inbuilt guns the F-100A had two wing hard-point mounts which could be fitted with pylons for two rakish drop tanks of high fineness ratio and a profile like an upside-down wing, with cruciform tailfins. Though seemingly carried at a marked nose-down incidence these 229 gal tanks were cleared for flight at Mach 1. Another startling fact was that the speed brake, a thing like a reinforced barn door hinged to the lower edge of the massive sculptured frame at the front of the wing box, could be slammed open at any speed the pilot chose. Though extended forwards by a ram of mighty proportions the brake merely opened until it was balanced by the air load, and could never be torn off or break the aircraft. As for the flight control system, the fully powered slab tailplane was protected against breaking the aircraft (or so everyone confidently imagined) by artificial feel, though the gearing chosen made it highly sensitive; the ailerons were powerful and light, and were again sensitive to a hamfisted pilot; and the rudder was similarly powered (in later versions it was fitted with a yaw damper). What seemed to be a trivial change—though actually it was worked out most carefully—was that the tall fin and high, narrow rudder of the first YF aircraft were cut down in the F-100A to reduce weight and drag. The production rudder was broad but squat, being arrested barely half-way up the fin by the sharply lowered fuel vent which in the first YF-100A had been on top of the tall fin. This little change was to have a major impact on the programme.

With these changes the normal gross weight of the F-100A was brought down to 28,935 lb (23,996 lb clean), much closer to the design estimate of 28,561 than the first aircraft which were cleared to 29,644 lb. By the autumn of 1953 production at Inglewood was ready to roll in the most spotless, air-conditioned, brilliantly lit plant it was possible to imagine. Though the rate of output was still low it was planned to build up rapidly during 1954; there was strong pressure to move even faster, and unbounded enthusiasm among almost everyone involved. Indeed the fact that the Air Force Phase II pilots sandwiched their work in between the contractor's Phase I tests—a most unusual and improper procedure—betokens the wish of the customer to clear away all deficiencies as quickly as possible and let the floodgates open. At the press demonstration, on 19 October 1953, the Air Force DCOS Materiél, Lt-Gen Orval R.

Cook, emphasised 'The important thing about this new airplane is that there are others like it on the production line'. He was already the author of the Cook-Craigie Plan (p. 173) for finding the best compromise between getting production going as soon as possible and avoiding the need to modify production aircraft because of a fault unearthed at a late stage. The plan was not applied to the F-100.

Though photographs of the F-100 had been released soon after the first flight, 19 October was the first time people outside the programme had been invited to see the actual aircraft, take pictures and ask questions. More than 125 newsmen came from film, radio, TV, newspapers and magazines across the nation, to what was then the remote and previously peaceful airport at Palmdale, in the Mojave Desert. There were two 'stars' on which many more than 125 cameras were focussed: George Welch and the first F-100A, number 756. This combination proved impressive. When you wait for a supersonic aircraft to appear at supersonic speed the tension in the air can well be imagined—and this was not to be, as it would be today, at contrail height but at about 100 ft altitude. The press had a brief vision of a weaving silver dot ahead of a black plume; then BANG! There followed a hushed rustling quietness, broken only by the tinkling glass of some of the windows in the airport administration building. Many newsmen claimed never to have seen the approaching fighter at all; others failed to see its departure, despite the winking afterburner. It was one of the happiest days ever for James H. 'Dutch' Kindelberger, NAA board chairman, and J. Leland 'Lee' Attwood, president.

Nine days later came the coveted record. The Air Force fraternity at Edwards had practically taken it for granted that something in their charge would always hold the world absolute speed record. Then, in 1953, the perfidious British had grabbed it, first with Neville Duke's Hunter at 727.6 mph and then with Mike Lithgow's Swift, stoutly flown in scorching heat in Libya to hit 737.7. Everest's lads could hardly wait to wrest the record back with the F-100. Though its supersonic speed at the 35,000 ft level was cut back to almost precisely Mach 1 at sea level, this was ample for exceeding the Swift's mark by the stipulated 1%. Then on 3 October the Navy wheeled out the odd bat-winged XF4D (p. 215), which the Air Force haughtily thought might perhaps touch Mach 1 in a dive, despite the terrible Westinghouse engine. One Jimmy Verdin climbed in and proceeded to set a record at 753 mph. To say this was unexpected by the boys in light blue is to understate the situation. After having for their entire lives felt slightly sorry for the Navy aviators, especially in recent months since the dark blues had had to borrow Air Force jets in order to go supersonic in a fighter, the situation was suddenly reversed. Everest was not at all sure he could beat Verdin, even with the F-100. But he had a go. On 29 October Everest pointed one of the YFs at the Salton Sea, the inland lake in Imperial Valley where, because it is below sea level, the summer noon-day temperature will fry an egg. Holding 75 ft above the mixture of hard salt and wet brine, Everest kicked in the afterburner and aimed to pass through two columns of black smoke from burning rubber tyres. Then, after a wide turn that had to keep within 150 ft of the ground, he made the return run. After a few victory rolls, with victory most uncertain, he headed back to the nearby Marine Corps station at El Centro.

The result was perhaps a half-victory. The average of the two runs was just over 755 mph. At the ambient temperature of a mere 29°C, typical for so late in the year, this was equivalent to over 0.96, and I think Everest had no reason to feel displeased. But it failed to beat Verdin's mark by the required 1%, and Everest offered to try again. The Fédération Aéronautique International, however, accepted Everest's attempt because it was submitted over a 15 km course, easily beating the existing F-86D figure of 707 mph, and it stands today as a world record; and NAA said they were well content with the figure, and described the F-100 as the 'fastest plane in the world'. (This seemed a bit tough on Bill Bridgman, who two weeks earlier had hit 1,272 mph in the Navy Skyrocket research aircraft; soon he did 1,327, and by the end of the year the Air Force X-1A had done 1,650, but these flights could not qualify under the FAI rules.) Everest's record, gained at full throttle in dangerous proximity to the ground, through turbulent air that not only caused supreme discomfort but came within an ace of causing ground and aircraft to meet, was the last record to be gained under the old rules drawn up in the days of stick-and-string. The next record was flown under new rules at 35,000 ft. On 20 August 1955 Col Horace A. Hanes, flying an improved F-100C (the second production version, described later), set up a figure just in excess of 822 mph. Everest could have done the same with his old YF prototype, had the FAI produced jet-age rules a little earlier.

Everest was naturally slightly peeved that the cooler weather had robbed him of a clear-cut win over the Navy, but he had no time to brood. When he got back to Edwards he found he was the centre of a hornet's nest. During the enthusiastically rushed Phase II testing Everest had appointed himself F-100 Project Pilot, backed up by Capt Zeke Hopkins. Wringing the F-100 out in deliberately harsh ways they discovered tendencies towards control sensitivity, divergence and 'coupling' between roll and yaw and between pitch and yaw of a nature which, though completely outside the boundaries of ordinary casual flying, or textbook aerobatics, seemed to be not merely undesirable in a combat aircraft but potentially even dangerous. Everest had finally considered that the F-100A ought not to be released for Air Force service until the deficiencies had been rectified. When this was set down in harsh black and white in Everest's formal Phase II report it caused no small stir. NAA took a very poor view indeed. George Welch gave formal evidence that the F-100 was one of the nicest and safest fighters he had ever flown. In Welch's own Phase I report he had formally recorded the measured compliance with the USAF specification requirements of supersonic speed in level flight, a service ceiling exceeding 50,000 feet and a combat radius exceeding 500 miles. He now testified that, in the opinion of the NAA test pilots, the F-100 was ready for production.

What happened next was, to my way of thinking, most odd. It would have seemed to me that, as the argument hinged about the behaviour of a new fighter which did not significantly change its behaviour between one flight and the next, the answer would be to carry out most searching trials with the most senior test pilots from the Air Force, NACA and possibly even rival manufacturers, with the maximum of on-board instrumentation. What was actually done was to let the user pilots from Tactical Air Command come and have a bash. The result was predictable. All of them eagerly awaited release of this splendid great supersonic fighter, and the chance to fly it ahead of time was just great. One after another they thundered off with afterburner blazing, poled it round the sky and came back saying 'Gee whiz!' Before all this the situation at Edwards had been anything but unanimous, with the majority either feeling Everest was nit-picking or coming out strongly against him with the openly expressed view that he was wrong. Poor Everest, though never exactly 'carpeted', found himself standing on quite a few eminent carpets, some of them in Washington, trying to explain the finer points of directional stability and hearing other chaps say that in their humble view the F-100 was just fine. It was a situation which, had it occurred in a Hollywood movie, would have made me cross that the script-writer should have so failed to mirror real life. Of course there is fine scope for dramatic emotion in the lone hero setting his grim jaw and fighting it out against the cigar-chewing generals and the politically powerful plane-maker, in reckless disregard for his career. But precisely why do we have test pilots? Everest must have felt that he was superfluous, and that, provided a big enough group of senior pilots from TAC squadrons said they thought the F-100 OK, then it was.

After a fine lot of argument the Air Force decided that, though no doubt Everest was correctly doing his job and was in no way mistaken in his findings, the important thing was that he was finding deficiencies in extreme corners of the flight envelope in conditions that would be unlikely to bother the user command. So they let Everest return to his post at Edwards, and told NAA the F-100 was released for full production and Air Force service. NAA got cracking in no uncertain way, and soon the first 110 A models were rolling off the line by day and night.

More had been ordered with both 1952 and 1953 funds to bring the immediate total up to 203. More money had been voted in 1953 for the first 70 of an improved model, the F-100C (NA-214), which had a structurally strengthened wing providing for a 7,500 lb external load on six pylons. NAA juggled with about ten balls in the air at once to sort out the pylon arrangement, because of the sharp wing sweep, the need to put the longest stores outboard of the main gears and the fact that the main gears had to retract behind the stores on the inboard pylons. The F-100C also introduced a quickly attached FR probe for overseas ferrying. TAC had adopted the British method of Flight Refuelling Ltd and calculated that with its widespread use it could even fly its fighters across the North Atlantic to Europe or the Mediterranean theatre in a matter of seven or eight hours. The F-100C was the first USAF aircraft to be designed with a probe.

Nor was this all. The F-100B, a major redesign with the bigger J75 engine for maximum capability in the ground attack role, was going ahead under the new number of F-107, while beyond the F-100C could be seen the F-100D (NA-223) with further improvements. The F-100C was announced on 30 December 1953, drawings were released on 19 January 1954, manufacturing began on 25 March and the first off the line was completed on 19 October 1954. And by this time the F-100 programme had called for a second-source for the F-100C and D models, to augment the engineering resources and almost double the rate of delivery. On 11 October 1954 this source was named as NAA's Columbus Division, the old Curtiss-Wright plant near the Ohio city of that name. Columbus had already shouldered a large engineering and manufacturing burden with the NAA products for the Navy and Marine Corps, including the whole design, development and manufacturing programmes of all the late-model Sabre developments (Furies) from 1952 onwards. Henceforth it was to play a large role in the F-100, which remained solely an Air Force aircraft.

On 29 September 1954, when about 60 of the original A models had come off the Inglewood line, the first TAC unit equipped with the F-100 was activated at George AFB, near Victorville, California. Even before the maiden flight of the YF-100 the 479th Fighter Day Wing had known it would be the first user, and it had watched the progress of the flight-test programme with intense interest—indeed its squadron commanders had been involved in the Phase VI evaluation and in the argument over the fitness for service of the F-100A without modification. I spent a day out at George in 1955, when everyone had successfully converted to the big new bird and the 479th Wing was hosting visitors from other units who had yet to receive their aircraft and training aids. My abiding memory of this trip out to the scorching Mojave desert was that on the return to Inglewood we made a detour up into the rugged Panamint range, far to the north, where the F-100s were authorised to exceed Mach 1. As a result I can confirm that in a Cessna you can hear a sonic boom generated about 30,000 feet higher up, and that the man who did it, flying F-100A No 31594, had no difficulty in formating on us later at about 120 knots, though with his nose so high he could not have seen directly ahead.

George AFB in 1955 had settled down to routine training, with the accent very strongly on safety rather than on the intensive flying that much later marked the introduction to service of the F-111. By the time I came visiting they had lost several months, and it is fair to record the early experience of the 479th after activation with the F-100 as frustrating in the extreme. During the summer and autumn (fall) of 1954 there had been four cases in which F-100As had seemingly suffered a loss of control leading to mid-air structural failure. In one case the pilot, who was killed, was a man of outstanding experience: RAF Air Commodore Geoffrey Stephenson, Commandant of the Central Fighter Establishment, who was giving the F-100 the most thorough work-out of all the US fighters that he was evaluating. The USAF were deeply disturbed, but worse was to come. Of all the manoeuvres an aeroplane can do, few have the drama and excitement of a high-speed full-power dive and subsequent pull-out. When I was a boy I was weaned on epic films about test pilots who seemed to delight in trying to pull the wings off; in one such celluloid classic the hero dramatically tore the instrument panel from the disintegrating pursuit ship in order to bring back the vital evidence! Modern test pilots sometimes have to do this kind of test, and on 12 October 1954 such a mission fell to the lot of George Welch. It was the last in a series of slow build-ups to the maximum structural test called for by the F-100 contractual specification.

At 10.46 Welch took off from Palmdale in 25764, one of the first F-100As to come off the line, and climbed into the warm blue sky. Everything had been most carefully checked for perhaps the oldest and toughest single flight test there is: a pull-out going right into one corner of the flight envelope, reaching the highest permissible speed and Mach number and then the limit load factor of 7.5 g. Earlier on the same day Welch had failed to hit exactly the required combination of airspeed, Mach number and g, and on this flight he was determined to succeed. At 10.58 he was ready to dive, and at 11.00 reported to NAA Flight Test at Palmdale that he was directly over Mojave, aiming at Rosamond Dry Lake. After some minutes the ground engineer found he was unable to make R/T contact. He was then told by Palmdale tower that two parachutes had been seen to open at about 20,000 feet over Rosamond and that there might have been a mid-air collision. Immediately the company despatched two

Navions—the lightplane NAA built after World War 2—which were circling the parachutes before they reached ground. One proved to be the F-100's drag chute, with a small piece of F-100 hanging from it. The other was the unconscious and dying pilot. It was soon established no other aircraft had been involved. What had happened?

Other F-100A aircraft had flown faster, though without pulling so many g; even greater structural loads had been borne, though at lower speeds and Mach numbers. Was there something new and unknown about this combination of speed and g which, even in a correctly executed symmetrical pull-out, would cause an F-100 to disintegrate? While every nut and bolt was picked off the desert floor, NAA interviewed 173 witnesses. They included two of exceptional reliability. A B-47 on its way home to Castle AFB from practice bombing at Salton Sea happened to reach Palmdale at 25,000 feet just at 11.00. The veteran pilots, a major and a captain, watched the fighter's white contrail arch over at 45,000 feet, less than five miles ahead, one pilot remarking that to make such a turn in their B-47 would need ten miles instead of about half a mile. Both watched the F-100 plummet down in a dive at 70° to 80° passing their own level so fast they could barely follow it with their eyes. Suddenly the fighter appeared to explode. Neither man was aware of any prior manoeuvre or any kind of warning.

There followed one of the most exhaustive accident investigations in the history of aviation, rivalled in scope only by the giant probe of the Comet 1 that was still going on in England. Many hundreds of engineers—one of them Harrison Storms who much later won for NAA the prime role in the Apollo programme—worked day and night to discover why a completely serviceable F-100 should suddenly come apart in mid-air. It was not difficult to salvage almost every part of the aircraft, mark exactly where in the desert it was found, determine which bits had hit others and when, and establish that until the disintegration started every item on board had been fully serviceable and functioning normally. The engine had been spinning at high speed even at ground impact, though long since severed from its fuel supply. Is there not a creepy feeling of the supernatural in an accident such as this?

Had ship 764 been a regular squadron fighter I doubt that an explanation would have been found. Salvation lay in the fact that it carried special instrumentation, and even though this was before the days of armoured crash recorders a surprising amount survived to yield vital evidence. One of the essential clues was provided by a camera mounted in the fin and focussed on the left tailplane. This camera continued operating under its own momentum for a second or two after disintegration had cut its electric supply, and the final frames showed that the sharp shadow of the fin and rudder had raced violently across the tailplane. After Griffith

Park Observatory had given the exact bearing and azimuth of the Sun it was possible to calculate the motion of the aircraft in its final few seconds Even more vital was the discovery that the badly fogged final inches of film from the oscillograph recording the control forces and positions could be made to yield a picture. The film was cut into small fragments and each piece was separately developed and printed, using the preceding one as a guide to the darkroom procedure, until a legible record was obtained. The tail shadow and the oscillograph film both showed that 764 had come apart as the result of a violent yaw to the right. Instead of flying the way it was pointing it had tried to make a flat turn to the right, resulting in a supersonic sideslip beyond the design limit of the airframe.

This was a complete answer to 'How?' but NAA still had to ask themselves 'Why?' It had been established that, as Welch pulled harder on the control column, the F-100 had yawed to the right. Ultimately he imposed a vertical acceleration of slightly more than 8 g (undoubtedly more than intended), and as this load was reached the yaw angle, which should have been zero, suddenly increased to 15°, stabilised for an instant and then went completely off the record. The F-100 had been built to survive an 8° yaw at maximum speed (strictly at 'maximum q', the dynamic head corresponding to maximum indicated airspeed), which in my view is indicative of impressive strength. Suddenly encountering more than twice this angle resulted in immediate total break-up, tragically causing fatal injuries to Welch. The final explanation was as fundamental a reason as one could find. An aircraft is made up of an assembly of masses arranged according to the shape found best for the mission. Older aircraft tended to have long wings and short bodies, but the F-100 was representative of the new breed of supersonic machines with stubby wings and long and heavy bodies. This inevitably tended to make the principal axis of manoeuvre the major longitudinal axis from nose to tail. Rotation about any other axis, such as pulling out from a dive, resulted in significant 'inertia coupling' between the three axes causing unwanted roll and yaw. Normally this was acceptable, though Everest warned of the possible consequences stemming from the marginal directional stability. In the severe conditions of Welch's last supersonic dive the coupling suddenly overcame the ability of the pilot, and the weathercock directional stability of the fin, to fight against it.

Thus 1954 left the twin spectres of fatigue (with the Comet 1) and inertia coupling (with the F-100) indelibly etched in the minds of designers. Neither was in any sense a new problem. Inertia coupling had nothing, *per se*, to do with supersonic flight or with any freak or previously unexplored environmental conditions on that October day high over California. Welch was doomed before he left the ground, because the test he was going to perform would be bound to destroy his fully serviceable aircraft, just as it would destroy any aircraft with its mass distributed mostly from front to rear and lacking in directional stability. Thus did aviation yet again learn in the hardest possible way about something already written down in musty textbooks. What made it harder was that the flashing F-100 was in volume production, 70 had been delivered and new wings were forming fast, with the 450th at Foster AFB, Texas, already busy with pilot and ground-crew training. What was to be done? After anxious discussions involving the Top Brass who had declined to listen too hard to Pete Everest the F-100 was grounded on 11 November 1954, save for aircraft engaged in special testing by NAA and the Air Force.

This was probably the most serious technical blow suffered by any Western military-aircraft programme since World War 2. With the F-100 Ray Rice's team had created what seemed to be a world-beating fighter, and done so with astonishing speed. Deep technical trouble and a protracted modification programme were just what the F-100 didn't want, especially at so late a stage and—from NAA's point of view—under circumstances in which the manufacturer would have to bear a heavy share of the considerable extra costs. In fact, the penalty on NAA was substantially lessened by the crucial fact that the production F-100A had been formally accepted by the Air Force. Had AFHQ conducted the searching examination that Everest's findings undoubtedly warranted I think it highly likely that the task of rectification would have had to be paid for by NAA down to the last nickel. The modification programme finally agreed, after an exhaustive elimination of alternatives, was chiefly confined to two visibly obvious changes to the airframe: the span was increased by just over 26 inches and the vertical tail (stabiliser) was increased in area by 27% by extending it upwards approximately back to the original shape.

These vital alterations were the simplest way of making the necessary redistribution of areas and masses to guarantee that, no matter what angular rate the pilot demanded, the F-100 would always point more or less the way it was going. It was 1955 before the new F-100A standard was agreed, and though the grounding order was progressively lifted from mid-January the need to rebuild 70 of the A models, and modify a further 90 on the line or awaiting delivery, took until the middle of the year. It affected Columbus because that plant was already tooling up for the forthcoming C and D models, and it also directly affected the first F-100C (53-1709) which since 19 October had been forlornly parked at Palmdale and subject to the grounding order. It was to avoid an extensive rebuild programme of this kind that the Cook-Craigie Plan had been devised, but not even the authors of that plan could guard against the extraordinary history of the F-100. In every big programme there has to come a time when the customer says 'She's OK, let her roll!', and—at least in those days of big numbers—new ships were soon thick upon the ground. What seems inexplicable, and I have tried hard to discover the answer, is how the Air Force signed formal acceptance of the F-100A and opened the floodgates nine months before the contractor had flown the most gruelling flight test! The best answer I can get was that it was a calculated risk—a gamble that failed to come off. I still cannot understand why the stability and control of the A model were not investigated to the limits in December 1953 instead of trying to discredit Everest by outvoting him with delighted chaps from TAC squadrons.

It was against this sombre background of a shut production line and a grounded aeroplane that Dutch Kindelberger went to the White House on 17 December 1954 to receive from President Eisenhower the Collier Trophy, jointly with Ed Heinemann who shared the award on account of his F4D (p. 215). This trophy can fairly be called the most prized honour in American aviation, and it is awarded for 'The greatest achievement in aviation in America, the value of which has been demonstrated by actual use during the preceding year'. In the fall of '54 there was no question whatever but that the F-100 was the correct choice, and NAA was accordingly notified by the National Aeronautic Association. Equally I think there is no question whatever that the 22 eminent men on that year's Collier Trophy Committee were right to stick to their guns with the F-100, but the trophy has never at any other time been awarded for an aircraft that (however temporarily) was deemed unsafe to fly. And Kindelberger's cup of ill-fortune was yet to take a further big drop, because two weeks later simmering labour trouble at Los Angeles degenerated into a major strike. NAA's press release said that, despite this, F-100 work was 'on schedule'; I'd give the man who wrote that a job any time, because there could hardly be a more encouraging way of reporting that the programme had come to a halt and the schedule had evaporated.

Before the programme picked up again there had been a further catastrophic incident which missed by a hair's breadth taking the life of another NAA pilot. On Saturday 26 February 1955 George F. Smith left his bachelor apartment to take out his laundry. Passing the plant he suddenly decided to drop by, though it was his day off, and finish writing the report on an F-100A he had flown late on the previous day. At the pilots' office the dispatcher hailed him and said '659 is ready for a first flight; why don't you do it, as you're here?' George agreed, and put on parachute and life vest on top of his sports shirt and slacks, not bothering about flight suit or boots. A few minutes later, at 35,000 ft over the coast, he was surprised and concerned to see and feel the 100 going into a dive. His immediate thought was 'runaway trim motor', but what really got him worried was that the control column was either locked solid or moving away from him. After radioing the symptoms he pulled with all his force with both hands, but could not stop the dive becoming ever steeper. As the dive went beyond the vertical he ejected. His last memory was the Mach reading of 1.05. After a fabulous bit of detective work NAA found the wreckage, 4,800 ft offshore, looking after its salvage 'like 50 barrels full of metal corn flakes'. Pinpointing the problem was thus hard (it was discovered to have been an obscure hydraulic fault). More important, from Smith's point of view, was that a series of lucky events saved his life after an incredible bale-out at over 780 mph at a mere 6,500 ft, just over five seconds from impact. As the first man ever to survive a supersonic bale-out —let alone in such frighteningly dense air—he was an object of intense interest. His list of injuries was awesome, and he 'approached close to the limit for human survival', but in an extremely unpleasant way he gave aerospace medicine new knowledge and supersonic pilots new confidence.

Flight development of the F-100C was allowed to begin on 17 January 1955, before the first example had been modified. The pilot was Alvin (Al) White, who almost a decade later made the first take off of the XB-70. The production programme got back into its stride gradually during the first quarter of 1955, aircraft coming off the line with wing tips and fins still lacking while NAA concentrated on fitting these parts to the machines previously grounded at George AFB. It was not until May that the 479th could start converting its young second lieutenants, and they had not finished conversion when I came visiting in July, though the programme was going beautifully. Certainly by that time there was not a single stumpy fin to be seen, either at George or at Los Angeles. The last A model was delivered late in 1955. All served as day fighters, and were replaced in the TAC inventory from 1957 onwards by C and D models, a batch of 80 being rebuilt in 1960–61 as D models and shipped to Nationalist China (Taiwan). Many improvements were introduced with successive blocks of A models, the most important being the J57-P-29 engine rated at 16,000 lb with afterburner.

A total of 476 C models were built, 25 of them at Columbus where the first Ohio-built machine flew on 8 September 1955. Deliveries began in July 1955 to the 322nd Group at Foster, and for the next 12 years the C served not only with the US Air Force but also with the Air National Guard before all had been passed on to other friendly air forces, notably that of Turkey. The first 100,000 hours in TAC service were completed in November 1956, by which time the accident record was: accidents, 95 (very bad); write-offs, 47 (fair); fatalities, 6 (outstandingly good). Why so many accidents? I think it is fair to put it down to the fact that, while other Century-series fighters flew relatively sedate missions, the Hun always had a rousing, boisterous life of tight formations, simulated air combat, supersonic passes at what I once saw in a programme (at Eglin AFB) as 'grass-blade height' and pull-outs with screeching tip vortices to release tons of assorted ordnance ranging from salvoed rockets to hot gouts of napalm. And, of course, I think you had to be pretty accurate with your landing. One of the least euphemistic descriptions I ever heard was that of a 20th TFW pilot in England who said an F-100 landing was 'a sort of controlled crash'. Drag chutes were mandatory.

Earlier I mentioned the F-100D. This was the ultimate type of single-seat F-100, and it marked completion of the process—which was equally marked with all production Century-series aircraft other than the F-102/106—of turning a 'fighter' into a tactical attack and close-support machine. Externally it looked much like a C except for having a kinked wing trailing edge with small flaps inboard of the ailerons, small fences starting behind the slats near the outer ends of the ailerons, and a further increase in fin height with more pointed tip and much deeper heat/vent outlet projecting aft just above the rudder. NAA would have liked to put the speed brake somewhere else because it prevented weapons from being hung on the fuselage, but this would have been a major redesign job. Inside, the changes were more extensive, and they reflected both the results of TAC experience with the A and C and also a willingness to spend considerable sums in buying a ground-attack fighter able to operate in both conventional and nuclear roles in bad weather. The major addition, apart from a 'wet' (integral tank) wing, was a Minneapolis-Honeywell autopilot, which in 1956 was a unique fitment on an aircraft still officially classed as a day fighter. It incorporated a LABS (low-altitude bombing system) facility for toss bombing with tactical nuclear weapons. Dan Darnell, who flew the first D model (54-2121) on 24 January 1956, said 'The autopilot lets you concentrate on the navigational and tactical aspects . . . it greatly reduces the chances for human error in split-second timings at supersonic speeds.' Afurther series of modifications concerned the underwing load. The pylons were unbraced and jettisonable, and NAA claim to have developed the world's first 'Buddy pack' refuelling system so that one fighter could refuel another in flight. This claim will be challenged by Flight Refuelling Ltd, who flew such a pack in 1955, and by Ed Heinemann who drew the very first such pack for the Skyhawk in 1954; but certainly the F-100D was the first Buddy-equipped supersonic aircraft. Oddly, once it had been cleared to do it the F-100 put away its Buddy packs and never used them in service.

No fewer than 1,274 D models were made, 334 of them at Columbus where the first was flown on 12 June 1956. This most numerous of all the Huns has been progressively updated by modifications which run into hundreds. Some were incorporated at first build; for example the final 444 from Los Angeles were equipped to fire AIM-9B Sidewinder air-to-air missiles, and all Ds were eventually converted to launch Bullpup air-to-surface guided weapons. Deliveries to TAC units began before the end of 1956, but approximately 300 D models were supplied new to the Armée de l'Air and Danish Air Force under the MAP.

On 3 August 1956 Al White flew an F-100C converted to a dual-control tandem-seater to serve as a development aircraft for the F-100F. The first F to come off the line, 56-3725, was rolled out on 7 January 1957 and flown on 7 March. The last of 339 Fs, all built at Los Angeles, was completed in October 1959, bringing the total run up to 2,294. This total was markedly lower than NAA had expected at the start of the programme, and shortage of work at Los Angeles considerably reduced the total built at Columbus. But it is probable that, had the Air Force in 1956 been able to look a decade ahead, it would have bought very many more F-100s than it did. The F model had only two guns and its external ordnance load was restricted to 6,000 lb, but it was fully operational and later served in action as well as in its original role of combat proficiency trainer. The pupil occupies the front cockpit, which is the only one fitted with armament controls; alternatively the F can be used for reconnaissance, FAC duties or RPV direction, with the observer or controller in the rear cockpit. Many new Fs were supplied to the Armée de l'Air and to Denmark and Turkey.

The subsequent story of the Hun is one of sustained global activity, and to a considerable degree hot-blooded action. It is doubtful that any other Western aircraft has introduced as many pilots to supersonic flight, or indeed to modern aerial warfare generally. It was on 12 March 1956 that the first supersonic fighter in Western Europe, an F-100C, arrived at Bitburg after an air-refuelled Atlantic crossing. On 25 May 1956 my colleague Mark Lambert suffered rainstorms, a babble of European tongues and the constant blast of J57s in full afterburner at Bitburg's first press day. The 36th Fighter Day Wing were busy converting, and the 23rd FD Sqn already had its F-100Cs. Col Brooks, 36th Commander, had quite a bit of PR work to do explaining why it was a comforting thing to have not only booming afterburners but also frequent sonic booms from the sky. Odd that, in 1956, the notion of defence against aggression was a sufficient and complete explanation, whereas in 1974 such defence must not annoy the public. Maj-Gen Robert M. Lee told me bluntly at his HQ at Ramstein 'We're just going to have to live with noise'. Honest and true, but nobody would dare take such a line today.

In June 1956 the Thunderbirds, the prime aerobatic team of the USAF, re-equipped with the F-100C, and in 1958 the Skyblazers, the team of USAFE, did likewise. Pilots will argue endlessly about the suitability of big supersonic fighters for this kind of show. Some said they preferred the F-86 Sabre, Fiat G 91 or Gnat; others welcomed the replacement of the old Hun in both those great teams by the even bigger and beefier Phantom.

Suffice to say that the first displays by both teams after they got their Huns were quite breathtaking, not so much on the score of precision as because the deafening noise and glowing afterburners added an element of drama that no rival could emulate. It was the smoky F-100 that introduced the tradition that the slot-man always flies with a sooty black fin, and I was solemnly assured by the Skyblazers PR man (whom I had facetiously asked about it) that 'The soot is deposited in the air, sir'.

On 19 September 1956 came Exercise Mobile Baker which neatly, and with surprisingly few 'hairy' moments, transferred the 322 FD Group from Foster, in Texas, to Sidi Slimane, Morocco, and thence to Landstuhl, another of the vast NATO 'basic operating platforms' in the Ramstein/Wiesbaden area where USAFE had its HQ. In its day this was no mean operation. The very technique of probe/drogue flight refuelling was still in its infancy, and crossing the grey Atlantic with a single jet—even a J57—behind you is calculated to make the most grizzled veteran imagine all sorts of incipient faults. The tankers were not yet the sleek KC-135s but lumbering KB-50s, which needed every last inch of Lajes, Azores, to become airborne, and then took over an hour to reach the height of the oncoming fighters—which, once they had succeeded in coupling up, hung at a drunken nose-up angle getting heavier and heavier and closer every second to the stall. The rest of the Group's gear came by C-124, which I seem to recall never took less than two days to fly *anywhere*. Having been sorry for the tankers and C-124s I might mention that the Hun pilots wore tight-sealed 'Poopy Suits' that would dehydrate a watermelon.

By June 1957 global deployment was making real progress. The USAFE force had almost reached its planned level of 18 squadrons, with the 48th, 388th and 20th wings converted to the F-100D. All were trained in flight refuelling. On 13 May 1957 six C models left London to fly back to the US, three landing at Jamestown, Virginia (scene of the first English settlement precisely 350 years earlier), and the other three going on to reach Los Angeles in 14 hours 5 minutes. Four days later the Air Force accepted its first F-100F, and four days after that (21 May) Maj Robinson Risner commemorated the 30th anniversary of Charles Lindbergh's epic flight from New York to Paris by flying the same route with the new F—which, after participating in the Paris Show, went to the 20th FB Wing. On the last day of the month Nellis AFB activated the F-100F training unit. In November 1957 Operation Mobile Zebra showed that 16 F-100Cs and 16 F-100Ds could fly non-stop from George to Yokota, Japan, in a pretty tiring 16 hours. Most Huns for the Fifth Air Force, however, went by a slower but probably cheaper route. The aircraft were flown from the NAA Los Angeles plant to McClellan AFB, partially de-equipped and repackaged, cocooned, towed on their un-cocooned wheels 15 miles on public highways to the Sacramento River, transferred to a barge for a

78-mile river journey to NAS Alameda, hoisted up to a US Navy carrier, off-loaded at NAS Yokosuka, transported by lighter across Tokyo Bay to Kisarazu AFB, de-cocooned, flown to Yokota AFB, picked up by pilots of the 8th FB Group and flown to their new home at Itazuke AFB—where, I should think, they were about due for a major overhaul!

I have never been able to discover why the British, who were the original pioneers of flight refuelling, should have ignored the technique except for two brief experiments until the US Air Force and Navy had demonstrated what it could mean in terms of enhanced global mobility. The F-100 was the first fighter in history to take fuel in flight as a routine squadron procedure. The pioneer transoceanic deployments mentioned above were extremely valuable in ironing out dangerous problems. They made it practical, in emergency, to fly out large TAC forces to trouble spots in a way that a few years earlier would have taxed the resources of SAC. Thus, in the Lebanon crisis of May-July 1958, one of the first American units to reach that overheated country was an F-100 wing which half a day earlier had been lounging in the sunshine at Myrtle Beach, N Carolina. Though they hardly had time to pack their tooth-brushes, and suffered terrible difficulties in mid-Atlantic hook-ups in severe thunderstorm turbulence, Gen Jim Hackler's outfit demonstrated once and for all that probes and drogues play a major role in global power.

Three developments in the first half of 1958 were the news that TAC F-100s could deliver tactical thermonuclear ('H') bombs, that nine A models had been delivered to the Air National Guard, and that a D model had made Zell launches. The tactical 'H' bomb was in its day a staggering accomplishment of the American weapons teams in miniaturising the thermonuclear bomb to sizes far smaller than the original fission bombs, about one-hundredth as powerful, had been five years earlier. Indeed, when the F-100 was designed the possibility of any fighter ever carrying any atomic weapon was problematical. The Air National Guard is the aerial reserve force organised by most American states, with fighter, bomber, transport, air-fuelling and other kinds of group attached to TAC, ADC or MAC. The first ANG unit in history to receive a supersonic aircraft was the 150th TF group of the New Mexico ANG, on 12 April 1958, reflecting not only swift delivery of later types of Hun but also introduction to the regular squadrons of later Century-series aircrafts. As for Zell, this name stems from the initials of Zero-Length Launch. NAA pilot Al Blackburn climbed a long ladder in March 1958 to reach the cockpit of an F-100D perched on a special mobile launcher at Edwards AFB. Main motive power for take-off was provided by a Rocketdyne M-34 solid rocket motor giving 130,000 lb thrust, enough for a 4*g* get-away to burn-out at 275 knots, when Blackburn could verify the release of the spent case, retract the gear and climb away normally. Later there were 20 further live Zells, including four out of a simulated bombproof shelter at Holloman AFB. The only snag was that on one occasion the pilot had to bale out because the rocket motor would not jettison. The final blocks of D and F models all had Zell provision, but obvious problems of logistic supply and cost kept the idea from ever being used, and today there are more convenient ways of making tactical aircraft independent of long paved runways.

A far more useful addition at this time was a tail hook, for picking up the cable of a runway arrester system. Such systems were gradually appreciated as being urgently necessary. The F-100 really needed its drag chute, and on a distressing number of occasions—I have heard it put at 1 in 20 landings—the chute failed to deploy properly. Until about 1958 this was just accepted as part of life, and twisted Huns and battered pilots were written off as part of the price of the Cold War. From then on a more thinking attitude emerged which insisted that the greatest possible care be taken of expensive hardware and men. Without runway arrester systems I doubt that many Huns would be around today.

Throughout the late 1950s the Hun equipped 16 USAF wings, and served on every front where the Air Force sought to counter anything that smelt like Red aggression. In 1964 the first Huns went to Viet-Nam. From then until 1971 the faithful F-100 bore a combat burden in SE Asia as heavy as that of any type, chiefly because it was quite good at doing everything. There was still a reluctance to realise that in Viet-Nam type operations Mach 2 is invariably irrelevant, and I think the success of the F-100 came as something of a surprise. Data on the performance of aircraft types, and Air Force units, are available by the ton because the Americans —unlike the British—consider that most knowledge harms nobody. The record in the SE Asia theatre of the F-100 is outstanding. Sortie rates better than 1.2 per aircraft per day continued for seven years, with availability consistently above 80% and turn-round time usually below 30 minutes. In the early days, before 1967, it was not uncommon for aircraft to be damaged or lost through premature explosion of their own ordnance, especially when a triple cluster of bombs became armed within seconds and then tumbled into each other. 'Flying through trees' also seemed to figure in many of the damage reports. By 1966 new ordnance was coming through the pipeline, and battle casualties tended to be due to Viet Cong guns.

Except for aircraft on special operations the F-100s in Viet-Nam were flown by four TF wings, the 3rd, 31st, 35th and 37th. Each had a combat strength of around 50 to 60 aircraft, though it could briefly top 80 or fall below 40. Some idea of how hard these units worked is afforded by the fact that the 3rd TF Wing alone had flown over 100,000 sorties by 1969, and the total F-100 figure in Viet-Nam slightly exceeded the figure of 259,702 combat sorties in World War 2 by nearly 16,000 P-51 Mustangs. As late as 1968 all but about 28 of the F-100s still on Air Force strength were in the active inventory, and it is particularly worth noting that the total number of flying hours of 5,100,000 at that time worked out to something approaching 5,000 hours per aircraft. Again this is a staggering comparison with the kind of fighter lifetime of World War 2 which averaged nearer to 50 hours. Most of the F-100D and F aircraft are still flying, many of them with the ANG.

Right up to the present time the F-100s have been continually updated and improved. They were the first aircraft to be maintained on the Air Force IRAN (inspect and repair as necessary) procedure, which aimed to cut the time and cost of overhauls and keep aircraft constantly in commission. Many is the overhaul shop, in Spain, Italy, Japan or even on Pacific Islands, where IRAN work on F-100s served to transform the capabilities of men who previously had never even seen an F-86. There was plenty of work to be done. The list of change orders and mods for Huns runs into hundreds, and in particular included various types of ECM (especially radar homing and warning systems for secure FAC in Viet-Nam), IFF installations, ILS receivers, a better (electrical) drag-chute control which was tested but never authorised, UHF RDF, secure speech capability and a major programme on structural integrity. Many Huns were taken from combat and turned either into special research aircraft or into RPV directors for use on Air Force missile ranges. One major scheme which did not materialise was to replace the old J57s by either the Spey 25R, as used in the British Phantom, or by the Rolls/Allison TF41 with reheat. The 'Rolls-Royce F-100', or F-100S, was conceived by NAA Los Angeles Division to meet a world need for a low-cost, reliable, long-range, multi-role combat aircraft (they said), with a 50% bigger external load, shorter take-off, 9,000 ft higher combat ceiling, improved rate of climb and 30% longer range. The idea was that engines should be changed during IRAN, but the NATO customers never got beyond saying 'What a marvellous idea?' The year 1964 was marked by the reheat Spey failing to get into the F-100, the Crusader and the F-104, partly because, in my view, top Rolls men did not have the capability of believing such a thing could actually happen.

As late as 1972 there was a combat-ready wing of Huns at RAF Lakenheath, Suffolk, wondering whether they had been forgotten. But they were not quite the last. That honour was reserved for the 524th TF wing at Cannon AFB, New Mexico, which in June 1972 put on an immaculate display with its last 18 F-100Ds, turned them over to the local ANG and replaced them by the ultimate F-111, the F-111F. As I write, in 1974, the Hun equips no fewer than 19 ANG TF groups and far outnumbers all other ANG equipment. Those booming take-offs and jarring landings will be part of the scene for quite a while yet. Thousands of today's Mach 2 pilots cut their supersonic teeth on this fighter. So did Mrs Zaddie Bunker, who in 1959 joined the Mach-Busters Club at the age of 72. There's really nothing to it.

Convair F-102 Delta Dagger

Consolidated Aircraft completed its first year of trading in June 1924, and the founder and president, Major Reuben H. Fleet, was able to announce a profit of $201.98—no mean achievement. Subsequently the corporation absorbed a shoal of other famous names in aviation—Fleet, Hall, Thomas-Morse, Vultee, Stinson and Barkley-Grow among them—and itself became owned by Avco and then by Atlas before becoming a division of General Dynamics in 1954. By this time it was a giant among giants, and one of its nine chief aircraft programmes was the supersonic interceptor which is the subject of this chapter. Winning the contract for the nation's first automatically guided, missile-armed supersonic interceptor was a mighty feather in Convair's cap, and one of the big reasons why General Dynamics had bought the biggest single block of Convair shares. It was therefore a considerable shock to discover that this supersonic interceptor would not fly faster than sound. No matter how the aerodynamicists fiddled with it, the peak Mach number attainable in level flight merely nudged closer and closer to unity, instead of storming past it.

This embarrassing shortfall in performance of the original F-102 is perhaps the most outstanding case in the history of aviation of full-scale drag proving to bear little relation to drag measured in the wind tunnel. It is bad enough when it hits something like a Belfast or VC10, but when it makes a supersonic fighter into a subsonic fighter you may be sure nobody close to the programme is going to get much time off. What subsequently happened was quite unpredictable: a brilliant aerodynamicist at the National Advisory Committee for Aeronautics (NACA) had hit on a simple rule for achieving minimum transonic drag. It happened to be perfectly applicable to the sluggish Convair interceptor, suddenly enabling it to take its proper place among the ranks of supersonic combat aircraft. Swiftly Convair altered all the production tooling and poured out hundreds of the properly shaped aircraft in a very quick time. The profit on the programme was tens of thousands of times $201.98, and the F-102 has ever since been rightly hailed as a great success story. But aerospace is a funny business. Whereas Convair did wonders with the extremely difficult B-58 Mach 2 bomber, flown in 1956, and with the fantastic Atlas intercontinental ballistic missile, flown in 1957, it again ran into a traumatic drag problem when it tried to build the CV-990, a perfectly ordinary four-jet transport looking like a 707 or DC-8. It was this entirely conventional subsonic jetliner that made Convair write-off a crippling $425 million. Among other things this involved a trading loss for the calendar year 1961 of $143 million, which set an all-time record. It made the F-102 look almost easy.

To start the story I must go back to 1945, when Convair shut down most of its 13 operating divisions across the nation yet still kept open huge plants at San Diego, Fort Worth, Wayne, Downey and Nashville. In sharp contrast to Britain and some other American companies, there was a wealth of active projects. One of these was a fighter with a turboprop at the front and jet at the back, and span greater than 50 feet, and the fairest comment on this is that it seemed like a good idea at the time. One of the reasons why this proposed long-range escort fighter slowly went off the boil is that the many teams of Americans that had probed a shattered Germany in the summer of 1945 had come back with a totally new perspective on the future of aviation. They could see that Convair's huge push-pull fighter was really just a piston-engined shape with new engines. The bold Germans had realised that the jet made possible a new realm of performance, which could be properly exploited only by throwing away old shapes and finding new ones. One of these shapes was the delta wing, of triangular form, flying apex-foremost. This had been investigated by Dr Alex Lippisch, who had not only done much tunnel testing of models but had even built a wooden research aircraft, the Dm-1, to test the delta configuration at low speeds.

There are several ways of using a delta wing. You can use it with a conventional tailplane, or with a foreplane. Lippisch proposed to use it without a tailplane, control in the pitching plane being provided by elevators or elevons on the wing trailing edge (which was the rearmost part of the aircraft). What are the advantages of such a layout? Much later Convair summarised them as: '1. Low transonic drag-rise, and reduction of peak drag made possible by low per-cent thickness; 2. Lift potential increases with Mach number to Mach 1 and then drops smoothly, with no lift divergence or abrupt variation in lift-curve slope (slope of lift plotted against angle of attack); 3. Gradual reduction of lift beyond angle for maximum lift, with no tendency to spin or drop out of control at stall; 4. Long wing chord permits greater depth for any low per-cent thickness, allowing light construction with efficient structure; 5. Greater fuel capacity without increase in weight; 6. Favorable structure aids in reduction of flutter, vibration and control problems . . . problem of aileron reversal is eliminated by the rigid wing . . . aeroelastic deformations are negligible; 7. Less shift of airplane neutral point in passing from subsonic to supersonic speeds, and absence of a horizontal tail eliminates erratic transonic stability changes; 8. Aerodynamic disturbances and compressibility effects are minimised; 9. Elimination of tail assembly and high-lift devices simplifies the design.'

This provided much food for thought in 1945. Today we might think it was making a virtue out of necessity to quote item 9, because if the early tailless-delta designer could have found a way of complicating his design by adding high-lift devices he would have jumped at the chance. Today nobody would build a plain delta, and even the ogival slender delta is just one way of doing things if you want to cruise at about Mach 2, but knowledge was more limited 30 years ago. The Army Air Force was glad to get its hands on friend Lippisch, and it took him and his Dm-1 to the United States as fast as it could. When he reached Washington he became a bone that was worried over by both the Army Air Force and the Navy. What happened to the Navy's Lippisch-inspired fighter is told on p. 215. Not to be outdone, the Army Air Force coolly placed a contract with Convair in September 1945 for a pure-delta fighter prototype capable of supersonic speed (Mach 1.2). This was at a time when no British firm was anywhere near to getting a contract for a swept wing for subsonic flight. If anyone had made the reasonable suggestion to the Americans that a supersonic fighter was too big a mouthful to bite off in 1945 the reply would have been 'Sure, we'll just find out the best shape as we go along'.

Convair's Model 7000, or XF-92, was to be powered by an afterburning turbojet and a rocket. It was to have a very big body, unlike Heinemann's Navy fighter, and in the mid position was to be the 6%-thick 60° delta wing, with a third surface of the same shape, and almost as large, serving as the fin and rudder. Perhaps fortunately, for the US taxpayer if nobody else, the fighter contract was cancelled early in 1946; but Convair retained a contract for a simpler full-scale research aircraft having the same aerodynamic form and control system, though of lower performance. The result was the Model 7002, XF-92A, which was a one-off with Air Force serial 46–682. It was trucked by night to Muroc (Edwards) and, after lengthy ground tests, it was lifted briefly off on 9 June 1948. The pilot was E. D. 'Sam' Shannon, chief of experimental flight test for Convair's San Diego division. About four experts out of five had predicted dire trouble, a typical malady being that the delta would be uncontrollable at high angles of attack—especially on landing—and would probably flip on to its back. These predictions proved to be unfounded, and Shannon and colleague Earle G. Martin flew hundreds of missions on white-painted 6682, reaching Mach 0.95 after the engine was fitted with an afterburner, before the first delta in the world was turned over to the NACA.

So successful was the XF-92A that I think it remarkable that so few other US design teams copied it. Certainly Convair, who were unable to patent the delta but got as far as taking advice on the matter, were of the opinion that they had a head start on everyone else and that with a 60° delta wing they could build a better supersonic aeroplane than anything with a wing of a different shape. The Air Force was in no position to disagree, and, as related in the companion book *Bombers of the West*, Convair soon had a major application for this wing in the world's first supersonic bomber. This was obviously a long-term programme; the most immediate application was surely a fighter?

Some of the factors involved in the interception problem have been discussed in earlier chapters. In the piston era it was a totally different problem. By day, in CAVU weather, a fighter pilot was vectored by ground control until he could see the distant speck(s) or trails that represented his enemy. Then he simply picked a target and tried to bring his guns to bear. At night or in bad weather the ground controller could do no more than bring the fighter within a mile or two astern of the enemy; then the fighter had to use its own radar to close in and effect a kill. Early radars were so temperamental and difficult to interpret that a navigator had to be carried to give steering directions to the pilot. This was a great advance in the winter of 1940–41, but by 1949 the US Air Force was looking for something better. By this time bombers could travel up to ten miles every minute, and with nuclear weapons in the bomb bay not one could be allowed to slip through. The old way, with a second man bending over a shaky radar scope, involved two possible sources of human error and unacceptable time-lags. Moreover, it could work only in the traditional curve-of-pursuit interception, in which the fighter tries to get 'on the enemy's tail'. Not only does this severely constrain the flight path and speed of the fighter but it also means that the fighter flies through any chaff dispensed by the bomber, and bears the full brunt of any other kind of rear-facing ECM.

It seemed to the Americans there ought to be a better way. Radar conferred the ability to see the enemy when he might not see you. If you were trying to intercept someone on foot over flat fields you would try to head them off. Instead of following in their footsteps you would look where they were going and make for the same place. In other words you would aim towards the target's future position, rather than the target itself. By 1949 this had crystallised as the 'collision-course' technique. It needed not only good radar vectoring from the ground, and a good AI radar, but also an airborne computer to work out the steering commands and pass these to the fighter's autopilot. Thus the fighter was steered by a synthetic servo-loop, with the pilot outside it just watching; no second man was needed. The radar/computer/autopilot loop would guide the fighter so that, at the ideal moment, armament would be fired towards the point in the sky that the target aircraft would occupy in a few seconds' time. Thus the cannon shells, FFARs or missiles would arrive at that point at the same time as the enemy. General Benjamin W. Chidlaw, Commander of CONAD (Continental Air Defense Command), said the new method would 'come on target instantly, accurately, and so destructively, day or night, in all weather, that no condition of utmost favour to the attacker will be able to put him out of reach to bring him down'. The hardware for collision-course was developed by the infant Hughes Aircraft Co. Howard Hughes had charged General Harold L. George with gathering 'a galaxy of talent' in advanced technology, and George succeeded so well that Hughes swiftly became world leader in AI radar. The first collision-course set was called the E-4. It could lock-on to a target 30 miles away and provide input for a sure-fire collision-course attack. It was fitted to the F-86D Sabre and, in modified form, to the F-89D Scorpion.

In May 1949 the US Air Force called a large conference to explain their thinking on interceptors to carefully screened senior technical staff from industry. The highly classified discussion, presided over by General Sherman H. Fairchild, was not all one-way. Convair was among the companies that expressed the results of their own findings, which tallied with the Air Force in believing that the speed and lethality of bombers of the immediate future would make a fully automatic interceptor essential. The Air Force did not at that time know how protracted and severe would be the development problems with the complicated radar fire-control fitted to the F-86D and F-89D, and even if it had known it would still have considered it prudent to press on with all speed with something even more complex.

At the conclusion of the conference Fairchild asked the engineers to study the problem and propose what kind of interceptor the Air Force ought to buy, primarily to defend the continental United States. It could be big or small, long or short-ranged, armed with guns or FFARs or self-guided missiles, crewed by two men, one man or none, and be subsonic or supersonic. The Air Force suggested it must be supersonic. Industry went away, thought hard and did many small unfunded research programmes, and came back with the answers. The Air Force compared the responses with its own views and sent out an RFP (Request for Proposals) for what it called 'The 1954 Interceptor'. It was stated that this was a full-blown design competition and that the winner would receive a contract for hardware.

Specific requirements laid down in the specification included: supersonic speed; extremely high rate of climb; armament to include either guided missiles (preferred) or multiple FFARs; high manoeuvrability; electronic controls equipped for remote operation; single human pilot; short take-off and landing runs; combat radius of 375 nautical miles;

combat ceiling of 60,000 feet; and very high probability of kill. This basic outline stands up well even today, yet five years later it was by implication condemned by the Air Staff in Whitehall who insisted that no all-weather interceptor could be any good if it did not have two men in it. (But they were hardly in a position to know, as neither they nor the British industry had sufficient information to reach a conclusion. Two years later still the British said no interceptor could be any good unless it had no men in it.)

Convair were invited to bid in what had become known as the MX-1179 programme by letter from Wright Air Development Center of 1 September 1950. The company proposed an aircraft derived directly from the XF-92A, but larger and with radar in the nose instead of a plain air inlet. On 31 August 1951 came a Phase I (design and mock-up) letter contract, followed by an amendment dated 19 December 1951 adding two flying prototypes. Earlier Hughes Aircraft had been awarded the prime contract for the MX-1179 electronic detection, guidance and armament system, which was an advanced development of the E-4. It was evident from the start that the Convair interceptor, known by the company as the Model 8 and by the Air Force as the F-102, was going to pose singularly difficult problems. These went beyond the usual ones of aerodynamics, structures, propulsion and systems; they even went beyond the problem of packaging, which looked like being more difficult than ever before. The fundamental problem was one of programme management. If I get across nothing else in this chapter I want to get across the significance of the fact that the Air Force and its contractors had the vision to see the problem and seek ways of solving it.

There were two parts to the problem. One was caused by the fact that a supersonic automated interceptor was likely to set a new high level in complexity. Traditionally, aircraft had first been designed in broad outline and then the detail engineering had been done and the various items of equipment accommodated. Most of these items were usually standard 'off the shelf' ones, and the aircraft designer merely shoved them in wherever they would fit. It very often happened that the result was not only a mess but also difficult to maintain, but the packing density was low enough for the thing to do its job. With the F-102 it looked as if a fundamental rethink would be necessary. The second part of the problem arose from the fact that complicated aircraft are never exactly right first time. When the prototype is built some parts may be found to need redesign, and many items of equipment may still be awaited. In 1952 the Cold War was icy, and the Korean War had revealed dangerous deficiencies not only in the West's capabilities but also in its whole procurement philosophy. Aircraft such as the F-102 were needed with extreme urgency, and the Departments of Defense and, especially, the Air Force, pondered long and hard on how to minimise the time between the emergence of an undeveloped prototype and the appearance of operational squadrons.

Standing well back to take in the whole scene, the Air Research and Development Command, as it was then called, recognised that what it was buying was not just an aeroplane into which would be stuffed a lot of equipment; it was buying what could only be called a 'weapon system'. The weapon system was the sum total of the things needed to fly the designated interceptor mission. It included the electronic detection and guidance, the armament, and all the supporting test gear, training devices, spares, replacements, tools and even pots of paint. It also included the aircraft, with all its supporting gear right down to special dollies for rolling out the engine or a special 100-foot range for boresighting the radar. It included every item of test and training equipment, and as well as the several volumes of engineering and instructional manuals it included a special mobile library in which to trundle them about neatly. Later the weapon system included a quick-alert hangar and a heat source for testing an infra-red seeker cell. Throughout, the unwavering philosophy was that everything was designed as a part of the whole. Obviously there were going to be occasions when it would be necessary to balance the grand design against cost to the taxpayer. The ladder to reach the cockpit would have to be part of the weapon system, because any old existing ladder would not do; but it might be a waste of taxpayers' money to buy special wheel chocks for each new type of aircraft.

Once the Weapon System Concept, as it was called, had been identified it was possible to do many things in a planned way which previously had been accomplished by a procedure not much better than trial and error. The new concept had one immediate effect on the whole approach to the programme. No longer was the F-102, or any other combat aircraft, thought of as just an aircraft. The thing that would thunder into the sky was merely a portion of the weapon system, and the basic air vehicle (comprising airframe, propulsion and aircraft systems) was merely to package and transport the MX-1179 system which was the heart of the weapon system. (Indeed, more than half the Air Force's weapon systems did not include an air-vehicle portion at all.) This revolution in thought was deliberately emphasised in 1952 to ensure that everyone in the Air Force and its suppliers understood the philosophy. It was really the only possible way to go.

Of course, it raised significant questions of timing, of priorities and of how compatibility was to be achieved. For example, the MX-1179 was specified to include a guided missile. Assuming that, to minimise aircraft drag, the missile(s) should be carried internally, there arose the question of trade-offs between the missile design and the aircraft missile bay. The spacing of the wing spars and fuselage frames might dictate a missile bay x feet long, while the missile might come out to a length of y feet. How much longer must x be than y? In a crunch situation, how does one assign numerical values to the penalties of having x too big or y too small? Looking far into the future, how will y grow to meet demands for extra missile range or warhead lethality? The missile bay would have to allow for future values of y. The objective was not only to achieve perfect compatibility, but to achieve sustained compatibility throughout the operational life of the weapon system by planning ahead to avoid future crises.

In a nutshell, it was intended to try to make the very first F-102 identical in all respects to the last. Though this worthy objective was not to come to pass—and indeed can hardly be more than a pious hope—it was not only a step in the right direction but also the only technique possible. Trying to design the F-102 in the traditional way would, I think, have been self-defeating. It would have taken twenty years of nitpicking to clear the first set of drawings, because several thousand modifications would have been needed each week. Even as it was, it was recognised that, in the real world, the F-102 could never be got right first time. Some changes were bound to be needed; the airframe might need aerodynamic improvement, the Air Force might ask for something new, the engine could change and a few hundred other things could alter even in the few short months of a 'crash programme'. It would thus be rash for Convair's engineering department to release the first set of drawings as production drawings. With the rate of production the Air Force had in mind there might be several hundred F-102s out of the door by the time the full list of modifications was compiled, and it would be a monumental task to rework all of them. At the other extreme one could build a single prototype in hand tooling, see how it worked, then build a second by hand a few months later and eventually, after two or three years, make the grand announcement that the F-102 was at last perfect and that it could go into production. A few more months would then be needed to make production tooling, after which the flood-gates could be opened—a few years too late!

Common sense suggested that neither extreme was the answer. A search was therefore made for what seemed to be the best answer. Lt-Generals Orval R. Cook (mentioned in the F-100 story) and Laurence Craigie, then DCOS-Development, were the architects of the plan that bears their names. Though it has frequently been bent to fit particular programmes, and on a few occasions has been ignored, it is still the ruling procedure for US military aircraft programmes, and has increasingly been adopted by makers of civil aircraft also. Broadly the Cook-Craigie Plan decrees that it shall be assumed that the aircraft is perfect from the start—with every possible effort made to ensure that this is indeed the case—and full 'hard' production tooling shall be made for manufacture at the peak rate. The production process shall begin in a carefully planned manner with a very limited number of aircraft, made in the production jigs, with a kind of funnelling technique, so that though materials and parts are readied for a large quantity, the final assembly effort is concentrated upon the first example. Then the effort switches to the second, and so on. As fast as modifications are agreed they are immediately incorporated in all the tooling. Gradually more and more of the tooling is brought into use, until the peak production rate is reached.

In practice there are many more details to the plan than this broad outline, but the basic objective remains that it attempts to strike the ideal compromise between fast development and minimal disruption. In any given programme the result obviously depends on how nearly right the crucial No 1 machine proves to be. If it is spot-on—and a few aircraft, such as the 727, have been generally better than prediction on the very first flight—then deliberately holding back the rate of production just wastes time. But if things go badly then, even with Cook-Craigie, lots of time and money must be wasted modifying hard tooling and aircraft. It is just a calculated risk, and with many types of aircraft it would be unhelpful to build hand-tooled prototypes because with modern airframes these cannot be truly representative of the production article. The F-102 broke important new ground in that its dense complexity, its timing and the urgency made it the first programme in history to follow the dictates of the Weapon System Concept and the Cook-Craigie Plan. It will be obvious that I think both a good idea. Neither is perfect, but each was an exceedingly carefully planned attempt to do the best thing possible in an imperfect world. It seemed strange that in Britain, where 28 out of 33 contemporary military-aircraft programmes were failures, not only was little attempt made to find out about the American methods but it became fashionable to pour scorn on them. Talking at the time with British officials it became clear that this was largely a reflex defensive mechanism to safeguard their own careers. Even today some people think a weapon system is just the armament carried by a fighter, and few people in British aerospace have even read the now-declassified documents describing how these two very important concepts came into being almost 25 years ago.

In December 1951 Convair were notified that the prototype weapon system would be designated MX-1554, and that the first two aircraft would be styled YF-102 (because with Cook-Craigie there could not be a pure 'XF' prototype). The Air Force also made it quite clear that the company that really called the tune in a crunch was likely to be Hughes Aircraft, because while their MX-1179 system could at a pinch be fitted into different aircraft (even an existing subsonic one, such as the F-89) it would not be a simple matter to find an alternative to it. Five companies had competed for the system, and the win of the still youthful Hughes team was further testimony to their advanced-technology talent. Hughes continued to pile up the No 1 track record in fighter fire-control systems, as well as in some other major areas of defence electronics.

During 1950–52 the MX-1179 went ahead with all possible speed, because it was recognised to be the pacing item in the weapon system. Hughes never included guns, and merely retained FFARs as an easy extra option. The primary armament was to be a completely new free-flying self-guided missile. By mid-1951 the design of this had been largely completed, and test rounds were in production at Culver City, with a big plant at Tucson, Arizona, earmarked as the future home of Hughes missiles. Known as the Falcon, the missile was a tube the size of a tall but slim man. At the front was a guidance package, signals from which governed the control actuators driving four fins on the trailing edges of the long, very acute delta wings. The aerodynamics of the Falcon family is a subject for a book in itself, and suffice to say here that the Falcon was the first of a totally new species of supersonic self-guided vehicle able to change trajectory in any direction without banking and able to outmanoeuvre any conceivable manned aircraft. The first Falcon had a solid-fuel rocket motor which accelerated it violently to about Mach 2.3 and then left it to coast while under full control for a range of about five miles. It had a warhead detonated by both impact and proximity fuses and powerful enough to destroy a large bomber by a near miss.

From those pioneer days in 1950–51 Hughes appreciated that it ought to be possible to use at least two methods of guidance. One was to make the missile home on to the heat (infra-red) radiation from the target. Tests showed that, though the hot gas actually forming the jet would be unhelpful, an IR seeker mounted at the focus of a Cassegrain reflector (like an astronomical telescope) could detect hot jet parts at a range of several miles. But there were many problems. Most seeker cells needed to be refrigerated, and were erratic in behaviour. They could lock-on to the Sun, or to the Sun's reflection on a lake or even to a friendly factory chimney! And in rain or thick cloud the effective range fell to an unacceptably short distance. So Hughes decided to make the first Falcon a semi-active radar homer. In the nose was mounted a sensitive radar receiver aerial able to pick up energy beamed by the fighter's radar at the target and reflected back towards the missile. Like all homing methods the accuracy of this kind of guidance system increases as the missile closes on its quarry, and Hughes judged it the best answer. Very nearly 2,000 lb of pressurised and air-conditioned electronics made up the rest of the MX-1179 system, including the extremely advanced radar operating in search and lock-on modes, autopilot links and weapon-control electronics.

Compared with the XF-92A the YF-102 was about 25% larger and twice as heavy. Instead of having a centrifugal Allison J33, rated at 8,200 lb with afterburner, it was planned around a two-spool axial engine rated at about 15,000 lb. For a while GE and Wright had candidate engines, but the wholly predictable choice was the big, robust and efficient Pratt & Whitney J57, the YF-102 receiving the P-11 version rated at 14,500 lb with afterburner. The airframe was noteworthy for the extensive use of machined skins and frames, most of the wing skin being 0.250 in light alloy sculptured down to 0.064 in to form large but shallow integral fuel tanks. There was no room for fuel in the big fuselage, because in addition to the 'black boxes', and the massive engine, the whole lower portion was occupied by a bay containing six Falcon missiles as described later. Electric power was generated by an alternator and d.c. generator driven via a reduction gearbox by an air-turbine motor running on engine bleed. Large fairings revealed the positions of the power units for the rudder and for the outer elevons, the inner-elevon power units being in the fuselage. The leading edges of the wing and fin were anti-iced by engine bleed air discharged through 'piccolo tubes' and, in the production machine, through novel sheets sintered from microscopic stainless-steel spheres by a new company called Aircraft Porous Media. Altogether the F-102 looked neat and workmanlike, but rather stumpy for a supersonic aeroplane.

Known as Air Force system MX-1554, and as the Convair Model 8-80, the first YF-102 bore Air Force serial number 52-7994 and it was trucked secretly from San Diego to Edwards in September 1953. Convair's chief project test pilot, Richard L. Johnson, flew the aircraft on 24 October, and on the whole things were satisfactory. On subsequent flights he, Martin and Shannon pushed out the performance envelope and found all kinds of trouble. There was severe buffet at Mach 0.9 and at about 0.93 uncontrollable yaw oscillations were met which appeared to endanger the aircraft. Urgent modifications were put in hand. Then, taking off for flight 7 on 2 November 1953 the engine flamed out soon after rotation, with the fighter sharply nose-up at a low altitude. Convair described what happened as a wheels-up landing, but as the machine was a write-off they eventually decided to call it a crash. This threw frantic pressure on to ship No 2 (52-7995) and on to the seven production-test aircraft ordered on 1 February 1952. All seven were on the line when the first YF-102 flew, together with the first half-dozen of an additional 33 production machines ordered in a definitive contract on 17 December 1952. The Air Force judged the F-102 such a bag of tricks that they thought all 42 might be needed to complete development in minimum time, and losing the first at the start of the programme was just what the Cook-Craigie plan didn't want.

The second YF flew on 11 January 1954. It was virtually identical to the first, and it was soon painfully apparent that it was indeed subsonic. The engine was giving its full rated thrust, yet at 26,000 lb (well under gross weight) at 35,000 ft the maximum level Mach number was 0.990. On 27 January 1954 it refused to go beyond 1.06 in a dive, whilst bucking and protesting violently. On 14 April it emerged with a new (Case X) wing with a cambered leading edge and reflexed tips. What had been done was bend down the leading edge of the wing to form a portion of the surface of a cone, the root rib being unchanged and the rest being progressively more rounded and drooped towards the tip. This improved performance at altitude, at moderate to high angles of attack. In addition the rear fuselage, where severe flow breakaway was obviously occurring, was extended aft and the elevon/fuselage fillet was modified. This greatly reduced the violence of the yaw oscillation, and 7995 was dived on 2 May 1954 to Mach 1.29. On the other hand the maximum level speed remained obstinately stuck at Mach 0.996. So 7995 went back into the Edwards hangar for more round-the-clock rework. The wing tips were again removed and replaced by fully cambered tips instead of the 10° reflex profile. A large elevon/fuselage fairing was added and the nose was extended, making it more pointed. Big deal! Level Mach number rose by 0.001 to 0.997.

In March the first so-called 'production F-102A', with serial 53-1781, made its first flight. This was obviously not going to be a production machine, any more than the rest of the aircraft to this standard, called Model 8-82. Ship 31781 and its sisters did good work in systems development, but it was painfully evident that the F-102 would have to be re-thought from stem to stern if it was to go into service with the Air Force. Poor Convair! Having done a good engineering job with the very challenging Model 8 they were victims of optimistic tunnel results which made them, alone among Western planemakers, incapable of exceeding the speed of sound with a product contractually committed to reaching Mach 1.5.

With some of their contracts the response of the Air Force would have been instant termination. Such a shortfall would have been ample grounds for doing so, but the Air Force badly needed the F-102—and so did Convair. While keenly looking at the engineering problems involved in packaging the MX-1179 system inside an F-100 or F-101, the best answer seemed to be to pull out all the stops to make the F-102 work. And it was sheer luck that the NACA had the answer all ready, to avoid more than a large hiccup in the programme, and certainly to avoid abandoning the F-102 and going through ulcermaking Congressional inquiries trying to pin down the blame for gross incompetence, in public.

Credit for one of the truly great discoveries in aviation goes to tousled, ebullient John Stack, who in 1949 was Assistant Director of the NACA Langley Lab. He devised a form of perforated working section for transonic tunnels, capable of bridging the vital gap between about Mach 0.9

and 1.2. By 1951 such a tunnel was fully operative at Langley, and young Richard T. Whitcomb, head of transonic tunnels, was given the job of exploring airflow patterns, shock-waves and drag of various wing/body combinations over this previously 'forbidden' range of Mach numbers. Early in 1952 Whitcomb confirmed one of the most useful little rules ever devised. He found that, within wide limits of shape and Mach number, a transonic body has minimum drag if its total cross-section varies in a smooth and regular way from nose to tail. Thus, if you add an excrescence, such as a wing, you must compensate for it by subtracting from the total (ie, by making the body slimmer). Thus was born the Area Rule, first formally stated (and classified, because of its defence implications) in December 1953. Broadly it states that, if you take transverse slices across a transonic or supersonic body, the plot of slice areas should make a smooth curve from nose to tail. This is a far more important rule than the discovery by Küchemann that a body ought to be waisted at the root of a swept wing, to conform to the optimum streamline directions, though in practice the two rules sometimes seem to have similar results.

Convair obviously wanted to slim down the F-102 above the wing. They did what they could, but the inside was full of engine and ducting, large air flasks and avionics. Underneath was the tightly tailored missile bay. The answer was self-evident: instead of waisting in the middle one could add at the ends. The result was the Convair YF-102A, Model 8-90. This was one of the most significant modifications ever made to any aircraft, and it was done by working day and night for 117 days. The first 8-90, serial number 53-1787, was known in the San Diego works as the Hot Rod. Compared with the 8-82 it had an area-ruled fuselage, with a length extended from 52 ft 5 in to more than 68 ft. The whole fuselage was redesigned, with greatly modified intakes, canopy and vertical tail, and with systems considerably redesigned and relocated. The acute vee windshield and nearly flat-sided canopy reduced drag but spoilt forward view, and this was not fully restored by drooping the nose radome and pointing the axis of the nose downwards. Later a thin black partition was added along the vertical centreline inside the windshield to get rid of annoying internal reflections. A further major improvement to the Hot Rod was the J57-P-41 engine with titanium LP section, rated at 15,500 lb thrust.

When the Hot Rod was rolled out at San Diego everyone noticed the huge streamlined fairings—officially called Yellow Canary extensions—which had been added on each side of the jet pipe to conform to the area rule. Someone likened these to Marilyn Monroe, but for years afterwards the press commonly thought the likeness stemmed from the supposed wasp-waisted fuselage; this was more properly likened to a Coke bottle, and 'to Coke' became a transitive verb. There was even some erudite discussion on hydrodynamics, wondering why girls are not faster swimmers than men.

Soon after the Hot Rod's roll-out the engine-runs and taxying tests were done openly at Lindbergh Field, because the appearance of the F-102 had been disclosed on 27 February 1954. Then on 16 December 1954 the longer, and far more shapely, fighter was trucked to Edwards, and there Dick Johnson made a shakedown flight on 20 December. On the following day he did a maximum level run at 35,000 ft and reached Mach 1.2, with remarkable absence of buffet and snags. You just have to get the shape right, and this was the most famous case in aviation history of getting it right second time.

On 29 December No 1787 exceeded 52,000 ft, and on 21 January 1955 it reached 55,130 ft, which I think may still be a record for the F-102. The same aircraft went on to complete Air Force Phase II (flying qualities, stability and control, and systems) development testing in the hands of Air Force pilots until March 1956. It went on to help with the development of the F-106, mentioned later. Not until the spring of 1955 could Convair and the Air Force breathe a sigh of relief and agree that they knew the production configuration, the Model 8–10. Initial testing for this began with one of the rebuilt YFs, 53–1791. It followed very closely to the standard of 1787, and flew on 24 June 1955. While 1787 had not explored the region beyond Mach 1.2, 1791 did; it immediately encountered severe aerodynamic buzz (high-frequency structural vibration excited by a buffet condition) and this took until January 1956 to cure. It was singularly difficult to trace the root causes, but after more than 100 flights 1791 had acquired an extended engine air inlet ramp, with a bifurcated duct wedge and stiffened duct internal wall. After a lot of refinement to the inlets the specification Mach number of 1.5 was satisfactorily demonstrated, about two years later than Convair had hoped. On 18 January 1956 this aircraft reached a level Mach number of 1.535, which again I believe to be a record for the type (and not a bad figure, because it is a good deal higher than the limit reached by the smaller F-100 with a similar engine).

Following Air Force Phase IV testing 1791 was modified in September 1956 for flight trials with a modest 192 gal tank on a pylon under each wing, and after extensive tunnel testing to predict success both tanks were jettisoned together at 36,515 ft at Mach 0.953—the highest speed attainable with tanks on—on 27 December. By this time more than 40 aircraft were flying, and the Cook-Craigie plan was letting rate of output build up at last. But there was still a major modification to come. On 10 December 1955 aircraft 53–1813 flew with a markedly taller fin, to provide increased directional stability and a better margin against roll-coupling. This programme was completed in April 1956 and the big fin was adopted for production on the 66th aircraft (55–3357), and fitted as a retroactive mod on nearly all the aircraft previously built. Further changes were made to the speed brakes hinged behind the tail, which were increased in area by extending them upwards, and the J57–P–23 was selected as the production engine. This retained a titanium front end but incorporated many improvements and was rated with afterburner at 17,200 lb thrust. Aircraft 54–1380 cleared the final production configuration on 2 April 1957. By this time roughly half the production batch had flown, and the 873rd and last F-102A Delta Dagger (57–909) was rolled out in April 1958.

Before I discuss the F-102 itself I should deal with two offshoots which do not really find a place in this book. One is the TF-102A side-by-side conversion trainer. Convair received a design contract for the TF on 5 May 1953, a contract for 20 in March 1954 and a letter contract on 12 April. The first TF, serial 54–1351, flew on 31 October 1955. The buffet problems were severe, and all sorts of canopy changes and fixes were tried, but eventually the aircraft was released for performance testing in November 1956. It proved to be persistently subsonic (0.985) but 63 of these pleasant dual-control machines were delivered, and I twice had the pleasure of trying one for myself so it must be a real old man's aeroplane. The other offshoot is a much hotter ship, and should be considered a second-generation machine. On 28 April 1955, after years of study mainly involving the Wright J67–W–1 (Americanised Olympus) engine, Convair received a contract for 17 of a redesigned fighter called F-102B, with the Pratt & Whitney J75. It was again planned as the air-vehicle portion of a Hughes weapon system, the new system being the MA-1 incorporating the Super Falcon missile and Genie nuclear rocket, and interfacing by automatic data link with the SAGE (Semi-Active Ground Environment) radar and communications net which was then being stretched over most of the continental United States. In 1955 the new fighter was redesignated F-106, and later named the Delta Dart. It flew on 26 December 1956 (a tandem-seat trainer followed on 9 April 1958) and eventually 345 were built, or about one-third as many as Convair had hoped. This was despite the fact that it proved a super all-weather interceptor, roughly twice as fast as the 102 (gaining a world speed record in December 1959 at 1,525 mph) and having a much greater range and ceiling. The 106 is still the standard ADC interceptor.

So let us return to 1955. In June I spent a day at Convair San Diego, a week after they had delivered the first service-cleared F-102A (53–1791) to the Air Force. Usually when I go plant-visiting the last thing I want to do is wear out shoe-leather tramping round the production line—I want to get in a huddle with the engineers and make legible notes—but I am grateful to Bernard F. Coggan, the genial general manager, for giving me no option. I had never before seen more than 100 seventy-foot fighter fuselages on the same line. Neither had I seen a US Air Force aircraft where the whole exterior was primed and then smoothly painted in a pale grey. Certainly it was new to find a fighter with an internal weapon bay longer than that of a B-17—indeed old Fort crews may find it hard to believe that the F-102 is, in side view, only fractionally smaller than their four-engined 'heavy'. Certainly it costs about 15 times as much, and today even that is cheap.

Most of what I learned in 1955 could not be printed, but no part of the F-102 is classified today. As initially released to the Air Force the MG-3 fire-control system was fitted, incorporating most of the MG-10 (MX-1179) but having a significantly lower capability in some respects. Huge electronics racks filled almost the whole cross-section in front of and behind the cockpit, In the cockpit the two dominant features were the big radar viewing hood and the dual joysticks, one for each hand. In the missile bay were six compartments, three in front and three behind, closed by long doors arranged to flip open for two seconds to release a missile. During those two seconds a pair of long hinged arms, the missile displacement gear, would swing down under the sudden thrust of a hydraulic ram to extend the chosen missile below the aircraft just before its release. The Falcon itself had originally enjoyed the status of a pilotless fighter, its designation being XF-98. Then it went into service as GAR-1 (Guided Air Rocket) and finally acquired a third title as AIM-4 (Air Interception Missile). About 4,000 of the original GAR-1 variety were delivered, most of these being used up in test and training programmes. The main production, chiefly for the F-102, was of two versions. The AIM-4A was a development of GAR-1 but with better manoeuvrability gained by carrying the control surfaces on outriggers well behind the wings; about 12,000 of these were built in 1956–59. The AIM-4C had an IR heat seeker inside its transparent nosecap. About 9,500 of these were delivered in the same timescale. Late in 1959 many thousands of 4C missiles were given the improved IR homing head of a later Falcon (AIM-4G) to produce the AIM-4D. From 1957 it became standard for a 102 to carry three AIM-4A radar Falcons and three 4C heat-seekers. Built into the four centre missile doors were tandem launch tubes for 24 2.75 in FFARs, but by 1957 the Air Force had ceased to regard these as worth having and later the tubes were blanked off.

How did one use the world's first supersonic interceptor? To its pilots it was always the Deuce, because to a card-player the number 102 is one-zero-deuce. Despite its size and shape the Deuce very soon became popular, for it was a formidable yet remarkably forgiving aeroplane. It entered combat service with 327 FIS at George AFB, which had been the first F-100 base a year earlier, in June 1956. By the end of 1958 the Deuce equipped 25 ADC squadrons, and the bulk of the early production—some 500 machines—were being recycled through Convair's production flight centre at Palmdale to receive the complete MG-10 fire-control system. In 1960–62 the final modifications were made, the MG-10 data-link aerial in the nosewheel door being coupled to interface the aircraft with SAGE (or, a decade later, with the Nadge system in Europe) and a small glass dome ahead of the windshield revealing the location of the new IR seeker cell, cooled by liquid nitrogen, which made it certain that no heat-homing Falcon could be launched until it had locked-on to the correct target. By his time the Deuces had largely been displaced by the F-106 in Stateside ADC squadrons, but they were very fully employed in the Air National Guard and in USAFE (US Air Force Europe) and PACAF (Pacific Air Forces). The F-102 was never equipped for flight refuelling, and so had to be sent overseas by ship. Several squadrons served in USAFE with the 86th Air Division, with HQ at Ramstein. Unlike many American tactical aircraft they were not much bothered by the leaden skies and drizzle of north-west Europe, and a dozen or two were always at instant readiness for a call to scramble and identify something that had been picked up by the Nadge system but which had not filed a flight plan with the West.

These Deuces on stand-by were parked inside Zulu hangars, special alert bases facing the active runway. Each Zulu typically comprised a central living quarters, with the predictable steak 'n eggs and air-conditioning, surrounded by four one-plane cells. Each Deuce had to be ready to go, with no inertial platform to run up and align. On a warning being sounded, the pilot would slide straight into the cell via a firemen's pole, and it soon seemed to have become fashionable for him to leave the partial-pressure suit behind. Up the ladder and he initiates the start sequence, assisted by well co-ordinated ground-crew hands fixing the seat harness and pulling and stowing the ejection-seat safety pins. Three minutes from the alarm the 102 is in full afterburner on the runway. At 31,500 lb, with three of each kind of Falcon and 891 gallons of fuel, a firm pull on the right-hand joystick makes the 102 rotate and lift off at about 220 knots. Then into a 'buster' (maximum cold thrust) climb, at 325 knots, up to wherever the controller says. Even without its drop tanks a Deuce is not the world's greatest climber, but it can get to 35,000 ft in well under 4 minutes.

Though the ground control can feed straight to the autopilot and thence to the flight controls, it is usual to have voice commands and fly manually. Pitch and yaw dampers are normally operative, and if desired the auto-pilot attitude-hold, heading lock or height lock can be engaged. Soon the pilot needs the radar. Today's airborne radars can have bright picture tubes which even in sunlight need no viewing hood. The Deuce, however, does need one, because the MG-10 is getting a bit long in the tooth. The pilot has to bend forward, extending his inertia-reel harness, until his eyes cover the top of the hood. With the left joystick he deflects the axis of the scanner in the search mode, rocking the little stick left and right while the beam sweeps the sky ahead from $37\frac{1}{2}°$ above to 20° below. Rocking the stick fore and aft sweeps the range gate and aligns it with the echo to be locked on. A small wheel, which he can feel for with the left hand, adjusts the scan elevation when the blip has been identified. Thus he flies, one hand on each stick and both eyes pressed against the radar hood. No chance of a mid-air collision; he'd see any conflicting traffic on the scope. The book says so.

With a bit of luck the Deuce pilot comes up behind the interloper and can identify it, reading out its identification marks over the R/T. It is, of course, some chap from a rival fighter outfit who has been sent over to provide practice. The F-102 jock may fire the WESM (Weapon Evaluation System Missile) at him. This is a Falcon painted bright blue. It flicks out at the opportune moment, but stays firmly attached to the swinging arms. Inside it a film cassette records the target and all fire-control parameters, and a second camera photographs the radar picture at the same moment. In a real attack the Deuce pilot would have selected IR or radar missiles, depending on the weather and a few other factors, and let the MG-10 system carry on by itself. All he has to do is press the trigger on the right stick to arm the firing sequence, and, in the case of an IR missile, link in the IR sight (though the old radar has fair IR capability, and that is all the Deuce had in its first seven years of service). Mission accomplished, he peels off and wishes it was permitted to make a sonic boom. Endurance is around 2 hours, and peacetime landing minima are 200 feet and half a mile, with ILS or GCA. It is possible to fly a light Deuce at 120 knots but the usual drill is to extend the runway hook, pull up the nose to 17° and cross the end of the runway at well over 140 knots. In no time he is back in the Zulu hangar and ready for debriefing.

All good things come to an end. Today the Deuce, still linked into the Nadge system, is serving in the air forces of Greece and Turkey. I do not believe they ever did fight each other, though Turkish F-102s were reported to have shot two Hellenic F-5s into the Aegean during the conflict of mid-1974. While these sad things were going on within the NATO alliance, the US Air Force was test flying an RPV (remotely piloted vehicle) PQM-102 in a programme called Pave Deuce. They chose the F-102 because of the immense amount of racking space available for the new black boxes, after removal of the original fire-control system. As I write, in late 1974, Sperry are converting a further 24, for the surprisingly modest sum of $11.5 million, for use as missile targets at Holloman AFB. It's far better than going to the silent graveyard not far away at Davis-Monthan where old combat aircraft gradually shrivel up in the desert air.

Lockheed F-104 Starfighter

In 1952, as the sunlight glinted from the swept wings of Mig-15s tangling with Sabres high over the Yalu river, Kelly Johnson sat doodling in his office in California. Clarence L. Johnson was then the chief engineer of Lockheed Aircraft Corporation, and in 19 years his doodles had helped lift the company from near-bankruptcy to become No 3 planemaker in the world. Now, he was trying to plan a new fighter—a fighter that would outperform all the opposition and suffer from none of the shortcomings that the Korean war had revealed in other American fighters. Like Ed Heinemann, 15 miles away in another part of Los Angeles, he was convinced that his country's combat aircraft had become too big, too heavy, too complex and too costly. They were deficient in ceiling, high-altitude manoeuvrability and ease of maintenance. He wanted to make exactly the right compromise that would provide a fighter that would not only make the American pilot supreme but would also sustain a huge production programme to succeed the F-80/F-94 family in the Lockheed works.

The result, the F-104 Starfighter, is one of the most controversial aircraft in history. In appearance it fully justifies its epithet of 'The missile with a man in it', for it was, and perhaps still is, the most breathtaking fighter ever planned for production. After overcoming serious development problems it demonstrated performance as high as pilots cared to experience, and a potential greater than engines could exploit. But it proved a disappointment in operational service. It was extremely limited in what it could do, was very 'unforgiving' and potentially dangerous in the hands of an inexperienced pilot, and suffered more than its fair share of teething troubles. Then, when it looked as if the programme would terminate at the 295th aircraft (about one-tenth as many as Lockheed expected), everything took off in a way that can fairly be described as fantastic. By turning the simple day interceptor into a dense-packed, complicated, all-weather, multi-mission aircraft Lockheed pulled off the greatest coup in aviation history. The new resulting Super Starfighter was built under licence in West Germany, the Netherlands, Belgium, Italy, Canada and Japan, and used as the chief aerial weapon system of these and other countries. Almost 2,000 of the 'Super' version were built; but again there were many problems, and in Germany the number of crashes and pilot fatalities became a national scandal. The sweeping success became just slightly tarnished, and various plans for developments of the F-104 bore no fruit until, late in 1973, Lockheed at last succeeded in sewing up an agreement with Italy to see what could be done.

Like so many other bold and enterprising aircraft, the F-104 seemed to be a good idea at the time. It would be making excessive use of the benefit of hindsight to try to fault Johnson's philosophy in 1952, and certainly I do not propose to criticise Lockheed's ability to engineer good hardware. The shortcomings of the F-104, in all its versions, stem from the over-riding design goal of reducing size and weight in order to increase performance. On the other hand, in 1952 there was not much else Johnson could do. It is the great development in thrust/weight ratio and specific fuel consumption of today's engines that have made possible really good fighters suffering from no deficiencies. And the cry of the top brass and the combat-blooded men from Korea for more speed and more height was so insistent that Johnson could scarcely have been expected to foresee that this view was slightly off-target.

After all, when you are in business selling aeroplanes to the military it is foolish not to pay the closest attention to what the customer says, and the combat pilot just back from operations is likely to tell it straight and in pretty plain language. Given the available technology of more than 20 years ago the F-104 seemed to be the one bold answer to the challenge of making a light simple fighter with highly supersonic performance, just as Heinemann's Skyhawk seemed to be the ideal answer for a Mach 0.9 attack machine. I am sure if anyone had told Johnson, or the US Air Force, 20 years ago that the most successful fighter would not be a light simple design at all but a complicated jagged monster weighing well over 25 tons and driven by two F-104 engines, they would have received the news in stony disbelief.

In fact, Lockheed's first major essay into the problem of finding the best new fighter to replace the very successful F-80 Shooting Star, F-94 Starfire and T-33 (T-bird) was a distinct step up the scale of size and complexity. Like the McDonnell XF-88 Voodoo, the Lockheed XF-90 was a big twin-engined 'penetration fighter' intended to fly long-range escort missions rather as the P-51 Mustang had done five years earlier. It looked good, but Westinghouse fell down on its propulsion and by 1951 the Air Force had in any case become disenchanted with the specification. But Lockheed's fighter projects multiplied. The company had the benefit of the extremely valuable classified flight data from both the Air Force X-1 and Navy Skyrocket families of supersonic research aircraft, and also was running its own programme of flight trials up to Mach 4.0 at over

150,000 feet using the X-7 ramjet test vehicles. This programme provided a solid bedrock of data on the aerodynamic and aeroelastic behaviour of a range of configurations and wing shapes, and in particular suggested that for Mach numbers greater than 2 a very good wing would be short, stubby, unswept and very thin indeed. Such wings seemed too difficult to many other companies, but Lockheed had already built and flown them on the X-7 vehicles and had lost its fears. It made a wing only 3% thick and tunnel-tested it on the XF-90, at a time when British designers were trying to make a thick swept wing for subsonic aircraft.

It is ironic that if the Korean war had never happened the XF-90 formula might ultimately have yielded a superb multi-role fighter. For example the XF-88 was developed into the F-101, and the XF-90 could eventually have been turned into something very like the Phantom II. Another promising project was the L-205, with a thin straight wing well aft and a big air duct on top behind the canopy. Johnson found this a very good configuration, and the air duct arrangement was later used successfully for the North American F-107 and Boeing's TFX submission. All these Lockheed projects weighed 25,000 to 45,000 lb. This is a very fair weight bracket for a fighter, and armed with their aerodynamic and structural knowledge Lockheed could probably have created the top multi-role fighter for the period 1955–70. But the sudden appearance of those shiny little Migs in Korea cast an almighty spanner into the works.

Johnson went across the Pacific to see on the spot how his F-80 was doing and what the Air Force was learning from combat experience. He found the cry for greater flight performance had reached such a pitch that pilots were rather strongly suggesting that a great many things should be 'left off' future fighters, and if possible removed from their own. It is hard to believe that the items regarded as expendable included ejection seats, wheel parking brakes, duplicated flying-control systems, armour and even fuel. Col 'Gabby' Gabreski, the top US 'ace' of World War 2, typified opinion by scorning the radar gunsight of the F-86, saying 'I'd rather sight with a piece of chewing gum stuck on the windscreen'. The general attitude was 'I want to fly faster and higher than the enemy, and pull tighter turns, and I'm prepared to sacrifice almost all the vital bits of my airplane to do it'. There were several things that could be done. Existing aircraft could be 'stripped' to improve performance. A new fighter could be designed to a similarly stripped specification. A new fighter could be designed that was not really devoid of anything yet which was much smaller and lighter than the machines in Korea. Or a new fighter could be designed that was bigger and heavier than the early jets yet which had a good flight performance and large payload. North American and McDonnell chose the last formula for the F-100 and F-101, and I do not think regretted it. But Johnson hearkened to the combat pilots and hitched his wagon to the star of minimum weight and maximum performance. He aimed at 15,000–18,000 lb gross weight.

He comments 'The large-airplane exponents claimed that equal speed, range and fighting power could not be obtained in a smaller airplane because such fixed items as the pilot size, canopy size, engine thrust per square foot of frontal area, and fixed equipment item weights, were a smaller percentage of the large-airplane weight than of the smaller one. Likewise, the fuselage cross-section and size, in general, would be unfavourable for the smaller airplane, resulting in lower ratios of lift to drag and thrust to drag, even if the same percentage fuel weight could be carried. There was not in existence a small engine which had as good thrust/weight ratios or specific fuel consumption as the larger engines then available. These factors were all true at the time; so it was necessary to make some rather major advances on practically all of these fronts before a successful light weight fighter could be developed.'

One instructive exercise carried out in early 1952 was to see what, in fact, could be accomplished by the stripping process. Johnson took one of his projects, a 31,849 lb machine (looking very much like a big F-104) powered by the proposed Wright J67 version of the Bristol Olympus, and removed 'half the armament, half the instruments, ejection seats, drag parachute, dual boosters, fire-detection equipment, and various other elements' while keeping the same mission radius and landing field length. The structure and fuel weights were reduced, but the engine was regarded as a fixed entity and not 'rubberised' in the way that is possible when things exist only on paper. The result was a reduction in weight to 28,100 lb and very marginal improvement in performance, indicating in Johnson's opinion that this game was not worth the candle. The process was done in a more subtle way by Heinemann in planning the Skyhawk, as related in that chapter of *Attack Aircraft of the West*.

There followed an intense year of parametric study, in which a project staff examined the effect of thousands of bigger or smaller changes in paper designs to see where the best compromise could be found. In 1953 aircraft speeds had been increasing much more rapidly than at any other time before or since. A year or two earlier there had been a 'sound barrier', and it still had considerable importance in Britain where such fighters as the Javelin, Vixen and Scimitar, all years away from service, were still irremediably subsonic. But in the United States Johnson was trying to decide whether to go for Mach 2 or Mach 3. In the end he chose 2.2, simply because this was the compressor-inlet duct limit of available engines; he was not bothered by the Mach 2.2 thermal limit of light-alloy structures, because interceptors do not 'soak' for very long at full speed. Indeed the central equations in the parametric analysis dealt with the interaction between fuel capacity, acceleration times (say, from Mach 0.9 to 2.2), maximum Mach number, and the combat time during which the aircraft could fly with full afterburner. Though the term specific excess power (SEP) had not then been coined, this was one of the crucial factors determining what this, or any other, fighter could do. It is a measure of the excess engine power available for climb, acceleration or manoeuvres at constant speed.

By 1953 the Lockheed project staff had arrived at the general form of a fighter having an extremely small and thin unswept wing and a large body housing a single engine and all fuel. In March 1953, after many discussions with the Air Force, a contract was placed for two prototypes of a day interceptor to exceed Mach 2 and have a combat ceiling over 60,000 feet. It was designated XF-104 (Weapon System 303A) and Lockheed called it the Model 83. A little later it received the Lockheed name Starfighter, which the Air Force adopted.

Johnson was fortunate in that the Model 83 appeared to be ideally sized and timed to use the outstanding X-24A engine being developed at General Electric for the Mach 2 B-58 bomber. This turbojet differed from the bigger J57 in having a single shaft, the high-pressure compressor being equipped with seven rows of variable-incidence stator blades to give good handling and fast acceleration. It was designed to be considerably lighter than the J57, at least as good in specific fuel consumption and not far short of the Pratt & Whitney engine in thrust, both dry and with full afterburner. Like the J57 the afterburner was planned to be all or nothing, with no intermediate settings. The production engine, designated J79, was to be available in 1956; this was too late for the F8U, F-101 and some other supersonic fighters, but Johnson was so impressed by the promise of high performance and light weight that he accepted the wait. Meanwhile he planned to use the Wright J65-W-6, an Americanised afterburning version of the British Sapphire rated at 10,200 lb, in the two XF-104 prototypes. During 1953 the research and engineering design pace on the XF-104 was as fast as anything in aviation history (this sort of phrase keeps cropping up, proving what a remarkable programme this was).

More than 290 configurations were explored, many of them in the form of detailed and fully instrumented models tested in tunnels at NACA Ames Lab and elsewhere. Many of the configurations were attempts to cure the problem of pitch-up, suffered in greater or lesser degree by almost all high-speed aircraft. Its cause may be that an increase in angle of attack (due to pulling g, or reducing speed) puts the horizontal tail in violently turbulent downwash from the wing; it may be due to strong vortices from the front fuselage or engine ducts, or in a swept-wing design may be caused by tip stall. Whatever the reason it must be searched for and guarded against, and the Lockheed aerodynamicists tried every conceivable position for the slab tailplane (stabiliser), as well as a T-tail plus a rectangular tailplane below the rear fuselage, foreplanes, strakes along the rear fuselage and even high-power boundary-layer control on large areas of the wing, fuselage and canopy. As other chapters of this book emphasise, many fighter designers found the answer to be a very low tailplane. With the XF-104 it was found that this almost always cured pitch-up 'but, when it did, the normal longitudinal stability, the directional stability, drag, weight and overall combat utility of the airplane were seriously compromised'.

This problem of pitch-up was almost insurmountable. Eventually it was decided to use a high T-tail and fit a special system to provide artificial warning and stability (just the sort of thing the Korean veterans wanted to leave out!). Research showed this APC (auto pitch control) system had to include not only an angle of attack sensor but also a second element sensing rate of pitch, because at high speeds it would be possible to add-on g at the rate of 5 every half-second. The final answer chosen in October 1953 was a fully powered, irreversible T-tail, made as one slab, with an APC system having two angle of attack vanes and a rate-gyro amplifier feeding a stick shaker and auto pitch actuator driving the tail. It was far more complicated than anything seen in earlier fighter control systems; and it still fell short of what was needed.

Undoubtedly the most radical feature of the XF-104 was the wing, measuring a mere $7\frac{1}{2}$ feet along the leading edge which had the unprecedented radius of 0.016 in (almost sharp enough to serve as a knife). Thickness was a fantastic 3.36%, giving a maximum depth at the root of a mere 4.2 inches. The leading edge was arranged to hinge down by electric screwjacks for take-off and landing, and the trailing edge was occupied by outboard ailerons and plain flaps. To drive the ailerons a novel 'piccolo' hydraulic booster was devised with ten rams spaced along the surface embedded in a single duralumin block fitting into the available depth of 1.1 in. The electrically driven flap was planned eventually to have boundary-layer control along the lines pioneered by John D. Attinello, with high-pressure engine bleed air expelled over the top of the surface from the leading edge. Tunnel tests were also done with blowing behind the drooped leading edge, again with good results. An inevitable result of the very stubby wing and quite high fin with T-tailplane was that the rudder would serve as a powerful aileron. The answer was negative dihedral (anhedral) on the wings. NACA Ames had lately fitted a CV-240 with black boxes giving it any desired degree of lateral stability, so that pilots could assess dihedral effect and directional stability and try to obtain optimised characteristics. Lockheed computed the predicted characteristics of the XF-104 at zero, 5° and 10° anhedral, and these were fed into the variable-stability computer system. Tony LeVier, Lockheed chief engineering test pilot (and one of the most famous racing and aerobatic pilots in history), then flew the NACA aircraft without being told which wing angle was being simulated. The zero setting brought the retort 'My God, what did you give me here?', but with 10° everything was fine.

There are countless other tales of technical pioneering in designing the F-104. One of the better ones concerns Johnson's conclusion that the best way to run flutter trials would be to launch instrumented and camera-equipped free-flight models riding on a 5-inch HVAR (high-velocity aircraft rocket). Lockheed soon found that private organisations were unable to buy HVARs (this was before the work was covered by any government contract), and Johnson mentioned the problem to an Air Force general he was visiting in Washington. His host turned to his aide and said 'Send a message to General Partridge in Korea and tell him to stop shooting 5-inch rockets for one morning and send them to Kelly'. When Johnson got back to Burbank he found a neat stack of some 400 HVARs, apparently without a bill attached. Lockheed then discovered they had no means of firing such things, or even of storing them properly, but all was solved when Edwards AFB was told the situation and the flutter models were soon roaring aloft. Ford Johnston was the top flutter man, and this work consumed one dollar in every eight spent on the original F-104 R&D programme.

Structurally the 104 was conventional, though Johnson recalls that 'several structural engineers threatened to commit suicide' when they saw the way the wings were to be bolted on to ring-frames forming the outside contour of the engine air ducts without any carry-through structure. In the XF-104 there were very few forgings, virtually no honeycomb, one or two chem-milled parts (such as the air ducts), a little titanium (in the rear fuselage), tapered sheet (for the four wing skins) but no major machined or integrally stiffened structure. On the other hand the Air Force agreed with Lockheed's proposal for a $400,000 producibility study, in which a team of about 20 engineers largely redesigned the aircraft in an extremely short time by studying the XF-104 in the minutest detail and then preparing new drawings for an eventual production machine which, while making no concessions in performance or ease of maintenance, would be easier and cheaper to make. Basing their sums on a run of about 2,500 aircraft, Lockheed reckoned the study saved $40 to $70 for each dollar it cost, and $10,000 to $12,000 per production aircraft.

This need to rethink the structure for production was because in building the XF-104s Lockheed had quite deliberately gone flat out in what they call the Special Project approach. Johnson's philosophy was to assign an *ad hoc* team of about 150 to engineer and build military prototypes in a security-protected area away from the main Burbank factory.

They worked three shifts, enjoyed the highest priority for supplies, services and materials, and aimed to do the job in an impossibly short time. Precisely the same technique was later adopted by Dassault, who tell me they invented it!

In fact the idea goes back to 1943, when Johnson's Special Projects team was working day and night to create the XP-80, the original Shooting Star. The Army Air Force had a Halford H.1 (de Havilland Goblin) turbojet and asked Kelly Johnson to build a fighter to use it. He decided the job could be done in 180 days, and beat this by 37 days. At one point in the hectic rush someone on the telephone asked a member of the highly secret outfit for the name of his department. Suddenly thinking of the crazy firm in the Lil' Abner strip cartoon the Special Projects man replied 'We're the Skunk Works'. The name stuck. Today the place is known as ADP, for Advanced Development Projects, and in the entrance foyer is a startling black and white mat that looks like an outsize skunk, though the air-conditioned atmosphere smells as sweet as anything can in the LA area. After rushing through the XP-80 the Skunk Works produced various advanced Lockheed projects before creating the XF-104 in the final ten months of 1953. Then Kelly became interested in the idea of a fantastically high-flying spy plane, amd switched ADP to what became the U-2. He never devoted much time to the F-104 again; to him this was history, and he lives ten years or so in the future.

Engineering design was thereafter managed by F-104 Project Engineer Bill Ralston. His assistant, Karl Achterkirchen, has stayed with the 104 ever since, probably knows the aircraft better than anybody else, and kindly read this chapter at the proof stage.

LeVier began taxying trials with the first XF-104, US Air Force serial 53-37786, in February 1954 at Edwards. On the 28th he made a 100-yard hop, and on 4 March, at about 9 am, he made a flawless first flight. Performance with the 7,200 lb of the temporary non-afterburning J65 was already extremely impressive. With his colleagues Herman 'Fish' Salmon and Joe Ozier he liked the sharp, pointed XF-104; but within a month they ran into handling problems. They began exploring pitch-up, and found it. They looked for inertia coupling (the F-100A had not then suffered its fatal accident due to this cause), and discovered problems at high rates of roll between Mach 1.4 and 1.6. They swore at the 'totally outmoded' Air Force mandatory requirement that a fighter had to demonstrate six turns of a normal spin. And as the engine had never before been used to propel an aircraft with its afterburner, they were not entirely happy with the Lockheed downward-ejecting seat which obviously posed problems in the event of trouble on take-off or landing. Downward ejection had been adopted for several reasons, including a supposed inability of existing seats to clear the high, sharp tail, and 'a much more reliable tie-in between the seat and the lower escape hatch than can generally be obtained with canopies which require ejection'. Perhaps most annoying of all was the realisation that pilots of all F-104s would be likely to have to wear the 'spaceman' partial-pressure suit lately developed for, and partly by, the Air Force, to protect the wearer from rapid decompression following engine flame-out at extreme altitude. This suit, though a great technical achievement, was torture to wear for anything much over half an hour. The aerospace medicine people down in Texas were even suggesting F-104 pilots would have to don their suit and then do half an hour pre-oxygenation before boarding the aircraft!

During 1954 Lockheed worked very hard indeed not only to sort out the problems of the XF-104 but also to build 15 YF-104A test aircraft which were ordered in January 1954. Sticking their necks out a bit it was decided all would have the J79 engine, and GE managed to qualify the YJ79-GE-3 engine, which differed considerably from the engine of the B-58, in time for the first YF-104A to roll out from Shop B-1 at Burbank on 23 December 1955. Its first flight, on 17 February 1956, was the first of any aircraft powered by a J79. Fish Salmon cut it short; some sixth sense had told him (correctly) that the engine was about to blow up.

This aircraft, 55–2955, had a bigger and longer fuselage to accommodate the larger engine and five bladder fuel cells, and the engine installation was much refined. Instead of plain intakes the inlets had half-cone centre-bodies to generate inclined shocks at supersonic speeds, the inner sides of the cones being cut away to let boundary-layer air escape. Downstream of the sharp-lipped inlet the air passed through a normal shock, jumping in pressure and temperature (guarded by a temperature gauge and warning light on the panel) and slowing to Mach 0.95. Most of this air passed through the engine, but there was a variable overspill by-passed around the engine to an air ejector nozzle around the afterburner nozzle. This offered good ram recovery, good jet expansion with afterburner on, cooling of the engine (within the limits of the ram adiabatic temperature rise) and fire protection (especially by blowing out a fire started by battle damage), and it eliminated the need for clever variable-geometry inlets. The new GE-powered machine introduced other changes such as a much more powerful a.c. electrical system (with two variable-speed engine-driven alternators and a third generator on a hydraulic constant-speed drive), and a nose landing gear retracting forwards instead of to the rear. Like the XF-104 it had a flat windscreen instead of a low-drag vee type. Other features progressively introduced included provision for wing-tip tanks, a series of minor improvements to the control system, a rear underfin and flap blowing. On top of these changes Lockheed had a vast amount of work to do to make their hot ship into an operational fighter.

In 1953 Lockheed had made a proposal, which was accepted by the

Air Force, for a lightweight radar sight system. This became the MA-10, incorporating the ASG-14 radar and, later, a simple infra-red detector for sighting at night. The company was in trouble because on the one hand they wanted a light and simple radar, able to fit in the pointed nose and of quite low power, while on the other the very high flight performance called for a radar having a usable range about ten times as great, of the order of 50 to 100 miles. Air-to-air search and tracking, with both radar and IR, was one of the fundamental tasks on which the whole concept of the F-104, as an air-superiority fighter, was based. I think it is fair to say that the radar and IR performance at no time matched the performance of the aircraft, so that the aircraft had to be used primarily as a day visual interceptor using such short-range weapons as the T-171 'Gatling' 20mm gun and the AIM-9B Sidewinder missile. In turn the concept of short-range in-fighting made it impossible to use the Mach 2.2 speed. A further problem was that the original J79 made no provision for modulated afterburning. In maximum cold thrust the speed stabilised very close to Mach 1, typically being subsonic except close to the tropopause where it reached 1.01 (owing to ASI error the speed was hard to measure; at 35,000 feet at Mach 1.04 the bow wave was an inch or so off the tip of the nose pitot boom, giving readings of Mach 0.95 and 33,000 feet, but acceleration to 1.05 pushed the pitot through the bow wave causing a sudden jump to the true readings). Moving the power lever beyond 'military power' eventually brought in the afterburner with a muffled WHOOMPH. Thereafter the thrust and drag curves did not again cross until about Mach 2.2 was reached at which point the engine temperature warning would illuminate. The pilot then had to throttle back; and as there was no way of throttling back except by returning to 'mil power' he would feel as if he had run into a brick wall. Thus it was impossible to stabilise at, say, Mach 1.5, or to make optimised interceptions. The early YF-104 trials were conducted according to an unnatural routine in which, depending on manoeuvre acceleration and vertical velocity, you had a choice of either Mach 1 or Mach 2.2. GE sweated day and night to perfect a modulated afterburner.

One aircraft that did not suffer from this problem was the first XF-104, which on 25 March 1955 hit Mach 1.79 to set what I believe was then a record for aircraft propelled only by a turbojet with a plain pitot inlet system. Unfortunately the other XF was destroyed late in 1955 in what Salmon called a 'hardware haemorrhage' believed to have begun with a blown belly hatch the moment he started firing the gun (he ejected all right and then got hurt arriving on some very nasty rocks). Two YF aircraft were also lost, one in a super-stalled pitch-up, and the other when the jettisoned tip tanks whipped violently in and struck the tail. On the other hand LeVier pulled off a fine dead-stick landing when a 20mm shell-case zipped into one of the intakes, punctured a fuel tank and doused the engine in kerosene. Pilots were excited with the 104; I hope Lockheed production test pilot Glenn Reaves will not mind if I quote the introduction to his hard-selling *Test Pilot's Notebook* for the F-104 where he describes it as the answer to the age-long cry of the fighter pilot for a mount that 'fits the pilot and fits the mission' and that 'could truly "dance the skies on laughter-silvered wings".' Certainly the 104 fitted the pilot; it was probably the first fighter that the pilot strapped on to him instead of the other way round. I do not think it really fitted the mission at all, and the laughter-silvered wings could have done with being a lot bigger. None of the YFs had a definitive flap-blowing system, which took an unexpectedly long time to perfect.

As finally agreed there was blow on the trailing-edge flaps only. High-pressure engine air was led through titanium ducts and expelled just above the leading edge of each flap through 55 slots each 0.55 in long and 0.09 in wide. The valve began to open at 15° flap and was fully open at the maximum angle of 45°. With full blow the velocity through the slits was 2,300 ft/sec, giving a thin sheet of very high energy air which entrained the flow above it and prevented breakaway and separation. This greatly increased the maximum lift, reducing stalling speed by about 15 knots. Blowing was noisy, and augmented the very distinctive sound of the F-104. The J79 is an almost constant-speed engine, running at about 7,460 rpm at all settings above flight idle. Thus, opening the throttle on take-off winds a Starfighter up to a constant note which hardly alters until the aircraft is parked at destination (with the Phantom you can do even better and get sonorous organ-pipe noises from the 'beat' interference between left and right engines). On the approach at low speed (say, below 170 knots) it is vital with the F-104 to hold high power to provide full pressure for blowing until the gear is about to hit the ground. View on the approach is good, because the F-104 wing in the high-lift regime does not need a high angle of attack. On the other hand, rate of descent is considerable, and in a no-flare arrival the main gears are brutally slammed out sideways—but the tiny shock struts, made by H. M. Loud to the patented Dowty Liquid Spring design, absorb all the energy. It is just one of several ways of recovering a supersonic fighter, and it is great to watch (from outside the aircraft).

By 1955 Lockheed had an order for 155 F-104A production interceptors for Air Defense Command. These followed directly on behind the YFs. The 15th and last YF was 55-2969; the first F-104A was 55-2970 and the second was -2971; then came the main batch ordered under 1956 funds, numbered from 56-730 to -882. Many of these had a zero inserted (thus 60834 instead of 6834), and the first hundred or so had a second number, just under the tailplane and on each side of the nose, running consecutively from the first YF (thus the first production machine was 16). This is a bit involved, but as many authorities report that there were 17 YFs (including the last two 1955-vote machines) I thought it worth going into the matter.

The first YF-104A reached Mach 2 on 27 April 1956 and came up against the compressor inlet temperature limit at 2.2. In the same month, on 17 April, Lockheed organised the biggest and most theatrical press show that I can call to mind. Rather surprisingly the Defense Department at this time took steps to protect design features of several supersonic aircraft, and one of these was the F-104A intake. As thousands of people at Burbank, Edwards and Palmdale had seen numerous YFs this seemed odd, but Lockheed cunningly got over the problem by photographing 52970 with the vital area obscured by the 21-inch waist of a well-chosen Lockheed employee in the foreground. But she could hardly do the same job at the vast press conference, so when Gen Otto P. Weyland (Commander of TAC) pressed the button at the heart-fluttering climax the curtains parted to reveal 52971 with the intakes covered by polished light-alloy fairings looking like strange hemispherical bulges. The Air Force also blanked over the J79 nozzle, having—they said—read my probe of the Russian Tu-104 jetliner which visited London the previous month. This nonsense did not last long, but for months afterwards the 'Flight Falsies' pictures kept appearing whenever a newspaper or non-aviation magazine wanted to illustrate a 104.

All the F-104As eventually had operative flap blowing, T-171 gun, wing-tip shoes for either tanks (of a new finned design) or Sidewinders, a definitive MA-10 system (though it did not please Johnson or the Air Force), a definitive lot of electronic racking behind the cockpit for radio, navaids, IFF and built-in test gear (though again Johnson was dissatisfied at the bulk and weight), the basic fuel capacity of 746 gal in three saddle tanks, an auxiliary cell and a sump, and a J79-GE-3A engine with an intermediate level of afterburning. The first 52 aircraft were occupied wholly in test programmes, involving more than 8,000 flights, in finding complete solutions to the pitch-up and other problems. One feature which gave no real trouble was the underfin. This was first fitted to the last YF, and its purpose was to add an extra bit of directional stability which became more and more important as the basic stability deteriorated from Mach 1 onwards. It acts as a large vortex generator, spoiling circular flow around the body, and as the centre of pressure of the differential across the left and right sides of the body (in yawed flight) acts through the fuselage, and not the fin itself, the F-104A underfin was made partly of plastics and used as an aerial. The need for this fin became evident during early tunnel testing, and was accentuated by the tandem-seat F-104B conversion trainer, first flown on 7 February 1957, but it was a remarkably long time being fitted. I have been looking at several Lockheed brochures and manuals dating from the late 50s (even up to March 1961) and it is surprising how many of the photographs have the underfin touched-in by an artist's airbrush!

The mighty F-104 flight-test programme, which took almost four years if one includes the XFs, exceeded in effort that of any other fighter in the world up to that time, proving that small and simple things are often the most difficult. The programme took twice as long as everyone had hoped, and cost more than $30 million, most of which was funded by the Air Force. I have a Lockheed document which tersely records 'As a result of the tests, the company determined that some internal airframe re-design was necessary'. The situation was not entirely happy, because the Air Force was no longer disposed to pay all the costs of this structural improvement, and in fact felt they were going beyond the line of duty in buying production aircraft which were deficient in several respects. It was clear that to rescue the programme Lockheed had to effect a major redesign not only of the structure but also of the equipment and systems to turn the very limited F-104A into an all-weather multi-mission aircraft. It was obviously going to occupy a further 18 months or two years, and Lockheed had to find most of the money. In the meanwhile the Air Force continued to buy interim aircraft in modest quantities.

Service clearance of the F-104A was received on 26 January 1958, when the first delivery was made to the 83rd FIS at Hamilton AFB. Unfortunately Lockheed were by no means out of the wood, and just at this time the J79 was going through a bad spell of misbehaviour caused by compressor stalls, incorrect fuel scheduling and other troubles. With the F-104 a flame-out, or loss of power for any other reason, was especially serious because a 'dead stick' landing was a hazardous business. Loss of flap blowing called for recovery at more than 225 knots, with a high rate of descent, and it was soon decided the correct procedure in these circumstances was to eject—though many dead-stick landings were demonstrated. Lockheed harboured nagging doubts about the downward ejection seat, and the Air Force bluntly described it as unacceptable. A group under Irwin Culver devised the D-type seat, with a forward-projecting skip-flow generator (to cause a strong bow wave in supersonic airflow well ahead of the occupant) and various fixed and retractable vanes to stabilise the seat in yaw and roll, but though this was fine at Mach 2 at high altitude the problem was what to do in an emergency near the runway. By April 1958 the situation was so bad the F-104A was grounded, except for aircraft flying special tests with Lockheed. Not until July were the aircraft restored to active status, re-engined with the GE-3B incorporating vital improvements.

This difficult period had its compensations. Flying Lockheed test aircraft at Palmdale, pilots of the 83rd took the world records for speed and altitude, the first time this had ever been done with the same type of aircraft. On 7 May Maj Howard C. Johnson reached 91,249 ft in a zoom, and on 16 May Capt Walter W. Irwin averaged 1,404.19 mph.

Experience with the F-104A continued to be worrying, and the true value of the aircraft was no higher than the Air Force had expected, though it would certainly have been better in other countries where short range and inability to link with the SAGE (semi-active ground environment) system were unimportant. In 1959 F-104As were withdrawn from the ADC inventory. Most were transferred to the Air National Guard, the state-organised reservist organisation which has always proved that part-time air and ground crew can cope with the most advanced aircraft (so Britain erred in disbanding the Royal Auxiliary Air Force, or at least in giving this as the reason). The ANG did surprisingly well with their very hot ships—despite the initials of the Puerto Rico Air National Guard, who were one of the recipients—and in 1963 the unexpected decision was announced that the ANG aircraft were being transferred back to the Air Force, equipping 319 and 331 Fighter Interceptor Squadrons of ADC. In 1968–71 about 30 of the surviving A models were re-engined with the very powerful (17,900 lb) GE J79-19 engine. The aircraft not assigned to the ANG in 1959 were: converted as target drones (24 QF-104s); fitted with a 6,000 lb Rocketdyne liquid rocket at the base of the rudder and HTP reaction controls for use by the Aerospace Research Pilots' School at Edwards at up to 130,000 ft (three (NF-104As), or supplied to Nationalist China (25), Pakistan (12) or, in 1968–69, Jordan (36). Pakistan re-engined its aircraft with the GE-11A engine fitted to later 104s, and after ten years, despite the war with India in 1965, still had nine left. One flew through the debris of its IAF victim, one hit the ground when attacking a ground target and the third was landing in a violent dust-storm; in no case was there an aircraft malfunction. Thus, even the old 104A could work perfectly well when it had finally shaken out its bugs. Unfortunately its early years were so troublesome that at the 100,000th flight hour (not reached until April 1961, seven years and two months after first flight) 49 USAF aircraft had been destroyed and 18 pilots killed, which was the worst record of any Century-series fighter (and the Phantom, Corsair II and F-111 were dramatically better).

Following the 170 A models in production came the 26 F-104B trainers and then—an order for 18 RF-104A reconnaissance versions having been cancelled in 1957—the F-104C fighter-bomber for Tactical Air Command. Powered by the GE-7 engine, with a 2 in increase in turbine diameter giving 15,800 lb thrust with reduced specific consumption, the C introduced a Lockheed probe for in-flight refuelling, which with its fairing could be added or removed on the ground only, and the option of carrying a range of tanks of up to 163 Imp gal size (about 1,500 lb) or offensive stores on two under-wing pylons, and a 2,000 lb rack on the centreline. The C was also the first type to have operative flap-blowing from the start. Clean gross weight went up from 17,350 to 20,500 lb, and maximum weight to 23,590 lb. Only 77 C models were built, equipping the 479th Tac Fighter Wing at George AFB from 16 October 1958. One aircraft was assigned to Capt Charles E. Tofferi, who represented the 479th at the 1962 William Tell fighter weapons meet at Nellis. He was the lone 104 pilot against ten flying the F-100 and three flying the formidable F-105; and he was regarded slightly as an interloper because the 479th was equipped and trained for tactical nuclear delivery as the primary mission, which most certainly does not figure in the William Tell programme! Lockheed were edgy at first, but at the end were jubilant. Tofferi scored a marvellous 19,018 out of a possible 24,000, almost 2,000 points ahead of the No 2 man. Three of his close-support missions were scored as perfect 1000s, and he picked up the maximum 3,000 for air-to-air gunnery by downing the towed dart target in 63 seconds. This splendid performance was undoubtedly the high point in the Starfighter's career with the US Air Force.

The C model served with TAC from October 1958 until the 479th re-equipped with the Phantom in 1965. Next came 22 F-104D trainers, which were essentially a mating of the B nose on an F-104C. Though they do not really qualify for this book the tandem-seat Starfighters often retained some offensive-stores capability, though the rear seat necessitated the removal of the gun, several electronics crates and about 30% of the internal fuel. Each cockpit had its own canopy, hinged to the left as on the single-seat versions. To improve directional stability the trainers also demanded a new rudder with greater chord and full hydraulic boost. Two export versions are the DJ and F, described later.

This takes the story up to the big redesign operation begun by Lockheed in 1956 to correct deficiencies and, at the same time, try to make the F-104 a true all-weather multi-mission aircraft. By this time the frantic wish to have light stripped-down aircraft had largely dissipated, and with the return of more considered and more carefully detailed reasoning the Air Force's enthusiasm for the F-104 had ebbed. This enthusiasm was never absolute. Though fighter pilots inevitably get a great kick out of having more performance, the 'wild blue yonder' kind of dream—laughter-silvered wings and all—must take second place to realistic scenarios of future wars, with real countries, real mission distances, real weather, and many other factors. Increasingly Air Defense Command said they wanted no part of the F-104; if they wanted a new fighter at all, after the F-106 Delta Dart, it would be very big and have radar and missiles reaching out 100 miles away. Tactical Air Command likewise looked at the breadth of the broad

Atlantic and Pacific Oceans, which in emergency their fighter and attack aircraft might have to cross in a matter of hours, and at the increasing vulnerability of big paved runways to enemy air or missile attack. They wanted a long-range delivery system carrying a big payload out of short rough strips. Mach 2-plus in the stratosphere seemed much less important than in 1953, and Lockheed realised it had to look for other customers.

Had Lockheed been a British company it would have sent out a hen-pecked salesman with some superficial brochures to try to sell a product that didn't exist and that his own country didn't want. This is hardly the way to get results. In contrast, Lockheed flooded the market with overwhelming confidence, generously offering to let friendly nations have a part of the world's greatest airplane. I quote: 'In 1956 Lockheed foresaw that Free World allies, vulnerable to attack by conventional weapons, had vital need for the high-performing F-104 as a multi-mission fighter. With Air Force approval we began negotiations on three continents on two proposals: 1. To license large-scale manufacture of internationally standardised advanced F-104s; 2. To supply participating nations with required quantities of ready-to-fly single-place and two-place Starfighters off our own California factory lines.' It was the biggest selling job in aviation history (there's that phrase again) and I hope someone has time to tell the full story one day, because the inside tale of this kind of selling uncovers fascinating insights into aggressive big business, the psychology of contrasting people (engineers, pilots, top brass, cabinet ministers and lots of much less obvious participants) from such dissimilar places as Germany, Canada and Japan, and countless splendid anecdotes which even now seem to be mostly unprintable.

To set the scene, Germany, Canada and Japan offered big markets, had nothing in this category later than the F-86 or F-84F, had ample funds and could build and operate the F-104. Almost every other NATO country was essentially in the same boat, except that Britain and France did not have the same replacement situation and in any case considered themselves self-sufficient (though both had been glad to clutch at such US fighters as the F-86 and F-100). By far the biggest market was Federal Germany, where there was an interesting situation. The Luftwaffe, reborn in 1955, had begun operations in 1958 with the Canadair Sabre 6 and the Republic F-84F. Though it indicated it would participate with Italy on the G 91 programme it also needed a supersonic multi-role fighter. It wanted it in very big numbers indeed—not far short of 1,000—and the Germans also urgently wanted to make this aircraft, in order to rebuild their manufacturing capability in airframes, engines and systems. Germany seemed the key to the whole situation. If Lockheed could sell Germany it would have most of Western Europe in the bag. By the end of 1958 there was a hotel in Bonn that became known as Lockheedshof, though I suppose it did have customers that were not from Lockheed, the Luftwaffe or the Deutschesbundesrepubliksluftfahrtministerium, or whatever it was called. The Lockheed team swarmed like ants, until at one point Defence Minister Josef Strauss let go a public blast that he couldn't open a drawer in his desk without a Lockheed man falling out of it.

Of course there were rivals: 7 (or 8) from the US, 3 from Britain, 2 from France and one from Sweden. At the start the favourite was probably a variant of the Grumman G.98 Super Tiger which was unique in actually being in existence. Lockheed's dominating man-power did not at first have the desired effect, and even made a few customers cross. By the end of 1958 most of the rivals had gone, including two potentially first-rate aircraft (the subjects of the first two chapters in this book) which could not have been more mishandled by their own government if it had set out to lose as a deliberate policy. France likewise fought with at least one hand tied behind its back in promoting (or not promoting) the Mirage III, but from the summer of 1958 every day brought Lockheed nearer to its goal and the Germans finally announced their choice of the Super Starfighter (as it was called) in February 1959, 'after evaluating nearly two dozen of the world's top fighter aircraft'. It was 13 or 14 actually, but that's about ten more than you could evaluate today unless you included the Russkies.

Pulling off this deal was one of the things that ought to be writ large in the Valhalla for salesmen, if there is such a place. Lockheed accomplished it mainly by sheer engineering fluency, a deep understanding of the Germans' combat missions and industrial aspirations, and by being able to convince their shrewd customers that they could make good on their claims. To the outside world it looked as if Germany had selected a top-line American fighter. In fact the aircraft involved did not exist, would not fly for almost two more years and had at no time even been considered by any customer in the United States! I could also make the point that it is misleading to call it a fighter. The original F-104 had not been much good as anything else, despite Capt Tofferi's runaway win of the William Tell trophy; in contrast, the Super Starfighter was bought by the Luftwaffe primarily for the all-weather precision delivery of tactical nuclear weapons, using advanced navigation techniques, and the rival aircraft were in the main eliminated because they were unable to fly the mission. Lockheed said their offering could.

When Lockheed began their redesign in 1956 the new aircraft was designated F-104-7 but in 1958, when the basic airframe was virtually designed, it was called F-104G (for Germany). Externally it was almost indistinguishable from, say, a 104C. Inside the structure was totally new, partly reflecting advances made in the five years since the original design and partly because it had to be made much stronger yet still fit into the same space. There were 36 new heavy-press forgings for fuselage frames and longerons, wing and tail root fittings, spars and ribs, structural joints and even some fuselage skin panels. About 60 small no-draught close-tolerance forgings were adopted at about half the price of equivalent parts machined all over. The big boosted rudder of the two-seaters was adopted, and tailplane power was increased. The engine was changed to the J79–GE–11A, rated at 15,800 lb, and the inlets were anti-iced by electrically heated Spraymat panels made in the US under British (Napier) licence. The drag chute was increased in diameter from 16 to 18 feet, the main wheels were given larger tyres and fully powered brakes of increased capacity controlled by an anti-skid system, and an airfield arrester hook was added under the rear fuselage. The flaps were given an intermediate setting, subject to an IAS restriction, for use as 'manoeuvre flaps' to reduce turn radii by 30–40% and thus help compensate for the increase in gross weight. By no means least, the downward ejection seat was replaced by the Lockheed C-2, which the company finally offered to the waiting air forces as the truly capable upward ejection seat the F-104 had always needed.

These changes to the basic aircraft enabled it to fly missions with no 'placard limitations' despite an increase in maximum gross weight from 22,400 lb to 28,780 lb. A major reason for the increase in weight was the fact that, far from stripping out essential items to save weight as had been requested in 1952, Lockheed had to stuff the Starfighter full of approximately a ton of complicated avionics. The main addition was a powerful and capable radar, the Autonetics F15A Nasarr (North American search and ranging radar), providing all the expected facilities for air-to-air and air-to-ground modes when used in conjunction with an optional fire-control computer. This not only provided the pilot with a display for search, tracking, terrain avoidance and bombing through cloud but also fed the new director gunsight for gun and missile firing by day and, with an additional input from a Lockheed infra-red sight, by night. Mergenthaler Linotype supplied the M-2 weapon-delivery computer. Minneapolis-Honeywell provided the MH-97 stick-steering autopilot, and Litton the LN-3 lightweight inertial navigation system. Other avionic 'jeep cans' contained the Position and Homing Indicator (PHI), a new uhf radio and other communications, an IFF (identification friend or foe), an air-data computer, ARN-52 Tacan, provision for a data-link time-division set, and provision for a reconnaissance pod under the fuselage.

Thus did Lockheed quietly perform a 180° change of course and turn their light simple fighter into a complicated and much heavier multi-role attack aircraft. With only 196 sq ft of wing there were nevertheless sharp limits to what was practical, and the maximum weight of armament was put at 4,800 lb. One of the primary needs of the Luftwaffe, with whom Lockheed planned the G model, was to carry a tactical nuclear store, and this was possible with the 2,000 lb rack on the centreline. A 1,500 lb pylon was provided under each wing, the tank/Sidewinder shoes were retained at the tips, and two further Sidewinders could be mounted on fuselage pylons in lieu of the main store. Obviously the whole exercise was a massive compromise. It resulted in a nuclear delivery system of minimal size, great penetrative capability, mission radius marginally adequate for most of the chief Luftwaffe targets, and well equipped for precision navigation in all weathers. In the clean condition the F-104G promised to have high performance and to prove a capable all-weather fighter.

On the other hand it was undeniably going to demand constant good flying by its pilot, and recovery in bad weather or after engine failure appeared to call for exceptional pilot skill and experience. A Lockheed pilot frankly said of the G 'This is an absolutely straight aeroplane; it will not forgive you a single mistake you make.' By no means least, the 104G was conceived just at the time NATO air forces were becoming deeply worried about the vulnerability of big paved runways, and were considering jet lift and other methods of V/STOL operation from short unimproved sites. I have it on the authority of General Bruce K. Holloway, and the Commander of TAC, General Frank F. Everest, that the F-104G did not appeal to the USAF either, and its characteristics often ran directly counter to the requirements later spelt out in the TFX specification.

But Lockheed were not aiming at the US Air Force. Indeed, in view of the urgent wish of the US Air Force to buy 650 Air Combat Fighters in 1974, in order to clinch the deal to replace the F-104G in four NATO countries, it is ironic to note that the F-104G found its huge worldwide sales without ever being adopted by its own air force!

Taking a long-term view I am surprised Lockheed did not increase the size of the wing, and the company also faced a basic problem in the diversity of their world market. Their prime target, the Luftwaffe, wanted a very well equipped and sophisticated aeroplane to fulfil particular challenging tasks, and they could pay for it. Most other air forces could afford to downgrade the equipment fit, and had less money to spend. Had Lockheed been able to foresee the huge export success of the Mirage they would probably have developed as their main Super Starfighter not the F-104G for Germany but a cheaper and simple version with a bigger wing, carrying a much heavier mission load and landing 20 or 30 knots slower. Such an aircraft could well have taken much of the market away from the Mirage, F-5 and Tiger II and would probably be in production today. But the Luftwaffe wrote the specification for the F-104G and Lockheed salesmanship did the rest. Federal Germany signed a contract for development of the F-104G and for licence manufacture on 18 March

1959, Canada followed on 17 September 1959, Japan on 29 January 1960, the Netherlands on 20 April 1960, Belgium on 20 June 1960, the US Air Force for MAP aircraft on 18 February 1961, Italy on 2 March 1961 and the US Air Force for additional MAP aircraft in June 1962. The 'mostest' phrase returns again here: this was the greatest international manufacturing programme in the history of aviation, yet its subject was designed in a country that did not want to buy any!

By far the biggest customer was Federal Germany, which bought 96 F-104Gs from Lockheed and 604 (later 654) from European sources. As finally arranged, when all the partners were in the programme, these 604 were made by Arbeitsgemeinschaft Süd (Arge Süd, or work group south), comprising Messerschmitt, Heinkel, Dornier and Siebel, with assembly at Manching, near Munich (210 aircraft); Arge Nord (north), comprising Hamburger, Weser, Focke-Wulf, Fokker and Aviolanda, with assembly at Schiphol, Amsterdam (350); a West Group, comprising Avions Fairey and SABCA, with assembly at Gosselies, originally with Italian participation, but later all-Belgian (188); and an Italian Group, comprising Fiat, Aerfer, Macchi, SIAI-Marchetti, Piaggio and SACA, originally with Belgian participation but later all-Italian, with assembly at Turin-Caselle (229, not including the later F-104S). Outside Europe the F-104G was adopted by the Royal Canadian Air Force as the CF-111, a designation later changed to CF-104, and put into production by Canadair as the CL-90 at Montreal. The CF-104 differs from the 104G in that it almost ignores the air-to-air role; the Nasarr is optimised to the attack role, and fuel replaces the gun and ammunition. Canadair made 200 CFs for the RCAF, supplied 121 sets of wings, aft fuselages, and tails to Europe, 40 sets to Japan and 40 sets to Lockheed, and then a further 110 MAP aircraft that conformed to the multi-role 104G standard. In Japan a different F-104 was selected, the F-104J, which is essentially a 104G with a Nasarr optimised in the air-to-air mode, a total absence of attack systems and a primary armament of the gun and four Sidewinders. Mitsubishi, assisted by Kawasaki, with assembly at Komaki, Nagoya, built 207, and the Japan Air Self-Defence Force also received three from Lockheed, as well as 20 Lockheed-built F-104DJ trainers. Lockheed also delivered the first 96 F-104Gs ever built to Germany, one G each to Italy and Belgium, and 81 MAP aircraft to participating nations. Lockheed also delivered 30 F-104F trainers, generally similar to the D, to the Luftwaffe; 38 CF-104Ds, similar to the D, to the RCAF; and 137 TF-104Gs, generally similar to a dual-control G but without the gun and autopilot, to the Luftwaffe, 14 to the Netherlands and 29 to MAP countries including Italy and Belgium. This is already a complicated list, but I ought to add that GE-11A engines for the European programme were made by MAN-Turbo, Fiat and FN, the IHI-11A Japanese engines came from Ishikawajima-Harima, and the

OEL-7 engines for Canadair were made by Orenda Engines. I shall discuss other components later.

Sorting out the programme is difficult, because hardly any manufacturer made the number it originally said it would, few air forces adhered to their original procurement plan and several new F-104 variants crept in along the way. For example there is the RF-104G of the RNethAF which has a reconnaissance camera installation in place of the gun and ammunition, the RTF-104G1 of the Luftwaffe which is a two-seat multi-sensor reconnaissance machine with vertical and oblique cameras, SLAR and IR linescan, and the F-104S described later. As for recipients, the Federal German Government received 750 F-104Gs (excluding two-seaters), the RCAF (now Canadian Armed Forces) 200, Italy 155 (excluding F-104S), Netherlands 130 and Belgium 100, while MAP recipients (including Norway, Spain, Nationalist China, Denmark, Greece and Turkey) took a further 191. The two-seat totals were Germany 167, Canada 38, RNethAF 14 and MAP recipients 29. I will not attempt a grand total until after discussing the F-104S.

To co-ordinate the giant European programme Lockheed used over 100 engineers, managers and other staff who demonstrated how American ruthless efficiency can get things done. Almost all were based in Germany, and by the end of 1959 the whole project was in full swing, even though most participants had yet to sign formal contracts. A central headquarters, the NATO Starfighter Management Office (NASMO) was established in Koblenz, under a German general manager, H. Sellschopp. By 1962 NASMO directed the production efforts of some 62,000 people, and the total involved full-time on the world-wide F-104 programme exceeded 100,000. Virtually all the work was on a fixed-price basis, and in the international consortia was carefully subdivided on a man-hours basis (thus in Arge-Nord Fokker had 33%, Hamburger 23%, Weser 18%, Aviolanda 17% and Focke-Wulf 9%). In terms of numbers of airframes more than 80% of the world total of F-104s for countries outside the United States were built by companies other than Lockheed. In every case the F-104 made new demands and taught new skills, and in the case of Federal Germany the acquisition of the F-104G as a weapon was almost a secondary consideration compared with the deep-seated wish of the Germans to rebuild a great aircraft industry skilled in advanced technologies. It was accepted from the start that this could be done only by building a foreign product, and from this point of view the F-104G served its purpose admirably. On the other hand only the Germans made the very great effort needed to build the entire weapon system. Germany wanted to acquire a total capability, and succeeded in becoming the source of almost all the avionics and system components for the European programme—though it was often done by getting the original US supplier to set up a German subsidiary. Acquiring new technologies quickly is usually hard unless you ride on the back of other companies in other countries.

Obviously it would have been nice for the Germans if they could have designed their own aeroplane, but they did not possess this capability at that time. Moreover, in 1958–62 there appeared to be an urgent need for a modern multi-mission fighter throughout the NATO air forces and there is no doubt that by jumping into bed with Lockheed the need was met, and met much faster than if any European design had been chosen. In 1958 the F-104G was no more a fully developed weapon system than any of its rivals, yet the development programme was carried through within the tight schedule Lockheed had promised. The first G flew at Palmdale on 5 October 1960. It was one of the 96 for the Luftwaffe, and delivery of these began in May 1961. The first European-built F-104G flew at Manching two months ahead of schedule on 10 August 1961, and A. P. Moll flew the first Arge Nord machine on 11 November 1961. In Canada the first CF-104 was completed on 28 March 1961, airlifted to Palmdale and flown there on 26 May. On 14 August 1961 the third and fourth off the Canadair line both flew at Montreal. The first Lockheed-built F-104J flew on 30 June 1961 and was then shipped for reassembly by Mitsubishi. The first F-104G from the European West Group was flown by Bernard Neefs at Gosselies on 4 December 1961 and the first Italian-built F-104G followed on 9 June 1962.

Most of the manufacturing programmes had been completed by the end of 1966, apart from that in Italy and a late buy of an extra 50 Gs by the Luftwaffe in 1968. Basic development of the F-104G, paid for almost entirely by Germany but carried out by Lockheed at Palmdale, was completed in 1962. German test pilots and Luftwaffe officers assisted, and to provide a supply of pilots the German government signed a large contract with the US Defense Department under the terms of which the main F-104G school was established at Luke AFB, Arizona, to which were supplied not only 30 of the Lockheed-built TFs but also 50 F-104Gs built by the Arge groups! Service clearance came in 1963 with the equipment of Luftwaffe Jabo G31 at Norvenich. The Kriegsmarine (German Navy), Netherlands and Belgian Air Forces had also formed F-104G squadrons by early 1964, and Italy followed in the course of that year. In the United States Miss Jacqueline Cochran finally achieved ascendancy over her long-time rival Mme Jacqueline Auriol by setting three world women's records, one of them being a straight-line speed of 1,429.3 mph which still stands. This was done with a TF-104G retained by Lockheed as a company-owned demonstrator registered N104L and emblazoned with an emblem bearing the legend FREE WORLD DEFENDER.

This did not seem too gross an exaggeration. In 1963 the first squadron of the powerful 1st Canadian Air Division began to arrive in Europe, the first three Japanese F-104J squadrons became operational in 1964, and the same year also saw the start of deliveries to MAP participating air forces. These early years were marked by intensely hard work by civil contractors' representatives, by pilots and by supporting military personnel at all levels, because even though the F-104G was not more complicated than other advanced combat aircraft of the time it marked a great advance on what its recipients had been used to. The Nasarr, the computers and the inertial navigation system were major headaches, not only to assimilate but also to keep serviceable. The Litton LN-3 was pioneering in a very real sense, because though inertial systems had flown in dozens of test aircraft from a DC-3 onwards, and in many pilotless aircraft and missiles, as well as operate in ships and submarines of the US Navy, no lightweight production system had gone into the arduous service of a front-line fighter squadron. True, the B-58 and A-5 bombers had reached the user with much bigger radar-inertial systems but this was fundamentally different and the experience did not read across. Litton began with an MTBF (mean time between failures) of the order of 15 minutes. Gradually over the years 1963–68 this time was extended to several hours, which was a very big achievement.

Even in the United States the F-104G broke a great deal of new ground, because it was the first multi-mission fighter equipped with what I would in 1974 call a modern nav-attack system; and as it was small and slim the packaging problem was severe. Lockheed bore a much bigger burden than they had expected, and to their chagrin could not pass on all the costs to customers. They had to make 1,167 flights at Palmdale to develop the basic nav-attack system, compared with the programmed 250. Probably the central problem continued to be the LN-3 inertial platform, which, though also fitted to aircraft of the US Navy, had to be developed mainly with the 104G. The MH-97G autopilot contained rate gyros but relied almost totally on the LN-3, and on the PHI and the Garrett air-data computer. In 1963 I had a long talk with Honeywell, ostensibly to discuss their pioneer automatic checkout trolley which in a few minutes could test several hundred F-104G circuits and instruments in the aircraft and indicate anything whose behaviour was outside specification. At that time the CEP (circular error probability) of the F-104G operating on the LN-3 and PHI and flying on autopilot was still consistently over 1 mile on the nominal strike mission, which was outside the guarantee. But things were getting better, and I believe that since 1967 it has been around 0.5 mile. A further big advance was in the warm-up time of the delicate floated gyro of the LN-3 system. Originally it took about ten minutes to warm up the nav-attack system and run the gyro up to speed with the platform exactly aligned, and in the sort of operational situation expected over Germany in wartime this was like saying 'Take the pills ten minutes before you feel the pain coming on'. What Litton managed to do was develop an alert-align mode which could be done at any time. Provided the parked aircraft was not moved more than an inch or two, or jolted by the pilot getting in (and above all not pointed in a different direction, the limit being 0.1°), the aircraft could be scrambled in 90 seconds and the inertial gyro spooled up in the process, with the platform already aligned. Another improvement was to replace the M-2 weapon computer by the simpler Lear dual timer.

From 1963 the Starfighters became a familiar sight and sound over much of the NATO airspace, and especially at low level over the conveniently flat North German Plain. Here the RF and RTF versions busied themselves on a highly classified task: making a finely detailed radar and optical map of every square metre, and as far East of the frontier as the sensing systems would look. They knew that if the balloon went up they would need the great armada of Starfighters to operate without ground aids and possibly without seeing the ground, and the pilots had to know every navigational feature both by its visual appearance and from its radar or IR signature. The important thing here is experience and familiarity with the terrain, but after a while many Germans began to wonder if Starfighter pilots were going to live that long. During the procurement competition rivals had naturally called the Starfighter dangerous; but not even the bitterest rival was prepared for the loss-rate suffered by the Germans in their first few years. In 1961 the rate was 80 per 100,000 hours, and in 1962 it went to a shocking level at 139. In 1963, though it fell to 30, partly because far more hours were flown, the actual number of losses rose. In 1964 the figure was 62, and in 1965 84.5, with a Starfighter write-off about every ten days. In an unacceptably high proportion of the crashes the pilot was killed.

Such a situation is unacceptable in peacetime, though it may be encountered and accepted when a nation is in the final phases of losing a war. The F-104G, Germany's double key to military strength and reborn industrial capability, became known as the Flying Coffin, the Widow-maker, and by other unkind names. An American rival distributed a brochure picturing the families of all the dead F-104G pilots. Possibly he thought they would buy his product instead. Sick jokes arose by the score—for example, the Luftwaffe's definition of an optimist was 'a Starfighter pilot who gave up smoking because he was afraid of dying of lung-cancer'. Pilots were found taking sedative drugs, and others were court-martialled for refusing to fly. After his court-martial one former 104 jock sued the Defence Minister, by now Kai-Uwe von Hassel, for wrongful dismissal. Another pilot's widow filed a petition against Lockheed. Von Hassel became personally identified with the Starfighter in a way that Strauss, who was the minister responsible for buying it, had avoided. By 1967

Von Hassel had become the object of bitter attack by millions of Germans; in 1970 he lost his own son in a Starfighter crash.

Undoubtedly the main reason for the violent political storm, and the screaming accusations of scandal, was that the Luftwaffe was thought to be denying its pilots a chance of escape by using an inferior ejection seat. When Lockheed began to design the F-104G the company had just completed the upward-ejection seat design which the US Air Force had long been demanding. The Lockheed C-2 seat was only a manual system but it did have rocket boost to throw the pilot clear of the T-tail. Lockheed took it for granted this would be the seat of the F-104G, but unexpectedly met resistance on the part of the Luftwaffe, their prime customer. The Luftwaffe's F-84F and F-86 fighters had gone into service with American seats. These had gained a bad reputation; Martin-Baker seats were bought from Britain, fitted in place of the early US seats and swiftly convinced the Luftwaffe that they were a thoroughly reliable and superior proposition. So when the German Defence Ministry specified its list of change orders for the F-104G one of the few major ones was a switch to the British seat. The Martin-Baker Mk 7 automatic seat was specified, ordered for the first batch of 96 aircraft built by Lockheed and duly fitted. But the Germans had no proving or trials establishment, and so they placed a contract with the US Air Force to clear the installation of the British seat in the new 104G. But the US Air Force was very anti-Martin-Baker, claiming the seat to be uncomfortable, fitted at the wrong angle and dangerous to the occupant if used. The Air Force refused to qualify the seat and brought great pressure to bear to have the Lockheed seat re-fitted—pressure which Lockheed did not exactly fight against. The Germans gave in and accepted the C-2 seat.

By the end of 1963 they had a growing dossier of pilot fatalities where it was judged the seat's performance had been deficient. Admittedly a number of fatalities could not have been saved by any pilot-operated escape system, because it was clear the pilot had become unconscious in the air. The Luftwaffe and the Dutch had incidents of this kind, and in some occasions accompanying aircraft held loose formation with the doomed pilot, shouting at him on the R/T, until the fuel ran out many hundreds of miles away. This series of losses was put down to oxygen contamination, but there was a much greater number of incidents where the pilot tried to escape and did not survive. From the start the Luftwaffe regretted the C-2 seat—though I am prepared to believe this may have been partly due to prejudice—and it insisted on the Martin–Baker seat for the tricky programme of Zell trials begun in 1963. Zell, a word formed from 'zero-length launching', involved raising an F-104G on a lofty inclined launcher and blasting it into the sky under the 120,000 lb thrust of a Rocketdyne solid motor of formidable dimensions. The idea was to make conventional aircraft independent of airfields, though the rocket motors posed almost impossible logistic and cost problems. The first Zell launch with a 104G was made at Edwards in June 1963 by Ed Brown under contract to the German government. Then the Germans bought GH-7 rocket-assisted automatic seats for nine 104Gs to be used in operational Zell trials at Lechfeld, from August 1966.

In fact the first people to fit a Martin-Baker seat to regular F-104G aircraft were the Danes. It so happened that they insisted on the British seat, and fitted them after delivery of their Canadair-built aircraft. For the poor Germans, however, the Starfighter became a nightmare. After the 65th crash, in December 1966, all Luftwaffe and Kriegsmarine Starfighters were grounded for urgent modifications to the C-2 seats. Released for operations again, the loss rate and fatality rate continued as before. Martin-Baker could see but one outcome, and began making long-lead parts of the GQ-7 seat, the latest type matched to the 104 cockpit. But the US Air Force and a few other far from disinterested parties continually sniped at Martin–Baker, claimed they would never be able to deliver, and even kept up the parrot-cry that the seat would not fit! Finally, the opposition collapsed on 8 March 1967, and in the greatest possible secrecy an order was placed for GQ-7 seats for the whole German 104 inventory. (The Italians, who had sat on the fence to see which way the wind blew, smartly zipped their order in first!) The entire conversion job was effected in Germany between October 1967 and October 1968.

To Martin-Baker's credit they never splashed this story, and even today are most reluctant even to mention it. They did agree to review this chapter, because they appreciated that I knew the story, but have said nothing at all about their F-104G seats because the last thing they wish to do is embarrass any of their customers. I think the tale is sufficiently important to be spelt out in full after all these years, and in any case bits of it have long been public knowledge. But if you look in the universal bible *Jane's All The World's Aircraft* you will never find the slightest mention of a Martin-Baker seat in an F-104G.

Few parts of the history of aviation have aroused such fierce emotion as the high loss-rate of German Starfighters. Even today it is not easy to set the tale down on paper without someone scenting bias or unfairness and hastening to point out that it was all the fault of the basic aircraft, or, alternatively, that it was nothing to do with the basic aircraft. The fairest assessment I can offer is that an experienced pilot would love the 104G and be unlikely to run into trouble, whereas the young Germans who made up the bulk of the Luftwaffe and Kriegsmarine Starfighter squadrons were far from experienced—and this goes for the ground staff as well as the pilots. On the other hand, there were numerous fatalities among older commanders who had been unable to keep their hand in and who might find themselves in an F-104G after years behind a desk. In the long term the best cure for the situation was the pilot-training programme at Luke AFB and the bringing in of Lockheed under contract to provide maintenance and to help train German ground engineers. The fact that the 104G did not really have to kill its pilots is shown by the Royal Norwegian Air Force, who went almost ten years before suffering a 104G fatality and who still use the aircraft quite successfully—and with the C-2 seat!

In recent years the loss-rate of German Starfighters has dropped sharply, to the 'acceptable' level of 10 to 20 per 100,000 hours. By 1970 the number of German write-offs had reached 124, but in the four years since there were only a further 40. This is due mainly to improved training and experience, and also to the whole weapon system shaking out most of its bugs. A further contributory factor is a generally reduced pressure to fly in marginal conditions, though in the interceptor role the big 104G force plays its full part, with aircraft at immediate cockpit alert status ready to scramble up and identify any unknown aircraft detected by the Nadge radar/computer system crossing into NATO territory. The Super Starfighter was not optimised as an interceptor, and in October 1965 Lt-Gen Walter Panitzki, Inspector-General of the Luftwaffe, said 'In interceptor squadrons the F-104G does not meet our requirements in performance, radar, weapons and all-weather capability'. Five years earlier such a pronouncement would have been inconceivable, but by 1965 the Luftwaffe was urgently wondering what it ought to do to procure a really good interceptor for the 1970s. It had reluctantly come to the conclusion that jet-lift V/STOL was not quite the great white hope it had believed it to be earlier (and I will say a bit more on this topic in a moment), and the all-German NKF (Neukampfflugzeug) studies were showing great reluctance to gell. Not altogether surprisingly the answer seemed to be to develop an optimised interceptor version of the F-104G, and plans went ahead with the Italians, as I shall relate.

What about V/STOL? If ever there was a non-V/STOL it was the F-104G, despite its blown flaps, yet it was conceived at a time when many military planners were becoming painfully aware of the extreme vulnerability of fixed, paved runways. Lockheed were as aware of the problem as anyone, and by 1960 they had begun to dish out confidential brochures for various startling V/STOL F-104s. One had four 'advanced GE J85' turbojets in pivoted pods on the wing tips. Another had a swivelling-nozzle lift/cruise engine on each tip, and again no engine in the body. But it was the issue of the NBMR-3 (NATO Basic Military Requirement 3) specification that really got all the Western planemakers jumping. Bids had to be in by 31 December 1961, and one of the submissions was the Lockheed-Short CL-704. This combined project was just what one might have expected. It was to a considerable degree an F-104G but with an

RB.168R (afterburning Spey) propulsion engine and with tip pods each housing seven RB.181 lift jets (scaled RB.162s of 2,600 lb each). Other features included low-pressure tyres for rough-field operation and a jet-reaction control and autostabilisation system derived from that of the Short SC.1. M. Carl Haddon, who then was president of Lockheed-California Co, told me the 704 'met or exceeded NBMR-3 in every respect'. But, to the chagrin of Rolls, who thought they could see about 99,000 engines coming, the whole project just faded away, though Lockheed never stopped thinking up ever-better ways of improving the F-104.

By 1966 the various F-104 users around the world were becoming used to receiving quite a lot of exciting proposals from Lockheed, the improved aircraft having a succession of CL (Lockheed-California) numbers from about 950 onwards. But the important air forces of Germany and Italy were not very interested, because they were already hard at work on their new fighter version, the F-104S. The letter S was chosen by the Italian Regia Aeronautica for Sparrow, the air-to-air missile the new version was to carry. The 104S was an active project as early as 1964. The airframe was identical with that of the 104G except that it was designed to incorporate many small engineering changes as a result of extensive experience with the 104G. The most obvious external change is the addition of canted ventral fins on each side of the ventral centreline fin. Far from obvious, a more important alteration is that the nav-attack system and weapons are totally different, being planned to launch the Sparrow air-to-air missile instead of to attack ground targets.

Panitzki said the S would meet the Luftwaffe's all-weather fighter needs until about 1980, whilst allowing all the G fleet to be used by the tactical strike and reconnaissance squadrons. Lockheed had previously done a study for a Spey F-104 with the CL-704, and were impressed by the great increase in all-round performance. But the price of the Spey 25R seemed excessive at £155,000, and then Henry Kuss, who swiftly won a reputation as the Department of Defense's top foreign salesman for US weapons, let it be known that he could offer various attractive kinds of support if the British engine was kept out. He recommended the J79–A1Q, and after some one-sided horsetrading the Italians agreed. The Germans rather lost interest, and by February 1966 walked out. But Italy liked the idea of developing a Mach 2.2 all-weather interceptor that seemed to pose virtually no technical risk, and pressed on alone.

Lockheed were awarded a contract by the Italian government just like the earlier German contract for the G; they undertook 'engineering and production design, prototype development and flight testing'. I must give Lockheed credit for the work, although shortly before I wrote this book I was assured by an Italian, in good faith, that 'when Fiat were given design status on the F-104 they proceeded to modify the 104G into the

104S'. They certainly collaborated, but Lockheed wrote the detail spec., negotiated it with the Regia Aeronautica, did all the engineering development at Burbank, built the first two S prototypes, and began the flight-test programme at Palmdale in December 1966. The first Italian-built S did not fly until more than two years later.

Another part of the programme that was entirely American was the collaboration between Raytheon, makers of the Sparrow, and Autonetics to make the missile compatible with the Nasarr radar. The missile was the standard AIM-7E, as carried by the Phantom, but the continuous-wave semi-active homing had to be altered to match the Nasarr scan, wavelength and other characteristics. This was no great problem, and the primary armament of the S is one Sparrow under each wing and the gun in the fuselage; unfortunately you cannot have both together (!) because some of the Sparrow auxiliaries are carried in the gun bay. In addition a Sidewinder can be latched on to each tip if tip tanks are not needed, and two more can be carried on big ventral pylons. The production engine finally turned out to be the J79–19, of 17,900 lb thrust, which can run a little hotter than earlier J79s though the 104S is still red-lined at Mach 2.2. Field length is about the same as that for a G, even though maximum weight is no less than 31,000 lb, more than double Kelly's original target, giving the rather daunting wing loading of 158 lb/sq ft.

Despite this, the S is a fine fighter, and for irrational reasons I like it and am not afraid of it whereas I frankly never entirely liked the earlier variants. Pietro Trevisan, chief test pilot at Fiat's Caselle plant, flew No 1 off the line on 30 December 1968. It was camouflaged in glossy green and grey, like all that have followed. The Regia Aeronautica placed five orders which brought the total run to a very useful 205 aircraft, with Aerfer making much of the airframe and with engine production in the good hands of Fiat assisted by Alfa-Romeo. Fortunately the success of the F-104S did not prompt Italian withdrawal from MRCA, and it is at present expected that the fighter version of that collaborative aircraft will supplement and then replace the 104S force from about 1981.

It would be simple to dismiss the F-104S as too much of a compromise, and an ill-conceived way of prolonging the life of a controversial old design. Indeed I have even heard one critic say it was designed, like the Aeritalia G.222 transport, merely to keep up employment in the Italian aerospace industry. I do not share this view. In the mid-1970s the 104S is capable of fulfilling a very important spectrum of roles, and though it could not safely dogfight with an ACF, or share the same 100-mile block of sky as a Tomcat or Eagle, it nevertheless represents a cost-effective answer to a basic defence problem, especially if you already happen to own a force of Starfighters. In 1974, when I wrote this, four members of the NATO alliance—Belgium, the Netherlands, Denmark and Norway—

were trying to decide on a replacement for their F-104Gs. They appeared to have come to the conclusion that they did not want an attack aircraft but an air-superiority fighter, which is a very questionable conclusion in itself; but at the same time none has shown the slightest interest in the cheap answer of converting their existing Starfighters into F-104S interceptors.

Typically, the only export customer for the F-104S so far has been a NATO country lately locked in combat with another NATO country. The customer is Turkey, whose air force has long since learned to operate the G model with considerable flair, and in its tragic conflict with Greece felt an acute need for a better interceptor. For seven years Turkey has been trying to create its own aircraft industry, Tusas—'Which', said an American observer who thought there were far too many planemakers already chasing a limited market, 'the world needs like it needs a hole in the head'. Tusas had been formally established by 1974, but had not come into tangible existence. It is planned to start life in partnership with a foreign company, such as Northrop, Lockheed, Dassault-Breguet or BAC, and to build one of the more obvious products of the chosen firm. To tide the Turkish Air Force over, an order was placed in August 1974 for 18 F-104S, plus a further 18 on option. The price quoted, 'just over US $16 million including spares', is so low that the engines and avionics must be priced separately. In my view the 104S is good value, and to try to keep it competitive Aeritalia has spent 1974 updating its avionics and weapons. The fundamentally obsolescent Nasarr R-21G radar is being much improved by CGE-Fiat, in partnership with Rockwell, with such new features as MTI, an improved aerial (still a scanning dish type, not a phased array) and some ECCM. The big Selenia electronics firm is also developing Aspide-1A, a high-performance air-to-air missile with semi-active radar homing especially for the 104S, to supplement or replace the Sparrow. One wonders where strife-torn Italy finds the money.

There remain just a few loose ends to tie up. German 104Gs are beginning to become slightly long in the tooth. In August 1971 the Germans signed a £500,000 contract for fatigue meters, choosing the British Negretti & Zambra/RAE design. Canada has already disposed of many CF-104s, 35 of them having gone to Norway. Several countries have been making enquiries for used Starfighters, and the going rate is around $400,000. This is not much help to Lockheed, who—having watched something like 2,439 Starfighters built in 15 years, nearly all of them outside the United States—have worked very hard to keep the programme going and retain a piece of the action for themselves.

Typical of the minor improvements was the CL-984, a ground-attack fighter of 1965–66, which was virtually a 104S changed back to ground attack. But by 1969 Lockheed accepted that they would do well to make the wing bigger, and the result was the CL-1195, with 250 square feet. Lockheed aimed it straight at the Netherlands the moment that country left the MRCA consortium. Having taken the major step of making the wing bigger, Lockheed then stood back some more and carefully planned a sort of 'optimised total redesign'. The company was anxious to retain as much commonality of F-104G tooling as possible, for obvious reasons, but could see that really the basic configuration of the Starfighter could be dramatically improved. The result was the CL-1200 Lancer, which Kelly Johnson himself announced in August 1970. This shows, to my way of thinking, how the 104 ought to have been at the start. Though the forward fuselage is the same as that of a G, and the avionics, ground-support equipment and nav-attack spares are all more than 80% common, the rest is quite new. The wing is bigger, has improved high-lift systems and is mounted on top of the fuselage. The vertical tail is new and tall, and the tailplane is mounted low! Kelly emphasised what an excellent dogfighter the Lancer would be, how it could come simple and cheap or as complicated as the G, and how effective it would be in the attack role also.

During 1970–73 the Lancer was greatly refined as a project, and Lockheed took the considerable step of switching to the Pratt & Whitney F100 engine, of 50% more thrust than the J79. But fate did not smile on the project. Northrop won the contract for the International Fighter Aircraft with the F-5E Tiger II in November 1970, the MRCA programme did not collapse, the US Air Force chose Northrop and General Dynamics to build its two beautiful little 'next-generation lightweight fighters', the YF-17 and YF-16, and the many users of the F-104 did nothing, other than politely look at Lancer brochures. Nothing, that is, until December 1973. Then Aeritalia, the big Italian combine which incorporates Fiat, Aerfer and Salmoiraghi, and thus includes virtually the whole F-104S and Italian MRCA participation, agreed to sign a contract with Lockheed for a lot of collaborative development and marketing. Included in the deal was the Lancer. The Italians insist this in no way conflicts with the MRCA programme, now very much into production hardware, nor with the 104S. Yet development of the Lancer would be a very big task indeed, and I would be prepared to bet it never gets off the ground.

Douglas F4D (F-6A) Skyray

I will not call the tailless Skyray a 'McDonnell Douglas' product, because it did not continue as an active programme to the end of the life of Douglas Aircraft as an independent company. Indeed it left front-line service during 1962, though it stayed long enough to receive the new Department of Defense designation of F-6A. Some of my readers will have only the haziest recollection of the Skyray, and it was not one of the 'great aeroplanes of history'—though it did win a world speed record. I have included it in this book for several reasons. One is that it was a unique and extremely effective answer to a very difficult problem. Another is that it makes an instructive and entertaining story. Perhaps the best reason is that I think it is fair to describe the Skyray as the first supersonic fighter in the world. One could argue about this indefinitely, but the design of the Skyray began as early as that of any other supersonic fighter, it flew much earlier than any other (though with a temporary engine of inadequate thrust for exceeding Mach 1), and when given a more powerful engine it did exceed Mach 1 on the level (though the F-100 and Mig-19 had done so previously). And it was also a successful programme, because more than 400 joined the US Navy and Marine Corps.

In 1945 Douglas had several very large plants. On the south side of what is now Los Angeles International Airport was the El Segundo Division, where chief engineer Ed Heinemann had directed the design of such war-winning aircraft as the Boston/Havoc, Dauntless, Invader and Skyraider. In May of that year El Segundo sent a team under DoD auspices to see what could be found of technical interest in Germany, the leaders being L. Eugene (Gene) Root and Amo (his initials) Smith; Dr Clark Millikan of the California Institute of Technology also joined. The whole team, and particularly Amo, returned laden with exciting information. Some of this had come from the research programmes of Dr Alex M. Lippisch, who had been investigating the possibilities of the tailless delta as a suitable shape for high-speed aircraft. During World War 2 the ignorance of aerodynamicists on what shape aircraft ought to be for flight at transonic or supersonic Mach numbers was profound. Though the existence of the turbojet made research into this huge unexplored field a matter of obvious urgency, nothing was done in Britain and almost nothing in the USA; but in Germany work proceeded frantically—even though it was unlikely to influence the course of the war. This pioneer work gave the world the swept wing, the variable-sweep wing and the delta.

Lippisch's deltas had wings that were more or less pure triangles, and they usually had hardly any fuselage. Typically there was a turbojet intake in the form of a shallow, flattened oval at the apex of the wing, and a small cockpit faired into the leading edge of a large triangular fin. The idea looked attractive and worth taking further, but though it showed to advantage over more conventional shapes in the medium-subsonic range its drag increased very sharply as the speed of sound was approached and crossed over the drag curve of a conventional jet well below Mach 1. In 1945 wind tunnels could not be operated in the transonic region because they became 'choked' by shockwaves and suffered violently unstable flow, though it was possible to run a supersonic tunnel successfully if adequate power was available to drive it. Heinemann's team spent much of 1945 trying to find a Lippisch-type configuration that would work for a fighter, if possible without a fuselage or tailplane in order to reduce drag. There were two seemingly insuperable problems. One was that the wing had to be fairly thick, just as were Lippisch's wings, so the transonic drag rise was disastrous. The other was that putting in a conventional cockpit and a powerful engine made the central part so deep that the net result was not so much the elimination of the fuselage as the gross thickening of the wing!

Heinemann's team were reluctant to drop this line of enquiry. It was a time of unprecedented broadening of horizons, when all sensible designers were urgently trying to pick the winners from countless radically new configurations. Already a P-63 Kingcobra had flown with a swept wing, North American were putting a swept wing on the XP-86 (later F-86 Sabre) fighter and Boeing were going for sweep on the B-47. Since 1943 Bell had held a contract for a rocket-propelled supersonic aircraft. Douglas did not wish merely to stick jet engines into a 'piston-engined shape' as most of their rivals were doing. But the El Segundo Division also had the opportunity to obtain a valuable and challenging high-speed research contract from the Office of Naval Research, and this kept the project and design staff very busy for several years. In fact the outcome of the ONR contract and its successors were the D.558-1 Skystreak, a small jet aircraft that in August 1947 twice broke the world speed record, and the D.558-2 Skyrocket that set a host of unofficial records for speed and altitude and in 1953 became the first aircraft to exceed Mach 2 (having reached 1.88 in August 1951). The data gathered with these very fully instrumented aircraft filled nearly 10,000 reports, and the Skyrockets, more than any other aircraft, removed the fear and mystery of supersonic flight and soon demonstrated it publicly right down to about 100 ft above the California desert.

The Skyrocket, in particular, was an outstandingly cost/effective project which put the Navy at least on a par with the Air Force (Army Air Force until 1947) in transonic and supersonic knowledge and experience. While the various D.558 aircraft were being designed in 1945–46 the El Segundo project staff continued to test tunnel models of tailless fighters, albeit in a low key. Heinemann and his chief designer, Leo J. Devlin, gradually refined the crude Lippisch form and overcame its drawbacks. It had really been obvious all along that there had to be a conventional fuselage, or at least a usable volume along the centreline shaped like one. It was also evident that the wing had to be thin. The breakthrough was the decision to blend the wing into the fuselage with a huge tapering fillet of increased chord. This concept gave the best tunnel drag measurements and also overcame the problem of finding space for adequate fuel tankage. (After the Skyray it was apparently forgotten until the Air Force FX programme of 1966 made several companies rediscover it, and it is today seen in the two most important Air Force supersonic aircraft, the B-1 and F-15, as well as the light fighters YF-16 and YF-17.)

By the end of 1946 it looked as if the tailless delta shape might lead to a practical fighter. The Navy had kept a close watch on the progress of the project, and early in 1947 the Fighter Branch Head, Cdr (later Admiral) A. B. Metzger had a formal discussion with Heinemann to ascertain whether Douglas was yet in a position to make a proposal. One handicap was that the sort of fighter they both had in mind would need an engine more powerful than any in existence, and neither Heinemann nor the Navy was at all keen on the idea of backing up the turbojet with a rocket; indeed even the new idea of an afterburner was likely to emphasise the difficulty of providing enough fuel capacity. After a lot of discussion and parametric analysis Metzger's team came up with a specification for a fairly short-range interceptor. It was, of course, to be capable of operating from a carrier, which in those days meant the *Essex* class. It was to be capable of reaching 40,000 ft within five minutes of taking off, and of there intercepting and destroying a 500 mph bomber. This specification was, I believe, the first formulated by any Navy in response to the threat posed by the jet bomber carrying nuclear weapons. Thus the Douglas design can be considered the first naval interceptor—as distinct from fighter—in history.

After World War 2 the National Advisory Committee for Aeronautics had collated and expanded American research into new shapes of wing, and Douglas El Segundo worked closely with NACA in trying to find the optimum shape for their Navy interceptor. Another organisation that played a major role was Millikan's Caltech, where two big tunnels were vital tools in proving the aerodynamic behaviour of the steadily refined shapes developed by Heinemann's chief aerodynamicist, Kermit E. Van Every. During 1947 and early 1948 Van Every refined the planform so that it was no longer a delta at all but a conventional swept wing redrawn to a very low aspect ratio. In fact the wing eventually adopted was essentially the same as that used for the A3D Skywarrior strategic bomber (see *Bombers of the West*), though the contrast in aspect ratio could hardly have been more extreme. By 1948 work had started on what later became the A3D, and it forms an instructive comparison with the tailless fighter. As the A3D had a tail, and was designed for long range, the right answer was a long, slender wing with high-lift flaps to give acceptable low-speed performance despite the extremely high wing-loading. With the fighter the best answer seemed to be to use an extremely low aspect ratio, making up in low wing-loading for the fact that the maximum lift coefficient of the tailless machine was approximately half that of the bomber. This was because, though it was possible to fit leading-edge slats, there seemed to be no way to use trailing-edge flaps because there was no tailplane further aft to trim out the pitching moment.

This problem of basic stability and control was a difficult one which proved too much for two major US fighter design teams at this time. In contrast, the basic components of the Douglas aircraft seemed to go together well. At the front was a radar and a comfortable cockpit with an ejection seat. Then came the two big engine inlet ducts, which curved inwards to feed the single turbojet, while the inboard part of the wing continued behind the ducts as a full depth fillet, tapering sharply from the body to meet the thin wing one-third of the way from the centreline to the tip. The unprecedentedly stubby wing held the span at a mere 33 ft 6 in, so only the tips needed to fold for carrier stowage. On the leading edge of the thin wing were slats; on the trailing edge were elevons, which were considered to need at least hydraulic boost if not full power control. Above the jet pipe was the tall, swept fin and rudder for good directional stability. The whole aircraft looked compact and very businesslike. It promised to have tremendous climb and outstanding manoeuvrability at all altitudes. Fuel capacity was adequate for the kind of interception mission the Navy had outlined. There was some difficulty in arranging the landing gear for the expected nose-high landing, and a more fundamental problem was the need to minimise trim drag and arrange the elevons for rapid manoeuvres about both the roll and pitch axes.

By December 1948 the Navy thought the time had come for a hardware contract. Though not yet entirely sold on the tailless delta formula, it respected Heinemann as probably the nation's No 1 designer of carrier aircraft, and it was prepared to fund two prototype fighters designated Douglas XF4D-1, with the name Skyray. Cdr Tommy Blackburn and

Lt-Cdr Sid Sherby, both later Heads of the Fighter Branch, were active in managing the programme on behalf of the Navy. At El Segundo Robert Donovan (later Charles S. Kennedy) was appointed XF4D project engineer, with Johnny Gorgenson his assistant. The Skyray fighter programme was now in being, joining the equally radical Chance Vought Cutlass (flown 1948), water-ski Convair Sea Dart (flown 1953), swing-wing Grumman Jaguar (flown 1953) and Lockheed XFV-1 and Convair XFY-1 tail-sitting VTOLs (both flown 1954). Clearly the Navy was prepared to fund a remarkable array of unconventional fighters to the stage of flying prototypes. Out of the whole lot, though the Cutlass did later see limited service, only the Skyray can be considered to have been a success.

Perhaps the most obvious problem facing Heinemann was the choice of engine. During World War 2 the leading engine firms, Pratt & Whitney and Wright, had been directed by the Defense Production Board to concentrate on war-winning piston engines, leaving gas turbines to a variety of other firms which had gained power experience chiefly in the field of steam turbines. Way out in front of the other turbine firms was the giant General Electric, but in 1948 this company's excellent J47 was judged too small for the Douglas fighter and the only visible alternative was the XJ53 which was likely to be much too big. Pratt & Whitney's J48 with afterburner could give up to 8,500 lb with water injection, but it was a fat centrifugal engine tracing its ancestry back via Rolls-Royce to Whittle. Pratts had a scheme to make a completely new and very advanced two-shaft axial engine, but this had not been settled even on paper. The best choice seemed to be the biggest engine in the Westinghouse series of axials, the YJ40, and this had two big advantages. It was already being planned with an afterburner for transonic fighters, and it was a Navy-funded engine. The predicted thrust level was 7,200 lb, with about 10,500 lb expected with afterburner.

Heinemann had not been in the aviation business 22 years for nothing. He reasoned that in the fullness of time he might wish he had chosen a different engine. Accordingly he arranged the fuselage interior so that it could readily accommodate any engine with a diameter below about 42 inches, no matter how it was suspended or where the accessories were. With the Westinghouse YJ40 the engine and airframe accessories were driven off the front of the compressor, and occupied a large bay projecting well ahead between the inlet ducts. But in 1948 this was all on paper, and no YJ40 had been built. Another thing Westinghouse had not built—perhaps understandably—was the radar. Unlike the muddled thinking in Britain, the US Navy had already decided that most fighters, especially expensive supersonic ones, were going to need 'night and all-weather' equipment in order to operate at the times they were most likely to be needed. Though it was from the start a single-seater, the XF4D was required to carry a complete AI radar with long-range search and lock-on facilities, though the armament specified was guns.

One of the most harassed members of the team was John Barter. His assignment was the flying-control system, and in 1948 not too much was known about how these should be arranged for a supersonic fighter in the form of a tailless delta. After a great deal of tunnel testing it was decided that the swept trailing edge of each wing should be filled by a one-piece elevon, serving as an elevator when both were moved together and as an aileron when the left and right surfaces were moved in opposition. The inner trailing edge curved back again to meet the fuselage about three feet ahead of the jet nozzle. It was decided to straighten this inboard trailing edge so that, at the point where the thin wing met the blended root fillet, there was a sharp kink. The inboard portion—the rear part of the fillet—was made in the form of a broad-chord trimmer, with a very sharp taper in both thickness and plan, with a final fixed inner section filling the gap at the boat-tailed rear fuselage. At take-off and landing this trimmer was locked full-up, to give a strong nose-up moment, whilst leaving the elevons in their most effective (neutral) position.

Douglas enquired diligently of such firms as Bendix, Sperry and Honeywell to find an autopilot and flight-data computer, and wondered where the boxes would fit when they were available. Barter had to scheme a 'q-feel' system, then a new idea, so that the pilot could sense the aerodynamic loads on the surfaces and thus avoid violent control deflections at very high speeds in dense air that could break the aircraft. To make matters much harder still, the Navy insisted on manual reversion, so that if the duplicated power units failed in any way the hydraulics could be cut out of circuit and the pilot could fly the aircraft with his muscles. Simple sums showed this to be possible only at low speeds, and even then it would be very hard work. To give the pilot greater leverage the control column was given a press-button which, when operated, extended the stick to almost twice its original modest length. This seemed a reasonable idea, and it worked satisfactorily on the ground system rig which the company's veteran test pilot, Larry Peyton, tried out several days a week.

The pretentious stick was not the only unusual bit of engineering. Though the blended wing/body fillet was structurally excellent, and served to distribute the very large wing loads round the engine through multiple V-shaped spars, Heinemann always had a passion for weight-reduction. Experience had taught him that this is the only way to accommodate all the added items and extra fuel that the customer later is sure to demand. To minimise structure weight the XF4D was given a novel skin over much of its area. The outer skin was made of very thin (0.0025–0.0030 in) light alloy sheet, and the necessary stiffening was provided by a 'pillowed' or double-corrugated reinforcing skin secured on the inside by spot-welding. The resulting panels were very light and stable, and showed excellent resistance to buckling.

Less happy was the realisation that Douglas would have to produce their own autopilot and flight-data computer. El Segundo had already learned in the hardest possible way about advanced avionics (a term not then coined for aviation electronics), mainly through the otherwise excellent F3D Skyknight. This twin-jet all-weather fighter for the Navy and Marine Corps had a huge radar containing almost 400 vacuum tubes (thermionic valves). Today electronics people have almost forgotten about such things, because it was in 1948 that the immortal Bardeen, Brattain and Shockley won their Nobel prize with the invention of the transistor. But it took a little while for semiconductor technology to percolate down to the level of the user squadrons, and with the Skyknight Marine radar crews worked all day and all night rebuilding radars on the spot and selecting individual tubes by hand to make the complex circuits behave. This was the same technology Heinemann had to use for the supersonic Skyray. The radar was Westinghouse's problem, but the autopilot and computer were his. He even had to sanction magnetic clutches in the control system, with different flux and gear ratios for different bands of indicated airspeed. Clearly he was going to have to use all his ingenuity to avoid the already radically unconventional Skyray becoming a disliked 'can of worms'.

More than this, Heinemann and his team had known from the start that with this interceptor they were sticking their necks out a mile. They were doing precisely the sort of thing Dassault would avoid like the plague, and to try to forestall trouble they nursed their radical offspring with a lot of tender care and racked their brains to think in advance of all possible ills. For example, as there was no horizontal tail it occurred to Heinemann that, following a stall, the XF4D might continue to autorotate end-over-end about the transverse axis. This seemed a valid worry, so suitably weighted free-flight models were released in different attitudes from the rafters of the highest building at El Segundo, and caught in a net. The air in the building was more or less still, and there was enough height for quite a few turns of a spin or whatever else happened. For comparative purposes two other types of tailless model—the El Segundo Model 25 bomber project and a rival fighter—were tested in the same way. The two latter aircraft, with dominant transverse axis, did not fare well; the one with the higher aspect ratio did indeed tumble autorotatively, with no recovery, at normal c.g. (and I cannot think of anything more unpleasant). But the XF4D, with its forward c.g. and dominant longitudinal axis, dropped its nose dutifully from all release positions and recovered well.

There were other snags of a blunter kind. In October 1949 the centre of activity was the impressive mock-up, which was to be inspected by a nit-picking Mock-up Review Board the next day. The mock-up, mainly of wood but complete with virtually all systems and equipment, was finished. On the wall in front was a huge drawing of a carrier, as seen on the approach, with little batsmen six inches high. When the mock-up was tilted by crane into the correct attitude for the approach the carrier vanished completely beneath the field of view of the worried pilot! This confirmed the worst fears of Admiral Trapnell, who had flown the mock-up a day or two earlier. Desperately, without drawings from the engineering department, structural design engineer Harry Gustafson led a crew which sawed off the nose and put on a completely new one which still accommodated the radar but had a sharply down-sloping top line. Nobody told the review board next day, which said the view on the approach was beautiful. There was another snag, too, which took longer to cure. Model testing from simulated catapults in a low-speed tunnel showed that the XF4D would not hold the altitude of the deck after launch. Instead it would sink until its continued forward acceleration—and also perhaps the worried pilot hauling back on the stick—had arrested the sink and started the climb. 'This problem alone', said Gorgenson, 'could have made the ship a turkey' (a technical washout)—which would have been a pity with 10,000 drawings released, 25,000 new items of tooling made and 2,000 subcontractors in the programme. When the Royal Navy bought the Phantom it cured a similar problem by doubling the length of the nose leg, so that the big bird could claw its way into the air from a British carrier at a greater angle of attack. Trying this with the XF4D would have rubbed the little tailwheel into the deck. The answer, found after exhaustive model tests by Harry Cornish's carrier-suitability team, was to select just the right location for the catapult hooks so that, as the fighter left the deck, it had rotated nose-up to the necessary 20° inclination. This sounds dicey but it worked.

A major nuisance, but a temporary one, was that Douglas built the first XF4D-1, BuAer No 124586, well in advance of Westinghouse getting flight-clearance on the YJ40 engine. So wide was the timing gap that Heinemann and the Navy agreed to use the much smaller Allison J35-A-17 engine in this first aircraft so that flight development could begin. The slim, non-afterburning J35 had to be mounted well aft to get the c.g. in the right place, and its thrust of 5,000 lb precluded any hope of exceeding Mach 1 for the time being, but when the midnight-blue prototype was finally readied for flight at the Navy facility at Edwards AFB in January 1951 I think it could be described as the first supersonic fighter ever built. After fast taxying runs, Peyton made a successful 30-minute maiden flight on 23 January 1951.

In their press release, which curiously was held up for six days, Douglas said 'The new interceptor is a swept wing with web-like planform'. I think this must have been some allusion to the feet of a duck, though the similarity is far from evident. Likewise, countless people described the Skyray as 'bat-winged' but though this sounds good I think a comparison with any species of bat will show it to be nonsense. Yet maybe these descriptions were preferable to calling the aircraft a delta. What was indisputable was that the Skyray had a singularly exciting shape, even more than other tailless aircraft.

One man who liked it was Robert O. Rahn, the big fair-haired fighter pilot who had been an El Segundo test pilot since World War 2. He was appointed XF4D chief engineering test pilot, and straight away began the long but intensely interesting task of getting rid of a host of 'bugs'. From the start the cockpit was comfortable, the very light and simple Douglas El Segundo ejection seat fitted well, the view was superb—even in the extreme nose-high attitude on landing—and the Hamilton Standard air-conditioning system pressurised and cooled the cockpit and instrumentation exactly according to plan. Handling was generally exemplary. Admiral Trapnell thought he was asking a lot when he insisted on a rate of roll of at least 500°/sec, but the measured figure was close to 1,000°/sec. This was before the days of bonedomes, and Rahn must have banged his head on the side of the canopy. I have never come across a higher normal rate of roll than this. But there were lots of bumps and buffets. On one early flight No 124586 suddenly yawed violently at 100 ft altitude at 400 knots. The cause was the peeling of the skin along the blister housing the retracted tailwheel. On another occasion Rahn had to haul back with both hands to stop the aircraft pitching into a bunt; eventually he was able to discuss the matter with the Edwards tower who told him to pull the powered-controls circuit-breaker. He was able to recover manually, but found the task no picnic, even with the stick extended.

These were transient snags, but it was soon apparent there was violent turbulence at the back end at high speeds. Tunnel testing revealed that this was due to complete flow-breakaway over the sharply tapered boat-tail surrounding the small J35 nozzle. It looked as if the much bigger original design of orifice for the afterburning J40 would do much to alleviate the problem, but the immediate cure was to redesign the back end. The modified rear fuselage was hardly tapered at all, but held its full diameter almost to the nozzle. The end of the small J35 jet-pipe was centred in a large outward-sloping periphery which inevitably increased the base-drag, cutting 10 knots off the cruising speed, but it raised the buffet boundary by 40 knots. On the other hand, the change resulted in the rudder and trimmers vibrating at their natural frequency. These surfaces were stiffened, and later they were completely redesigned. Below the rudder was added a pointed 'pen nib' fairing. The trimmers were extended far behind the nozzle in the form of even more sharply tapered surfaces, so that the nozzle was surrounded by huge aft-pointing spikes at 9, 12 and 3 o'clock. This rear-fuselage buffet grew in violence when the afterburning YJ40 engine was finally fitted in 1953, and required at least 150 flights to cure completely.

During 1952 both XF4D-1s (124586 and 124587) were cleared to use the Westinghouse YJ40-WE-6, without afterburner, rated at 7,000 lb, which gave rather better performance but suffered from very short time between overhauls and persistent mechanical failures. There was also abundant evidence that the thin-gauge skin, despite its pillowed inner reinforcement, was not robust enough to stand up to normal wear and tear. Very soon the outer skin showed numerous depressions, dents and even punctures, which are highly undesirable on a supersonic fighter. Heinemann was also deeply troubled at the unreliability of the autopilot and computer—though these were no worse than other complex avionic systems of more than 20 years ago—and at the very slow progress of Westinghouse with the radar. But the biggest problem of all was the unreliability of the J40, and the succession of diverse failures suffered by the development engines on the test bed. There were engines running at the main test station at Kansas City, at the headquarters of the Gas Turbine Division at South Philadelphia and at the Naval power-plant lab at Camden and Trenton. The fact that Philadelphia and Kansas City were so far apart was only a small factor in a very distressing situation. Westinghouse will appreciate that I cannot avoid re-opening this old wound, but the gigantic corporation had never acquired the necessary skills and facilities to develop aircraft turbojets. It so happened that their 24-inch engine worked quite well, and was able to go into production for several aircraft as the J34. This helped to mask the company's development weaknesses and when the bigger J40 was found to be a design and engineering disaster there was no way of remedying the situation.

For a long time Westinghouse attempted to present a brave face to the Navy and to their several anxious customers. One programme that was badly hit was Heinemann's own Skywarrior, which could not take the air until flight-cleared YJ40-WE-3 engines were available, which extended the time from start of design to first flight from the planned 24 months to 36 months and 9 days. Some other programmes were abandoned, and the excellent near-Mach 1 McDonnell F3H Demon suffered the most depressing experience of any fighter that comes to mind. In 1953–55 a total of 58 F3H-1 Demons were completed, some being test-flown; 21 of them were then taken away from St Louis on barges in drab primer paint and used for ground instruction or any other non-flying duty the Navy could think of. The only alternative engine that would fit was an urgently contrived afterburning version of the Allison J71. With this McDonnell and the Navy finally managed to salvage the Demon programme by developing the very fine F3H-2, which became the first aircraft ever to go into operational service with advanced radar-directed air-to-air guided missiles. Fortunately for Heinemann things were easier for the Skyray; his foresight in planning for a possible alternative engine paid off. On 15 March 1953 the Navy took the decision to replace the J40 in both the Skyray and the Skywarrior with the J57, the excellent Pratt & Whitney two-spool axial engine that had been only a piece of paper at the start of the Skyray programme in 1948.

While the harrowing power-plant story unfolded in the east, Rahn and his colleagues in California continued to do their best to fly the two XF4Ds on the Westinghouse engines. By the end of 1952 both had been much modified in detail and repainted white, and despite a not inconsiderable list of snags and deficiencies neither had suffered any major set-back. On the contrary, the combination of light weight and low wing-loading promised to make the Skyray a first-class interceptor as soon as it acquired a good engine. The very thin skin could by now be fairly judged a mistake, but there was nothing lacking in the strength of the airframe. On one memorable occasion Rahn overstressed the whole wing—which is virtually the whole structure—while doing high-g manoeuvres. On recovery it was found that 'the whole ship looked like a prune—it was deeply wrinkled all over'. Had it been a conventional airframe one wing would have jack-knifed upwards, and if it had had a single spar the wing would probably have come off. As it was, the multiple spars and unusual skin panels allowed the wing to deflect upwards in the bending mode about the neutral axis with all the failures on the compression (upper) side. Heinemann thinks this was the first time such a thing had happened. It was good for Rahn, though the first XF4D was a write-off.

Early in 1953 the YJ40-WE-8 was at last cleared for limited experimental flying. This massive engine was rated at 11,100 lb (later 11,600 lb) with afterburner, and it madc a big difference to the performance of the Skyray and pushed the level speed up close to Mach 1. In doing so it sharply accentuated some of the buffet troubles, requiring further reshaping and reinforcement around the tail, and Heinemann also devoted increased attention to the engine air inlets. In 1953 the design of inlets and ducts for supersonic air-breathing engines was still in its infancy. Most of the manned flight experience at Mach numbers greater than unity had been gained by rocket aircraft, and the many trial launches of supersonic ramjet vehicles had been with intakes which did not have to operate at low speeds or (so the story went) at large angles of yaw or pitch or any other off-design condition. To avoid trouble the XF4D had been designed to begin its development with simple plain inlets of rounded triangular form, with a generous radius round the edges. These fat lips did avoid trouble, but with the afterburning engine it was clear they were taking a bit off the speed.

One day in August 1953 Rahn returned to Edwards slightly disappointed that he had been unable to push through what was in those days still a fairly tangible 'sound barrier'. He and the Douglas/Navy team at Edwards were not exactly unaware of the triumph of the rival NAA/Air Force team in exceeding Mach 1 on the very first flight of the YF-100. Rahn had made a level run at medium height with sustained full afterburner, but the Machmeter had stubbornly refused to move beyond about 0.98. He taxied up to his parking place, opened the clamshell canopy and was surprised to find himself surrounded by exuberant chaps trying to shake his hand and pat his back. As later happened to several other test pilots, he had gone supersonic with an imperfect pitot/static system which did not record the fact. That the Skyray was supersonic there was no doubt; the watching crew at Edwards said the shock wave 'nearly knocked us off our feet'.

This made the rivalry between the Navy and Air Force reach fever-heat, with the added excitement that both teams were unable to stop thinking about the world speed record. It was that unique time in history when the world speed record was being squeezed up into the last subsonic extremity by choosing hotter and hotter weather on which to fly. As the speed of sound varies with air temperature, a record contender capable of reaching a given subsonic Mach number can fly significantly faster in summer than in winter. In fact in the summer of 1953 the record was held by an Air Force pilot who had taken an F-86D to the Salton Sea, deep in the California desert, where not only was the summer temperature extremely high but the flat terrain was below sea level, making the air still hotter. Lt Col Barnes had reached 715 mph, which the Skyray could beat easily. Douglas and the Navy discussed the matter, and it was decided to complete further vital test programmes and gain more experience, especially with the troublesome engine, rather than risk an abortive attempt. Had the Skyray been raced in the height of summer it would almost certainly have set a startling world record, and it would also have dashed the hopes of two Englishmen. On 7 September 1953 Neville Duke averaged 727.6 mph in a special Hunter with an afterburning engine. At once the Navy decided to 'have a go' with the Skyray, with their own F4D project pilot, Lt Cdr James B. Verdin. Swiftly plans were made to detach a crew to the Marine base at El Centro and to set up the instrumented course over the nearby Salton Sea. Unknown to them, the Vickers-Supermarine works at Chilbolton in Hampshire had already sent a crew to the scorching Libyan desert at Azizia, together with a Swift 7.4 flown by Mike Lithgow. On 25 September, just as the XF4D crew were leaving for the record course, Lithgow set a record at 735.7 mph. This would not be simple to beat.

Though the XF4D was troubled by various airframe deficiencies, by its undeveloped engine, and by the fact that it was not designed for full-throttle flying at 'nought feet' (or, in this case, possibly even a minus altitude), the attempt went ahead. Unfortunately, the mercury stood at a mere 27.5°C, and Verdin found he could only just better Lithgow's speed (gained in air at 49°C) by the necessary 1%. But on 3 October the ambient temperature reached 37°C and Verdin climbed into the stubby white Skyray determined to do the best he could. For once, the J40 ran faultlessly and the average for his two runs was 752.9 mph. This made the Navy whoop with delight, and caused shocked surprise to the Air Force who had never dreamed the world record could be gained by anything designed to fly off a carrier. For good measure, on 16 October Bob Rahn flew the same aircraft round a 100 km closed circuit at Edwards to set another world record at 728.11 mph. The Navy was cock-a-hoop; no longer were they second-class citizens where air speed was concerned.

These records did wonders to Navy morale, which had been badly hurt by the J40 engine situation. Moreover, during the XF4D flight development, in early 1953, the BuAer had become so intensely interested in the Skyray that they asked Douglas for production quotes. Heinemann tells me 'We didn't think we were quite ready, but our reluctance wasn't exactly overwhelming and we submitted a bid. It was accepted, and we were given a production contract with deliveries starting in 1955. This, with add-ons, totalled 412.' Thus, while the surviving XF4D-1 was breaking the sound barrier and speed records in 1953, the Douglas plant at Torrance, Los Angeles, was tooled-up to make the unusual interceptor and a big manufacturing programme began. Final assembly took place on a single ten-station line with a continuous floor at wing level, the floor sections between one aircraft and the next as far out as the main legs being hinged to allow aircraft to move to the next station. Production was found to be particularly easy, Douglas claimed, partly owing to the 'one-piece manufacture of the wing and fuselage allowing speed and economy in assembly'.

Everything hinged on the J57–P–2 engine, which ran on the bench at Hartford in June 1953 at ratings of 10,500 lb dry and 14,500 lb with afterburner. Engine troubles had almost crippled the Douglas programme, and Westinghouse had also consistently failed to develop the complex and densely packed AI radar. Heinemann recalls he 'was about ready to commit hara-kiri over Westinghouse' because the big Skywarrior was likewise held up for engines and radar, but in the course of 1953 the production F4D-1 was planned around a new simplified radar by GE and this broke the second stumbling-block. (It is only fair to add that Westinghouse never gave up, and many years later it was partly their completely different and much better APQ-72 radar that clinched the decision of the Air Force to buy the Navy Phantom.) The performance of the new GE radar was comparable with that of the missing Westinghouse set. The armament of the F4D-1 was four 20mm Mk-12 cannon, and there were two under-wing pylons each stressed to 2,000 lb. Later five more racks were added to give a range of tank/FFAR/missile/bomb options, though the load limit stayed at 4,000 lb. The basic build-standard was decided in 1952, before the Navy became interested in probes for in-flight refuelling.

I ought to mention here that, early in 1953, Heinemann had decided in favour of undertaking a thorough structural and systems redesign of the F4D in order to eliminate all its significant deficiencies. This work made good progress during 1953, and in December the Navy authorised a go-ahead on the improved aircraft which was designated XF5D Skylancer. This will come into the story later on.

Jimmy Verdin did far more for the Skyray than gain a world speed record. He played the major role in early evaluation on behalf of the customer, and it was his enthusiasm that assured the BuAer the potentially outstanding performance was not gained at the expense of losing docile handling. His first encounter with the XF4D had been early in 1953 at the Naval Air Test Center at Patuxent River, Maryland. He told *Bee-Hive*, the magazine of United Aircraft (which includes Pratt & Whitney), 'Like most pilots I had to find out something for myself. Through my own error I put the airplane into a spin. I spun all right—six times. I got out of that one, and I went on to fly the airplane with a lot of success that day. In spite of that introduction, I've grown to have more confidence in the F4D's performance than in any other airplane I've ever flown.' In another context he said 'When you are climbing at the rate possble in the F4D you are almost flat on your back. In that situation it is all airplane, almost like instrument flying, and everything in the way of pilot assistance helps.' The sustained-climb angles reached by afterburning Skyrays had never before been equalled, and this not only required good judgement if the maximum rate of climb was to be achieved but it also caused air-traffic problems, as related later.

Between 26 and 30 October 1953 Verdin flew the XF4D through its carrier qualification trials. The ship was USS *Coral Sea*, off Norfolk, Virginia. Verdin relates 'The landings and take-offs were made during windy weather and the deck was pitching considerably. This made for a good test of the F4D's low-speed characteristics, especially its stability.' The Skyray retained its automatic slats, half on the fixed wing and half on the curved folding tip, because these markedly improved lateral control on carrier approach. They slightly degraded pitch stability, however, and Heinemann kept researching for ways to eliminate them. They were open on both take-off and landing, and were certainly over-worked during the 36 approaches made by Cdr Marshall Beebe during carrier qualification when, in heavy rain squalls, he simulated in an exaggerated way the worst carrier landings conceivable. At the end of the trials Verdin made a maximum-rate climb to 40,000 feet, disappearing on full afterburner at a seemingly impossible angle. This demonstrated compliance with the requirement to climb 40,000 feet in five minutes; indeed, in 1958 the operational Skyray set some world record times-to-height which showed it could get up there in much less than half the time!

The first production F4D-1 (No 130740), with J57-P-2 engine, exceeded Mach 1 on the level on its maiden flight by Rahn on 5 June 1954. This was the first time the Skyray had flown with the J57, and at last it looked as if the Navy had a bug-free aeroplane. The available thrust was almost three times as great as that on the first flight in 1951, and it made a wonderful difference. Like Air Force J57 engines the P-2 cut in its afterburner in one sudden booming jerk, and Rahn was reported to have likened this to 'getting kicked in the rear-end by a well-fed mule'. Rahn came from Illinois farming country, so he probably knew what he was talking about; but can he really have been so scrupulously polite as to say 'rear-end'? More seriously, Rahn was one of the first pilots in the world to have an aeroplane that could operate far up the back of the drag-curve, where increasing speed reduces drag and vice versa. Some early deltas, such as the Avro 707s, lacked engine thrust and could easily get into impossible situations at low speeds from which there was no recovery without drastic loss of height. In contrast Rahn found he could reduce speed to the minimum-drag point—which I guess may have been around 160 knots—and then pull the nose up further, going slower and slower and opening the throttle wider and wider. He reported he had 'often amazed myself, and some of the boys, by taking the airplane down and flying formation on a Navion', a lightplane which cruises at around 125 knots. It is a funny feeling to fly straight and level with your nose pointing so high in the sky.

The J57 engine at long last enabled the El Segundo and Navy pilots to explore the combat manoeuvring envelope at all altitudes, at transonic and supersonic speeds. Protected by the q-feel from folding up like a prune a second time, the production fighters showed excellent behaviour and could out-turn any other jet aircraft. Not unexpectedly, pulling g at altitude did cause some buffeting with the more powerful engine, and Heinemann himself said it was a problem at 'Mach 1 plus 2 or 3 tenths' in maximum-rate turns. On the other hand, not even the Skyray could hold both the turn and the speed. Studies had confirmed that, although at supersonic speeds a fighter could manoeuvre better with a tailplane, 'manoeuvres initiated at low supersonic speeds mostly decelerate the F4D quickly into the transonic region where its configuration is clearly superior'. The higher performance of the production machine emphasised the advantage of a yaw-damper, though there was never any serious tendency towards Dutch roll or inertia coupling such as that experienced by the original F-100A. Almost the only continuing nuisance was the problem of engine stalls, largely due to the inadequate knowledge of how to install a high-pressure engine, especially with a short and curving inlet duct. On the other hand the Skyray was better than many other aircraft, partly owing to its fat-lipped inlets, and it was far better than the F-111 was in 1964–67.

In January 1955, as the production Skyrays were really beginning to roll, Jimmy Verdin was killed. He had joined Douglas as a test pilot, and on 13 January he ejected at high altitude from an early A4D Skyhawk but was later found with his parachute unopened. Selling safety equipment is a touchy business, but it may be fair comment that not long after this the Navy came to England and bought Martin-Baker seats. The F4D-1, however, stayed with the lightweight Douglas seat, and so did the Skyhawk. The production F4D-1 was put through a brief programme of carrier landings by Lt Cdr Franklin T. Stephens, the ship being USS *Ticonderoga.* On 19 February 1955 an unexpected world record was set in a climb from Edwards to 10,000 ft in 56 seconds. Another bonus that is very hard to achieve without luck was that the F4D-1 proved to be an outstandingly good platform for gun-firing, weapon release or any other roles involving ordnance. Squadrons began to form with both the Atlantic and Pacific Fleets in 1955, when 32 aircraft were delivered. They each carried their guns and two 300 US gal drop tanks, with options of six packages each containing seven 2.75 in FFARs or four packages of 19. The 2000 lb bombs were seen mainly on Skyrays assigned to the Marine Corps. The one thing that at first was lacking was the hook-up between the GE radar, the fire-control and flight-data computer, and the autopilot, to allow the Skyray to perform automatic track, lock-on and firing at unseen aerial targets. The vast assemblages of vacuum tubes were persistently troublesome, just as they were in the Air Force F-86D and F-102 all-weather interceptors.

In service the Skyray was exceptionally popular with its pilots and it soon established a good name for itself—apart, perhaps, from the electronics and thin skin. Deliveries totalled 91 in 1956, 136 in 1957 and 158 in 1958. Most were embarked aboard carriers, but there was a shore-based Navy interceptor squadron at NAS North Island, San Diego. It was the only interceptor outfit on US soil not run by the Air Force. It was also a very exceptional outfit indeed, partly because of the quality of its pilots and partly, perhaps, because it flew the F4D, but I think the crux of the matter is that the CO was Cdr Eugene Valencia. He was an outstanding ball of fire. One of his precepts was 'The bigger they come, the harder I work 'em', and he insisted on a flight of three Skyrays being at near-instant readiness every minute of the year. He had a habit of hitting the alert button at about 3 in the morning, and there would be trouble if the 'burners were not blasting on the runway inside 2½ minutes' (2 minutes was expected). Each year the North American Defense Command (later NORAD) Trophy was eagerly competed for by every home-based Air Force interceptor squadron and the F4D boys from North Island. Each year at the presentation at Oxnard Gene Valencia would stand out vividly against the light blue of the Air Force top brass. In 1957 the sole Navy man proudly stepped up to receive the Trophy. In 1958 he collected it again. This also says quite a lot about the F4D.

Earlier I commented on the amazingly steep climb possible with the F4D. Though this demanded a new piloting technique, and a new presentation on the horizon, it was soon accepted as just good fun, as it is on Lightning squadrons. The angle was, in fact, 70°. It was only when an F4D-1 squadron was shore-based at NAS Alameda that trouble was encountered. Anyone who knows the San Francisco Bay area will readily agree that things that go skywards at 70° are going to bother lots of other traffic at all sorts of flight levels, and before long there were formal complaints from the airlines serving the busy international airport across the bay that their pilots were apparently being 'buzzed' from directly below and had no way of seeing what was coming. The only answer was to abandon the optimum climb angle and reprofile missions to a 25° climb-out at a much higher speed. To confirm what the F4D-1 could do, on 22 and 23 May 1958 Major E. N. LeFaivre, US Marine Corps, set world official climb records, reaching 3,000 m (9,843 ft) in 44.39 sec, 6,000 m (19,685 ft) in 1 min 6.13 sec, 9,000 m (29,530 ft) in 1 min 29.81 sec, 12,000 m (39,370 ft) in 1 min 51.23 sec, and 15,000 m (49,215 ft) in 2 min 36.05 sec. It is worth recalling that when the design went ahead in 1948 several experts considered that the requirement to reach 40,000 ft in 5 minutes would be impossible to meet. LeFaivre passed this level in approximately 1 min 53 sec!

I last saw Skyrays, by then re-styled F-6A, aboard the super-carrier *Independence* in 1962. The Marine Corps all-weather fighter squadron VMF(AW)-115 was embarked, still with slats, with the paintwork surprisingly fresh after years of transonic all-weather flight and with probe-equipped Buddy stores under their left wings. It was not long after this that I read that Lt Col Atwater and his men had re-equipped with the F-4B Phantom.

Before I round off this chapter I must hark back to December 1953 when El Segundo were authorised to go ahead with the XF5D Skylancer (which for a very short time was styled F4D-2N). This was the Skyray that had been re-engineered from stem to stern. The exterior shape was lengthened and refined. The wing was made thinner, the inlet ducts flattened and extended forwards, and the deep blended wing/body fillets replaced by shallower fairings filling in from the ducts to the new trimmers.

The latter did not reach as far aft as the big propelling nozzle of the J57-P-20 rated at 18,000 lb with afterburner. Internal fuel capacity was increased, despite the reduced thickness of the wing, by adopting integral tankage and adding fuselage fuel. The vertical tail was enlarged and moved aft, and to reduce drag the canopy was redesigned with a vee windshield and knife-edge top using toughened glass. Convair sent engineers to El Segundo to find out how to solve the severe problems they were having with the F-102/F-106 (p. 166), which had windshields and canopies of similar design.

Most important of all, the pillow-reinforced skin was discarded and replaced by integrally stiffened skins milled from light-alloy plate. The machining was all done at a single pass by multi-gang cutters on a horizontal miller cutting the whole depth in one operation, which gave a good result and was many times faster than the vertical-spindle profiling adopted by certain other US fighter firms at this time. The finished panels had skin 0.1 in thick, with stiffening webs 0.25 in × 1.25 in spaced every 2 in. Experience in the machine shop and with production tooling indicated that the F5D set a new record for low total man-hours per pound of airframe.

Douglas had a contract for ten Skylancers, and these came through final assembly in 1956. Bob Rahn flew the first, No 139208, on 21 April 1956. The first flight was a dream, and Mach 1 was easily exceeded even though fat-lipped inlets had been fitted a day or two previously as a result of a sudden message from the Navy that they would cancel if there were any engine-stalls or duct flow-separation problems such as the F4D had been prone to.

The Skylancer was planned as a largely automatic all-weather interceptor. Compared with the Skyray it had higher speed, about 30% greater range and much better systems, and in particular it would eventually have had a radar fire-control and autopilot of a later generation with solid-state circuits. It goes without saying that the manual reversion and extensible stick had also been left behind, and altogether it promised to be a cheap, robust and extremely effective aircraft. But the programme was terminated through lack of funds, along with that of the very attractive Grumman F11F-1 Tiger, leaving the interception role to the Crusader (p. 234). Four XF5D-1 and F5D-1 Skylancers were flying at the termination in 1956, and all were turned over to the NACA (NASA from 1958) who used them in numerous research programmes at Moffett Field. Douglas had flown the first Skylancer to Mach 1.35, and NACA aerodynamicists calculated that with improved inlet ducts the speed would be well in excess of Mach 1.8. In fact it was said at the time that, as the F5D was likely to beat the Crusader in speed, range, manoeuvrability, climb and low cost (a claim with which Vought are not quite in agreement), the reason for dropping it must have been that Douglas already had supplied 80% of the carrier-based aircraft and had to let someone else have a share of the business! The last time I heard of a Skylancer was in 1961 when a remarkable series of NASA trials for the Air Force required that an F5D should simulate a Dyna-Soar spacecraft aborting on the pad. The aircraft had to fly slowly at very low level and then pull vertically upwards, or even past the vertical, and explore the possible trajectories. This work, which was flown mainly by Neil Armstrong—in 1969 the first man on the Moon—showed that much smaller escape rockets could be used.

Today we would not build a tailless fighter, unless it had a foreplane, but in some other ways the basic conception of the Skyray was very much more right than some of the things that came later. If you want to clobber surface targets then big bodies and small wings make sense, but for air-superiority combat you need something with plenty of area in plan form—preferably something which looks as if it has been slightly run over and squashed flat. If the Skyray formula could have been carried on with a foreplane or tailplane into the Mach 2+ era it might have given all the other fighters a run for their money. But in January 1951 the first Skyray was a very long way ahead of the technology needed to back it up.

Vought F-8 Crusader

Today the Crusader seldom gets into the papers. Indeed, though on one or two occasions it did make front-page news, it was never well-known even to the American public, and I suppose there are a few young aviation enthusiasts who have never heard of it. I hope in this chapter to do what I can to redress the balance, because this fighter was from the very first a wholly outstanding technical achievement. At a time when no fighter could fly faster than sound in level flight, and only a select few could briefly do it in a dive, the Crusader was planned to be significantly faster than any supersonic land-based machine, and also to have greater range, despite its obvious severe restrictions in having to operate from quite small carriers. On top of this it was beautiful to fly, was a splendid dogfighter and lacked no armament the pilot wished for. As if all this were not enough, the design, development and clearance for service set a cracking pace that no other post-war jet fighter—in the West, at least—has equalled.

Such a performance suggests that the Crusader was created by a pretty remarkable team, and this is certainly the case. Chance Vought himself was a fine engineer, and one of his early designs, the VE-9 of 1923, was the first type ever to be operated from a carrier of the US Navy. Two years later Vought talked to Frederick B. Rentschler, who had broken away from Wright Aeronautical with a small team in order to make a new and better engine, and the result was the first of a long series of Navy biplanes called Corsairs. Rentschler's new company was called Pratt & Whitney Aircraft. In World War 2 both Pratt & Whitney and Vought were divisions of United Aircraft Corporation, and they worked together to create what many knowledgeable people say was the finest carrier-based fighter—if not the greatest fighter of all—of the pre-jet era. This also was called Corsair, but it was a far cry from the old biplane. It was as strong as a battleship and in front of its inverted-gull wing projected a Double Wasp which with water injection gave 2,500 hp under emergency combat conditions. When this power was translated into thrust by the broad 'paddle' blades of the HamStan propeller it was urge enough for short free deck take-offs with three 1,000 lb bombs, for steep climbing and for pulling all the g the pilot cared to experience. Indeed the great F4U Corsair was so good it was not easy to replace. Early jets were faster—often only marginally—but they were deficient in range and weapon load. Korea found the piston-engined Corsair working as a fighter and ground-attack aircraft, both by day and by night. When it was over more than 12,000 Corsairs had been built, and the final models soldiered on into the 1960s, setting a service record unrivalled by any earlier US fighter, in the matter of both longevity of production and longevity of service.

In September 1952, when Vought still had several hundred Corsairs to make, the US Navy issued a formal requirement for a new single-seat day fighter. Obviously it was to be a jet, and the Navy could be relied upon to need large internal fuel capacity, extremely robust structure and a slow landing speed. In addition the requirement stipulated supersonic speed in level flight. This also was not unexpected. Thanks to Ed Heinemann and his team at Douglas El Segundo the Navy had been one of the leaders in exploring supersonic flight with manned aircraft, and in November 1953 the Navy Skyrocket became the first aircraft ever to exceed Mach 2. Heinemann's Skyray (p. 215) was potentially a supersonic Navy fighter already in being. But this was a time when the fighter art was changing with extreme rapidity. In aerodynamics, structure, propulsion, avionics and weapons the possibilities were changing almost daily, and the Navy judged it ought to be possible to plan a completely new air-superiority fighter significantly better than anything seen before. They judged correctly.

Proposals were received from eight companies. Though the effort in terms of engineering man-hours needed to make a proposal for a supersonic jet fighter was far greater than anything known in the piston era it was still possible, by working day and night, to get the job done very fast indeed by 1974 standards. Under the urgent pressure of the Korean war the customer was also likely to take decisions fast. This was especially the case with the US Navy Bureau of Aeronautics, which had an evaluation staff of outstanding ability. The Navy was heavily engaged in Korea, needed superior aircraft badly and also longed for a jet that could lift its pilots out of the third row and put them right up front. Until quite recently the naval aviator in every country inevitably tended to have an inferiority complex; though it would be misleading to describe his aircraft as 'inferior', he could never forget that for several fairly obvious reasons the carrier-based fighter was usually of lower performance than its land-based counterpart, and invariably also suffered other shortcomings. Sometimes, as with the Corsair, the balance had not been too one-sided. With the F8F Bearcat parity had been achieved, but at the expense of weapon load and range. In the jet era, despite great efforts by Grumman and McDonnell, the Navy had been quite unable to come up with anything to rival the performance and glamour of the Sabre, and had finally decided to buy some Sabres itself (it called them Furies). Chance Vought had had even less success. The F6U Pirate was underpowered, and the F7U Cutlass—a radical design, with nothing aft of the wing!—flew surprisingly well but took a long time to develop. Both the Vought jets were first powered by small J34 axial engines from the Navy firm of Westinghouse, and this giant company ran into great engineering difficulties, as explained in the preceding chapter. It was partly because of this that the Cutlass saw only limited service.

Chance Vought very much wanted to win this promising Navy programme. In late 1952 the last contract had been placed for the Corsair, the Cutlass looked a highly uncertain project, Westinghouse was no longer able to hide its desperate engine problems, and the future of Chance Vought was looking rather bleak. On top of this the Vought organisation itself was going through major changes. At the instigation of the Navy it had in 1949 moved more than 1,000 miles from Connecticut to a Naval Industrial Reserve plant at the Dallas, Texas, Naval Air Station. In 1952 Congress had decided that United Aircraft was in breach of Anti-Trust legislation in making both engines and aeroplanes (they didn't seem to mind about Sikorsky's helicopters), and poor Vought was going to be chucked out in the cold as an independent company. The severance from United Aircraft, which took place in the summer of 1953, made it doubly desirable for the Dallas team to win the supersonic Navy fighter if they were not to go out of business.

What sort of an outfit was this newly created Chance Vought Aircraft Inc? It was slightly unusual in several ways, but one that is especially worth mentioning is that it did not believe that big aerospace companies should be run by financial men. Every time an accountant retired at the top he seemed to be replaced either by an engineer or by a pilot. When Fred Detweiler retired as president his place was taken by Paul Thayer, who had been chief experimental test pilot, and by the end of the decade Vought's management and engineering staffs contained a higher proportion of ex-fighter pilots than any other large American company. Vought was also very strong technically. Fred Dickerman, chief engineer, was a graduate of MIT, and so was his assistant and eventual replacement, Russ Clark, who led the team on the new fighter. Let us put ourselves in Clark's shoes for a minute as he considered how to go about the most important task he, or anyone else in Chance Vought, had ever tackled.

In September 1952 nobody could say how a supersonic fighter of any kind, let alone a carrier-based one, should be designed. Should it have a delta wing? A tail? Just one, two or several engines? Should it have boost from ramjets or rockets? Should it be small and nippy, and handy for carrier operations, or big and long-legged and fully equipped? Should it have a second crew-member? Ought one to be bold and use the new metal titanium, in secondary or primary structure? Almost the only thing one could be sure of was that one would add an afterburner to the engine(s), but beyond this the design was wide open. I saw some of the studies made for this project by one of the unsuccessful contenders and they included a tailed delta, a tailless delta, a tailed swept-winger, a variable-sweep design and a canard! Some had one engine, most had two and one had three. Vought might have been expected to be as radical as anyone, in view of their considerable, and not unsuccessful, flight experience with the tailless Cutlass, and with the earlier 'Flying Saucer' XF5U, but divine providence undoubtedly guided Clark and his team.

The two vital choices, taken in the first month, were to use a traditional configuration and a single Pratt & Whitney J57 engine. The engine was crucial. Had the RFP been issued six months earlier there is a chance the Dallas engineers would have become wedded to the Westinghouse J40, which in early 1952 was still the official Navy high-power engine for advanced combat aircraft. The extra time was just enough for this engine's fundamental design weaknesses to become manifest to all, and throughout this period the new two-spool engine running at Hartford, and already delivered to Boeing for the B-52, gained swiftly in stature and importance as a 'wonder engine' that for the first time promised not only high speed but also extended range, because of its high pressure-ratio. Vought in 1952 were still partners with Mr Pratt in United Aircraft, and thus had a bit of an inside edge over their rivals where the new J57 was concerned. The fine new engine had already been chosen for the supersonic F-100 (p. 138), and was fast being prepared for that aircraft in a re-stressed supersonic form with an afterburner and variable nozzle of advanced conception. The Navy had already chosen the original, subsonic J57 as the replacement for the J40 in the A3D Skywarrior bomber, and was in the process of adopting the supersonic version for the Skyray fighter. It all happened at precisely the right time for the J57 to fit the new Vought fighter from the start.

But for Clark's project engineers to choose the right shape for the new fighter was not so much luck as judgement. They knew the F-100 had a conventional shape, they knew it was becoming fashionable to keep a tail-plane and they also knew that the tailplane ought to be mounted low down to avoid transonic pitch-up problems. But any designer will recall the vast room for error that existed in 1952 in choosing the shape of the wing and body. Moreover, Dick Whitcomb at the NACA had yet to complete his work on the Area Rule, and this did not become fully available as a design tool for more than another year. Yet the wing/body shape of the Vought proposal was unbelievably right. It even looks right in 1974, and in 1952 it was a generation ahead of every other fighter. This is despite the almost unique decision to put the wing on top of the body. Today fighter designers favour the high wing, but in 1952 it was almost unheard-of.

Vought chose it because they wished to hinge the wing to the body so that its incidence could be varied in flight.

This was extremely bold, because the wing of an air-superiority fighter needs to be fastened on very firmly, and in 1952 no variable-incidence wing had gone into production; indeed only three or four prototype or experimental aircraft had been built with such wings, and the engineering had in each case been cumbersome and heavy. Vought wished to incorporate this feature not in order to achieve extreme STOL performance but so that the wing could fly at an angle of attack exceeding 12° with the fuselage remaining almost level. With the body in a level attitude the pilot would retain an excellent view for carrier landings, and a short main gear could be used able to fold into a restricted bay in the fuselage. Vought calculated the improved pilot view on the approach was alone worth the complication and weight penalty of the variable-incidence wing, and that the reduced weight of the landing gear would more than cancel out the penalties. When I saw the first Crusader I happened to comment that I thought the Lightning should have been designed the same way. Later Freddie Page seemed somewhat needled by this, and figuratively 'shot me down in flames', but I am unrepentant. I still think the Lightning should have had a wing and landing gear like a Crusader; it would have been recoverable with the gear up and would have room for more internal fuel.

Internal fuel loomed very large in the design of the Vought fighter. I am never able to decide whether the US Navy want more fuel than the Air Force or vice versa, but certainly they both used to make European fuel capacities of the pre-1960 era look silly. Clark's engineers put fuel in every nook and cranny, though in fact the fuel system came out beautifully simple. The long box-like body was schemed with a long afterburning J57 at the rear, fed by a duct from a chin intake. All the lower part of the body was filled with flexible fuel cells. The entire wing, apart from the leading and trailing edges and the hinged tip portions, was made in the form of an integral tank. This tank forms the structural box on which everything else is mounted, and though natural today it was very advanced in 1952. There are multiple spars and integrally stiffened aluminium alloy skins, bolted together with what was then exceptional precision. Though plenty of aircraft in 1952 had tapered skins or sandwich construction I cannot think of a contemporary fighter with machined integral stiffening. T/c ratio was 5%, a very low value yet not so low that structure weight became excessive and fuel capacity insignificant. Indeed half the fuel was housed in the wing, and the total internal capacity came to 1,165 gal, or double the capacity of an early Lightning. While I am on the subject, a folding flight-refuelling probe was incorporated at the very start of the programme. It was not fitted to the prototype, nor to one or two special variants, but in conformity with a Navy ruling of September 1955 was a standard feature on every aircraft delivered for combat use. This again contrasts sharply with the Lightning and every other aircraft to reach the RAF or RN up to the Jaguar, which at last shows that a neat folding probe can be housed in a European aircraft—damn it, we invented it!

To this splendid shallow box of fuel that formed the basis of the wing were hinged leading and trailing devices which again would not look out of place today. On the front were separate hinges carrying a large one-piece leading edge which, when the wing was tilted to the high-incidence position, was pulled down by a mechanical interconnection to droop 25°. On the rear edge were hinges for a large flaperon, or drooped aileron, which (as in the F-100) was put there to avoid the feared problem of control reversal from outboard ailerons. Tilting the wing up automatically drooped these surfaces 15° relative to the wing, thus, with the drooped leading edge, greatly increasing the camber and giving excellent lift in the low-speed regime. Inboard of the ailerons were small flaps, made of magnesium, which automatically drooped 20° in the high-lift regime. The outer panels, which were made to hinge upwards hydraulically, had fixed trailing edges but drooped leading edges having greater chord than the inboard portions. The discontinuity at the joint is what is called a dog-tooth. It was just coming into use in 1952; the tiny delta FD.1 had extended outboard slats which gave a dog-tooth effect, the Grumman F9F-8 Cougar had very definite dog-teeth when it flew in 1953 (design, late 1952, contemporary with the Vought fighter), and in 1954 dog-teeth were hastily being fitted to Swifts and Hunters. The Vought fighter was, I believe, the first completely new type to have them from the start. The discontinuity works like a fence in preserving chordwise flow; it induces a strong attached vortex which swirls back across the wing and prevents the flow from curving sharply out towards the tips. Unlike most fenced or toothed aircraft the Vought fighter had no control surface further outboard. Usually the main reason for fences, saw-cuts (Lightning) and dog-teeth was to preserve good control from outboard ailerons at high angles of attack, but in the Vought wing the ailerons were wholly inboard. The wing/fuselage attachment was a plain fail/safe pair of forged aluminium hinges at the bottom rear edge of the centre box. An irreversible hydraulic ram positioned the wing at 0° or 7° according to a cockpit lever. In the 7° position the bluff front face of the centre section is exposed to the slipstream. I have read that this 'acts as a large speed brake'. In fact the Vought engineers put a barn-door speed brake under the fuselage, very like that of the F-100. The extra drag of the cocked-up wing was not needed but hard to avoid.

This wing, with 5° anhedral and 35° sweep at the quarter-chord line, was the complement to the J57 with afterburner in ensuring an excellent design. Vought owed a lot of its aerodynamics to the NACA, and in fact it was almost scaled from a NACA research wing. My opinion is that it was the best fighter wing of the first half of the 1950s; indeed I am not sure it is even beaten by the wing of the original Phantom which was designed after the middle of the decade. Without wishing to criticise Dassault it is also instructive to compare the Vought wing of 1952 with the delta wing of the Mirage III of 1956 and then with the dramatically superior wing of the Mirage F.1 of 1966. With the F.1 Dassault at last created a wing similar to that designed at Dallas 14 years previously, the only significant advance being that in those 14 years engineers had lost their fear of outboard ailerons, so the French team were able to fit the inboard part of their wing with double-slotted high-lift flaps. Of course, the F.1 does not have variable incidence, and neither does any other modern fighter, but that in no way invalidates Vought's philosophy. Vought have been unable to tell me a meaningful figure for the weight penalty of this feature, but it was in the order of 500 lb or less, not allowing for the 'more than 500 lb' saved on the main gears. Since the Vought team made variable-incidence respectable it has been carried much further in the tilt-wing V/STOL aircraft where the range of incidence is around 100°.

Compared with the wing the body of the Vought proposal was straightforward. The pilot was placed in the extreme nose. Vought had put the pilot as far forward as possible in both their previous jets, the Pirate and Cutlass, perhaps because in the old Corsair he was rather far aft and had a lot of aeroplane getting in the way of his forward view. Certainly the nose location of the Crusader cockpit, allied with the tilting wing, gave the pilot the best view for landing of any jet fighter I can think of—save perhaps the Northrop XP-79 where he lay on his tummy and looked ahead through a completely transparent bubble. On the other hand, the canopy was an upward-hinged clamshell, so it had to be shut even on accelerated take-off and carrier recovery. Ahead of the instrument panel Vought put an APG-30 gunsight radar, and the fact that they put this in a proper nose, instead of in the thin upper wall of the duct (as on the F-100) later facilitated the installation of much more powerful radars with bigger dish aerials. Armament was a difficult question. The Navy had requested guns, and the capability of carrying FFARs which in 1952 were at the height of their fame as a seemingly effective air-to-air weapon pending the availability of guided missiles. Vought's choice was four traditional Mk 12 Colt-Browning 20 mm guns, the same as they were fitting to the Corsairs, at first with 84 rounds each but later with 144, plus a shallow box forming part of the belly containing launch tubes for 32 'Mighty Mouse' 2.75 in FFARs. The box was hinged at the rear and thus could be pivoted down for less than a second while the rockets were 'rippled away' by electrical signals from the fire-control system. Much development was needed to make the rocket pack work properly. After trying various schemes it was installed in the form of a single large tray occupying most of the underside of the body between the nose and main gears, and on its underside was hinged the big speed brake. The main development difficulties were how to get rid of the rocket gas quickly enough and how the fire-control system could pull up the nose of the fighter so that the down-tilted FFARs should point exactly at the target intercept point.

There were hundreds of other design choices that might have gone differently. Vought chose to use airborne power systems energised by shaft-drives off the engine, and to add a ram-air turbine that could be quickly extended into the slipstream to supply emergency hydraulic and electric power for safe recovery after flame-out or engine failure. This was a new idea in 1952 and Vought adopted it largely because of the impressive image presented by Roy E. Marquardt whose young firm had developed the first RAT (ram-air turbine) and swiftly got it qualified. I might comment that one European supersonic aircraft was almost fitted with a RAT as late as 1970 after one had crashed following main-engine failure because the pilot could not move the flying controls. Another area where Vought had plenty of choice was in structural materials and techniques. I have mentioned the machined wing skins; another bold choice was titanium for almost the whole of the rear fuselage. Vought proved titanium can be spot-welded. Some major items, including large areas of forward and mid-fuselage and the small inboard flaps, were of magnesium, a metal of very low density which eventually gave a lot of trouble in the marine environment. Other interesting choices were the knife-edge air inlet without variable geometry or blow-in doors, the steerable nose gear, the catapult hooks and sting arrester hook hinged to the lower longerons, and the general superb shape and cleanliness of the whole design.

It would be incorrect to suggest that Vought's entry was the only one worth looking at, but the Navy came to a favourable decision very quickly indeed. The speed at which the programme moved was remarkable, and I do not think such a pace would be possible today. Several of Vought's rivals had submitted developments of such existing aircraft as the Fury, Skyray and Demon, and these might have been expected to pose less technical risk than the radical Vought proposal, and to fly sooner. When he was head of BuAer, Admiral Jim Russell told me the fairly large risk inherent in the Vought entry had not been ignored, 'but this design seemed to be the *only* one that would do what everyone in the Navy had been hoping would result from this fighter competition: put the Navy right in the front rank.' The Navy was obviously concerned with what might succeed the Mig-15, which had been a nasty surprise the previous year, but perhaps a sharper competitive spur was its deep desire to acquire a fighter that could beat the best in the Air Force. When the eight competing proposals were evaluated only that from the Dallas company seemed likely to beat the F-100 while having the range and weapons and docile flying qualities the Navy needed.

Vought had other things going for it. In the five months they had worked on their fighter they had made more tunnel models, logged more tunnel hours and built more test rigs than any rival company. They alone had collaborated closely with the NACA to ensure that their submission, when built, would fully conform to the Area Rule, and they assisted in refining the rule to take it up to the supersonic regime beyond Mach 1.5 where the shockwaves are significantly inclined. And in 1954 they followed English Electric in devising, making and logging 500 hours on a flying-control rig, called the Flight Simulator (though this was a confusing name), which faithfully duplicated the complete powered flight-control system. Never before in the US industry had it been possible to measure before first flight the flight-control characteristics with such precision and reliability at all altitudes and speeds, and over a very wide range of manoeuvres. The simulator paid off handsomely. It enabled really major advances to be made at the design stage in perfecting stable high-power servomechanisms, it highlighted a deficiency in the control system as originally designed (saving the possible loss of the first aircraft) and it was instrumental in enabling the eventual prototype to set a new record for the industry in its number of flights and the quantity of useful data logged in the first six months of flight testing.

It was early in May 1953 that the Navy announced Vought as the winner. I have already given plenty of reasons why they were chosen, but yet a further reason which certainly carried some weight is that the newly independent Vought had to win or face possible extinction. Douglas El Segundo, on the other hand, had six major Navy programmes and was already supplying approximately 80% of all American carrier-based aircraft, so its excellent Skylancer (p. 231) could hardly have been chosen even if it had been coated with anti-gravity paint. But I do not wish to imply that the Navy did not think the Vought submission the best; they rated it not merely the best but way out in front.

Detail design began in May 1953, and at the end of June Vought received a contract for two prototypes, designated XF8U-1. During 1953 there were minor structural and equipment alterations, and refinement to the external shape to conform more closely to the newly developed Area Rule for flight well beyond Mach 1. Dr Hugh L. Dryden, head of NACA, commented that, as the Vought fighter had been designed to conform to the rule from the start, it had been applied 'in a discreet manner'—in other words, there were no voluptuous bulges and wasp-waists. Despite these changes, and the fact that the first aircraft—BuAer No 138899, but always referred to at Dallas as 'One-X'—had to be trucked dismantled over 1,400 miles to Edwards AFB for assembly, the job of building the first XF8U was completed as early as February 1955. By this time the type had been given the official name Crusader, which followed quite nicely after Corsair and Cutlass. The mock-up review board had been held the previous October, with singular success. For this mock-up Pratt & Whitney had supplied a replica of the chosen engine, the J57-P-12, but this Navy engine was not flight-cleared in time for the One-X and the first engine fitted was therefore an Air Force P-11 rated at 9,700 lb dry and 14,500 with full afterburner. John Konrad made the first flight on the afternoon of 25 March 1955. Before he landed 52 minutes later he had comfortably flown significantly faster than Mach 1—about 1.2.

Taking stock of the XF8U in March 1955 it can be seen to be a most remarkable aircraft. Exceeding the speed of sound on its maiden flight was encouraging but no more than the YF-100 had done (and, the Air Force/Navy ball game running at fever-pitch, Konrad was determined to do likewise). What was significant was that the Crusader promised to be faster than the F-100 on equal power. It was also to demonstrate longer range, faster climb, more rapid rate of roll, smaller turning circle at all speeds and heights, and, of course, slower and shorter landing. Looked at another way, de-navalising it would have resulted in a world-beating land-based fighter! As it was, its importance was even greater. A Russian once told me that, of all the Western aircraft of the late 1950s, the Crusader seemed to bother the Kremlin the most because it was liable to turn up anywhere on Earth and start commanding the air-space over every distant trouble-spot. His argument was quite plausible. The giant weapons of the strategic nuclear forces could be cast into the background because they were unlikely to be used, but the carriers of the US Pacific Fleet, and the 6th Fleet in the Mediterranean, were a thorn in the Soviet side and the Crusader was likely to give those fleets command of airspace even in the face of the latest Communist fighters.

He was speaking of how his people regarded the original Crusader, before it had begun to develop. Subsequent years were to see it develop so much that, said Vought, 'no other fighter has ever realized as much growth from its original airframe'. If this means no other fighter has ever developed so much without changing its airframe, this may well be true. In the course of its career the Crusader has grown in weight by 10,000 lb, or 45%. It has been equipped with higher-thrust engines, air-to-surface weapons, radar, ECM and other devices, and has even found room for more internal and external fuel.

Throughout 1955 the XF8U-1 flew intensively and well both at Edwards and at the Marine Corps Air Station, Mojave. On 30 September it was joined by the second prototype, and shortly thereafter, on a non-stop ferry flight from Dallas, there arrived the first production F8U-1. The whole programme seemed to lead a charmed life. Not only was the fast pace maintained but everything seemed to be right first time, and the production fighter hardly differed at all from the One-X. It did have the definitive Navy engine, the J57-P-12, rated with full afterburner at 16,000 lb, but this required no airframe alterations. The main changes over the One-X were to add a retractable flight refuelling probe, housed in a shallow bulged compartment aft of the cockpit on the left side, and a launching rail on each side of the fuselage for a Sidewinder. This slim, snake-like air-to-air missile had not existed when the requirement for the new fighter was drafted. Its development, 'in house' by a tiny team at the Naval Ordnance Test Station at China Lake and Inyokern, California, is often cited as an example of cost/effective weapon technology. Its timing was brief, the cost miniscule and the result the cheapest self-guided missile that there has ever been. It is little more than a gyro-stabilised rocket motor carrying a warhead group and a seeker head with four control fins moved by signals from an IR heat-homing cell in the nose. The Crusader was the ideal carrier for it. As it needed hardly any equipment in the parent aircraft it was fitted to almost every other Navy fighter as well, and then percolated through the Air Force and Allied forces, but the Crusader was teamed with Sidewinders from the start. They soon became the primary armament for interception missions.

From the original requirement it had been known that the Vought fighter was supersonic, a member of the still exclusive family of aircraft to which such terms as drag-rise Mach number and critical Mach number meant little, but which could slip through Mach 1 as if it were no barrier at all. Nobody knew publicly how fast it could fly until 21 August 1956 when one of the first F8U-1 production aircraft was flown by Cdr R. W. 'Duke' Windsor at 36,000 feet over a 15 km course at China Lake to set a national speed record. If the Navy had done this a few months earlier it would have been a world record, and taken much of the excitement away from Peter Twiss's great achievement in setting a mark of 1,132 mph with the FD.2 the previous March. The Navy refused to disclose Windsor's exact figure, but said it was over 1,000 mph. Later, when the speed was revealed as 1,015 mph, the Crusader pilot was awarded the 1956 Thompson Trophy. This flight was the first officially observed flight by a US aircraft, other than experimental models, at over 1,000 mph, and the first performance record to be won by a carrier-based aircraft. By this time the Crusader was indeed carrier-based, the fourth production machine having completed carrier qualification aboard USS *Forrestal* in April 1956.

By the end of 1956 the F8U-1 was being produced at the rate of three per month, and this rose to the planned level of eight per month by March 1957. The first aircraft for inventory service was accepted by the Navy on 28 December 1956, a mere four years and three months from the original draft requirement. Deliveries built up fast during 1957, and the first operational Crusader squadron, VF-32, joined the 6th Fleet aboard USS *Saratoga* in February 1958. Later in the same month a squadron became operational with the 7th Fleet in the Pacific aboard USS *Hancock.* The latter ship was significant in confirming that the supersonic fighter could be deployed aboard CVS (supplemental) carriers, of the *Oriskany* class, as well as aboard the big CVA ships such as the *Midways* and giant *Forrestal*s. Quite soon, in 1957, Crusaders began to reach the Marine Corps. Indeed it was a Marine major who gained the biggest headlines ever won by the Crusader. On 17 December 1956 Vought flew the first unarmed photo-reconnaissance Crusader, the F8U-1P. On 16 July 1957 one of these, straight from Dallas and with its six cameras installed and loaded, was taken off by the major from Los Angeles in company with a standard F8U-1. The pair flew with full afterburner to rendezvous over New Mexico with an AJ-2 Savage tanker. Letting down at well over Mach 1 from 35,000 to 25,000 feet the pair then had to kill speed to the refuelling limit of 320 knots. The unfortunate pilot of the fighter damaged his probe and was forced to land at Albuquerque, but the major refuelled successfully and went back into afterburner and up to 35,000 ft. Twice more he made a refuelling rendezvous, in between whiles operating his cameras to provide a complete overlapping mosaic of pictures of his route. He landed at Floyd Bennet Field, New York, after crossing the United States in the unprecedented time of 3 hr 23 min 8.4 sec, which worked out to about 726 mph or Mach 1.1 at cruising height (speed between refuellings was actually around Mach 1.7). The major received the DFC for this feat which was the biggest thing in his life until, five years later, as Lt Col John H. Glenn, he became the first American to orbit the Earth. Later he retired from the astronaut team and became president of Royal Crown Cola—where I am told he would dearly like to fly a Crusader again.

There were many other fine flights in 1957. One which closely rivalled Glenn's, and actually took place five weeks earlier, was the formation dash by Capt Robert G. Dosé and Lt Cdr Paul Miller Jr from the deck of USS *Bon Homme Richard,* steaming with the Pacific Fleet, right across the United States to land on USS *Saratoga* at sea off Florida. Their time, for a marginally shorter trip than Glenn's, was 3 hr 28 min, but the flight was not observed officially—though President Eisenhower and his Cabinet watched from *Saratoga*'s bridge. On 17 December 1957 Vought received the highest honour a US planemaker can receive, the Collier Trophy, jointly with the Navy for sponsoring this notable design. In March 1958 the Navy BuAer presented Vought with the first Certificate of Merit ever awarded an aircraft manufacturer for the design, development and production of the Crusader. Meanwhile the Dallas production line steadily worked through 318 F8U-1 fighters and 144 photo versions, each priced at about $1 million, while squadrons formed at the rate of one every six weeks. 'Crusader College' at Dallas and NAS Moffett Field was working at full pressure converting pilots and ground engineers, who then went on to the Caribbean and Nevada to learn how to use the Crusader in combat. At sea the Air Development Squadron not only explored 1,000 mph interceptions but began to look at other missions and possibilities that were to bear fruit in new versions of the Crusader.

One aircraft—hardly a mere 'new version'—was the so-called F8U-3 or Crusader III (also called Super Crusader). This was in fact a totally new design forming a seemingly obvious next generation. Powered by a Pratt & Whitney J75-P-2 rated with afterburner at about 21,000 lb, it had a redesigned airframe of steel (part honeycomb sandwich) and titanium for briefly reaching flight Mach numbers up to 2.7. Wing and tail had a reduced thickness/chord ratio and aspect ratio, compared with the Crusader, and there were two very large fins hinged below and ahead of the tailplane which, once in the air, could be swung down to give extra keel surface below and aft. The inlet duct was fed from an inclined attached-shock inlet beneath the conical nose radome, and primary armament in the air-to-air mission was three Sparrow III missiles semi-submerged into the fuselage. Five of these impressive machines were built, but only three had flown when the Navy judged that the Crusader III would have been fine if only McDonnell had not done even better with the Phantom. The surviving F8U-3s were turned over to NASA and are reckoned to be the only single-engined fighters in the West to have sustained Mach 2.4. I believe the claim is correct.

At this point, to avoid confusion, I must jump to 1962 when the Department of Defense rationalised the numbering of its aircraft. It altered the Navy numbers drastically, though wherever possible the new number had an affinity with the old one. Thus the F8U-1 became the F-8A, and the F8U-1P became the RF-8A (R for reconnaissance). And the next fighter version, the F8U-1E, became the F-8B. The 1E had been planned in 1955 when it was realised that there was no law of physics or anything else forbidding a single-seat all-weather naval fighter. The original Crusader had been planned with the APG-30 gunsight radar which had no relevance to either guided missiles or bad weather. All-weather radars were available, but they were old and bulky and had poor reliability. As an interim step the Navy produced the APS-67 set which fitted into the Crusader very well, but needed a bigger radome. This gave the F-8B version limited all-weather capability. The new radar was fitted to a standard F8U-1 which flew on 3 September 1958. The switch in production came only three weeks later, and the final 130 'dash 1' fighters were bought as 1Es, to make the total 'dash 1' buy 448. The last was delivered in May 1959.

The original squadrons of F8U-1 day fighters had a busy year in 1958. Over 150,000 hours were flown by the Atlantic and Pacific Fleet squadrons, the training bases and the Marine Corps, and some units established such good records that they wrote official communiqués reading like advertising copy. For example, the CO of VF-211 ended a magnificent report with 'In summary, the F8U-1 has provided an optimum combination of reliability and performance.' It was certainly given a thorough working out. Carrier service is no picnic at the best of times, and in 1958 there were major crises that caused violent activity in both the 6th and 7th Fleets. The former sent *Saratoga* to steam off the Lebanon shore in July, and by the time a stable government was restored in that country in mid-August VF-32 had flown 1,295 hours in full battle kit, fortunately without having to join combat. Shortly before this flare-up four aircraft of another *Saratoga*-based squadron cut weeks off their delivery by flying the 5,850 miles from Virginia with the aid of aerial fuelling and a stopover at a USAF base in Morocco. The Lebanese must have been impressed by the Crusader because six years later they tried to buy a squadron of rebuilt F-8As (eventually to discover the Navy could not spare them). The other panic of 1958 occurred in the Formosa Strait, and around the Quemoy islands, as prickly Nationalist Chinese set up defences against the giant from the mainland who seemed to be bent on invasion. Many Crusaders actually tangled with Communist Chinese fighters, presumably Russian-built Mig-15s of Korean vintage, but I have no record of any 'kills' (such as were gained at that time by Nationalist Chinese pilots flying F-86Fs converted to fire Sidewinders).

During 1958 the F8U-1 and -1P (F-8A and RF-8A) went into wide service with the Marine Corps, equipping five fighter squadrons and one photo squadron at El Toro, California, and Beaufort, SC. Late in the year the next member of the family completed its Navy Preliminary Evaluation Program with impressive results; this was the F8U-2 (F-8C). The main advance was installation of the 16,900 lb J57–P–16 engine, first flown in a converted -1 fighter in December 1957. This had a notably hot afterburner (the specific fuel consumption rising to no less than 2.35) and to cool the surrounding structure the -2 introduced two small ram intakes above the rear fuselage which were retained in all subsequent Crusaders. It was also given a pair of large ventral fins, or rather strakes, to improve stability at extreme Mach numbers; but 1.7 remained the limit in normal operation because of stability deterioration and engine temperature. The extra thrust was valuable in assisting take-off, climb and, above all, combat manoeuvrability. Improvements were made to the fire-control system, the radar was modified to give greater scanning sharpness and operate in new modes, the missile pylons were twinned to carry two Sidewinders on each side and the wing tips were clipped by three inches on each side. The -2 flew on 20 August 1958, and the 187th and last was delivered on 20 September 1960.

So far Vought's experience with the Crusader had been more successful than any other modern military aircraft I can call to mind, save perhaps the Nimrod. There was just one cloud in the sky. For various reasons pilots seemed fairly often to be having to eject, and the neat lightweight seat designed by Vought had shown itself to have shortcomings. Though the Air Force continued to let airframe manufacturers design and make their ejection seats if they so wished, the Navy came to the conclusion that it was a job for specialists and that the best specialist was Martin-Baker Aircraft in England. The little Denham firm had given convincing demonstrations to the Navy and fell over backwards to co-operate, and the upshot was that the Navy standardised custom-tailored Martin-Baker seats in most of its combat aircraft (other than those, like the Skywarrior, which had escape chutes). By this time there were over 400 Crusaders and it was a big job re-seating them, but Martin-Baker did the job over a period of two years with field reps assigned to the user squadrons on airfields and carriers. At first the Mk F5 seat was used, one of the prolific automatic Mk 5 series, but later the F7 was substituted.

On 16 February 1960 the F8U-2N (F-8D) made its maiden flight. This model remains the greatest performer of the entire series, having a low gross weight of 27,700 lb, a very powerful engine and clean exterior; level speed reaches 1,067 knots (almost 1,230 mph), service ceiling is 42,900 ft and combat radius 394 nm with full weapon load. This is due to the 18,000 lb Pratt & Whitney J57-P-20, at that time the most powerful engine in the entire J57 family, together with the replacement of the belly FFAR pack by a new fuel tank bringing the capacity up to 1,348 gal. Pilots rated loss of the rockets no loss at all, and infinitely preferred the four Sidewinders. But by far their biggest gain in the -2N was the inclusion of a Vought-developed autopilot. For a planemaker to do his own autopilot has always been exceptional, even in the United States. This one was a very good autopilot, meeting severe demands on racking space and g loading yet offering a wide range of facilities including push-button heading hold, height lock, and fixed orbit in the fleet-defence loiter mode. By this time the Crusader could fairly be described as an all-weather interceptor. The -2N introduced an appreciably better radar, the APQ-83, and a new instrument panel, and the net result was to offer greatly improved all-weather capability with much reduced pilot workload. It was customary to launch the -2N with a mix of infra-red Sidewinders and the lately introduced AIM-9C version, by the Motorola company, which had semi-active homing on to the target while the latter was illuminated by the fighter's radar. The APQ-83 had sufficient beam power for this to work well. Crusaders of this type reached the Navy on 1 June 1960, and the 152nd and last arrived in January 1962.

By 1960 Vought had delivered more than 500 Crusaders, and the two batches of -2N models (priced at about $99 million and $68 million) running in parallel with the end of the -1P and -2 production took the total by mid-1961 close to the magic figure of 1,000. And by mid-1961 new business was coming from several directions. In October 1959 Vought had begun to rebuild and update early -1 fighters, under a $9.5 million contract, and thus started a remanufacturing programme which ultimately rivalled in magnitude the work of making the Crusaders in the first place! In addition Vought had made several proposals for new versions which in two cases struck immediate sparks from the Naval Air Systems Command (formerly BuAer) and in one case led to the biggest single operational advance in the entire family and to a very big extension of the manufacturing programme for new aircraft. This was extremely welcome to Vought, who from 1958 had viewed the big Phantom as a formidable competitor. The Phantom, winner over their own F8U-3, cost almost twice as much as a Crusader and drained the Navy's budget for fighters rather fast. Vought, which in August 1961 merged with Ling-Temco-Electronics to form Ling-Temco-Vought (LTV), and was henceforth known as LTV Aerospace, were eager to extend the potential of the Crusader to the uttermost, to enable it to remain cost/effective in the sharpening battle against the Phantom. The immediate possibilities were to improve the all-weather fire-control equipment yet again and to equip the aircraft to carry weapons for attack on surface targets.

The two big improvements that could be made at the front end were to fit yet a fourth radar set and a completely new device, an IR scanner. The latter, originally developed for the Air Force F-102 interceptor, consists of an extremely sensitive seeker head able to detect the heat radiated by an enemy aircraft at a distance of up to 15 miles, though when flying through cloud, rain or a snow blizzard the range shrinks to a very small distance indeed. The pilot can thus acquire the target by infra-red methods as well as by radar and pass the IR signals to the seeker head of the Sidewinder missile(s). This ensures that, before a missile is launched, it has positively locked on to the target, so that in theory no missile flops down to the ground, locks on to the Sun or does any other silly thing (such as turning round and joyfully discovering the fighter that launched it). The AAS-15 fitted to the new Crusader version consists of a neat electronic package plus a seeker head protected by a thing like a miniature radome of special IR-transparent material which projects ahead of the pilot's windshield (in the early Phantoms the IR seeker projected below the radome and in the F-102 it looks like a miniature astrodome of glass above the nose). The new radar was the APQ-94, which has considerably greater power than any previous Crusader radar. Like other long-range sets it works at a longer wavelength than those previously fitted, and the considerably bigger dish aerial necessitates not only a much larger radome but also a reprofiled fuselage nose. This might have been expected to spoil the efficiency of the engine air intake, but in fact Vought claim they actually achieve better pressure-recovery in the duct than before!

The AAS-15 and APQ-94 made the new version of the Crusader, the F8U-2NE (F-8E) a true all-weather aircraft, still unable to match the radar performance of the F-106 or Phantom but capable of defending the fleet under all weather conditions or at night in a way that the F-8D could not accomplish. It retained the powerful P-20 engine and augmented fuel capacity of the F-8D, but its greater weight reduced level speed to 984 knots and cut a little off the range and ceiling. The first -2NE was produced by taking the second F8U-2N and converting it up to the new standard. This aircraft flew on 30 June 1961, and following very successful trials an order was placed for 94. Subsequently two further large batches were bought, at a unit price only 55% higher than that for the first batch of simple F8U-1s, to take the total F-8E procurement up to a valuable 296 aircraft. The 142nd E model happened to be the first to be delivered as an F-8E, rather than with the old Navy designation F8U-2NE. I shall use nothing but the new DoD designations in the rest of this chapter.

Back in 1959 Vought had talked to the Navy about the possibility of equipping the Crusader to carry two Bullpup missiles, which entered service in that year. The original Bullpup was not much more than a 250 lb bomb to which had been added a solid-propellant rocket motor and radio-command guidance. The Navy had demonstrated that it could be steered to its target, which could be a surface vessel, bridge or any other discrete 'point' objective, by the pilot of a single-seat aircraft. Successful trials were flown with A-4 Skyhawks and FJ-4B Furies, and though the pilot had his hands full and could not steer away from the target nor take evasive action, he could steer the missile as well as could a second crew-man. At that time no decision was taken, and the Crusader remained a pure fighter, but the possibility continued to simmer. During 1961 the decision was taken to evaluate one Crusader in a more general surface-attack role, carrying not just Bullpup but iron bombs, Zuni rockets and various other stores. The first production F-8E flew in September 1961, and if the Navy had made up its mind earlier it could have been a multi-role aircraft. As it was, nearly 90 had been built before LTV were able to convert a single trials machine, and over 180 had been delivered before attack capability became standard. Then they all had to have the wing racks and missile guidance fitted as a field modification, which is most untypical of the way the Navy likes to do things. Originally the anticipated load was two early Bullpups weighing 571 lb each, but the standard finally agreed was a long pylon under each wing stressed to 2,000 lb and capable of carrying tandem triplets of 250 lb bombs. The electronic pack for Bullpup guidance was installed above the wing centre section under a prominent humpback fairing. The Sidewinder pylons on the fuselage were replaced by new ones able to carry launch tubes for eight Zuni rockets. Carrier trials were held aboard *Forrestal* in the summer of 1963, in the course of which the attack-converted aircraft, 149159, was catapulted with full fuel, two 2,000 lb bombs and eight Zunis at 34,000 lb. As a result the F-8E became a multi-role strike fighter, with wing bomb and fuselage missile pylons quickly bolted on or removed to suit the mission. I do not claim the Crusader is the only aircraft in history to have progressed from being a day fighter to a night and all-weather fighter and then a multi-role attack machine, but I claim it has done it better than anything else.

Attack capability was one of two big improvements which interested the Navy. The other, which caused instant interest yet never led to a production order, was the tandem two-seat version. In 1958 Vought began to scheme two such developments, both having slightly less internal fuel in order to preserve the original fuselage length. One was an all-weather attack fighter with the rear seat occupied by a navigator and missile-operator, as in the Phantom. The other was a dual-control trainer for pilot conversion and weapons training. It was the latter that most interested the Navy, and in fact it was a bigger conversion job. To give the rear man a good view he had to sit about 15 inches higher than the original pilot, and there were geometric and c.g. problems in installing the two Martin-Baker seats, and in such details as protecting the rear man from supersonic airflow if the single, very long canopy should be lost in flight. Originally styled F8U-2NT, the trainer was finally simplified and planned as an F8U-1T; after 1962 it was called NTF-8A. The prototype was the 74th production F8U-1, No 143710, and it also happened to incorporate a lot of F-8E equipment added during an earlier rebuild in 1961. The NTF-8A flew on 6 February 1962. It retained two guns, and its P-20 engine was de-rated to extend life. A braking parachute was added to reduce brake wear and keep landing roll within about 2,700 ft.

The NTF-8A proved extremely useful, and became a popular hack at the Naval Air Test Center at Pax river, but owing to a sudden cut in the 1964 budget it never went into production. During the past ten years it has been hard at work at the Naval Test Pilot School. During its career it has been used not only for the normal type of test-pilot student research programmes but also for a host of trials and special purposes. At various times it has had low-pressure tyres for rough-field operations, a flying boom refuelling receptacle (it does not have a probe) and a profusion of advanced navigation and weapon-delivery systems beyond anything carried by other Crusaders.

This conversion of the 74th Crusader completed the manufacture of new aircraft for the US Navy and Marine Corps, but it is by no means the end of the story. Indeed LTV even found an export customer, which is a rare thing when your product is a Mach 1.8 aircraft for use from carriers. This part of the story begins in 1959 when Vought took the sixth production aircraft, 140449, and used it for STOL research with BLC (boundary-layer control) from blown flaps. The aircraft was freely bailed back by the Navy, but the work was funded mainly by the company as the Navy had not issued any requirement for such a development. Various schemes were examined, including blowing from above the rear of the drooped leading edge, but the arrangement tried in flight was to use engine bleed to blow the small flaps and the drooped ailerons, while adding double-hinged leading-edge droops. The speed on the approach could be reduced by about 10 knots, but nothing more could be done at that time. Vought regarded this research as an insurance against a future substantial increase in weight or a requirement for emergency recovery with both fuel and weapons.

At the same time the French Aéronavale was looking keenly at the Crusader as the best replacement it could see for Vought's own F4U-5N Corsair (the piston-engined one) and the Aquilon (developed Sea Venom), which were obsolescent and could not last beyond the mid-1960s. The Crusader in its later all-weather form appeared ideal in every respect save that its approach speed was rather fast for France's small escort carriers *Clémenceau* and *Foch*, and it seemed a bit too much for these severely limited ships to handle. Vought's experiments to reduce the landing speed were exactly what the French wanted to hear about, and in 1962 the new customer was engaged in detailed discussion at Dallas. Not unnaturally the French wanted everything: the flight performance of an F-8D, the radar and weapons of an F-8E and a landing slower even than had been achieved with the BLC-equipped F-8A. In a matter of days LTV said 'No sweat'. Tunnel testing had suggested that much greater low-speed lift could be obtained by relatively simple trailing-edge blowing coupled with a fairly considerable modification to the drooped leading edge.

The main change as finally agreed—which took several months to refine in detail—is a drooped leading edge made in front and rear sections of approximately equal chord. When fully down the rear section is depressed 35° and the front section a further 8.9° or almost 44° in all (compared with 25° for the regular aircraft). On the outer (folding) wing the angles are even more remarkable: 35° and 20°, giving an aggregate deflection of 55° instead of the original 27°. On the trailing edges the deflection angles are almost doubled, the ailerons going to 30° and the inboard flaps to 40°, with engine-bleed BLC blowing to prevent the airflow from breaking away from the upper surface. To maintain good pitching control at reduced airspeeds the slab tail is slightly larger, and the angular travel of the wing is held to the 5° position. These changes were all incorporated in an F-8D, 147036, which flew on 27 February 1964. Though it crashed the following 11 April it had amply demonstrated the effectiveness of the modifications, which reduce the stalling and approach speeds by some 15 knots. Whereas the basic design case for the Crusader landing gear had been a descent rate of 20.5 ft/sec, the modified aircraft could reliably arrive at sink rates close to 11 ft/sec, and arrested landings seldom experience more than 3.3 g, compared with almost 4 g for ordinary Crusaders.

This clinched the deal with the French, who independently confirmed that the modified Crusader would be compatible with their carriers. In August 1963 the French government placed a contract with the US Department of Defense for 42 Crusader F-8E(FN) aircraft, the extra initials being obvious. Apart from the new high-lift system they were equipped to a standard slightly different from the US Navy F-8E and the fuselage racks were changed to rails compatible with either Sidewinders or the far bigger and heavier Matra R.530, which has to be carried further away from the fuselage wall. The first F-8E(FN) flew on 26 June 1964 and the last—the last Crusader of all—in January 1965. Flight tests and initial carrier trials aboard USS *Shangri-La* were completed by October 1964. The main bulk of the French order were delivered to Lann-Bihoué by *Foch* and the non-operational carrier *Arromanches*, and carrier qualification aboard *Clémenceau* in the Mediterranean was completed in May 1965. Today 36 of these excellent aircraft are still in use as all-weather interceptors. It is difficult to see what could replace them, though Dassault are pushing naval versions of the Mirage F.1.

LTV tried hard to make a sale to the British, though it never got into the papers. It so happened that the US 1964 budget was cut just at the time the Royal Navy was beginning to get ulcers over the commonality and carrier-compatibility problems of the Hawker Siddeley P.1154 (described in the companion volume *Attack Aircraft of the West*). As the situation became increasingly critical LTV sent a team over to see their Lordships, and in May 1963 sent the NTF-8A itself, and demonstrated not only to the Fleet Air Arm but also to the RAF, and at the Paris Salon. Late in 1963 LTV schemed an advanced British development of their original two-seat study of five years earlier. Called F-8F(RN) it would have been slightly longer than other Crusaders, would have had a pilot and observer in tandem at the same level (unlike the trainer) and would have matched the BLC and double droop of the French aircraft with the better fuel economy and increased urge of a reheat Spey engine. LTV were obviously prepared to bend over backwards to meet RN requirements and even to help fund development, but in February 1964 their Lordships said that nothing would do but the Phantom (with two Speys instead of one) and LTV were told they had won the Navy VAL contract, with the prospect of making at least 1,000 of these new attack machines derived from the Crusader (the A-7 Corsair, likewise described in *Attack Aircraft of the West*) and so stopped bothering about a few dozen rather difficult Crusaders for Britain.

On the other hand nobody with such a successful fighter programme would fail to see how far it could be extended, and from 1963 to 1972 LTV tried hard to find a new market-opening. One obvious possibility was to upgrade the basic F-8 and see who showed the most interest, and the resulting V-1000 would have had the wing of the F-8E(FN), a J79-GE-17 engine, increased internal fuel capacity, two M-39 revolver cannon (not Gatlings but the gun used in the F-100) and an ordnance payload of 6,000 lb. A variant of the V-1000 was considered as a candidate in the International Fighter Aircraft (IFA) competition conducted by the US Air Force to find a successor to the F-5 as a standard fighter to sell to friendly nations. LTV were told the IFA had to be 'non-provocative' in character, which means it must be a defensive aircraft. LTV need not have worried about taking the bomb racks off the V-1000 because the winning IFA, the F-5E Tiger II, has a bomb load of 7,000 lb!

This is almost the end of the tale of the Crusader, except that there are five more versions! This is because the refurbishing and remanufacturing programme, which began in 1960, has continued in a way exceeding anything seen with any other aircraft I can call to mind. A cynic might say it is exceeded by the B-52 programme, but in that case it has been done to stop the big bombers from falling apart as the combined result of low-level turbulence and the crew chiefs having to buy book-ends for the aircraft log-books. The rebuilding of the F-8 fighters has been to update them and keep them on the top line. Nothing like it was done with rival types because none had to stay young for so long. The reason, to quote a few thousand US Navy and Marine pilots, is because 'When you're out of F-8s you're out of fighters'. Perhaps these jocks would think again now they have the F-14 Tomcat, but some of them remained unimpressed by the Phantom.

First of the rebuilt versions was the RF-8G. The big inventory of RF-8A reconnaissance aircraft had more than proved their worth. Was it not one of them that secured the vital film revealing the presence of Russian ballistic missiles in Cuba? VFP-62 and the Marines' VMCJ-2 received Presidential Commendations for their sustained low passes across Cuba at that crucial time in 1962, doing more than any other aircraft to keep the Pentagon and White House supplied with minute-by-minute intelligence. But they were rather old aircraft, and technically were contemporary with the F-8A. The RF-8G is a total rebuild, with reinforced and strengthened wings and fuselage, doppler navigation, new camera installations, ventral fins, new engine, stores pylons, moulded-harness electrics and a beefed-up landing gear. The first 53 were completed in 1967, and the remaining 20 followed in 1970.

The F-8H is a remanufactured F-8D. It has a completely new wing designed for a 4,000-hour service life, a beefed-up landing gear, very greatly improved weapons similar to those of the F-8J (described below), a P-20A engine, strengthened arrester hook and other minor improvements. Though it is slower, has shorter range and a lower ceiling than the F-8D it remains a first-class dog-fighting aircraft. It was the first type of remanufactured F-8 to see combat in Viet-Nam, and the H remains the alleged top-scorer in that theatre with almost twice as many Mig kills as the Phantom. (In saying 'alleged' I do not dispute the combat reports but recall that Allied claims in World War 2 were often very wide of the mark, and I think the same may be found to apply, in lesser degree, in SE Asia.) Navy pilots will thump the table, or whatever is handy, when they tell you that this good combat performance was to a large extent due to the F-8H's four guns, which, though generations out of date in design, are something the Phantoms in Viet-Nam noticeably lacked.

F-8J is the designation of the 'fightin'est' F-8 of all. It is the rebuild of the F-8E, and the conversion gives it: the extended-service 4,000-hour wing, but with the addition of the entire BLC and double-droop system (plus bigger tailplane) of the French aircraft; APQ-124 MAGDARR radar, new fire-control and much enlarged missile-acquisition envelope; underwing drop tanks; beefed-up gear and hook; and minor changes included an improved cockpit. First of 136 J models flew on 31 January 1968, six months after the first of the 89 F-8Hs. More recent changes to the F-8H and J have included the fitting of the J57-P-420 engine, giving almost 19,000 lb thrust, and fatigue clearance for 2,000 catapult launches and carrier arrested landings.

The remainder of the rebuild programme worked its way back through the Cs and Bs, the F-8C being turned into the F-8K and the old B models emerging as F-8Ls. This programme involved a complete structural rework, with the new wing (as in the H) and stronger landing gear, underwing stores pylons, and systems improvements such as the moulded-harness electrical system. The radar and other weapon equipment fits are not brought up to F-8J standard but are suitable for day training roles. By 1970 some 446 Crusaders had been rebuilt, at a contract price of around $200 million, which is really gilt on the gingerbread when one recalls how long and profitable the original first-build programme was.

Though they are oddballs outside the main story of the Crusader fighter, I must also mention two research conversions that are making significant contributions to the art of the fixed-wing aeroplane. The first is an F-8A which became the first aircraft ever to fly with a supercritical wing. This is a wing of a radically different section profile, with a rather fat front part, bulged bottom, flattish top and down-turned trailing edge. At first glance it seems to make nonsense of elementary wing theory, and to be very much like a conventional wing—or the popular image of a conventional wing, which has far more camber than most real wings—arranged upside-down! In fact the supercritical wing gives a marginally worse low-speed performance than an ordinary wing but can fly much closer to the speed of sound with less drag-rise and better efficiency. Rockwell got the contract to design and build the completely new, fixed-incidence wing for this NASA Crusader, which since early 1971 has given excellent results at Edwards. The other aircraft, also flown by NASA at Edwards, is a conversion of an F-8C to have electrically signalled ('fly by wire') flying controls. Vought did this conversion, complete with computer and an inertial measuring unit similar to that used on the Apollo lunar module. Applied to transport aircraft 'the concept is expected to eliminate discomfort to passengers in turbulent air and ease the workload on the pilot. It may also reduce the size required for large structural components such as tail surfaces; they may be relocated to reduce the basic weight and drag of the aircraft and offer improved flight performance and increased payload.'

I can hardly think of anyone saying a cross word about the F-8. Admittedly there were times when everything seemed to go wrong. The Achilles heel of this aircraft, if it had one at all, was the landing gear which has been greatly strengthened in the big remanufacturing programme. Properly flown, it gave no trouble, but aircraft such as the F-8 often have to be flown in lousy weather by dog-tired pilots and make recoveries at high weight, and the gear sometimes failed. I recall one occasion not long ago when one of the greatest ships in the world lost five Crusaders on five consecutive nights. Each hit the deck, appeared to suffer main-gear damage, overshot into the blackness, went off the air and was never seen again, on radar or by anyone else. But this is not at all typical of the F-8. Four hours' steaming by carrier from where that happened is Naples, from whose Capodichino runway a young Navy pilot thundered aloft in his F-8A on a fine day in August 1960. At about 5,000 ft he noticed an excessive forward stick pressure was needed to level off. I'm glad he noticed this because a minute earlier he had failed to notice, as he opened up for take off, that his wings were still folded. For the first time in history this was of no great consequence. Our cool friend explored the handling, dumped fuel and considered the possibilities of spreading the wings (perhaps while performing a carefully judged slow roll at close to zero g) and finally made a perfect—but very fast—recovery on the same runway with the wings still pointing skywards. As a story among pilots it's practically impossible to cap, so I'll finish on it.